D1532037

Reference Guides in Literature

Ronald Gottesman, *Editor*

Sherwood Anderson:
A Reference Guide

Ray Lewis White

G. K. HALL & CO., 70 LINCOLN STREET, BOSTON, MASS.

R813.52
Anderson

Copyright © 1977 by Ray Lewis White

Library of Congress Cataloging in Publication Data

White, Ray Lewis
Sherwood Anderson: a reference guide

(Reference guides in literature)
1. Anderson, Sherwood, 1876-1941--Bibliography
Z8035.6.W52 (PS3501.N4) 016.813'5'2 76-46388
ISBN 0-8161-7818-6

This publication is printed on permanent/durable acid-free paper
MANUFACTURED IN THE UNITED STATES OF AMERICA

Contents

Introduction

Stuart Pratt Sherman was wise about Sherwood Anderson when he predicted in 1926 that literary historians would someday point to Anderson's dramatic escape from his paint factory into literature and call that escape symbolic, prophetic, and historic. Not often sympathetic to Anderson's writings, Sherman was in 1926 being less prescient than observant, for Sherwood Anderson (1876-1941) had already made his abandonment of commerce into a well-known story. I should say into a well-known fiction, because in 1913 Sherwood Anderson did not go directly from being a full-time paint manufacturer to being a full-time bohemian literary artiste. Instead he gave up managing a small distribution company in Elyria, Ohio, in order to return to composing advertising copy in a Chicago office--hence, from one business to another, from one duty-filled life to another less regimented but no more exciting. And Anderson did not so deliberately or so craftily feign insanity in November, 1912, in the office of his warehouse as he in truth suffered a psychological dysfunction, disappearing for three days into amnesia, wandering over the cold Ohio countryside lost and soon thereafter finding himself freer and in the fringes of the Chicago Renaissance in American letters.

Yet--as Anderson himself would say--essence of truth is in this legend. Instead of (or along with) the conscious change of habit and goal in middle-age, Anderson had by 1912 started forming his life as raconteur, as questioner of American assumptions, and as storyteller of the untold lies and truths of buried, ignored lives of grotesque, unhappy people. I do not know why Anderson first wanted to write fiction and poetry, but I suspect that he recognized *nada* and sought through creative writing to fill the moments of life between awareness of nothingness and ending in death with temporary coping. Financial security (or indebted struggle toward mogulship), middle-class family life (lovely wife, three fine children), and macho comradeship and country-club fellowship were illusory as fulfillment; in some art such as writing fiction could be sought the momentary pleasures of craft, the occasional shock of critical praise for good stories beautifully told.

Encouraged by the younger and more formally educated admirers he found in the Chicago artistic world after 1913, Anderson tried to write what tradition and friends told him was important--novels about great movements of society or self, novels such as Windy McPherson's Son (1916) and Marching Men (1917)--works actually drafted by the unhappy businessman in Ohio before 1913. Of interest now only to Anderson scholars and devotees, these early novels about unfulfilled businessmen or lawyers who become labor organizers or adoptive fathers were praised by several critics--to Anderson's sure joy. Those Chicago critics who knew the author liked the crudity of his prose and the obvious questioning toward moral answers amid cultural chaos, modern commercial life; critics unfamiliar with the background and personality of the writer assumed from the publicity photographs accompanying the novels that the youthful author would someday learn to add polish and sophistication to his obviously sincere and socially-conscious fiction.

Sherwood Anderson believed both groups of critics--those who praised him and encouraged him to become the untutored, bardic Whitman of Midwestern prose, and those who expected the Great American Novel to appear from some Midwestern genius. The missionary critics got what they wanted in Mid-American Chants (1918) and A New Testament (1927)--free verses (often psalms) about fertilities in Midwestern cornfields and souls; and the encouraging (if condescending) critics got a whole line of novels from Poor White (1920) to Kit Brandon (1936)--novels in which Anderson sought narrative power and found structural flaws, novels into which he poured his developing (or borrowed) philosophies and found "muddlement." I cannot blame Anderson for believing his critics when they called on him for the great novel, for critics then as now seemingly must rank genres and create hierarchies of authors. Yet I regret that not one of the Anderson novels can be read now for enjoyment instead of analysis, for expression instead of autobiography. The reputation would, I wager, be as greatly favorable if Sherwood Anderson had not published a single novel.

By accident, then, Sherwood Anderson found his craft, his genre--the short story. Finally ignoring friends who wanted novels from his pen and critics who could hope that the naive young author (or the embarrassingly naive man of forty) would write the great social novel of the age, Anderson in a moment of inspired self-reassurance sat in his rented room in Chicago in the winter of 1915 and looked at the lights of Chicago's Loop and (not long after having read Gertrude Stein and Edgar Lee Masters) decided to tell stories of the frustrated lives of puzzled, unknown people--stories written in cadenced, colloquial prose. These Winesburg, Ohio stories, collected into book form in 1919, gave creative joy to Anderson, who in these ostensibly simple sketches about grotesque small-town Ohioians in the 1880's expressed for the first time in American literature the secrets of all inward-turning souls who long for community, human touch, and the flavor of significance in outwardly barren lives.

Introduction

These were stories new in subject and style, for Winesburg, Ohio creates from outside literary tradition the modern American short story, the sketch without obvious plot or expected development but with entire interest on revelation of character, on the baring of secrets through thrusting of hands, as Edmund Wilson would say, into the very bowels of life . . . hands clean and sympathetic and sure. At publication in 1919 (in England in 1922) many wise critics of Winesburg, Ohio saw and said what Anderson was trying to accomplish in these stories; others became mired in charges of plotlessness and obscenity and missed the moral beauty before them. The work was reviewed widely and generally favorably, a fact that Anderson later tended to forget. Yet the author never became financially secure from Winesburg or other works, although he lived by royalties and commissions (and patronage from a collector of manuscripts) from 1925 until his unexpected death in 1941.

Still--even after Winesburg, Ohio--the critics said that they wanted novels, and Anderson provided them, each one given much attention and publicity and each one quickly forgotten. If they wanted Winesburg updated and in novel form, they got Poor White (1920). If they wanted ultra-modern style and shocking treatment of marriage and duty and sex, there was Many Marriages (1923). If they wanted Huck Finn in the Industrial Age, there was Dark Laughter (1925). If they wanted social, radical concern for politics, there was Beyond Desire (1932). And if they wanted romantic fiction with the shell of the Jazz Age (Southern Appalachian style), they got Kit Brandon (1936).

But Anderson knew to return always to the short story for true expression. In three collections--The Triumph of the Egg (1921), Horses and Men (1923), and Death in the Woods (1933)--he published impressive and important sketches from life as he observed it, not fiction written on critical order. These three story collections were widely reviewed and generally well understood, and I have come to regret having once commented that Anderson found it impossible to continue writing Winesburg stories; I now wish that he had written ten such volumes.

Thus, in spite of having seemingly wasted his time in writing novel-length fictions and several volumes of essays and personal newspaper material or social observations, Anderson produced several volumes of great short stories and memoirs. He enjoyed a wide press and esteem, even if the novels and poetry and plays brought forth charges of artistic death as early as 1929. Anderson had become a public figure, his career entwined with those of Faulkner and Hemingway and Stein and his influence felt by Saroyan and Welty . . . and . . . .

Sherwood Anderson: A Reference Guide is the most complete bibliography about the author to date, consisting of 2550 references to criticism published from 1916 through 1975. All of these entries are references to writings about Anderson, not references to writings by him. While there is yet no definitive bibliography of Anderson's own numerous publications, useful lists are provided in Eugene P. Sheehy and Kenneth A. Lohf, Sherwood Anderson: A Bibliography (Los Gatos, CA: Talisman Press, 1960); and Douglas G. Rogers, Sherwood Anderson: A Selective, Annotated Bibliography (Metuchen, NJ: Scarecrow Press, 1976).

Because Sherwood Anderson: A Reference Guide is limited to writings about Sherwood Anderson, I have not included editions or translations of the author's works. Such editions and translations often do carry valuable introductions, prefaces, forewords, afterwords, and notes; but lists of such materials properly belong in primary bibliographies. I have, however, included commentary about such editions and translations of writings by Sherwood Anderson.

This secondary bibliography contains almost every item of criticism listed in previous bibliographies about Anderson, his literary associates, and the movements in literary history in which he took part. I have tried to include all autobiographical or memoir material by the writer's famous and obscure friends and associates. I have made useful for the first time all identifiable newspaper clippings filed among The Sherwood Anderson Papers at The Newberry Library of Chicago--an already enormous archive that is to include my own large collection of clippings about Anderson from the 1930's through the 1960's. I maintain that all such references to Sherwood Anderson in the popular and scholarly press are of high importance, creating means of reliving with the writer the high and low times of public approbation or neglect--and then the course of the reputation after the author's death. I estimate that the materials listed in this book triple the previously known writings about Sherwood Anderson.

I cannot alone take credit for all of the material enumerated and annotated in Sherwood Anderson: A Reference Guide. All previous Anderson scholars have contributed through their own published and unpublished studies references to the discussions of multiple other scholars. Unpublished dissertations and theses (herein enumerated) have often opened new sources of Anderson material. To two kind scholars I owe all of the entries for Anderson published in their homelands--Professor Takashi Kodaira of Japan and Professor Tauno Mustanoja of Finland; entries provided by these scholars are presented with my pleasure and with their names after each contribution.

I am glad that Sherwood Anderson: A Reference Guide provides for the first time extensive commentary on Anderson in non-English languages. For aid in preparing material from German I wish to thank Girard Steichen of Saalfelden, Austria; for aid with materials in Dutch, Swedish, Norwegian, and Danish I thank Heidi Butler of Illinois State University; for signed annotations of many materials in Russian and Polish I thank Professor James Cradler of Illinois State

University. I must assume personal responsibility for materials in French, Spanish, Portuguese, Italian, Romanian, and Hungarian.

Sherwood Anderson: A Reference Guide is arranged chronologically, entries being listed under each separate year from 1916 through 1975. Within each year, entries are arranged alphabetically by author's name. Items of anonymous or unidentifiable authorship are grouped under the heading "Anon."; these entries occur wherever "Anon." occurs alphabetically in each annual list.

Entries under each year are divided into two sections: "A" contains books, pamphlets, theses, and dissertations dealing solely with Sherwood Anderson or with Anderson and one other writer; "B" contains newspaper stories, reviews, articles, and chapters about Anderson, along with sections of books, theses, and dissertations that deal with Anderson and other subjects or authors.

All entries are identified by year of publication and order of presentation; cross-references guide the researcher to reprintings in whole or in part, translations, and pseudonyms. The entry numbers are used instead of page numbers in the index, which is exhaustive in references to authors, periodicals, individuals, Anderson's publications, and works of a creative nature. The index otherwise contains two headings--Biography and Bibliography.

Finally, the wealth of newspaper material about Sherwood Anderson (presented with page numbers where available) requires that papers published in towns and cities of obscure or ambiguous location be identified by two-letter United States Government abbreviations for states.

My indebtedness to librarians for materials and information is so great that I must reluctantly here thank only the staff of The Newberry Library of Chicago and Joe Kraus and Sharon Hartzell of Milner Library of Illinois State University. For aid of various kinds I thank William Linneman and Charles A. White of Illinois State University.

Writings about Sherwood Anderson, 1916 - 1975

1916 A BOOKS - NONE

1916 B SHORTER WRITINGS

1 ANON. "Windy McPherson." New York Times Book Review (8 October), p. 423.
Windy McPherson's Son pictures Midwestern life as well as Dostoevski pictured Russian life. The novel is more truly American than any recent work by others.

2 ANON. "Fiction." Athenaeum, no. 4611 (November), p. 543.
Windy McPherson's Son is sordidly repellent and excessively long.

3 ANON. "Windy McPherson's Son." Times Literary Supplement (9 November), p. 536.
Anderson has written Windy McPherson's Son too much from the mirror image of his imagination and too little from direct observation of reality.

4 ANON. "Windy McPherson's Son." North American Review, 204 (December), 942-43.
In Windy McPherson's Son Anderson unsuccessfully combines realistic detail with romantic questing, and the ending lacks intellectual credibility.

5 ANON. "The New Books." Review of Reviews, 54 (December), 679.
Windy McPherson's Son is the powerful biography of a man who seeks riches and finds ashes.

6 BOYNTON, H. W. "Some Outstanding Novels of the Year." Nation, 103 (30 November), 508.
Windy McPherson's Son is a remarkable first novel. The old theme of questing for happiness is given fresh American treatment.

7 _____. "Some Stories of the Month." Bookman, 44 (December), 393-94.

In Windy McPherson's Son Anderson resembles the constructively realistic Russians more than the destructively naturalistic Dreiser and Dostoevski. Close in style and intent to Spoon River Anthology, the novel verges on parody and must be read as more poetic than realistic.

8 DELL, FLOYD. "A New American Novelist." Masses, 9 (November), 17.
An advertising writer has created a great novel of quest for life's meaning in America. As in the works of Turgenev, Tolstoi, Dostoevski, and Gorki, Anderson answers no questions in Windy McPherson's Son; but he does ask wise questions. Reprinted: 1924.B14.

9 FRANK, WALDO. "Emerging Greatness." Seven Arts, 1 (November), 73-78.
Windy McPherson's Son, flawed by an ending too joyously heroic, heralds an honest use of American life hitherto absent from American fiction. Reprinted: 1924.B18; 1966.A7; 1974.A3.

10 [HEAP, JANE]. "Windy McPherson's Son." Little Review, 3 (November), 6-7.
In Windy McPherson's Son Anderson strives too earnestly to create a totally American novel. Like Dreiser, he produces only the homely.

11 HECHT, BEN. "A New Novelist." Friday Literary Review (8 September), p. 11.
The author of Windy McPherson's Son is a great new American artist with the poetic vision to write heroically of America. Anderson admits to having read Nietzsche and Dostoevski, but this novel is more vitally emotional than stylistically finished.

12 [JONES, LLEWELLYN]. "Sherwood Anderson." Friday Literary Review (8 September), p. 11.
Anderson follows Dreiser, Masters, and Sandburg in writing of Midwestern small towns; and in Windy McPherson's Son he rises beyond surface detail to give unstylistic vitality to his characters.

13 M., D. L. "From Newsboy Upward." Boston Evening Transcript (25 November), 3, p. 6.
Perhaps the author's inexperience in writing fiction excuses the happy ending of Windy McPherson's Son, or perhaps external forces coerced Anderson to write this cheap conclusion.

14 MENCKEN, H. L. "The Creed of a Novelist." Smart Set, 50 (October), 144.

In Windy McPherson's Son Anderson writes realistically of rejection of business yet implausibly of human crises. In vitality and sincerity, Anderson promises to create better stories.

15 PHELPS, WILLIAM LYON. "Three Not of a Kind." Dial, 61 (21 September), 196-97.

Windy McPherson's Son has crude vitality but lacks artistry. The characters are too detailed and hence unreal.

1917 A BOOKS - NONE

1917 B SHORTER WRITINGS

1 ANON. "Notes on Names." Seven Arts, 1 (January), inside front cover.

Anderson's stories of "Winesburg" are based on his boyhood town; when the series is "gathered into a volume, America will see that a prose complement to E. L. Master's 'Spoon River Anthology' has been created."

2 ANON. "Current Fiction." Nation, 104 (11 January), 49-50.

Anderson uses incident and detail well in Windy McPherson's Son, but his hero's ending is romantically weak narration.

3 ANON. "Chronicle and Comment." Bookman, 45 (May), 307.

An autobiographical publicity release about Anderson now demonstrates that the early parts of Windy McPherson's Son are based on the writer's life.

4 ANON. "For the People." Nation, 105 (11 October), 403-404.

In Marching Men the proletariat shows strength through order instead of through socialism or labor organization. Anderson's novel is both mystical and vague.

5 ANON. "Dignifying Labor." New York Tribune (27 October), p. 9.

Losing courage to give Marching Men an honest ending, Anderson abandons the good effects of setting and thought.

6 ANON. "Marching Men." New York Times Book Review (28 October), p. 442.

Neither the hero nor the plot of Marching Men makes progress enough to repay the reader.

1917

*7 BEFFEL, J. N. Review of Marching Men. New York Call (11 November), p. 14.
Cited: Book Review Digest 1917, p. 13.

8 BOYNTON, H. W. "A Stroll Through the Fair of Fiction." Bookman, 46 (November), 338.
In Marching Men Anderson invents a mystical hero of the working classes who shall lead the oppressed toward non-violent revolution.

9 DONLIN, GEORGE BERNARD. "Discipline." Dial, 63 (27 September), 274-75.
Anderson creates Marching Men to celebrate the need for order in society and thus writes of masses instead of individuals, of passion instead of intellect.

10 GOULD, GERALD. "New Novels." New Statesman, 8 (6 January), 330-31.
In Windy McPherson's Son Anderson first writes realistically and then melodramatically. Only in fragments of the story is there "pathetic beauty."

11 H.[ACKETT], F.[RANCIS]. "A New Novelist." New Republic, 9 (20 January), 333-34, 336.
In Windy McPherson's Son Anderson aimed to write of life's meaning and innocently fell short. Blessed with veracity of character, the novel is crude in dialogue and narrative development. Reprinted: 1918.B5.

12 _____. "To American Workingmen." New Republic, 12 (29 September), 249-50.
In Marching Men Anderson succeeds in conveying his sympathies for working classes, in making visible in fiction the neglected workingman; but his idea of mankind marching toward revolution is more poetic than practical. Reprinted: 1918.B5; 1966.A7.

13 MENCKEN, H. L. "Critics Wild and Tame." Smart Set, 53 (December), 143.
When Anderson removes his hero from Pennsylvania in Marching Men, the author's credibility and the hero's aim are blunted.

14 WEBB, DORIS. "Labor in Life." Publishers' Weekly, 92 (20 October), 1372.
Anderson's dialogue in Marching Men is so stilted as to be unnatural, but the author's passionate feeling for suffering masses is clearly presented. Reprinted: 1917.B15.

15 [_____]. "Fiction." Pittsburgh Monthly Bulletin, 22 (November), 748.
Reprint of 1917.B14.

1918 A BOOKS - NONE

1918 B SHORTER WRITINGS

1 ANON. "Poetry and Drama." New York Times Book Review (14 April), p. 173.
Picturing the Middle West in Mid-American Chants, Anderson adds prophecy and mysticism to free verse.

2 B., W. S. "The Lutanists of Midsummer." Boston Transcript (5 June), 2, p. 6.
In Mid-American Chants Anderson has material for poetry but not finished poetry.

3 CONKLING, GRACE HAZARD. "Book Reviews." Yale Review, New Series 8 (January), 437.
Mid-American Chants are not poems but perhaps subject-matter for future poems. Anderson has written "half-utterances, improvisations on life."

4 COOK, HOWARD WILLARD. Our Poets of Today. New York: Moffatt, Yard & Co., pp. 203-204.
"Spring Song" from Mid-American Chants "is one of the most admirable poems to come from this writer of the Mid-west." Now residing in New York, Anderson is "a short story writer of unusual and unique style."

5 HACKETT, FRANCIS. Horizons. New York: B. W. Huebsch, pp. 50-61.
Reprint of 1917.B11; 1917.B12.

6 H.[ENDERSON], A.[LICE] C. "Mid-America Awake." Poetry, 12 (June), 155-58.
Mid-American Chants expresses Anderson's countryside in verses deceptively crude and awkward. The poet longs to recapture American dreams obscured by industry.

7 JONES, LLEWELLYN. "Nascent Poetry." Friday Literary Review (26 April), p. 10.
Mid-American Chants are "the nascent poems of an unterrified romanticist," often "the inchoate verbal outcomes of inchoate feelings." If Anderson learned more about art, he could indeed write true free verse.

1918

8 UNTERMEYER, LOUIS. "A Novelist Turned Prophet." Dial, 64 (23 May), 483-85.

In Mid-American Chants Anderson is more sincere and passionate than prophetic. Compared to Anderson's novels, these poems are forced and vague and unrealistic.

9 WALSH, THOMAS. "Poets, Rose Fever and Other Seasonal Manifestations." Bookman, 47 (August), 461-62.

Anderson's poetry in Mid-American Chants shows poor education and culture boasted of in "honest expletive for the most part rather than singing."

1919 A BOOKS - NONE

1919 B SHORTER WRITINGS

1 A.[NDERSON], M.[AXWELL]. "A Country Town." New Republic, 19 (25 June), 257, 260.

In prose "homely and unemphatic," Anderson tells in Winesburg, Ohio of rebellion against convention. These stories give to American short story writers a new form that replaces the old plot-story. Reprinted: 1966.A3; 1966.A7; 1971.A2.

2 ANON. "A Gutter Would Be Spoon River." New York Sun (1 June), p. 3.

Whereas Masters wrote simply and subtly of wholesome characters, Anderson writes obscenely of the "nauseous acts" of abnormal, perverted people, changing his material "from human clay to plain dirt." Winesburg, Ohio comes from the gutter. Reprinted: 1971.A2.

3 ANON. "Winesburg, Ohio." New York World (1 June), E, p. 6.

Winesburg, Ohio shows the hero growing to maturity; such a subject unifies the twenty-four stories. Someday Anderson may learn to censor his unnecessarily ugly stories.

4 ANON. "Books of the Fortnight." Dial, 66 (28 June), 666.

In Winesburg, Ohio Anderson has written honestly but acridly of pathological characters to form "a prose Spoon River Anthology."

5 ANON. "Aspects of Mid-America." Nation, 108 (28 June), 1017.

In Winesburg, Ohio Anderson has created real characters, but he may have distorted his imaginary town for literary effect.

6 ANON. "Winesburg, Ohio." Springfield Republican (20 July), A, p. 15.

Anderson's sketches in Winesburg, Ohio lack obvious feeling and life, for the author writes impressionistically and buries beauty under realism. Reprinted: 1966.A3.

7 B., W. S. "Ohio Small Town Life." Boston Transcript (11 June), p. 6.

Anderson's Winesburg, Ohio stories, beneath the facade of ordinary small-town life, tenderly reveal the deepest layers of human nature. In these fictions Anderson is "an artist with vision and sensibility, with comprehension and the capacity to test reality with imagination." Reprinted: 1971.A2.

8 BEFFEL, JOHN NICHOLAS. "Small Towns and Broken Lives." New York Call (21 September), p. 10.

After the disaster of Marching Men, Anderson has unexpectedly created a masterpiece of exposé, boldly showing the sensational, shocking secrets of a small Midwestern town.

9 BOYNTON, H. W. "All Over the Lot." Bookman, 49 (August), 729-30.

In Winesburg, Ohio Anderson makes sex the motive for his small-town characters' actions, but his use of psychoanalysis is more in line with the work of Stevenson than with the "spiritual grossness of the Russian naturalists and their imitators." Reprinted: 1966.A3.

10 B.[ROWN], H.[EYWOOD]. "Winesburg, Ohio." New York Tribune (31 May), p. 10.

In Winesburg, Ohio Anderson mars his "clear insight into character" with over-writing, lack of humor, and obsession with neurotics.

11 CRANE, HART. "Sherwood Anderson." Pagan, 4 (September), 60-61.

Anderson has shown flawless style in Winesburg, Ohio, opening for readers "the windows, alleys, and lanes of the village . . . to find what epics, tragedies and idylls we may." The nation should welcome this book, for "it constitutes an important chapter in the Bible of her consciousness." Reprinted: 1948.B32; 1966.B12.

12 D.[ELL], F.[LOYD]. "American Fiction." Liberator, 2 (September), 47.

In Winesburg, Ohio Anderson has avoided Joyce's overemphasis on neuroticism to produce a great collection of

1919

(D.[ELL], F.[LOYD])
stories "vivid and in spite of some grotesqueries, beautiful, and in all but the finest sense true."

13 FRANK, WALDO. Our America. New York: Boni and Liveright, pp. 136-44.
Anderson felt dirt and boredom as a businessman, abandoned his fascination with wealth in order to write fiction, was first published with the help of Floyd Dell, and uses "escape" as the motif of his novels. In Winesburg, Ohio Anderson fictionally recreates his boyhood town with "that impalpable marriage of substance and of human spirit which is art."

14 H.[ENDERSON], A.[LICE] C. "The Soul of Man in Chicago." New Republic, 17 (4 January), 288-89.
Mid-American Chants is Anderson's struggle to "sing" in the midst of an industrialism that damages nature, physical and human. The writer knows more of poetic technique than he would have readers think.

15 JONES, IDWAL. "Winesburg, Ohio." San Francisco Chronicle (31 August), S, p. 6.
Only Ethan Frome is comparable in American fiction to the excellence of Winesburg, Ohio. The work is "a revelation of men's motives by psychoanalysis, with the purpose of revealing that human existence is not necessarily a deadly commonplace, but that in every life there comes, even if but once, moments of dramatic climax."

16 JONES, LLEWELLYN. "The Unroofing of Winesburg." Friday Literary Review (20 June), p. 9.
In Winesburg, Ohio Anderson treats the significant episodes of lives instead of writing well-constructed stories. His poetically told stories are frank revelations of small-town citizens without spiritual or sexual outlet. Reprinted: 1966.A3; 1971.A2; 1972.A2.

17 MENCKEN, H. L. "Novels, Chiefly Bad." Smart Set, 59 (August), 140, 142.
Winesburg, Ohio creates a new form for the short story. Writing "pure representation," Anderson evokes the secret buried life in sketches that are "half tale and half psychological anatomizing, and vastly better than all the kinds that have gone before." Reprinted: 1966.A3; 1968.B25; 1971.A2.

18 O'SULLIVAN, VINCENT. "Précisions sur la Littérature Américaine." Mercure de France, 136 (1 December), 535.
Winesburg, Ohio is perhaps the best novel published since the World War. Anderson demonstrates that fixed rules for storytelling produce formulaic fiction--a fate which he avoids in this work.

19 [PHELPS, WILLIAM LYON]. "Excellent Fiction for Summer Reading." New York Times Book Review (29 June), p. 353.
In Winesburg, Ohio Anderson writes with understanding love of lives comprehended through the new psychologies of Jung and Freud. Reprinted: 1971.A2.

20 RASCOE, BURTON. "Winesburg, Ohio." Chicago Tribune (7 June), p. 13.
In contrast to Masters in Spoon River Anthology, Anderson loves his characters in Winesburg, Ohio and shares their humanity. More important for Americans than Chekhov and Dostoevski, Anderson's stories are powerfully suggestive constructs chiefly of the sexual lives of a Midwestern village. Reprinted: 1971.A2; 1972.A2.

21 SMITH, WALLACE. "Civilian Communique." Chicago Daily News (3 September), p. 6.
Winesburg, Ohio does not contain the Russian violence of Chekhov, but it is full of neurotics and psychopaths whose stories are told in too-naive simplicity and perhaps for shock value. Reprinted: 1972.A2.

22 WEAVER, J. V. A. "Sherwood Anderson." Chicago Daily News (11 June), p. 12.
In Winesburg, Ohio Anderson precisely shows the emotional heart of a small town, doing for America what Gogol and Dostoevski have done for Russia. This book gives a "panorama, with souls instead of trees, with minds in place of houses." Reprinted: 1972.A2.

1920 A BOOKS - NONE

1920 B SHORTER WRITINGS

1 ANON. "Anderson, Sherwood." Who's Who in America: A Biographical Dictionary of Notable Living Men and Women of the United States. Chicago: A. N. Marquis & Co., p. 90.
Married to Tennessee Mitchell on August 1, 1916, author Anderson now lives at 12 East Division Street in Chicago; and his office is in Chicago's Brooks Building.

1920

2 ANON. "The Epic of Dulness." Nation, 111 (10 November), 536-37.
In Poor White Anderson tells of Midwestern characters drained of vitality by an insufficiently beautiful civilization. Compared to Main Street, however, Poor White "lacks fire and edge, lucidity and fulness."

3 ANON. "Latest Works of Fiction." New York Times Book Review (12 December), p. 20.
Poor White is "a careful, conscientious study of certain phases of the industrial development of America, and especially of the Middle West."

4 ANON. "Feast of Unleavened Realism." New York Sun (24 December).
Poor White in style and theme resembles all other Midwestern towns in realistic fiction.

5 BROUN, HEYWOOD. "Books." New York Tribune (13 December), p. 8.
Anderson's madness in Poor White may be divinely inspired, for in the midst of a totally serious novel he verges on burlesque, on crudity, and on sentimentality. Anderson lacks humor, and he invents an incredible age of pre-machine contentment for his Middle West.

6 EDGETT, EDWIN FRANCIS. "An American Zola of the Middle West." Boston Transcript (1 December), p. 8.
Poor White lacks sensible structure. No Midwestern Zola yet, Anderson tells his hero's life crudely. Perhaps the author's youth will excuse his unwisely used ambition.

7 GERSHOM, ERIC. "The Factory Comes to Ohio." Publishers' Weekly, 98 (18 December), 1888.
Poor White describes a time when Midwestern pioneers turned from farming to building factories. In this important novel Anderson visualizes the spirit of this American era.

8 HACKETT, FRANCIS. "The American Novel." On American Books: A Symposium by Five American Critics as Printed in the London Nation. Edited by Francis Hackett. New York: B. W. Huebsch, pp. 52-59.
All vitality in current American fiction comes from the Midwest. In his first three books Anderson appears to be "a naturalist with a skirl of music haunting him."

9 H.[ACKETT], F.[RANCIS]. "Poor White." New Republic, 24 (24 November), 330.

Poor White is a flawed novel in spite of Anderson's admitted intentions and abilities, for the writer lacks values for form and structure and language.

10 HANSEN, HARRY. "The Book of the Week." Chicago Daily News (1 December), p. 12.

Poor White is "a truthful, well written study of the middle west by a western writer."

11 JOHNSON, NUNNALLY. "The Real America." Brooklyn Daily Eagle (11 December).

The theme of Poor White is the turning point of mechanization and its human damage. Anderson uses vignettes to present an entire community and thus excels any purely historical treatment of his subject.

12 JONES, LLEWELLYN. "Anderson: His Novel of Invading Industry." Friday Literary Review (19 November), p. 12.

Unlike Anderson's two previous novels, Poor White has a satisfactory ending; and here Anderson presents good background description and small-town grotesques.

13 MENCKEN, H. L. "Chiefly Americans." Smart Set, 63 (December), 138-39.

Poor White reflects the two sides of Anderson--the poetic describer of his scenes and people, and also the reformer of society. While Winesburg, Ohio will surely be the great model for future storytelling, in Poor White Anderson's moralizing almost obscures the writer's descriptive genius. Reprinted: 1968.B25.

14 _____. Prejudices, Second Series. New York: Alfred A. Knopf, pp. 27, 55, 100.

The unfortunate young critic learns from Stuart Sherman that Anderson, along with Dreiser and Cabell, is not academically admirable. Such authors as Anderson, Frank, Dreiser, and Cabell are teaching America healthy scepticism.

15 PEATTIE, ELIA W. "Sherwood Anderson's 'Poor White.'" Chicago Tribune (18 December), p. 10.

Poor White is "a novel of abortive power, telling with a certain limited lucidity" the story of a Midwestern industrialist; but Anderson has defamed pioneering Midwesterners, picturing them as stupid, brutal, and ignorant.

1920

16 ROURKE, CONSTANCE MAYFIELD. "A New Middle West." New York Evening Post Literary Review (4 December), p. 4.
Poor White is written by a poetic novelist, one who uses "the flexible naturalism" of Winesburg, Ohio to create characters that are at once specific and representative. In effect, Anderson approaches more closely to Whitman than to Howells.

17 SANDBURG, CARL. "Portrait (for S. A.)." Smoke and Steel. New York: Harcourt, Brace and Co., p. 174.
". . . he has / cried a heart of tears for Windy McPherson's / father; he pencils wrists of lonely women. . . ."

18 WOOD, A. L. S. "Agates and Migs." Springfield Union [MA] (26 December).
Poor White is irregularly excellent, Anderson telling a lucid story of industrialism; but the style and the philosophy are often confused.

1921 A BOOKS - NONE

1921 B SHORTER WRITINGS

1 ANON. "Fiction." Booklist, 17 (January), 155.
In Poor White Anderson tells a loosely woven, often sordid story about industrialization, yet his characters are defined well.

2 ANON. "Poor White." Springfield Republican (2 January), A, p. 5.
Anderson leads in protesting fictionally against the self-satisfaction of America, but in Poor White he has written hastily as though carving wood with a hatchet instead of with a knife.

3 ANON. Review of Poor White. Washington Times (26 March).
There is much of Anderson's life in Poor White. Having tried painting and now soon off for Europe, Anderson may return a less indigenous writer.

*4 ANON. "Interview with Sherwood Anderson." Brentano's Book Chat (April), pp. 18-19.
As Anderson could not invent plots because of laziness, he began writing plotless stories of character made from real life. Cited and quoted: 1923.B25.

5 ANON. "Editorial." Double Dealer, 1 (May), 172.
On the question of American qualities in American literature, "The best work of Sherwood Anderson and Willa Cather seems exotic--it, too, partakes of the eternal moods."

6 ANON. "Poor White." Times Literary Supplement (8 September), p. 582.
Based on peculiarities of possible behavior, Poor White is told in an unemotional style, giving an effect of "watching, through a magnifying glass of high power, the perturbations in an ants' nest which has been stirred up with a stick."

7 ANON. "Accusation." Nation, 113 (23 November), 602.
Anderson finds only despair in American life, filling The Triumph of the Egg with bitterness and contempt, "immitigable ugliness and meanness." Yet his stories must be faced for being true to the writer's vision.

8 ANON. "Fiction." Saturday Review, 132 (26 November), 621.
Only Mansfield could have produced such Chekhovian stories as Anderson does in The Triumph of the Egg. While Anderson writes stories that ignore the popular plot formula, the author's true medium is the novel.

9 ANON. "'Triumph of the Egg'--Or Perhaps the Ego." Springfield Republican (11 December), A, p. 11.
Influenced by Whitman, Dostoevski, and Freud, Anderson must someday learn to write of characters not based solely on sexual urges and repressions. The author is not dull in The Triumph of the Egg; he is merely blind to other motivations than sex.

10 ANON. "Winner of National Prize a Scion of Camden." Preble County News [OH] (15 December).
Although no one in Camden, Ohio, remembers Sherwood Anderson, one citizen remembers a harness-maker of the 1870's with that last name. Anderson has confirmed that he was born in Camden, and the town is proud of its former citizen's winning the Dial prize.

11 BAILLY, ALBERT. "Sherwood Anderson: Romancier Américain." La Bataille Littéraire (25 September), pp. 182-85.
Poor White is Anderson's story of the development of the United States and the effects of that development on individuals. Anderson's technique is cumbersome; his story is long and tiresome but perhaps fitting the current taste in America.

1921

12 BENCHLEY, ROBERT C. "Heroes of Industrialism." Bookman, 52 (February), 559-60.

Like Dell's Moon-Calf, Anderson's Poor White is already a historical novel about the dull middle class. Yet Poor White is written well with little narrative action; someday there will be a novel "in which the hero is a young man of no attainments at all, who will not bear watching, and who gets nowhere."

13 BENÉT, WILLIAM ROSE. "The Spirit of Pity." New York Evening Post Literary Review (26 November), p. 200.

Anderson's main effect in The Triumph of the Egg is pity "stronger even than his stark desire for truth or the spirit of irony that is in him." Seldom does prose so closely approach poetry as in these stories of "psychoanalytic groping."

14 BISHOP, JOHN PEALE. "The Distrust of Ideas: D. H. Lawrence and Sherwood Anderson and Their Qualities in Common." Vanity Fair, 22 (December), 11-12, 118.

Anderson of all American writers most resembles Lawrence, but only in sharing a common intuition about life and in writing of repressed lives. Always an accurate observer, Anderson in The Triumph of the Egg becomes the subtle craftsman missing from his earlier books. Reprinted: 1948.B6.

15 BROOKS, VAN WYCK. "Current Comment." Freeman, 4 (14 December), 315.

Anderson deserves the Dial writing award for starting to fulfill the promise of Whitman.

16 BROUN, HEYWOOD. "It Seems to Me." New York World (6 December), p. 11.

The characters of The Triumph of the Egg suffer from having idealized sexuality. Were Anderson less "literary," he might become the nation's foremost writer of fiction.

17 C., A. E. Review of Poor White. Manchester Guardian (16 September).

Although Poor White is better than Main Street, the characters are not really human portraits, the plot is thin, and the "behavior is improbable."

18 COLUM, MARY C. "Literature and Journalism." Freeman, 4 (30 November), 281-82.

The Triumph of the Egg contains almost no action except the psychological action in the characters' minds, for

Anderson's characters "must be the loneliest people in literature" crying out against "the winglessness of their lives." Anderson is now America's "most significant writer of imaginative prose."

19 COURNOS, JOHN. "A Welcome Guest." London Daily Herald (5 October), p. 7.
Poor White is an epic novel about the waste of human energy. "One of the best novels that has come out of America," the work can teach a lesson to Europe. The publisher should also bring out Winesburg, Ohio, "a collection of short stories of exceptional beauty and appeal."

20 CRANE, HART. "Sherwood Anderson." Double Dealer, 2 (July), 42-45.
Anderson excels as artist by having no philosophy of life or literature to impose on his stories that are told from sophisticated realism. His first two novels did threaten to become propaganda, but in Winesburg, Ohio and Poor White Anderson does combine thought with actions and characters. Reprinted: 1948.B32; 1966.B12.

21 F.[ARRAR], J.[OHN]. "Prose Poetry." Bookman, 54 (December), 378.
Anderson commands attention, in The Triumph of the Egg, for voicing "the tragedies of starved lives."

22 H., G. "Out of the West." World Tomorrow, 4 (January), 29-30.
Poor White describes well the process and psychology of industrialism, although Anderson's style shows lack of polish and evidence of hasty composition.

23 HANSEN, HARRY. "Sherwood Anderson--And Others." Chicago Daily News (30 November), p. 2.
The winner of the Dial award completed his first manuscripts in Chicago. Writing slowly and about common people, Anderson "has the great gift of pity that distinguishes Thomas Hardy," for Anderson loves his characters.

24 [HARRIS, FRANK]. "Books." Pearson's Magazine, 47 (August), 87-88.
While Main Street is dull although an American sales success, Winesburg, Ohio suffers, having no "typical characters," for Anderson seemingly cannot "find anywhere a generic typical figure that shall represent in itself more than a townfull of mediocrities."

1921

25 HAWTHORNE, HILDEGARDE. "A Prize Winner's Ironical View of Life." New York Times Book Review (4 December), pp. 10, 23, 29.

Anderson's stories in The Triumph of the Egg are lyrical tales of the inner lives of moments of intense experience. To read Anderson's stories is to walk with "someone who is tired," for the author recreates the lonely, the frustrated, and the suffering, giving no sense of hope.

26 HIND, C. LEWIS. "Sherwood Anderson." Authors and I. New York: John Lane Co., pp. 19-23.

Compared to Henry Adams, Anderson is of the dynamic and the future. Dell helped Anderson to publish Windy McPherson's Son, getting Anderson a contract for three books. Anderson should not have listened to friends' advice to rewrite the end of Marching Men. Whereas Spoon River Anthology is historical, Anderson's Winesburg, Ohio is prophetic.

27 JEWETT, ELEANOR. "Riddle is Posed for You to Read in Arts Club Show." Chicago Tribune (23 January), 7, p. 7.

Anderson's paintings--his "color impulses"--need poetic explanation to clarify the artist's imagination. Anderson saw a lovely tropical storm and simply sat down to paint it. Thus learning to paint, Anderson has exhibited works that are "queer, a round of color, a chaos of design. . . ." Reprinted: 1927.B46.

28 JONES, LLEWELLYN. "Anderson: Short Tales His Best Manner." Friday Literary Review (16 December), p. 15.

The Triumph of the Egg demonstrates that Anderson should be compared to Chekhov instead of to Dostoevski, although he lacks Chekhov's humor and forced artlessness. Anderson's humor in person is Rabelaisian, but these stories are of grotesques bound by repression and convention. Unlike Lewis, Anderson does not create sociological studies; rather, he observes and describes life without diagnosing it.

29 LeVERRIER, CHARLES. "Dernières Publications." L'Europe Nouvelle (26 February), pp. 287-88.

Set in the 1880's, Poor White is Anderson's study of a new orientation in the American destiny. Anderson has the sociological and historical knowledge to attempt this project successfully.

30 LOVEMAN, AMY. "The Masquerading Tract." Saturday Papers: Essays on Literature from The Literary Review. Edited by Henry Seidel Canby, William Rose Benét, and Amy Loveman. New York: Macmillan Co., p. 79.

Why is it that "our novels with a moral, like 'Main Street' and 'Winesburg, Ohio,' will in all probability in a few years [sic] time have gathered the cobwebs of literary history?"

31 LOVETT, ROBERT MORSS. "Elemental Things." New Republic, 28 (23 November), 383-84.

The Triumph of the Egg is as unified as is Winesburg, Ohio. Still groping in artistic ability, Anderson unifies these new stories through "singleness of purpose and unity of result."

32 _____. "Mr [sic] Sherwood Anderson's America." Dial, 70 (January), 77-79.

In Poor White Anderson creates the hero as "a distinct human type--a sort of sub-conscious Lincoln" who symbolizes America in "industrial progress and spiritual impotence." Better at creating naturalism than Norris, Anderson here formulates "realism, enlarged and made significant by symbolism."

33 [McCOLLOUGH, MARTIN]

See TAIT, SAMUEL W., JR. 1921.B36.

34 S., H. J. "Reviewing an Author Face to Face." Chicago Daily News (19 January), p. 12.

In Poor White Anderson shows his humanity through sympathy for "the morons, the cretins, the hookworm victims, the ignorant lovers, the misers, the slaves of certain American towns." In style this novel could be a translation from French or a Scandinavian language.

35 SCOTT, C. KAY. "Books." Freeman, 2 (5 January), 403.

While Poor White shows again that Anderson cannot structure a novel, the author creates beautiful characters from his poetic vision. Anderson errs in trying to determine a philosophy from observing and describing life.

36 TAIT, SAMUEL W., JR. Letters on Contemporary American Authors. Boston: Four Seas Co., pp. 15, 97.

Anderson is part of the Chicago Renaissance and his first novel, Windy McPherson's Son, "had an unmistakable ethical stink." Freeing himself from tradition in Winesburg, Ohio, Anderson "achieved a work that, for sheer

1921

(TAIT, SAMUEL W., JR.)
originality, is unrivalled by anything that any American has ever done." Yet this work lacks the needed bitterness of its setting.

37 UNTERMEYER, LOUIS. "Books." Liberator, 4 (February), 32-34.
Poor White is an enlarged Winesburg, Ohio, a novel full of powerful contradictions. In his subjective realism Anderson is closer to Sandburg and Lawrence than to Dreiser, giving high significance to isolated episodes in his novel. Yet as poet and prophet Anderson has led in warning civilization of industrial evils.

38 VAN DOREN, CARL. The American Novel. New York: Macmillan Co., p. 271.
Not a naturalist, Cabell belongs with such new writers as Anderson--writers willing to create new forms for new subjects.

39 _____. "Contemporary American Novelists--X. The Revolt from the Village: 1920." Nation, 113 (12 October), 408-409, 410, 412.
The heroes of Anderson's first two novels escape from their villages on quests for meaning, happiness, and money. In Winesburg, Ohio--Anderson's prose imitation of Spoon River Anthology--he makes use of beauty, whereas Masters utilized irony. Anderson loves these village inhabitants, as he later shows similar affection for the characters of Poor White and The Triumph of the Egg. Reprinted: 1922.B45.

40 WHITE, WILLIAM ALLEN. "The Other Side of Main Street." Collier's, 68 (30 July), 7, 18.
Anderson's stories in Winesburg, Ohio are "the picture of a maggoty mind; a snap-shot from a wapperjawed camera." The true artist would have presented a likeable picture. Using French literary methods on American materials creates untrue fiction.

1922 A BOOKS - NONE

1922 B SHORTER WRITINGS

1 ANON. "Sherwood Anderson's Two-Thousand-Dollar Prize Stories." Current Opinion, 72 (January), 96-98.
The Triumph of the Egg joins the unhappy literature America has abundantly produced. The work is "a veritable

chamber of horrors," pervaded by sex and futility, peopled by the atypical; and yet many critics find it valuable literature.

2 ANON. "The Gossip Shop." Bookman, 55 (March), 90-91.
Anderson's oral stories are richly drawled, but his public speeches, says Floyd Dell, are the words of a businessman.

3 ANON. "Sherwood Anderson, Interpreter of the Folks that Men Forgot." Kansas City Star (6 March).
Although accused of imitating Dostoevski, Tolstoi, and the French naturalists, Anderson is neither foreign nor imitative. Thoroughly American in style and subject, Anderson expresses universals about "the submerged world in mid-America"--all without propaganda or message.

4 ANON. "An Exponent of the New Psychology." Literary Digest, 73 (1 April), 33.
Anderson should now be immortal, if foreign opinions matter, for Rebecca West has praised his psychological fiction in an issue of The New Statesman.

5 ANON. Review of The Triumph of the Egg. Irish Independent (29 May).
Anderson, who won the Dial award, will publish Winesburg, Ohio and The Triumph of the Egg in England soon.

6 ANON. "Sherwood Anderson." Observer (4 June).
Anderson excels in creating characters sensitively abnormal. In Winesburg, Ohio and The Triumph of the Egg he sometimes describes the merely provincial; and he cannot always give significance as Chekhov can.

7 ANON. "Literature." Glasgow Herald (8 June), p. 4.
In both Winesburg, Ohio and The Triumph of the Egg Anderson shows "remarkable powers of observation, together with quick analytic skill and ability to compass definite precision of statement."

8 ANON. Review of Winesburg, Ohio and The Triumph of the Egg. London Daily Express (18 June).
In Winesburg, Ohio and The Triumph of the Egg Anderson writes of unhappy people who need sex and love.

9 ANON. Review of Winesburg, Ohio and The Triumph of the Egg. Edinburgh Scotsman (22 June).
In Winesburg, Ohio and The Triumph of the Egg Anderson's thirty-nine stories are vivid and sharp but depressing.

1922

10 ANON. "Fiction." Spectator, 128 (24 June), 789-90.
With the best artistic intentions, Anderson's The Triumph of the Egg handles sex uneasily and makes the reader uneasy. Reprinted in part: 1922.B20.

11 ANON. "Young America." Hull Daily Mail (26 June).
As Anderson is not obsessed with money, he writes ironically of unattractive people, promising in Winesburg, Ohio and The Triumph of the Egg to overcome his forced quality and help raise the standards of American literature.

12 ANON. "American Sketches." Yorkshire Post (5 July).
The Triumph of the Egg fails when Anderson becomes too much the impressionist poet, but many of these stories "stimulate us to explore difficult and unaccustomed ways."

13 ANON. "American Stories." Aberdeen Daily Journal (10 July).
Being a young writer, Anderson in The Triumph of the Egg is sex-obsessed--a quality that damages the style and philosophy of his stories about "dreary, often unlovely figures."

14 ANON. "An Unequal Story-Teller." Times Literary Supplement (13 July), p. 457.
The Triumph of the Egg is "more striking" than Winesburg, Ohio, although in both Anderson's characters are dreamlike, being known by their inner lives. Anderson "can penetrate to those roots of emotion with a sureness which makes them profoundly real--more real than the cramping world outside them." Reprinted: 1957.B3.

15 ANON. "Books to Read." London Weekly Dispatch (16 July).
The Triumph of the Egg contains uneven but striking stories "by a famous United States writer."

16 ANON. "The Candid Critic: Real People or Grotesques?--Only One Side of Life." London Evening Standard (26 July).
Anderson's stories in Winesburg, Ohio and The Triumph of the Egg are depressing and monotonous, "records of the most casual sex encounters, episodes of adulterous wives and faithless husbands, of sex-ridden bachelors and hungry spinsters."

17 ANON. "Young America." Liverpool Daily Post and Mercury (28 July).
Anderson's stories in Winesburg, Ohio and The Triumph of the Egg are worthy of admiration and dislike. Sometimes the author assumes simplicity but fails as he mixes Whitman, Chekhov, and fudge.

18 ANON. "The Short Story in America." Westminster Gazette (12 August).
Not so good as Chekhov but able to write symbolically about small-town characters, Anderson in Winesburg, Ohio and The Triumph of the Egg shows promise of becoming great.

19 ANON. "Friends and Acquaintances in the Book World: Keeping Hens." Humorist (29 August), p. 92.
In The Triumph of the Egg Anderson "speaks with the rude vigour of a man who has seen a family literally annihilated by broodies. . . ."

20 ANON. "An English View of Sherwood Anderson." Life and Letters, 1 (September), 12.
Reprint in part of 1922.B10.

21 ANON. "Other Novels." Spectator, 129 (16 September), 375.
So unified is Winesburg, Ohio that the origin of the work as separate stories is almost unapparent. In comparison to The Triumph of the Egg, the stories in Winesburg, Ohio "exhibit more of artistic restraint and less of a certain passionate crudeness. . . ."

22 B., I. "Mr. Sherwood Anderson's Tales." Manchester Guardian (23 July).
When Anderson forgets his obsession with sex, he can write with Chekhov's understanding of the commonplace. In Winesburg, Ohio and The Triumph of the Egg Anderson lacks narrative power but demonstrates a certain power of observation.

23 BODENHEIM, MAXWELL. "Psychoanalysis and American Fiction." Nation, 114 (7 June), 684.
Psychoanalysis has ruined fiction, for now there is room for one idea only--sex determines life. In Anderson's stories and novels, "young men lie upon their backs in cornfields and feel oppressed by their bodies. . . ."

24 COURNOS, JOHN. "Diagnostician and Artist." London Daily Herald (14 June), p. 2.
In Winesburg, Ohio and The Triumph of the Egg Anderson "writes extraordinarily about ordinary people," finding treasure inside inner lives, equalling Chekhov and de Maupassant.

25 CRAWFORD, NELSON ANTRIM. "Sherwood Anderson, the Wistfully Faithful." Midland, 3 (November), 297-308.
Anderson's writings are "the most significant contribution to American literature" because his style is

(CRAWFORD, NELSON ANTRIM)
colloquial, he feels the tragedy of modern life, and he writes symbolically. Either Winesburg, Ohio or Spoon River Anthology is the greatest work since Leaves of Grass.

26 FAŸ, B.[ERNARD]. "Sherwood Anderson." Vie de Peuples, 7 (10 August), 920-26.
Born on the banks of the Mississippi River, abandoned by his parents, accidentally named, married to a school superintendent, magnate of department stores--this is the Anderson legend. The real Anderson is half the simple townsman and half the cultured man of letters.

27 GARNETT, EDWARD. "A Note on Two American Novelists: Joseph Hergesheimer and Sherwood Anderson." Friday Nights: Literary Criticisms and Appreciations, First Series. London: Jonathan Cape, pp. 342-46.
Poor White shows that Anderson has educated himself in writing fiction so that now his very inability to tell conventional stories in usual ways gives play to the humanity of his characters and situations.

28 GILMAN, LAWRENCE. "The Book of the Month: An American Masterwork." North American Review, 215 (March), 412-16.
The reception of The Triumph of the Egg suffers because the book won the Dial award and because Anderson tells truthful stories. Anderson uses words magically in these stories that are unified by tone in order to have the reader reexamine the apparently, deceptively familiar.

29 H.[EAP], J.[ANE]. "Words." Little Review, 9 (Autumn), 37-38.
Anderson's "impression" of Paul Rosenfeld is from friendship more than objectivity. Critics are wrong to claim that Anderson "writes of the soul of the American people," for he treats an America that pre-dates current materialism and cheapness. Anderson is "more inevitable than conscious" and creates "absolute achievement, experiments and existences." Reprinted: 1953.B18.

30 HECHT, BEN. "Don Quixote and His Last Windmill." A Thousand and One Afternoons in Chicago. Chicago: Covici-McGee Publishers, pp. 31-34.
Anderson and Hecht once drank with a Mr. Sklarg, owner of a factory in Chicago.

31 _____. "Literature and the Bastinado." Nonsensorship. Edited by Heywood Broun et al. New York: G. P. Putnam's Sons, p. 17.

Each year it becomes "more obvious that the duly elected commissioned and delegated high priests of the nation's morale are growing blind to the dangers which assail them. If not, then how does it come that such enemies of the public weal" as Sherwood Anderson "are not in jail?"

32 [LeVERRIER, CHARLES]. "Dernières Publications." L'Europe Nouvelle (11 February), p. 186.
Like Russian writers, Anderson in The Triumph of the Egg finds life full of perplexes and surprises, for he is drawn to grotesques troubled by strange sexuality.

33 _____. "Le Sommeil du Roman Américain." La Revue Hebdomadaire (15 April), p. 298.
As the United States awakens from literary sleep, Anderson (who has not read Freud) finds hidden emotions in sex.

34 LEWISOHN, LUDWIG. Up Stream: An American Chronicle. New York: Boni and Liveright, pp. 149-50.
When the popular novels of 1910 were read, they lied about real life. Even in 1922 "an eminent artist like Sherwood Anderson finds the conventional periodicals inaccessible and suffers the obvious consequences."

35 LOVETT, ROBERT MORSS. "The Promise of Sherwood Anderson." Dial, 72 (January), 79-83.
The Triumph of the Egg marks progress for Anderson in mastering narrative technique, but he has yet not succeeded totally. Unified by cosmic instead of geographical forces, these stories of the ultimate pain and despair of life show Anderson to be a very conscious craftsman. Reprinted: 1934.B24; 1974.A3.

36 MAIS, S. P. B. "Young Writers of America." London Daily Express (22 June).
Trying for new methods of expression in his stories of blindly wandering, miserable people, Anderson has become a new literary force with publication of Winesburg, Ohio and The Triumph of the Egg.

37 MANLY, JOHN MATTHEWS and EDITH RICKERT. "Sherwood Anderson." Contemporary American Literature: Bibliographies and Study Outlines. New York: Harcourt, Brace and Co., pp. 6-8.
[Brief biography, five study questions, brief list of primary and secondary readings].

38 MENCKEN, H. L. "Sherwood Anderson." Smart Set, 67 (February), 143.

(MENCKEN, H. L.)
Although Anderson still seems indecisive in handling ideas, in The Triumph of the Egg the stories are completely original and "full of a strange beauty and an unmistakable power."

39 RASCOE, BURTON. "A Bookman's Day Book: August 9." New York Tribune (20 August), 5, p. 4.
At dinner with Rascoe and Edmund Wilson, Anderson told of his brother Karl's reading Stein's Tender Buttons to a group and laughing. But Anderson reacted amazedly to the book, realizing that Stein was creating new literature by using words as painters produce modern art.

40 [_____]. "The Literary Spotlight--VII: Sherwood Anderson." Bookman, 55 (April), 157-62.
While Anderson passes for humble, his ego as person and writer is huge. His stories and his paintings are good automatically because they are his. Very shrewd and calculating, Anderson listens to everyone, acts superior, and ranks among the country's greatest authors. Reprinted: 1924.B39.

41 ROSENFELD, PAUL. "Sherwood Anderson." Dial, 72 (January), 29-42.
Anderson's genius is to take ordinary English words and structures and transmute them into lovingly crafted art. Son of the Midwest, Anderson has known and loved the life of which he writes. He becomes a "phallic Chekov" [sic] in showing sexuality as life's greatest force. Reprinted: 1924.B40.

42 [SUGITA, MIRAI].
See TAKAGAKI, MATSUO. 1922.B43.

43 TAKAGAKI, MATSUO. "On Sherwood Anderson." Rising Generation, 46 (1 February), 284.
Now introduced for the first time to Japanese readers, Anderson is the author of Windy McPherson's Son, Marching Men, Mid-American Chants, and Winesburg, Ohio. Anderson has been praised by Francis Hackett for Poor White and by Louis Untermeyer for his general realism. The writer's newest work is The Triumph of the Egg. [Takashi Kodaira]

44 UNTERMEYER, LOUIS. Heavens. New York: Harcourt, Brace and Co., pp. 70-72.
Hugh McVey and the doctor in Main Street discuss Hugh's right to live in heaven. [Parody of Poor White]

45 VAN DOREN, CARL. "Sherwood Anderson." Contemporary American Novelists: 1900-1920. New York: Macmillan Co., pp. 153-57.
Reprint of 1921.B39.

46 WEST, REBECCA. "Notes on Novels." New Statesman, 19 (22 July), 443-44.
Although Winesburg, Ohio is not so distinguished as The Triumph of the Egg, this poetic book finds "beauty in anything, in absolutely anything." With illogical plots and delightful inconsequences, ". . . Anderson moves about his ugly little town and watches his dull ugly people. It lives, it glows, they exist as immortal souls."
Reprinted: 1966.A3.

47 WHIPPLE, T. K. "Sherwood Anderson." New York Evening Post Literary Review, 2 (11 March), 481-82.
Whether an author can recreate his native scene is irrelevant; and Anderson errs in saying that he tells stories instead of creates fiction, for his works should be read without regard to environmental verisimilitude. Anderson's generalized landscape of futility, his deformed characters, and their passionate outbursts are beautifully imagined, not cleverly photographed.

1923 A BOOKS - NONE

1923 B SHORTER WRITINGS

1 AARON, MANLEY. "American First Editions: A Series of Bibliographic Check-Lists Edited by Merle Johnson and Frederick M. Hopkins." Publishers' Weekly, 103 (27 January), 251.
[Brief bibliographical descriptions of Anderson's books from Windy McPherson's Son through Many Marriages]

2 A.[DAMS], F.[RANKLIN] P. "The Conning Tower: The Diary of Our Own Samuel Pepys." New York World (24 February), p. 11.
On Sunday, February 18, Adams read Many Marriages and "found the toyle humourless and tedious."

3 ANON. "Latest Works of Fiction." New York Times Book Review (25 February), p. 10.
In Many Marriages Anderson uses stream-of-consciousness technique to present the boring story of a dull man's unprofound rebellion toward freedom.

1923

4 ANON. "Many Marriages." Manuscripts Number Five (March), p. 3.
Perhaps Anderson himself went through a cleansing experience similar to his hero's in Many Marriages--his poetic liturgy of union of mind and body.

5 ANON. "Memorandum on Gertrude Stein." Manuscripts Number Five (March), p. 3.
Anderson's foreword to Geography and Plays by Gertrude Stein wisely assesses Stein's aim of making the word supreme.

6 ANON. "Many Marriages." Boston Transcript (7 March), 3, p. 6.
Dull enough to be harmless, Many Marriages, a "crudely constructed, crudely written story of the beastly amours of a married man," cannot add to Anderson's fame.

7 ANON. "New Novels." Times Literary Supplement (8 March), p. 158.
In Windy McPherson's Son Anderson presents too much ugliness and flatness, turning his narrative occasionally into plot-summary. The author tries to discuss life without showing enough of life.

8 ANON. "Anderson's 'Many Marriages.'" Springfield Republican (11 March), A, p. 8.
Many Marriages disgusts the reader with Anderson's obsession with ugliness. The reader recognizes morbidity and subconscious festering.

9 ANON. "Advertising Bad Books." New York Times (15 March), p. 18.
The public is perhaps threatened by books that appeal to base emotions, but the larger threat is from books that appeal to "pretentious and solemn minds." In Many Marriages Anderson is humorless and naughty and devoid of much idea.

10 ANON. "Purging the Reading Public." New York Times (24 April), p. 20.
Some authors must write for expression, and some publishers must publish for art, and Professor Bliss Perry must wish for more wholesome books. Yet anyone "so solemn as to take 'Many Marriages' seriously was beyond hope."

11 ANON. "The Mind of America." Spectator, 130 (28 April), 714-15.
In Windy McPherson's Son Anderson uses great energy to create "with almost oppressive realism the heavy, sordid

atmosphere of a small town in the Middle-West." The author here tries to give the American novel aspiration toward poetry.

12 ANON. Review of Many Marriages. Binghampton Morning Sun [NY] (14 June).
Many Marriages makes Anderson "the outstanding figure in the rabbit school in America. . . ." The sensitive reader will be more inspired than offended by this novel.

13 ANON. "'Many Marriages' Seems Literary Neurasthenia." Columbia Missourian (16 June).
Without humor but with sincerity, Many Marriages is "a sort of apotheosis of the flesh . . . overstrained and unnatural."

14 ANON. "Many Marriages." Times Literary Supplement (2 August), p. 518.
Anderson's simplistic emphasis on nudity in Many Marriages belies his growing perception and subtlety since he wrote Windy McPherson's Son.

15 ANON. "An American Book in British Courts." Literary Digest, 79 (24 November), 30.
An English publisher is accused of "obscene print" for publishing part of Many Marriages.

16 ANON. "Sherwood Anderson's Unfettered Tales of Unlettered Men." New York Times Book Review (25 November), pp. 7, 25.
Horses and Men are not stories of the lovely aspects of Midwestern life, but they are occasionally powerful versions of the sordid brutality of that area's history.

17 ANON. "Sherwood Anderson." Know Thyself, 1 (December), 15.
Reprint of 1923.B34.

18 ANON. "Fiction." Boston Evening Transcript (19 December), p. 4.
Perhaps Anderson's dedication of Horses and Men to Dreiser is the best part of this book, stories both inchoate and "overloaded with sex."

19 ARVIN, NEWTON. "Mr. Anderson's New Stories." Freeman, 8 (5 December), 307-308.
Anderson's genius is his mythopoetic quality of concern strictly for the inner life. In Horses and Men the writer is trying to be "bardic poet" of the bewildered and frightened. Reprinted: 1924.B19.

1923

20 [BECHHOFER, C. E.].
See ROBERTS, CARL ERIC BECHHOFFER. 1923.B53.

21 BOYNTON, H. W. "Man the Blunderer." Independent, 110 (31 March), 232.
Having passed from bold Midwestern novelist to anti-Puritan, Anderson in Many Marriages tries to be the worldly writer, producing instead "a pretentious tract upon a trite theme, the slavery of the marriage bond."

22 BROUN, HEYWOOD. "It Seems to Me." New York World (24 February), p. 11.
Anderson did not, as perhaps accused, invent the subject of sex in his fiction, for he "is hardly more interested in it than was Walt Whitman nor is he any less disposed to reticence."

*23 _____. Review of Many Marriages. New York World (23 February), E, p. 6.
Cited: Book Review Digest 1923, p. 12.

24 COLLINS, JOSEPH. "Certain Novels, Pleasant and Unpleasant." Literary Digest International Book Review, 2 (December), 43-44.
Anderson's lyrical prose reminds the reader of Walter Pater, although men and works differ vastly. In Horses and Men Anderson triumphs with the American word, basing his new stories on his intuition and his experiences.

25 FAGIN, N. BRYLLION. Short Story Writing: An Art or a Trade? New York: Thomas Seltzer, pp. 16, 17, 79, 81, 128, 129.
Brave young authors might foolishly be content with praise such as given to Anderson instead of money. If Anderson wrote less about filthy sex, he would be more popular; and his talent is wasted on his subjects, for he is a "heretic" for abandoning "the technical and moral pattern of the magazine tradition. . . ."

26 FITZGERALD, F. SCOTT. "Sherwood Anderson on the Marriage Question." New York Herald (4 March), 9, p. 5.
Many Marriages culminates the expression of Anderson's personality and his philosophy of sexual freedom. Using "transcendental naturalism," Anderson has written a book that is "not immoral--it is violently anti-social."
Reprinted: 1971.B14.

27 GOULD, GERALD. "New Fiction." Saturday Review, 135 (17 March), 375.

Again in Windy McPherson's Son Anderson wastes great talent, providing great amounts of dull prose sometimes enlivened with worthwhile parts. He lacks the ability to give form to the novel.

28 _____. "New Fiction." Saturday Review, 136 (8 September), 281.

Both Anderson and Lawrence should never have heard of psychology. In Many Marriages Anderson tries to express a simple philosophy simply and simply fails.

*29 GREGORY, ALYSE. Review of Horses and Men. New York Evening Post Literary Review (8 December), p. 333.

Cited: Book Review Digest 1923, p. 11.

30 _____. "Sherwood Anderson." Dial, 75 (September), 243-46.

Anderson lacks artistic restraint, clear technique; he has not cultivated his native talent through discipline. Better at stories than novels, Anderson yet gropes toward meaning instead of flashing with insight.

31 H., R. B. "The Best of the New Type of Novels." Harvard Crimson (7 April), p. 5.

Many Marriages counters American economics and social orthodoxy. The novel is healthily dangerous and depressingly revolutionary.

32 HANSEN, HARRY. Midwest Portraits: A Book of Memories and Friendships. New York: Harcourt, Brace and Co., pp. 6-7, 12, 103, 109-79, 183, 188, 193, 202, 291, 310, 314-15, 321-22, 323.

When Anderson joined the Chicago Renaissance he produced and defended new forms of writing, partly for self-protection. After dramatically resolving his own problems with business, Anderson sought to write of characters facing similar crises; but his earliest books were modeled on reading more than on direct observation. Later he wrote of the buried lives of types he had known--most of them from Chicago. Today Anderson must decide whether to remain the artist writing truly in isolation or to become the easy social figure. It is Anderson's total concern with mind over outward detail that shall mark his importance.

33 HASTINGS, WILLIAM T. Syllabus of American Literature. Chicago: University of Chicago Press, p. 72.

In Winesburg, Ohio and The Triumph of the Egg Anderson has produced distorted reality through "extreme realism, or naturalism. . . ."

1923

34 [HECHT, BEN]. "Andante Con Amore Face to Face With Artist Anderson." Chicago Literary Times (15 April), pp. 1, 2.
Garrulous as a small-town barber, Anderson has a very charming personality. Fame has not affected Anderson, who is even less intelligent while famous. Hating sentimentality, Anderson is cold and shrewd. Reprinted in part: 1923.B15.

35 [_____]. "Anderson Soars on Phantom Wings and, Alas! Flops." Chicago Literary Times (15 March), p. 2.
In Many Marriages Anderson tries to be both priest and philosopher and fails. Should he fly, he shall perish.

36 [_____]. "A Pair of Windows." Chicago Literary Times (1 March), p. 2.
While drinking with Hecht, Anderson asked Hecht to be not a literary friend but a literary enemy.

*37 J., G. W. Review of Many Marriages. Greensboro Daily News (13 May), p. 24.
Cited: Book Review Digest 1923, p. 12.

38 JONES, LLEWELLYN. "Sherwood Anderson's Biggest Achievement." Chicago Evening Post Literary Review (2 March).
Many Marriages is Anderson's poetic novel of joyful acceptance of life's freedoms. Condemned by moralists, this book is ironically an entirely spiritual document.

39 LAWRENCE, D. H. Studies in Classic American Literature. New York: Thomas Seltzer, p. viii.
"Two bodies of modern literature seem to me to have come to a real verge: the Russian and the American. . . . And by American I do not mean Sherwood Anderson, who is so Russian."

40 LEARY, EVE WOODBURN. "Six Novelists Rewrite Mother Goose: VI--After the Manner of Sherwood Anderson." Literary Digest International Book Review, 1 (September), 7, 12.
Natalie Muffet, bored by her husband and tempted by her employer, escapes into the quiet woods to sit naked eating curds and whey. Dejected by a sudden spider, she abandons the woods and the food to go tempt her employer.

41 L.[EWISOHN], L.[UDWIG]. "Novelist and Prophet." Nation, 116 (28 March), 368.
Many Marriages is flawed by the very passion of the author in stating his subject of sexual liberation. This novel is "imperfect, ragged, absurd, at moments dull; it is also electrically alive, tragic, stirring, memorable."

42 LITTELL, ROBERT. "Many Marriages." New Republic, 37 (11 April), 6-8.

Many Marriages should have been left the long short story that Anderson published in the Dial. Now Anderson has lost his interest in individual characters in order to present theses of sexual behavior.

43 _____. "Rich and Strange." New Republic, 37 (19 December), 99-100.

Horses and Men shows that Anderson "continues, with crude instruments and painful zeal, to work at his unreclaimed land, a fascinating, mysterious place, but a marsh none the less."

44 MAIS, S. P. B. "Sherwood Anderson." Some Modern Authors. London: Grant Richards, pp. 17-31.

In contrast to Fitzgerald, Anderson interprets America instead of just picturing it. Winesburg, Ohio is "one of the most significant books of our generation." Anderson sounds "a clarion call to a new sweet philosophy."

45 MARKEY, GENE. Literary Lights: A Book of Caricatures. New York: Alfred A. Knopf, p. [3].

Caricature captioned: "Sherwood Anderson wondering if the report be true that he is a greater realist than Zola."

46 MENCKEN, H. L. "H. L. Mencken Gives Meed [sic] of Praise to Anderson's Stories." Baltimore Evening Sun (8 December).

Horses and Men redeems Anderson from his literary downfall in Many Marriages. Always here original, Anderson's stories yet show descent from Dreiser. These new characters Anderson knows, and their problem of "dreadful normalcy" is lyrically expressed.

47 _____. "Some New Books." Smart Set, 71 (July), 138-39.

In Many Marriages Anderson shows again that he cannot handle lengthy narration or ideas. Reprinted: 1968.B25.

48 MORTIMER, RAYMOND. "New Novels." New Statesman, 21 (4 August), 500-501.

Many Marriages is "a really silly book," Anderson being totally unable to compromise with commercial success and now stripping his fiction of all but minimal realistic detail. Usually Anderson describes heroic quests for meaning; here he describes becoming free to search.

1923

49 O'BRIEN, EDWARD J. "Sherwood Anderson and Waldo Frank." The Advance of the American Short Story. New York: Dodd, Mead and Co., pp. 247-65.

Anderson rebels against the "mechanical efficiency" of O. Henry's fiction and against Puritanism; and his stories measure gropings toward new life, the author becoming speaker for his people.

50 PERRY, BLISS. "Address on Pernicious Books." Forty-Fifth Annual Report of the New England Watch and Ward Society, 1922-23. Boston: [n.p.], p. 24.

Although sex is "an integral part of human life," some modern authors may think it is all of life: "Walt Whitman was touched with this disease, for a time, but he got over it. I hope that Sherwood Anderson will."

51 RASCOE, BURTON. "The Once-Over." New York Tribune Book News and Reviews (25 November), p. 20.

Horses and Men shows Anderson's "limitations of form and clarity" and his "power, which is certainly that of intuitive genius, the like of which is not to be found among any of the contemporary writers."

52 _____. "Psychology, Realism and Rhapsody." New York Herald Tribune Book News and Reviews (25 February), p. 17.

Anderson's great gift is to tell stories well in the colloquial style; yet he fails in the novel form. In Many Marriages Anderson is too mystical and too close artistically to his hero.

53 ROBERTS, CARL ERIC BECHHOFER. The Literary Renaissance in America. London: William Heinemann, pp. 92, 116-25, 128.

Perhaps Anderson will be the great writer from the American Midwest. In The Triumph of the Egg he returns to the form of Winesburg, Ohio, and Anderson's progress from 1919 to 1921 "shows the distance in self-interpretation that America has travelled in the last few years."

54 SELDES, GILBERT. Announcement of Dial Award. New York Times Book Review (4 December), p. 10.

Anderson has received the Dial award to enable him to continue writing at some leisure, not with the assumption that his best writing is finished.

55 SINCLAIR, UPTON. "Sick Novels of a Sick World." Haldeman-Julius Weekly (31 March), p. 4.

Many Marriages is "a sick book, written by a sick man about a sick world"; yet the author is also "a very gentle, patient and loving human soul, who is also caught in a trap." With no knowledge of the economic facts of life, Anderson writes of a hero needing to free his body. What such people need is clear-headed thinking.

56 STEIN, GERTRUDE. "Idem the Same: A Valentine to Sherwood Anderson." Little Review, 9 (Spring), 5-9.
"Very fine is my valentine and mine, very fine very mine and mine is my valentine." Reprinted: Sherwood Anderson / Gertrude Stein: Correspondence and Personal Essays. Edited by Ray Lewis White. Chapel Hill: University of North Carolina Press, 1972, pp. 28-32.

57 STONE, PERCY N. "Novels à la Carte." Bookman, 57 (April), 210-11.
Many Marriages shows in its clarity and strength that Anderson has mastered narrative.

58 [SUGITA, MIRAI].
See TAKAGAKI, MATSUO. 1923.B59.

59 TAKAGAKI, MATSUO. "New Stars in the American Literary World--Chicago as the Center of the American Literary World, Masters, Dreiser, Sandburg, and Anderson." To, 6 (January), 37-47.
Takagaki was in the Chicago Public Library in 1920 or 1921 when he found Marching Men; he had not before heard of Anderson. He outlines that novel and then adds that he considers Anderson realistic and also poetic. Although Anderson offers criticism of society, the keynote of his work is the agony, hope, and contemplation of a youth sensitive to nature and life, as in Winesburg, Ohio. [Takashi Kodaira]

60 VILLARD, LÉONIE. "La Vie Américaine d'après le Conte et la Nouvelle." Mercure de France (1 December), pp. 322-27, 328.
Winesburg, Ohio taught American authors to care about character more than facts. Anderson builds his book about "moments" that reveal everyday lives. The Triumph of the Egg gives beautifully simple form to themes more fully treated than in Winesburg, Ohio.

61 W., C. Review of Many Marriages. Stanford Spectator (June).
In Many Marriages Anderson avoids didacticism by being poetic. Using a Babbitt-like hero, the author states his belief in combining spiritual and bodily love.

1923

62 WARD, CHRISTOPHER. "The Triumph of the Nut or Too Many Marriages." The Triumph of the Nut and Other Parodies. New York: Henry Holt and Co., pp. 1-9.

All bodies being houses and houses not to wear clothes, John Webster strips, lectures his wife and daughter about sex, and tries to escape with his secretary. Now he resides in a Wisconsin asylum. [Parody of Many Marriages]

63 WILSON, EDMUND. "Many Marriages." Dial, 74 (April), 399-400.

In Many Marriages Anderson is pale, dull, and repetitive; yet even in this poor novel the reader feels "disturbed and soothed by the feeling of hands thrust down among the deepest bowels of life--hands delicate and clean but still pitiless in their explorations." Reprinted: 1952.B23.

1924 A BOOKS - NONE

1924 B SHORTER WRITINGS

1 ANON. "Horses and Men." Times Literary Supplement (7 February), p. 78.

Anderson frequently drops (or rises) from faithfully realistic detail to poetic unreality, making uneven results of Horses and Men.

2 ANON. "Sherwood Anderson and a Parisian Critic." Living Age, 320 (1 March), 429-30.

French critics of American literature, such as Charles LeVerrier, do not understand the relationship between American authors and American Puritanism.

3 ANON. "S. P. Sherman Calls This Great Literary Period." New York Herald Tribune (12 December).

When Sherman addressed the American Academy of Arts and Letters, he praised Anderson for leading modern literature into "new vistas of human experience." Fifty years hence, Anderson's sudden departure in 1912 from his factory will be "one of the historic moments in American literature."

4 ARMSTRONG, MARTIN. "Fiction." Spectator, 132 (9 February), 210-11.

Anderson's attempts in Horses and Men to struggle with inarticulate expression descend into boredom.

5 BALDWIN, CHARLES C. "Sherwood Anderson." The Men Who Make Our Novels. New York: Dodd, Mead and Co., pp. 26-33.

In all of his works Anderson explains the need for a revolution from the drab routines of life toward the excitement of the creative life.

6 BENÉT, WILLIAM ROSE. "The Dark Field." Saturday Review of Literature, 1 (18 October), 200.
A Story Teller's Story lags when Anderson descends into unimpassioned speculation; it sparkles when he narrates his life and impressions of people. Reprinted: 1934.B11.

*7 BLEI, FRANZ. "Tisch mit Büchern." Prager Presse (20 February).
Cited: 1960.B24.

8 BOYD, ERNEST. Portraits: Real and Imaginary. New York: George H. Doran Co., pp. 39, 54, 84, 167.
Many Marriages, cynically viewed, has disrupted family life; it was anticlimactic to Winesburg, Ohio. Snobs will compare Anderson to Henry Fielding to Anderson's loss; and Mencken's praise of Anderson is for the latter's anti-Puritanism.

9 BOYNTON, PERCY H. Some Contemporary Americans: The Personal Equation in Literature. Chicago: University of Chicago Press, pp. 52, 53, 168, 185.
Sandburg, Dell, Masters, and Anderson led the Chicago Renaissance and forced their countrymen to see Midwestern culture anew.

10 BROMFIELD, LOUIS. "A Shelf of Recent Books." Bookman, 60 (December), 492-93.
As Anderson is "of all writers . . . one whose work is drawn out of himself," A Story Teller's Story is the apotheosis of the author's excellent fiction.

11 CALVERTON, V. F. "Sherwood Anderson: A Study in Sociological Criticism." Modern Quarterly, 2 (Fall), 82-118.
The oppression of the proletariat by capitalists is the background out of which Anderson and his writing come. When the author tries--as in his later novels--to write from beyond his own experience of social reality, he fails in art and produces incoherent and puzzling literature. Poor White is almost a great American novel, and Anderson should return to such realistic study of social forces. Reprinted: 1925.B22.

1924

12 CANBY, HENRY SEIDEL. "Sherwood Anderson's 'Many Marriages.'" Definitions, Second Series. New York: Harcourt, Brace and Co., pp. 242-48.
Reprinted: 1930.B15.

13 COLLINS, JOSEPH. "Sophism and Mr. Sherwood Anderson." Taking The Literary Pulse: Psychological Studies of Life and Letters. New York: George H. Doran Co., pp. 29-47.
Anderson has completed his contributions to literature; he will write nothing more new or valuable. Whereas Lawrence has written of sex perversion, Anderson has written of sex obsession. To give sex dominance over life is "absolute denial of the facts of civilised life." Even when he writes stories better than his novels, Anderson's ideas are "fragmentary, incomplete, unbalanced."

14 DELL, FLOYD. "Sherwood Anderson, His First Novel." Looking at Life. New York: Alfred A. Knopf, pp. 79-84.
Reprint of 1916.B8.

*15 DINAMOV, S. "Uainsburg, Ogaio." Knigonosha, No. 22-23, p. 10.
Cited: 1969.B29.

16 DREWRY, JOHN E. Some Magazines and Magazine Makers. Boston: Stratford Publishers, pp. 46, 157-59.
Through his contributions to magazines, Anderson has aided such periodicals as The American Mercury, The Dial, and The Nation. Although his early books and poetry are excellent, Winesburg, Ohio "and several of his short sketches and essays will, in time, become permanent additions to the best class of American literature."

17 FAGIN, N. BRYLLION. "The Feet of Sherwood Anderson." Double Dealer, 6 (July), 167-69.
Horses and Men, Anderson's eighth book, is still full of brooding, groping characters, this time mostly adolescents. The author's subjectivity is his strength.

18 FRANK, WALDO. Salvos: An Informal Book about Books and Plays. New York: Boni and Liveright, pp. 31-40.
Reprint of 1916.B9.

19 The Freeman Book: Typical Editorials, Essays, Critiques, and Other Selections from the Eight Volumes of the Freeman, 1920-1924. New York: B. W. Huebsch, pp. 359-62.
Reprint of 1923.B19.

20 FRIEND, JULIUS WEIS. "A Story Teller's Story." Double Dealer, 7 (November-December), 71-73.
Being "a modern who has absorbed the Freudian psychology," Anderson in A Story Teller's Story presents the emotionally remembered parts of his life which made him an author.

21 GORMAN, HERBERT S. "How One Story-Teller Saved His Soul." Literary Digest International Book Review, 2 (December), 15-16.
A Story Teller's Story may be Anderson's most profound book, giving the author's growth from businessman to author, from fact to imagination.

22 GOULD, GERALD. "New Fiction." Saturday Review, 137 (2 February), 111.
The colloquial style and adolescent characters in Horses and Men do not give consistent success.

23 HANSEN, HARRY. "Sherwood Anderson's Autobiography." Nation, 119 (10 December), 640-41.
Standing almost alone among autobiographies of American authors, A Story Teller's Story describes "the mental growth" of a valuable author.

24 KELLOGG, ARTHUR. "Telling Tales on Life." Survey, 53 (1 December), 288-89.
In A Story Teller's Story Anderson gives stories of famous and unknown people who aided the artist in gaining his individualistic view of life.

25 LeVERRIER, CHARLES. "L'Adolescent Attardé." L'Europe Nouvelle, 7 (5 January), 12-13.
Many Marriages is more naive than vulgar, Anderson being a childish author more emotional than rational.

26 LEWIS, SINCLAIR. "A Pilgrim's Progress." New York Herald Tribune Books (9 November), pp. 1-2.
A Story Teller's Story is the pilgrimage of the creative writer and the Midwestern teller of tales, picturing the soul of an author hurt often by his detractors.
Reprinted: 1953.B22.

27 LEWISOHN, LUDWIG. The Creative Life. New York: Boni and Liveright, pp. 54, 67-68, 116-17.
Anderson and other writers are haunted by the goal of the mythopoetic novel. The hero of Anderson's Many Marriages is an extreme example of the decadence of recent

(LEWISOHN, LUDWIG)
fiction. And all of Anderson's works may be denied "classic" status because of his lack of universality and acceptable speech.

28 _____. "The Grandeur that Was. . . ." Nation, 118 (30 April), 510-11.
In Horses and Men Anderson is bringing into fiction the buried minds of the forgotten American, hunting for the earthy secret of life.

29 LOVETT, ROBERT MORSS. "Horses and Men." Dial, 76 (March), 274-76.
Horses and Men demonstrates Anderson's ability to let his fiction base itself on character, with theme or moral distinctly secondary. As Winesburg, Ohio was unified by setting, so these new stories are unified by method--the author's entering imaginatively into his characters' minds.

30 _____. "Sherwood Anderson." English Journal, 8 (October), 531-39.
Anderson has produced a large and largely unified body of work in ten years. In the forthcoming A Story Teller's Story he explains his trust of reality and his faith in imagination. Most like Chekhov of all American writers, Anderson is far better in the story genre than the novel.

31 _____. "A Story Teller's Story." New Republic, 40 (5 November), 255-56.
A Story Teller's Story is not a chronological autobiography but instead "a story of spiritual adventure, a fascinating and moving revelation of the artist's mind."

32 MENCKEN, H. L. "Three Volumes of Fiction." American Mercury, 1 (February), 252.
Horses and Men is "largely a set of variations on Dreiserian themes" and is a tonic to Anderson's mysticism in Many Marriages.

33 MORRIS, LLOYD. "The Education of Sherwood Anderson." New York Times Book Review (12 October), pp. 6, 22.
Along with The Education of Henry Adams, A Story Teller's Story is a searching to understand America and the role of the individual in current society.

34 MORTIMER, RAYMOND. "New Novels." New Statesman, 22 (9 February), 513-14.

As Anderson is "the only living American novelist whose prose it is often a pleasure to read," his stories are disappointing when they leave ordinary reality for fancy. The stories in Horses and Men somehow are about searching for truth.

35 POLETIKA, JURIJ. Review of Winesburg, Ohio. Russkij Sovremenik, 3 (1924), 283.
Winesburg, Ohio marks the possible decline of the sentimental, romantic line of short stories and the resurgence of the psychological type. [James F. Cradler]

36 R., M. "Horses and Men." Vient de Paraître (May), p. 264.
A Paris newspaper had to stop printing Anderson's stories because French readers were offended by his adolescent characters' sexual lives. France has not often been more prudish than the United States about such stories as those in Horses and Men.

37 RANSOM, JOHN CROWE. "Freud and Literature." Saturday Review of Literature, 1 (4 October), 161-62.
Of American writers Anderson exhibits Freud's influence--an influence repulsive to the public but enriching to literature. At the publication of Winesburg, Ohio, ". . . it almost seemed as if for the first time in our history American humble folk were depicted in the possession of their inalienable human rights, by virtue of exercising frankly those radical and immitigable passions which are the most that human beings can possess. . . ."

38 RASCOE, BURTON. "Contemporary Reminiscences." Arts & Decoration, 21 (August), 66-67.
Basically mystical, Anderson succeeds in his stories in separating "the mystically poetic and the realistically prosaic." He admits to having deep religious feeling that "Christ was the rightest man I know anything about." He hears confessions from simple folk instead of enjoying literary crowds, and his oral tales such as the one about Mama Geighen are full of robust humor. Reprinted: 1937.B42.

39 [_____]. "XXIII: Sherwood Anderson." The Literary Spotlight. Edited by John Farrar. New York: George H. Doran Co., pp. 232-40.
Reprint of 1922.B40.

1924

40 ROSENFELD, PAUL. "Sherwood Anderson." Port of New York: Essays on Fourteen American Moderns. New York: Harcourt, Brace and Co., pp. 175-98.
Reprint of 1922.B41.

41 SHERMAN, STUART P. Points of View. New York: Charles Scribner's Sons, pp. 132-33, 136, 263-68.
Anderson and other unhappy Midwesterners have brought their locality into prominence in American literature. And Anderson has written a sensible introduction to his own favorite author, Gertrude Stein; but Geography and Plays is incomprehensible.

42 STALLINGS, LAWRENCE. "The First Reader: A Legendary Hero." New York World (23 October).
A Story Teller's Story is an autobiography with "gusto" and with the humor that Anderson has often lacked.

43 [SUGITA, MIRAI].
See TAKAGAKI, MATSUO. 1924.B44.

44 TAKAGAKI, MATSUO. "Introduction to 'War.'" Study of English (November), pp. 19-26.
No other contemporary American writer could write a story so rich in universality as Anderson has done with "War." His work is unforgettable; his setting is as symbolic as in drama; Anderson tries to express the voice of the soul: his effect is gripping. [Takashi Kodaira]

45 _____. "A New Star in the American Literary World: Sherwood Anderson." Shincho (April), pp. 26-35.
Anderson's work has three stylistic characteristics: simplicity and little dialogue, rhythm based on thought, and digressions. Reprinted revised: 1934.B38. [Takashi Kodaira]

46 W., R. D. "The Voice of an Author." Boston Transcript (31 December), p. 4.
A Story Teller's Story is basically a story of escape into imagination and reverence for all life.

47 WERTH, ALEXANDER. "Letters to the Editor: Sherwood Anderson." New Age, 35 (19 June), 94-95.
Although Anderson can write well, he has produced some of "the most obvious rubbish." When Anderson is good, he expresses life itself in his writings.

48 WILSON, EDMUND. "Mr [sic] Hemingway's Dry Points." Dial, 77 (October), 340.
Anderson, Stein, and Hemingway now almost form a "school" of literature by themselves; and Hemingway is the only other American writer but Anderson to have been influenced by Three Lives. Reprinted: 1952.B23.

49 _____. "Mr [sic] Lardner's American Stories." Dial, 77 (July), 69-70.
How to Write Short Stories by Ring Lardner contains pieces almost as good as examples by Anderson and Lewis, for in vernacular and outer realities he excels Anderson. Reprinted: 1952.B23.

50 YOUNG, STARK. "The Prompt Book: New Mine for Dramatists." New York Times (16 November), 8, p. 1.
The American theater needs a dramatist to achieve what Anderson has in A Story Teller's Story--American material, precision, tenderness, comedy, and natural feeling.

51 YUST, WALTER. "The Essence of Things." New York Evening Post Literary Review (1 November), p. 4.
Wise in groping toward the essence instead of the surface of life, Anderson in A Story Teller's Story has written "the most significant book of the year."

1925 A BOOKS - NONE

1925 B SHORTER WRITINGS

1 A., E. H. "Library Notes." Marine Base Weekly (3 August).
Influenced by Whitman, Anderson's informal autobiography is subtly formed. Careless of praise or blame, Anderson in publishing A Story Teller's Story shows that "while other modern authors concern themselves with freakishness and filth, Anderson goes on quietly working as the true artist always works. . . ."

2 ANON. "Biography." Booklist, 21 (January), 147.
A Story Teller's Story is Anderson's autobiography of his imaginative life, giving the origins of several of his stories.

3 ANON. "The Artistic 'Urge.'" Springfield Republican (4 January), A, p. 7.
Anderson's own life, as described in A Story Teller's Story, was of bleak poverty until his middle-age rebellion

1925

(ANON.)
toward the creative life. Despite frequent poor taste, Anderson's stories have emerged from this hard life.

4 ANON. "Sherwood Anderson Well Known Writer at M'Vicar Chapel." College Hill News, No. 9 (15 January), p. 1.
Anderson will speak in Topeka, Kansas, on "America, a Storehouse of Vitality"; and he is "a pleasing speaker and really has something to say about American life and letters."

5 ANON. "Anderson Here Tonight." Topeka Daily State Journal (16 January).
After two years of being hard to get as a speaker in Topeka, Anderson will present "America, a Storehouse of Vitality." Knowing people and how to write great stories, Anderson is the "most significant voice now heard in America."

6 ANON. "The Word Fellow." London Morning Post (16 June).
Product of hard Midwestern life, Anderson sees the world clearly and coldly in A Story Teller's Story--especially the interior world of the United States.

7 ANON. "An Artist in Revolt: The Autobiography of Mr. Sherwood Anderson." Yorkshire Post (17 June).
A Story Teller's Story shows Anderson cutting through the face of industry for creative living by the individual in the inner world.

8 ANON. "A Story Teller's Story." Times Literary Supplement (20 August), p. 541.
When Anderson gives fictional form to his vision of life, he creates often good stories; when he theorizes his vision, he creates a muddled narrative. A Story Teller's Story shows Anderson's failure to create his characters and himself in society.

9 ANON. "Sherwood Anderson Contemplates Life on the Levee." New York Times Book Review (20 September), p. 9.
Realizing that the buried parts of lives must be acknowledged, Anderson in Dark Laughter creates sensual rebellion amid primitivism; yet the entire novel degrades humanity.

10 ANON. "Noted Author to Hear Nickname." Toledo Times (15 November), p. 14.

George S. Richards of Toledo, for whom Anderson worked as a boy, may call him "Job Lots" because in his three years of selling goods for Richards in Clyde, Ohio, Anderson was a "queer sort of boy" who showed little promise in life.

11 BENCHLEY, ROBERT. "A Ghost Story (As Sherwood Anderson Would Write It If He Weren't Prevented)." Life, 86 (December), 21, 64.

David Perk, contemplating the sex of potatoes, awaits a midnight ghost--hopefully he will have a girl ghost. Remembering niggers singing on Boston Common, he escapes into freedom with his girl ghost.

12 BERG, RUBEN. Moderna Amerikaner. Stockholm: Hugo Gebers Förlag, pp. 113-25.

From Dreiser Anderson could have learned a psychological approach; from Masters he may have gotten the idea for Winesburg, Ohio. Desiring to be the poet of Mid-America, praising nature more than small towns, Anderson, unlike Dreiser, could not write sympathetically of capitalists. He deals better with the frustrated misfits who suffer as Anderson himself did. In his later books, Anderson attacked the standardization brought to American life by technology.

*13 BOND, GEORGE. "Sherwood Anderson Chats at Length About Books and This Changing Age." Dallas Morning News (24 October), Magazine.

Cited: 1964.A2.

14 BOYD, ERNEST. "Readers and Writers." Independent, 115 (12 September), 302.

Using the usual triangle of lovers, Anderson in Dark Laughter again treats his two subjects of sexual liberation and artistic isolation.

15 BRAND, KARL. Letter. Ohio State Journal (8 December).

Contrary to reports, Anderson's lecture in Columbus, Ohio, on December 7, 1925, was well understood by the audience, even though the speaker was at times confusing.

16 _____. Letter. Ohio State Journal (13 December).

Anderson's lecture in Columbus, Ohio, was quite good; the charge that he is neurotic is not new. Winesburg, Ohio is "an authoritative and excellent study of the spiritual and moral life of a small American community."

1925

17 BREWSTER, DOROTHY and ANGUS BURRELL. Dead Reckonings in Fiction. New York: Longmans, Green and Co., pp. 10, 11.

Why should one care what authors are remembered--Anderson or Tarkington or H. B. Wright? Behaviorist critics would prescribe Anderson and Lawrence for the repressed, but immorality in literature can create immorality in life.

18 BRICKELL, HERSCHEL. "An Armful of Fiction." Bookman, 62 (November), 338-39.

In A Story Teller's Story Anderson gives his familiar story of rebellion and escape. The use of Negro laughter is a "daring experiment," and Anderson's preservation or recapture of a past American scene is well handled in Dark Laughter.

19 BROUN, HEYWOOD. "It Seems to Me." New York World (29 September).

Anderson might become the best-known novelist of his day, his books might be taught in colleges (perhaps in 2022), and his reference in Dark Laughter to Heywood Broun might immortalize that newspaperman.

20 BUTCHER, FANNY. "Reviewer Twines No Bay Wreath for Sherwood Anderson." Chicago Tribune (10 October), p. 14.

In materials and results, Dark Laughter is filthy and ugly. Great in neither poetry nor in psychology, Anderson here has thrown words on his pages, with no regard for style or logic.

21 C., W. R. "Thoughts on Solitude." Spectator Literary Supplement (24 October), p. 712.

In A Story Teller's Story Anderson has shown "the exasperation . . . of genius with a society whose ideas and whose goods are all equally 'ready made.'"

22 CALVERTON, V. F. The Newer Spirit: A Sociological Criticism of Literature. Introduction by Ernest Boyd. New York: Boni & Liveright, pp. 52-118.

Reprint of 1924.B11.

23 _____. "Sherwood Anderson Not At His Best In His Latest Novel." Baltimore Evening Sun (12 September).

Science and technology have destroyed the beauty and spirituality extant before the modern age, Anderson claims in Dark Laughter, a novel without form or acceptable character or restraint.

24 CANBY, HENRY SEIDEL. "The Woman Takes. . . ." Saturday Review of Literature, 2 (10 October), 191.
Perhaps a further phase of Anderson himself, the hero of Dark Laughter desires freedom to be creative in a mechanized society. Wanting other than women, this hero is captured by a woman. Anderson brilliantly senses and dramatizes the buried lives and the repressed desires of his countrymen.

25 CESTRE, C. "Sherwood Anderson: A Story Teller's Story." Revue Anglo-Américaine, 3 (December), 175-78.
Winesburg, Ohio was bolder than the fiction of Zola. Instead of the expected emphasis on sex, in A Story Teller's Story Anderson gives more essence than fact from his life. His style here is slow, boring, repetitive, and nonchronological.

26 COLLINS, JOSEPH. "The Doctor Looks at Biography." Bookman, 61 (March), 22-25.
Only Cellini and Rousseau have excelled Anderson's revelations in A Story Teller's Story, in which he gives "the gestation and travail of the poet's fancy, the birth and growth of poetical form" and his later great escape from business into literature. Of manic-depressive constitution, Anderson's primary characteristic is the forming of expression about beauty. Reprinted: 1925.B27.

27 _____. Litterateurs: American Writers." The Doctor Looks at Biography: Psychological Studies of Life and Letters. New York: George H. Doran Co., pp. 63-68.
Reprint of 1925.B26.

28 DeWOLFE, CHUB. "Good Evening: Sherwood Anderson." Toledo News-Bee (17 November), p. 4.
Anderson could be named for a Toledo congressman; being from Clyde, home of kraut and perhaps Winesburg, Ohio, the author will speak in Toledo on "America, a Storehouse of Vitality." Preferable would be a speech by Anderson on the originals for Winesburg, Ohio.

*29 DINAMOV, S. "Torzhestvo Iaitsa." Knigonosha, No. 10, p. 18.
Cited: 1969.B29.

30 EMERSON, R. H. "Sherwood Anderson Fails in Profundity." Springfield Republican (11 October), A, p. 5.
Anderson's method in Dark Laughter is symbolism, an attempt to express in lyric prose the author's plea for simple, joyous living. Yet philosophically Anderson fails through ignoring totally any rationality.

1925

31 FAGIN, N. BRYLLION. "Sherwood Anderson: A Middleaged Adolescent." Guardian, 1 (April), 246-55.

Anderson is the grim, earnest "product of middle-aged America," with the "soul of an adolescent." A very subjective writer, lyrical and elegiac, Anderson wants America to mature. Reprinted with slight revision: 1927.A2.

32 _____. "Sherwood Anderson and Our Anthropological Age." Double Dealer, 7 (January-February), 91-99.

The race's first literature is cosmological--"What is the physical world?" Next is anthropological literature--"What is man, singly and socially?" Being motivated anthropologically, Anderson questions American characters and society mystically, adolescently, obliquely--all in order to understand and record the inner, buried life. Reprinted with slight revision: 1927.A2.

33 FAULKNER, WILLIAM. "Prophets of the New Age II. Sherwood Anderson." Dallas Morning News (26 April), 3, p. 7.

The characters in Winesburg, Ohio, Anderson's first book, are alive, and then Anderson's characters and stories begin to decline. Horses and Men causes one to ask whether stories not novels are Anderson's métier. While with Anderson on a boat out of New Orleans, the writer told a good dream-story with humor an ingredient. Reprinted: 1957.B10.

34 FRANK, WALDO. "Laughter and Light." Dial, 79 (December), 510-14.

Having been taken into American literature, Anderson's early chapters in Dark Laughter are a continuation of his themes and style. Yet in overall narrative craft, Anderson shows maturity, combining romantic escape again with assumed Negro primitivism.

35 _____. "Meditation: On Reading 'A Story Teller's Story.'" Guardian, 1 (February), 97-99.

A Story Teller's Story must be accepted, not analyzed. Read with simple faith, this book is a "naif relation of fresh religious values." Moved by spirit alone, Anderson is godlike.

36 GALANTIÈRE, LEWIS. "A Storyteller's Story." Vient de Paraître (May), pp. 262-63.

Not a classically written autobiography, A Story Teller's Story has little form but good episodes. In it French readers will find an unfamiliar American world.

37 [GUTTERMAN, ARTHUR]. "Fiction." Outlook, 141 (21 October), 288.
If readers are shocked by Dark Laughter, when Anderson calls for irresponsible primitivism, they must simply accept this author's anti-social view.

38 HARRIS, JULIA. "The Story of an American Artist." Columbus Enquirer-Sun [GA] (4 January).
Gifted in telling truth frankly, Anderson in A Story Teller's Story need be read by only open-minded and poetic souls.

39 HEAP, JANE. "Books and Other Matters." Little Review, 10 (Autumn 1924-Winter), 19-21.
Anderson is redeeming himself with A Story Teller's Story after Many Marriages, which may belong to the "whisky [sic] school of prophecy and art." Much of the value of A Story Teller's Story is Anderson's frequent disregard for factual truth.

40 HEMINGWAY, ERNEST. "A Story Teller's Story." Ex Libris, 2 (March), 176-77.
A Story Teller's Story shows Anderson's humor and contains beautiful episodes. As the book is made up of sometimes interrelated tales, Anderson is here using his best genre, producing "as good writing as Sherwood Anderson has done and that means considerably better than any other American writer has done." Reprinted: 1974.A3.

41 HERVEY, JOHN. "Sherwood Anderson." All's Well, 5 (March), 9-11.
Having liked the promise shown in his early works, the reader now finds disappointment in Anderson's writing and only with trouble can finish reading A Story Teller's Story. Even Winesburg, Ohio is an inferior imitation of Spoon River Anthology.

42 KREYMBORG, ALFRED. Troubadour, An American Autobiography. New York: Boni & Liveright, pp. 221, 222, 225-27, 229, 287-88.
From the Midwest, Anderson had to fight no established culture but could bloom among common people; and Chicago critics prejudicially promoted him. Anderson was friendlier and mellower than Masters or Sandburg. Resembling a kindly businessman, Anderson obviously had experienced deeply and was almost ready for literary expression.

1925

43 KRUTCH, JOSEPH WOOD. "Vagabonds." Nation, 121 (2 December), 626-27.

Mistaken for a philosopher, Anderson is a poet able to describe vagrant souls like his own; in Dark Laughter he succumbs to primitivism--too easily, perhaps. Reprinted: 1926.B51; 1966.A7.

44 LANGFIELD, WILLIAM R. "Sherwood Anderson Pursues Elusive Emotions." Literary Digest International Book Review, 3 (November), 805, 808.

As a romantic realist, Anderson creates mythical, symbolic characters. In Dark Laughter he clothes his bare characters with aspects of himself--thoughts, hopes, and escape to freedom, especially in sex.

45 LOVETT, ROBERT MORSS. "Dark Laughter." New Republic, 44 (21 October), 233-34.

At last Anderson proves in Dark Laughter that he can manage a novel-length fiction, based on his direct experience of life and his devotion to art as a basis for life.

46 MacLEISH, ARCHIBALD. Review of Dark Laughter. Atlantic Monthly, 136 (December), Bookshelf.

In Dark Laughter Anderson tries to mold the technique of Ulysses and conventional narration, succeeding in structure but forgetting to have the Joycean internalization occur in the minds of the characters instead of in Anderson's own mind.

47 MARPLE, ALLEN. Letter. Ohio State Journal (12 December).

The writer of this letter did not hear Anderson's lecture in Columbus, Ohio, but wishes the newspaper had sent a better reporter.

48 MENCKEN, H. L. "As H. L. M. Sees It: Why Sherwood Anderson Puzzles All the Academic Critics." Baltimore Sun (5 January).

Traditional literary critics dislike Anderson because his works cannot be studied scientifically. Anderson has no final answers: "The agony of man in this world interests him immensely, but he doesn't know what causes it and he has no remedy for it."

49 _____. "Fiction Good and Bad." American Mercury, 6 (November), 379-80.

In protagonist and setting, Dark Laughter is Anderson's finest long fiction. The writer is too wise to give ready explanations; he simply presents his characters dramatically.

etry. Edited By Peter H. Lee.
ty Press Of Hawaii,1980.

. The Sound Of Thunder.
ng-o-sa, 1990.

The Waves: Four Modern Korean
ranslated By Sung-Il Lee.
manities Press, 1989.

Wrens Elegy, A Prose : The
An Epic & Other Poems.
d, 1980.

dBond

Publica

Fiction Kim — Kim, Dong-ni
Paul Ir

895.7 Silence — The Silence
Korean
Univers

Fiction Kim — KIm, Chu-Yor
Si-sa-y

895.714 Wind — The Wind And
Poets.
Asian I

895.714 Mo — Mo, Yun-Suk
Pagoda
Larchwo

SELECTED BOOKLIST OF KOREAN A
TRAN

895.7 Silence	The Silence Korean Univers
Fiction Kim	KIm, Chu-Yon Si-sa-y
895.714 Wind	The Wind And Poets. Asian F
895.714 Mo	Mo, Yun-Suk. Pagoda, Larchwo

50 MORRIS, LLOYD. "Skimming the Cream From Six Months' Fiction." New York Times Book Review (6 December), p. 2.
Anderson's major flaw in Dark Laughter is the mysticism which simply appears important or thoughtful.

51 POWYS, LLEWELLYN. "Half Truths." Dial, 78 (April), 330-32.
In A Story Teller's Story Anderson writes careless prose and tells half-lies about himself, redeemed somewhat by his vignettes from life.

*52 RAMM, E. "Shervud Anderson. Torzhestvo Yaitsa." Novy Mir, No. 8, pp. 155-56.
Cited: 1969.B29.

*53 RED. "Sherwood Anderson." Novinki Zapada, No. 1, p. 95.
Cited: 1969.B29.

54 RICHARDS, V. K. "Uplift the World? Not My Job, Says Sherwood Anderson." Toledo Blade (19 November), p. 3.
Never having read a psychology book and claiming that his work has no social message, Anderson states that "When a man sets out to reform the world he should have something to offer which he is sure is better. And I haven't."

55 S., K. "Dark Laughter." Boston Transcript (10 October), p. 4.
Literary radicals should realize that revolution against tradition does not lead to happiness. Dark Laughter adds little "to the reputation of Sherwood Anderson, nothing to American literature, not a whit to the enjoyment of life."

56 SCHÖNEMANN, FRIEDRICH. "Der Arme Weisse." Das Literarische Echo, 28 (April), 372-73.
Anderson has slowly gained a reputation although he has the flaws of desperate ideas, primitivism, and an often bizarre style. Yet--as Poor White demonstrates--he has the virtues of independence, keen ability, and direct observation of life. Poor White now stands as Anderson's best novel to date.

57 SELAH. Letter. Ohio State Journal (11 December).
As Anderson's lecture in Columbus, Ohio, leads one to hope, his literary works--products of a "diseased mind"--will soon be forgotten.

58 SHERMAN, STUART P. "Sherwood Anderson's Tales of the New Life." New York Herald Tribune Books (4 October), pp. 1, 2.
Now that Anderson has been living in New Orleans, he tries in Dark Laughter to show possible rejuvenation for

1925

(SHERMAN, STUART P.)
American letters. In itself, however, the novel is another of Anderson's businessman-escaping-to-freedom stories. Reprinted: 1926.B67.

59 STEIN, GERTRUDE. "A Stitch in time saves nine. . . ." Ex Libris, 2 (March), 177.
A Story Teller's Story is not the story of Anderson's personal facts but instead the story of his existence. Here as always Anderson renders life permanently. Reprinted: Sherwood Anderson/Gertrude Stein: Correspondence and Personal Essays. Edited by Ray Lewis White. Chapel Hill: University of North Carolina Press, 1972, p. 45; 1974.A3.

60 TOE, MISS L. Letter. Ohio State Journal (11 December).
Anderson's recent lecture in Columbus, Ohio, was not well received; the lecture was indeed "a farce."

61 TUGWELL, REXFORD GUY. "An Economist Reads Dark Laughter." New Republic, 45 (9 December), 87-88.
The creator and citizen of the modern orderly world reads Dark Laughter uneasily, for Anderson is subversively calling for humanism among progress, mechanization, and comfort.

62 V.[AN] D.[OREN], C.[ARL]. "O Pioneers!" Century, 109 (March), 717-18.
In A Story Teller's Story Anderson tells of fighting against conventional life in order to create. For the first time in a long narrative, he has sustained his purpose and technique to make this work one of "the few best American autobiographies."

63 _____. "Sinclair Lewis and Sherwood Anderson: A Study of Two Moralists." Century, 110 (July), 362-69.
Both Lewis and Anderson study individuals repressed by societies from escape or growth into happier ways of living. In Anderson's stories characters who remain in conventional societies are warped, tortured, made grotesque. While Lewis sees society clearly and comedically, Anderson's vision is blurred and poetic.

64 VAN DOREN, IRITA. "A Fugue in Words." Forum, 74 (December), 955-56.
Telling always one story and obsessed always with words, Anderson triumphs in only one way in Dark Laughter: his choral effect from Negro laughter is finely handled.

65 WANN, LOUIS. "The 'Revolt From the Village' in American Fiction." Overland Monthly and Out West Magazine, 83 (August), 299.

The revolt against provincialism in American literature has not come from the foreign-born, but from natives. In Winesburg, Ohio and The Triumph of the Egg, descended from Spoon River Anthology, Anderson has come to stand for revolt against small-town Ohio.

66 WILBUR, SUSAN. "What Mark Twain Left Out." Chicago Evening Post Literary Review (25 September), pp. 1, 3.

Dark Laughter is Anderson's best book to date, giving first clearly-focused pictures of modern life and then dream-like escape into liberation.

67 WOOLF, VIRGINIA. "American Fiction." Saturday Review of Literature, 2 (1 August), 1-3.

Anderson is among the most popular American authors read in England, and A Story Teller's Story can illustrate books that can cause problems for English readers of American writing. Anderson is strongly patriotic in subject, language, genres, and depth, making success out of his defensiveness. Reprinted: 1948.B33.

68 YUST, WALTER. "Anderson's 'Dark Laughter' Only Novel in Name, But Has Peaks of Rare and Charming Magic." Philadelphia Public Ledger (26 September), p. 14.

Because Anderson is "the most important living short story writer," certain parts of Dark Laughter are fine literature; but the novel as a whole is structurally flawed.

*69. _____. Review of Dark Laughter. New York Evening Post Literary Review (26 September), p. 2.

Cited: Book Review Digest 1925, p. 14.

1926 A BOOKS - NONE

1926 B SHORTER WRITINGS

1 ANON. Four Addresses in Commemoration of the Twentieth Anniversary of the Founding of the American Academy of Arts and Letters. [New York]: American Academy of Arts and Letters, pp. 11, 186-88.

Paul Shorey has heard told that Anderson put aside reading others' books and thus wrote Winesburg, Ohio. Stuart Sherman predicts that someday literary historians

1926

(ANON.)
will point to Anderson's dramatic escape from business and call it symbolic, prophetic, and historic.

2 ANON. "Fiction." Booklist, 22 (January), 161.
Dark Laughter is an "intimate, rather wandering, but on the whole a finely written story of a man and a woman."

3 ANON. "Good Typography From San Francisco." New York Times Book Review (10 January), p. 14.
In The Modern Writer Anderson blames literary failures on commercialism, industrialism, and cheap writing.

4 ANON. "Sherwood Anderson MS. Burned In Excitement Caused by Fire." New York Times (26 January), p. 29.
The manuscript of "Sherwood Anderson's Notebook"--scheduled for spring publication--was burned in a fire at the office of Boni & Liveright.

5 ANON. "Dark Laughter." Times Literary Supplement (29 April), p. 320.
Although Dark Laughter is Anderson's anti-intellectually-presented plea for joyous, spontaneous living, his thought becomes dissipated and confused.

6 ANON. "In Brief Review." Bookman, 63 (May), 361.
The Modern Writer contains Anderson's idea that industrialism has led to the fakery and dullness of much recent writing.

7 ANON. "Sherwood Anderson's Notes." Springfield Republican (16 June), p. 12.
Reading Sherwood Anderson's Notebook shows the author to be of "virile, outspoken [,] crude, powerful personality. . . ."

8 ANON. "New Books in Brief Review." Independent, 116 (26 June), 751.
Sherwood Anderson's Notebook is an uneven collection, often acutely perceptive, frequently blind in judgment--especially in self-criticism.

9 ANON. "Essays and Criticism." Outlook, 143 (21 July), 420.
Sherwood Anderson's Notebook reveals more of the writer's inner life than do his novels, for the writer is here revealed as passionately life-seeking and mystically realistic.

10 ANON. "Books in Brief." Nation, 123 (18 August), 155.
The pieces in Sherwood Anderson's Notebook are critical and often autobiographical, for "he has never written more engagingly."

11 ANON. "Freer Verse Than Usual." New York Times (10 September), p. 20.
As Dreiser has "appropriated" some Anderson material for one of his poems, the matter could interest a psychologist more than a literary critic, although Dreiser's adaptation of Anderson's prose aids the debate over free verse.

12 ANON. "Literature." Booklist, 23 (November), 68.
Anderson's impressions of people are mixed with thoughtful essays on life in Sherwood Anderson's Notebook, for the "working of the writer's mind becomes almost a visual process in the course of the disclosures set down here."

13 ANON. "Sherwood Anderson's 'Tar.'" New York World (5 December), M, p. 11.
Although flawed by Anderson's occasional didacticism, Tar is a lovely, gentle picture of the author's youth. Anderson "is still the only writer who regards the soil lovingly, who gets the tang of it into his writing."

14 ANON. "Notes of a Rapid Reader." Saturday Review of Literature, 3 (18 December), 451.
Tar is Anderson's brooding over the flavor of significance in his own youth, "born curious as to how (and why) the human machine works."

15 BEACH, JOSEPH WARREN. The Outlook for American Prose. Chicago: University of Chicago Press, pp. 9, 11, 12, 15, 17, 25, 59-60, 118, 204, 211-14, 247-80.
Future American prose will probably be modeled on Anderson's style, for Anderson writes simple prose "in the interest of feeling and design." A Story Teller's Story is important as both autobiography and literary criticism. Whereas Henry Adams wrote in resignation, Anderson writes inspired and energetic prose. He writes from his senses and from his mystical imagination to reflect the size and complexity of his nation. His stories are carefully crafted but resemble the oral, unprofessional storytelling tradition. From Stein and from his own experiments Anderson has learned to use words to capture the mysterious souls of characters.

1926

*16 BERGE, ANDRÉ. "Le Cahier de la Rédaction. Les Cahiers du Mois (1 January), pp. 151-54.
Cited: 1971.A1.

17 BODENHEIM, MAXWELL. "The Pagan Meditates." Oracle, 2 (July), 12-13, 22-23.
Product of poverty and Freud, Anderson has brooded on the matter of repression until his fictional philosophy is merely guise for his paganism. If all humanity at once stripped and had sex, he once said, all troubles would end.

18 [BRADLEY, W. ASPENWALL]. "Dark Laughter." Vient de Paraître (April), p. 194.
Dark Laughter shows Anderson becoming less a storyteller than a moralist. When he leaves the autobiographical and the observed in favor of the psychological, he loses authenticity.

19 BROCK, H. I. "Sherwood Anderson Reports on Life and Letters." New York Times Book Review (9 May), p. 2.
Usually without humor, Anderson scolds America about industrialism in his Notebook, an anthology of his published essays with autobiographical supplements.

20 BROOKS, VAN WYCK. "Day-Dreams." Forum, 76 (October), 637.
In his Notebook Anderson describes dreamily people he has known and goals for which he has strived--ultimately the goal of an "America of the future that has outgrown commercial values and seeks for a spacious, gracious, leisurely life."

21 BURROW, TRIGANT. "Psychoanalytical Improvisations and the Personal Equation." Psychoanalytic Review, 13 (April), 173-86.
In "Seeds" Anderson recounts a quarrel about psychiatry--that the human mind cannot be understood scientifically, only subjectively. Anderson could err in missing the professional analysis of behavior, and the doctor could err in limiting his data to observable behavior. Both author and doctor must add themselves to their methodology.

22 CALVERTON, V. F. Sex Expression in Literature. Introduction by Harry Elmer Barnes. New York: Boni & Liveright, pp. 275-76, 282-83, 305-306.
Now that psychoanalysts have rediscovered sexuality in life, the works of Dreiser, Joyce, and Anderson express the anti-bourgeois sexuality of literature. With exclusion of all life but sex, however, absurd books like Many Marriages can result.

23 CATEL, JEAN. "Lettres Anglo-Américaines." Mercure de France (15 March), pp. 733-34.
In A Story Teller's Story Anderson tells in crude but powerful language of his Midwestern youth; in Dark Laughter there is new form--the epic--in the writer's attempt to present an entire civilization in a plot of only symbolic value.

24 CESTRE, C. "Sherwood Anderson: Note Book." Revue Anglo-Américaine, 4 (October), 85-86.
Anderson reveals his personality in his Notebook, and he gives hope that he will now write of modern life and avoid the crudity of his earlier works and the revolutionary fervor of some of these essays.

25 COLTON, ARTHUR. "Life, Suave and in the Raw." Saturday Review of Literature, 2 (17 July), 933-34.
Without the humor of sophistication, Anderson presents in his Notebook "what he has seen and felt." His irony is personally developed and somewhat heavy.

26 CUPPY, WILL. "Here Are Essays." Bookman, 63 (July), 599-600.
In Sherwood Anderson's Notebook the author often falls prey to the very slickness he expounds against, and his call for crude literature is unacceptable. Occasionally, Anderson is healthily ironic or perceptive.

27 DEUTSCH, BABETTE. "A Writer's Testament." New York Herald Tribune Books (20 June), p. 7.
The essays in Sherwood Anderson's Notebook both demonstrate and discuss the writer's extreme care about craft in fiction. When Anderson is faithful to describing, he is good; when he theorizes, he is muddled.

*28 DINAMOV, S. "Tri Amerikanskikh Pisatelia. Sinkler L'iuis--Shervud Anderson--Dzhozef Gerzhkheimer." Knigonosha, No. 44-45, pp. 14-17.
Cited: 1969.B29.

29 DONDORE, DOROTHY ANNE. The Prairie and the Making of Middle America: Four Centuries of Description. Cedar Rapids, Iowa: Torch Press, pp. 406, 410-13, 420, 423.
Lewis, Dell, and Anderson led the Midwestern revolt for literary freedom, Anderson being most concerned with the development of industry in his first three novels. In short stories, however, Anderson presents a pessimistic view of the same Midwest, this time dealing with individuals' "hidden tragedies." In his poetry Anderson expresses the hopeful yearnings of Midwesterners.

1926

30 DREISER, THEODORE. "The Beautiful." Moods, Cadenced and Declaimed. New York: Boni and Liveright, pp. 143-45.
Woman is a quality called Beautiful--"the quality of being strong to be loved." [Imitation of Anderson's "Tandy"] Reprint of 1926.B31.

31 _____. "Recent Poems of Love and Sorrow." Vanity Fair, 27 (September), 54.
[Dreiser's "The Beautiful" is an imitation of Anderson's "Tandy"]. Reprinted: 1926.B30.

32 DREW, ELIZABETH A. The Modern Novel: Some Aspects of Contemporary Fiction. New York: Harcourt, Brace and Co., pp. 136-38, 143, 147-48.
Anderson writes of the environment against which he is actively in rebellion, questioning the alleged moral law of the universe. Potentially of great literary significance, Anderson lately is "struggling to give expression to a drama of inner realities which he feels behind the mechanistic civilization he lives in" and which requires expression in innovative forms.

33 FAGIN, N. BRYLLION. "Sherwood Anderson Explains the 'Modern' Writer." Literary Digest International Book Review, 4 (August), 593.
The Modern Writer, one of Anderson's published lectures, shows that this author is not puzzled and groping in his understanding of writing. The troubles in recent literature Anderson lays to industrialism and the popular magazines.

34 FARRAR, JOHN. "Sex Psychology in Modern Fiction." Independent, 117 (11 December), 669.
The psychology of sexuality is this century's contribution to the novel, producing the totally subjective Ulysses and the "sex-symbol romances" of Hecht and Anderson. Anderson is losing pre-eminence because he lacks a sense of humor.

35 FAŸ, BERNARD. "Vue Cavalière de la Littérature Américaine Contemporaine." Les Cahiers du Mois. Paris: Éditions Émile-Paul Frères, pp. 161-62.
The best of Anderson's work to date compares to and shall endure as do Whitman's poems. Anderson has invented a new form for his work--"une mélopée en forme d'histoire"--for he is truly but not solely a poet.

36 FITZGERALD, F. SCOTT. "How to Waste Material: A Note on My Generation." Bookman, 63 (May), 263-64.
Although Anderson started to decline with Horses and Men, Hemingway echoes him in In Our Time. Anderson's critics have caused waste of literary material, speaking of Anderson as "an inarticulate, fumbling man, bursting with ideas--when, on the contrary, he is the possessor of a brilliant and almost inimitable prose style, and of scarcely any ideas at all."

37 FORD, COREY. "Three Rousing Cheers!!! The Parody Adventures of Our Youthful Heroes VI: 'And Here Let Us Say Good-By' or, Beer and Light Winesburg." Bookman, 62 (February), 682-84.
Mr. Thomas Beer writes of the Rollo Boys, "presenting for the first time the Suppressed Desires of our Boyhood Heroes in the manner of Mr. Sherwood Anderson."

38 FORD, JAMES L. "Sherwood Anderson's Notebook." Literary Digest International Book Review, 4 (September), 654-55.
Being a confirmed realist is Anderson's excuse for publishing his Notebook, "the pent-up broodings of a lifetime," crude in origin and intent.

39 GLASPELL, SUSAN. The Road to the Temple. London: Ernest Benn, pp. 167-68.
One of the pleasures of Chicago in its Renaissance was to hear "the good stories of a fellow named Sherwood Anderson, who had a trunkful of novels somebody might one day publish. . . ."

40 GORMAN, HERBERT S. "Sherwood Anderson's Fancy Of His Youth." New York Times Book Review (21 November), pp. 2, 12.
Naiveté exists in Tar, but this innocence is appropriate to Anderson's subject and above all sincere. Here Anderson is not strained, and his expression flows purely.

41 HALDEMAN-JULIUS, E. "Sherwood Anderson." A Book of Persons and Personalities: Paragraphs and Essays. Foreword by Lloyd E. Smith. Girard [KS]: Haldeman-Julius, pp. 77-78.
Anderson's first critics categorized him as influenced by Russian authors, whereas his greatest influence was from life itself. In A Story Teller's Story Anderson jokingly discusses the alleged Russian influence by crediting inspiration to his boyhood cabbage soup.

42 HANSEN, HARRY. "Anderson's Scrapbook." New York World (9 May), M. p. 6.

1926

(HANSEN, HARRY)
In Sherwood Anderson's Notebook are most of the man's ideas--passionate writers love well, craft in writing requires clarity and gives nobility, and rich life comes from rich living.

43 HARRIS, JULIA. "Enthusiasm for Sincere Craftsmanship Marks Sherwood Anderson's Note Book." Columbus Enquirer-Sun [GA] (23 May).
Sherwood Anderson's Notebook more closely relates to the autobiography of the author than to his fiction, for these essays are Anderson's thoughts on imagination and art.

44 [HARRIS, JULIAN]. "Forty Most Important American Books in 1924." Columbus Enquirer-Sun [GA] (23 February), p. 4.
According to the International Book Review, the American Library Association includes A Story Teller's Story and a publishers' symposium includes Dark Laughter as top-rated books for 1924 and 1925.

45 HARTLEY, L. P. "New Fiction." Saturday Review, 141 (24 April), 546.
The characters in Dark Laughter are motivated--if at all--by malaise of the spirit. Anderson reduces all emotion and thought to vague yearnings for relationships in modern unrest.

46 HAVILAND, WALTER. "Fiddlededee, Fiddlesticks!" American Parade, 1 (April), 186-88.
In spite of his reputation among misguided intellectuals, Anderson writes illogically, feebly, boringly--and Dark Laughter confirms this charge.

47 HEMINGWAY, ERNEST. The Torrents of Spring. New York: Charles Scribner's Sons.
Scripps O'Neil and Yogi Johnson feel spring coming in Petoskey, Michigan. Diana, local waitress, reads advanced journals and criticisms to hold Scripps' interest--all in vain. Yogi escapes into nature with a naked Indian woman, as two male Indians pick up his discarded clothing. [Parody of Anderson's novels through 1925]

48 HURLEY, JOHN. "The Ambler of the Middle Western States." Manitoba Free Press (5 April), p. 1.
Without a hero but with authentic detail, form, and charm, Poor White "discovers and understands America."

49 KARSNER, DAVID. "Sherwood Anderson, Mid-West Mystic." New York Herald Tribune Magazine (16 May).
In youth "an Ohio peasant boy," Anderson grew up to own a paint factory. Abandoning his successful business in the midst of dictating a letter--an "entirely personal" revolt--Anderson moved to Chicago, was published, and now concurs with many of Whitman's ideas about common people and human values. Reprinted: 1928.B29.

50 KENNEDY, P. C. "New Novels." New Statesman, 27 (5 June), 199.
Leaving wives--in moments of "turgid . . . morbid psychology"--seems to be a favorite American occupation. In Dark Laughter the hero's next step is adultery. Cleverly written but made of unreal people, this novel illustrates Anderson's decline since Windy McPherson's Son.

51 KRUTCH, JOSEPH WOOD. "Vagabonds." American Criticism, 1926. Edited by William A. Drake. New York: Harcourt, Brace and Co., pp. 108-11.
Reprint of 1925.B43.

52 MACAFEE, HELEN. "Some Novelists in Mid-Stream." Yale Review, 15 (January), 349-51.
Anderson is more humorless than sentimental, and his special hatred is "civilization," meaning repression, mechanization, and cheapness. Without fondness for society, Anderson shall never write comedy. Dark Laughter is his best novel to date.

53 MENCKEN, H. L. "America's Most Distinctive Novelist." Vanity Fair, 27 (December), 88.
Anderson tries to understand his own ideas, lately finding his way clearly and promising "an ordered and plausible rationale of life." Never indebted for literary forebears, Anderson is an artist of integrity.

54 MICHAUD, RÉGIS. "La Révolte Intellectuelle aux États-Unis." Les Nouvelles Littéraires (5 June), p. 6.
Son of immigrants, Anderson writes in Chicago, the literary center for American fiction. Not optimistic and growing toward mysticism, Anderson writes stories that deal with youthful rebellion.

55 _____. Le Roman Américain d'Aujourd'hui: Critique d'une Civilisation. Paris: Boivin et Cie, pp. 126-68.
Reprint of 1926.B57; 1926.B58. Translated: 1928.B37.

1926

56 MICHAUD, RÉGIS. Panorama de la Littérature Américaine Contemporaine. Paris: Kra, pp. 153, 170-73, 244, 254.
A mystical sensualist, Anderson draws upon reality for only his theme of dreams and emotions. His heroes leave depressing jobs to pursue spiritual adventures, becoming apostles and ascetics. In Winesburg, Ohio Anderson deals with the subconscious better than anyone since Hawthorne.

57 _____. "Sherwood Anderson, ou le Rêveur Éveillé." Revue des Cours et Conférences, Second Series 27 (30 June), 521-40.
Like Whitman, Anderson writes mystically about common Americans from direct knowledge. Not educated for literature, Anderson awoke to free himself from business life to write. His imagination--all-important to the awakened dreamer--is pessimistic, for he has dealt with the secret, buried lives of his world. Reprinted: 1926.B55.

58 _____. "Sherwood Anderson, Psychanalyste." Revue des Cours et Conférences, Second Series 2 (15 July), 627-42.
Poor White showed Anderson starting a new style and obsessing himself with sex, whereas Winesburg, Ohio is very fine psychology, dealing with neuroses created by changes in social orders which deaden grotesque characters. By the time of Many Marriages Anderson was combining his mystic and erotic tendencies, and in Dark Laughter he joined psychology to lyrical prose. Should the United States ever create a literature, Anderson will have been the leader. Reprinted: 1926.B55.

59 PERRY, F. M. "Sherwood Anderson." Story Writing: Lessons from the Masters. New York: Henry Holt and Co., pp. 184-94.
Being an expressionist writer and concentrating on "moments" of revelation, Anderson does not penetrate to inner lives directly and clearly; he approaches obliquely and with struggle. When Anderson approaches subjects directly, he falters, as in his abhorrence of industrialism.

60 POWYS, LLEWELLYN. The Verdict of Bridlegoose. New York: Harcourt, Brace and Co., pp. 137-38.
To remember Alfred Stieglitz' group of artistic friends and admirers in New York is to imagine a Salvation Army band, with Anderson, "the new convert, giving a heart-to-heart prayer at every market-conduit" as "they pass down the great highway to an enviable immortality."

61 RICHARDS, I. A. "Reading Novels." Forum, 76 (August), 319.
Using free association in Dark Laughter, Anderson creates formlessness and confusion, "a record of disorder, not a new ordering of our responses."

62 ROZENTAL', L. Review of Winesburg, Ohio. Pečat i revoljucija, 1 (1926), 242-43.
Anderson's affected naiveté in Winesburg, Ohio is not always successful. While bold in attacking the illusory optimism of American society, Anderson is generally boring. [James F. Cradler]

63 _____. "Servud Anderson." Bol'šaja sovetskaja énciklopedija, 2. Moscow, 729.
Anderson's use of autobiographical dreamers and intellectual vagabonds undercuts any possible protest value of the depression and routine that he depicts in portraying contemporary America. [James F. Cradler]

64 S., K. "Sherwood Anderson." Boston Transcript (29 May), p. 5.
In his Notebook Anderson proves that he is better at stirring up troublesome thoughts about life than in proposing adequate answers to life's problems. He is speaker for all who suffer to no solace.

65 SCHRIFTGIESSER, KARL. "Sherwood Anderson and His Boyhood." Boston Transcript (11 December), p. 4.
Anderson, who tells fables beautifully, in Tar tells poetically of the inner world of his Midwestern child hero.

66 SEAVER, EDWIN. "Theodore Dreiser and the American Novel." New Masses, 1 (May), 24.
Anderson writes fiction for self-therapy, a "secretive" instead of an "accretive" kind of authorship.

67 SHERMAN, STUART P. "Sherwood Anderson's Tales of the New Life." Critical Woodcuts. New York: Charles Scribner's Sons, pp. 3-17.
Anderson has always repeated fictionally his own escape at forty from the constraints of business life. To ordinary American realism Anderson brings certain gifts--almost religious sincerity, colloquial style, originality, healthy nationalism, seriousness, and mysticism.
Reprint in part of 1925.B58.

68 SPRATLING, W[ILLIA]M and W[ILLIA]M FAULKNER. Sherwood Anderson & Other Famous Creoles: A Gallery of Contemporary New Orleans. New Orleans: Pelican Bookshop.

1926

(SPRATLING, W[ILLIA]M and W[ILLIA]M FAULKNER)
[Caricature of Anderson by Spratling, p. [3]; "Foreword" by Faulkner (pp. [1-2]) parodies Anderson's prose style]

69 TAKAGAKI, MATSUO. "American Literature Today." Rising Generation (1 July), pp. 16-18.
From the early story "Sister" through Tar, Anderson's three characteristics have been that his works are humorous, that his pure nature is expressed in his writing, and that he is fanciful. [Takashi Kodaira] Reprinted: 1927.B63.

70 [VAN DOREN, CARL]. "Short Cuts." Century, 111 (January), 384.
Dark Laughter, another of Anderson's escape stories, proves that the author can create a long narrative.

71 W., G. F. "Sherwood Anderson's Best." Springfield Republican (20 December), p. 6.
Autobiographies of childhood have changed from adventure to introspection, and Tar becomes a poetic story of Anderson's own early inner life and a joy to read.

72 WEST, REBECCA. "Sherwood Anderson, Poet." New York Herald Tribune Books (21 November), pp. 1, 8.
Winesburg, Ohio and The Triumph of the Egg are "two of the most interesting books of short stories ever written," but some of Anderson's longer fictions are laughably naive when he deals psychologically with sex. In Tar Anderson pales his child hero into drabness and fake reticence. Reprinted: 1928.B53.

73 WILLIAMS, STANLEY THOMAS. The American Spirit in Letters. New Haven: Yale University Press, pp. 293, 299.
Possessing "a marked psychological bias," Anderson attacks the novel structure in his own Many Marriages. Putting sex back into literature is essential, and Anderson's autobiographies aid this goal.

74 YUST, WALTER. "Refreshingly Frank Confessional Notes By Sherwood Anderson." New York Evening Post Literary Review (22 May), p. 3.
The quality of continued groping for truths endears Anderson and his Notebook, a delightful work of his many impressions of life.

1927 A BOOKS

1 CHASE, CLEVELAND B. Sherwood Anderson. New York: Robert M. McBride & Co., 85 pp.

Anderson's achievements are great: he has written daringly and deeply about basics, until recently ignored in or forbidden to literature. However, he frequently fails through sentimentality, not recognizing that his stories are about escape from modern life into defeat and evasion. Winesburg, Ohio is successful because Anderson uses psychology and craft to avoid this sentimental escapism; in The Triumph of the Egg and Horses and Men he often avoids even sex-obsession. The novels fail because the author knows too little about life and tries to create imaginary characters that are unrealistic. A Story Teller's Story will remain important as the psychological record of a sensitive, expressive rebellion against industrialism. When Anderson learns to write only when he has something to say, his work will become consistently good. Reprint of 1927.B29.

2 FAGIN, N. BRYLLION. The Phenomenon of Sherwood Anderson: A Study in American Life and Letters. Baltimore: Rossi-Bryn Co., 156 pp.

In a middle-aged nation Anderson has an adolescent soul that makes him the most subjective American author. He tries to write of the meaning of all lives and all aspects of each life, hoping that the lost spirituality of America can be regained through understanding and acceptance. The heroes and heroines of Anderson's novels learn to question received opinion and convention. His stories reveal his desire to explore psychologically the buried lives of ordinary people, for Anderson mystically and symbolically prefers to find truths beneath objective facts. Winesburg, Ohio, The Triumph of the Egg, and Horses and Men will remain Anderson's best work to date. These stories represent a new, organic short story form that Anderson has invented to give expression to the inarticulate characters that he understands intuitively. [Useful bibliography, pp. 153-56] Reprint of 1925.B31; 1925.B32; 1927.B37.

1927 B SHORTER WRITINGS

1 AIKEN, CONRAD. "With Life's First Principles." New York Evening Post Literary Review (9 July), 3, p. 8.

Anderson's stories are good because they are childlike and mystical, but A New Testament is beyond transcendence; these pieces are amorphous, humorless, and structureless. Reprinted: 1958.B1.

1927

2 ANON. "Briefer Mention." Dial, 82 (January), 74.
The publication of Sherwood Anderson's Notebook so soon after A Story Teller's Story and just before Tar causes concern that Anderson "is somewhat precipitately making himself fabulous."

3 ANON. "Fiction." Wisconsin Library Bulletin, 23 (January), 24.
Parts of Tar have appeared in periodicals, and in book form the work is a "series of incidents and impressions as recorded on the mind of a sensitive boy."

4 ANON. "Tar." Outlook, 154 (12 January), 60.
The main character of Tar is less vivid than secondary characters, and the reader must guess how truly autobiographical Anderson is being.

5 ANON. "Receive O. Henry Prizes." New York Times (19 January), p. 25.
Anderson won the second O. Henry Memorial Award of $250 for "Death in the Woods."

*6 ANON. Review of Tar. New York Evening Post Literary Review (22 January), p. 2.
Cited: Book Review Digest 1927, p. 16.

7 ANON. "Biography." Booklist, 23 (February), 224.
Deliberately naive but with verisimilitude, Tar "gives an uncommonly convincing picture of childhood, with its peculiar psychology and sociology."

8 ANON. "Better Books for All-Around Reading." World Tomorrow, 10 (February), 89.
The first half of Tar, written beautifully and whimsically, is superior to the second half.

9 ANON. "Briefer Mention." Dial, 82 (March), 256.
Without the simple early Anderson style, Tar is written with "the studied simplicity of his later novels" and about Anderson's "Hegelian mannerism--all about being, and not being, and becoming."

10 ANON. "Sherwood Anderson In a Lyric Mood." New York Times Book Review (12 June), p. 9.
Always lyrical in his fiction and autobiography, Anderson reveals in A New Testament his mystical connections with people and things met.

11 ANON. "New Books in Brief Review." Independent, 118 (18 June), 641.
A New Testament expresses Anderson's mind in rhythmic and opiate prose-poetry.

12 ANON. "Sherwood Anderson's New Testament." Boston Transcript (22 June), p. 4.
Inarticulate groping for expression is hardly meaningful, and A New Testment shows Anderson fallen into mere self-love and ignorance of his true audience.

13 ANON. "Prose Poetry by Anderson in New Book." Denver News (3 July), Society, p. 7.
A New Testament, which lacks the regularity of traditional poetry, is composed of lyrical fragments of thought, tentative metaphors of Anderson's quest.

14 ANON. "A Writer's World." Springfield Republican (21 August), F, p. 7.
About various subjects and in different styles, the poems of A New Testament reflect Anderson's "deeply subjective reaction towards life, people, places, ideas."

15 ANON. "Tar." Times Literary Supplement (13 October), p. 712.
The virtue of Tar is Anderson's attempt to overlap in a child's mind the real and the imaginary worlds.

16 ANON. "Novelist Buys Papers." New York Times (19 October), p. 10.
Anderson has bought and will personally operate two newspapers in Marion, Virginia.

17 ANON. "'Triumph of the Egg.'" New York Times (23 October), 3, p. 4.
Anderson claims that editing his Virginia newspapers will put him back among the common people about whom he writes fiction.

18 ANON. "Back to Ole Virginny." New York Times (20 November), 3, p. 4.
No one is so purely southern as a former Midwesterner, such as Anderson in his adopted town of Marion, Virginia.

19 ANON. "Sincerity." Daily Express (27 November).
Not over-sentimentalized but based on emotions, Tar pictures a youth's imaginative life.

1927

20 ANON. "Briefer Mention." Dial, 83 (December), 524.
Inspired in manner by Whitman and Nietzsche and in subject by Anderson's desire to prophesy, A New Testament is merely disarmingly sincere and poor poetry.

21 ANON. "An American Childhood." New Statesman, 30 (17 December), 330, 332.
Written as impressionist fiction instead of biography, Tar is a sensitive story of escape from the poverty and frustration of childhood into the imaginative life.

22 AURIOL, JEAN-GEORGES. "The Occident." Translated by Elliot Paul. transition (May), pp. 158-59.
Anderson's robust tales of American life "touch us to the marrow."

*23 B., M. "Un Païen de l'Ohio." Comoedia (20 April), p. 2.
Cited: 1971.A1.

24 BOYNTON, PERCY H. "Sherwood Anderson." More Contemporary Americans. Chicago: University of Chicago Press, pp. 157-77.
Reprint of 1927.B25.

25 _____. "Sherwood Anderson." North American Review, 224 (March-May), 140-50.
Anderson has grown in understanding and technique from thinking for his characters to letting his characters think as part of their stories. Reprinted: 1927.B24; 1940.B24.

26 BROMFIELD, LOUIS. "La Nouvelle Découverte de l'Amérique." Bibliothèque Universelle et Revue de Genève (March), pp. 338, 342.
Child of obscure poor parents, Anderson grew up in a strongly elemental culture. In his best works he uses his mystic insight to view life with entire originality.

27 CANFIELD, MARY CASS. Grotesques and Other Reflections on Art and the Theatre. New York: Harper & Row, Publishers, p. 9.
Is it possible that creation of grotesque characters such as Anderson's might "spring from a too long endured aesthetic disappointment, some starvation of the artist's soul among the avidities of materialism and the distracting hideousness of a machine-driven civilization"?

28 CATEL, JEAN. "Lettres Anglo-Américaines." Mercure de France (1 July), pp. 225-26.
With no pretension to being literature, Sherwood Anderson's Notebook is written spontaneously enough to hush criticism. Setting imagination against materialism, Anderson aims beyond his ability; but he creates dreams of the multiple visions of this age.

29 CHASE, CLEVELAND. "Sherwood Anderson." Saturday Review of Literature, 4 (24 September), 129-30.
In Winesburg, Ohio and some few other writings Anderson exhibits his "interpretative imagination"; more often his imagination is revealed as mere wishful-thinking for a better or more convenient world: "He writes to escape from life and, as a rule, life escapes from his writing." Reprinted: 1927.A1.

30 CLEELAND, ANNE. "Father of the Man." Forum, 77 (April), 636.
Tar mingles past, present and future as a child's mind could to give the inner life of a juvenile--an ordinary but important boy's life.

31 COBLENTZ, STANTON A. The Literary Revolution. New York: Frank-Maurice & Co., pp. 23-24, 25, 26.
Anderson is among converts to the new creed of psychology according to Freud, and "I'm a Fool" illustrates well the author's use of "the modern conversational style."

32 COLTON, ARTHUR. "Reminiscences." Saturday Review of Literature, 3 (19 February), 593-94.
Anderson's rough style in Tar--and his rough subject-matter--are unpleasant, and the author is no longer to be discussed with other, truer realists.

33 CRÉMIEUX, BENJAMIN. "L'Homme qui Devient Femme . . . Winesburg en Ohio . . . Un Paien de l'Ohio." La Nouvelle Revue Francaise (1 November), pp. 694-98.
Evoking a lost America that was rustic and stable, Anderson uses a monotonous style to present descendants of pioneering settlers in a world where adventures, dreaming, and repressions have replaced original vitality.

34 DEUTSCH, BABETTE. "Betrayal." New York Herald Tribune Books (24 July), p. 2.
Anderson's stories are so good that restraint prevents mockery of his so-called poems. A New Testament shows only Anderson's quality of bewilderment and resembles "the free monologue of a psychiatrist's patient whose reading matter has been limited to Whitman and Djuna Barnes."

1927

35 EVANS, ERNESTINE. "A Lively Sculptor." Nation, 124 (16 February), 192-94.

Tennessee Mitchell Anderson began sculpting near Mobile, Alabama; and her early pieces served to illustrate her husband's The Triumph of the Egg. Her "clay people" have always had the believability of characters in Winesburg, Ohio.

36 FADIMAN, CLIFTON P. "Endless Adolescence." Nation, 124 (2 February), 121-22.

Tar illustrates Anderson's habit of giving "a genetic process, never . . . a creative process." All of his books are juvenile in style, subject, and thought.

37 FAGIN, N. BRYLLION. "Sherwood Anderson: The Liberator of Our Short Story." English Journal, 16 (April), 271-79.

Anderson comes to storywriting with such intensity that mechanical traditions and conscious artisanship are forgotten, for Winesburg, Ohio even alone has remade the definitions and scope of later short fiction. Reprinted revised: 1927.A2

38 FARRAR, JOHN. "The Testament of Neuroses." Bookman, 65 (August), 710-11.

Resembling Blake's prophetic works, A New Testament is "fragments of distilled ego."

39 FAULKNER, WILLIAM. Mosquitoes. New York: Boni and Liveright, pp. 242-43.

Julius (Paul Rosenfeld) says of Dawson Fairchild (Anderson) that the latter writes of a confused world in fumbling, humorless style with the purpose of expressing inhibitions and confusions.

40 GEROULD, KATHARINE FULLERTON. "'Stream of Consciousness.'" Saturday Review of Literature, 4 (22 October), 233-35.

When Anderson--a minor novelist--tries to use stream-of-consciousness in his fiction, he creates laughably poor results or disgusting characters.

41 GREEN, PAUL and ELIZABETH LAY GREEN. "General Topic: Sherwood Anderson." Contemporary American Literature: A Study of Fourteen Outstanding American Writers. Revised edition. Chapel Hill: University of North Carolina Press, pp. 27-30.

In his works Anderson uses grotesque actions by grotesque characters as "symbols of a mental state"--generally sexual repression and boredom in small towns. Whereas Masters makes use of irony, Anderson shows poetic love for his characters. [Brief biography, lesson plans, paper topics, and bibliography]

42 HANSEN, HARRY. "The First Reader: Herr Sherwood Anderson." New York World (6 September), p. 13.

Sentimental Germans like translations of Poor White, The Triumph of the Egg, and A Story Teller's Story. In Germany recently Hansen saw Anderson's picture in a bookstore.

43 _____. "Sherwood Anderson Writes His Testament." New York World (19 June), M, p. 8.

Carl Sandburg says that A New Testament is the only such work dedicated to Horace Liveright. Anderson imitates Biblical poetry to reveal "truths" which the author has discovered about himself and others' inner lives.

44 HARTLEY, L. P. "New Fiction." Saturday Review, 144 (19 November), 709-10.

In trying to create even a child's thought patterns, Anderson in Tar verges on simple-mindedness. Reared among "the rubbish heaps of the Middle West," Anderson's hero has a story without progression or meaning.

45 HAZARD, LUCY L. The Frontier in American Literature. New York: Thomas Y. Crowell Co., pp. 74, 177, 204, 286, 290-98, 300.

Anderson's early years are close to Horatio Alger's myth of work-success; then he rebelled against sterile success and sought artistic freedom through imaginative writing: "He is the first of American writers to comprehend the full paradox of the failure of success and the success of failure."

46 JEWETT, ELEANOR. "Color Impulses: Water Colors by SA." From the Top of My Column. Chicago: Ralph Fletcher Seymour, p. 18.

Reprint of 1921.B27.

47 JOLAS, EUGÈNE, ELLIOT PAUL, and ROBERT SAGE. "First Aid to the Enemy." transition (December), p. 165.

Wyndham Lewis has made Anderson one of his literary victims.

*48 KULLE, R. "Khudozhestvennaya Proza Sovremenovo Zapada." Sibirskiye Ogni, No. 1, p. 128.

Cited: 1962.B6.

49 LALOU, RENÉ. "Sherwood Anderson--Winesburg en Ohio." Europe, 15 (15 September), 114-16.

In Winesburg, Ohio Anderson shows his strengths and tastes--rebellion, simple truths, penetrating analysis--and his genius for seizing characters just when they become representative in value. Continued revelation of secret lives gives this book a music of heavy vibrations, of reticent confessions.

50 LANN, JEVGENIJ. "Standartnyj janki." Krasnaja nov', No. 1, pp. 252-54.

Anderson's hero, in his desire to reach out to his fellows and in his search for self-awareness, contrasts with the sullen, money-seeking representative of "standard America." [James F. Cradler]

51 LEGOUIS, ÉMILE. "Dark Laughter." Revue Anglo-Américaine, 4 (August), 568.

Using the cinematographic technique of flashback in Dark Laughter, Anderson traces his hero's longings for freedom with verve; but even Freudian psychology does not save these characters from being boring. Perhaps as analysis of war's aftereffects this novel is worthwhile.

*52 LEVINSON, ANDRÉ. "Sherwood Anderson et le Dilemme Américain." Comoedia (13 March), pp. 20-28.

Cited: 1971.A1. Reprinted: 1929.B66.

53 LLONA, VICTOR. "Sherwood Anderson." Les Nouvelles Littéraires (1 January), p. 6.

From Anderson's personal appearance he does not resemble an author; but from hearing him talk, one learns of his debt to Europe and of the writer's life in an excessively intense society.

54 MAINSARD, JOSEPH. "Sherwood Anderson." Études, 190 (8 February), 303-25.

Anderson is the "historian" of the Chicago Renaissance writers, having witnessed the growth and change of the Midwest. Deeply pessimistic, a disciple of Freud, Anderson presents his characters as conditioned by environment or representative of social classes. After searching for truth, Anderson's heroes find only deep sadness; their only happiness must, therefore, be in themselves.

55 MENCKEN, H. L. "Literary Confidences." American Mercury, 10 (March), 382-83.

Tar is nearly puerile at times, repetitious frequently, and not of new material. For Anderson to assume the amateur pose is charming, and parts of Tar are answers to Anderson's detractors.

56 MILES, HAMISH. "From an Inner Fever." Saturday Review of Literature, 4 (3 September), 85-86.
Lacking order and doctrine, A New Testament falls short of its title, being instead incomplete ideas in rhythmic form to celebrate lack of cerebration.

57 MORRIS, LAWRENCE S. "Sherwood Anderson: Sick of Words." New Republic, 51 (3 August), 277-79.
Having achieved success by living and writing of an emotional adolescence, Anderson cannot seemingly go beyond that stage, now using words for their value as words and stories for pride in being their teller: "The author of 'Winesburg, Ohio' is dying before our eyes."

*58 P., B. D. "Loshadi i Liudi." Chitatel' i Pisatel' (1 December).
Cited: 1969.B29.

59 SAGE, ROBERT. "The Mysticism of Reality." transition (September), p. 167.
Marcel Jouhandreau is "actually a gallic Sherwood Anderson x-raying the troubled souls of people whose desires, exceeding the available normal fulfillments, become petrified as misshapen makeshifts."

60 SELIGMAN, HERBERT J. "An American Testament." New York Sun (11 June).
A New Testament, influenced by the Bible, Whitman, and Gertrude Stein, lacks the broader background of European civilization but succeeds as innocent American "dreamlike avowals in psalmodic prose."

61 SINCLAIR, UPTON. "Muddlement." Money Writes! New York: Albert Boni, pp. 119-23.
Reading Anderson's novels shows the author to be the "victim of a dissociated personality," but no American can arise to proclaim that capitalism and class-struggle has caused this overwhelming neurasthenia in this author and his characters.

62 T., R. "Sherwood Anderson: Un Païen de l'Ohio." Bibliothèque Universelle et Revue de Genève (June), pp. 830-31.
Jolas is wrong, in his preface to The Triumph of the Egg, to think that all of Anderson's characters suffer from

(T., R.)
repressions; perhaps Europeans too easily assign vices to Americans.

63 TAKAGAKI, MATSUO. "Two Novelists: Sherwood Anderson and Sinclair Lewis." American Literature. Tokyo: Kenkyusha, pp. 221-36.
Reprint of 1926.B69.

*64 UREÑA, PEDRO HENRIQUEZ. "Veinte Años de Literatura en los E E U U." Nosotros. Anniversary Issue.
Cited: 1966.B10.

65 YOSHIDA, KINETARO. "On Anderson." Jiji Shinpo (26 January), p. 10; (29 January), p. 4; (1 February), p. 4.
Anderson is the representative of a new spirit in America after the World War. His stories as well as his legend symbolize the first step of an American Renaissance. It is true that he is a realist, but he is somewhat an idealistic romantic and a surrealist. He is like Chekhov but more hopeful and humorous. Those who read Anderson can know what is man, what is the truth of life, and how to love one's neighbors. [Takashi Kodaira] Reprinted in part: 1928.B55.

1928 A BOOKS - NONE

1928 B SHORTER WRITINGS

1 ALEXANDER, DAVID C. "Sherwood Anderson: A Study of the American Realist Whose Work Reflects the Mental Awakening of the Proletariat." Letters, 2 (February), 23-29.
Whereas Calverton bases Anderson's characters in applied sociology, these characters are more accurately understood through common-sense psychology. Exalting the proletariat, Anderson writes of circumstances that inhibit, repress, or forbid the growth to full artistic awareness of the worker.

2 ANON. "Šervud Anderson--provintcial'nyj redactor." Vestnik inostrannoj literatury, 2 (1928), 155-56.
Anderson's purchase of two newspapers may reflect the bourgeois act of (as The New Republic termed him) "a dying artist." [James F. Cradler]

3 ANON. "Is Sherwood Anderson's Art 'Integrally American'?" New York Times Book Review (19 February), p. 2.
In Sherwood Anderson Cleveland Chase denies Anderson his Americanism because of foreign influences. Anderson fails

because he is "soft," his characters question existence, and he often philosophizes instead of tells stories.

*4 ANON. Review of Chase, Sherwood Anderson. Pratt Institute Quarterly (Spring), p. 26.
Cited: Book Review Digest 1928, p. 144.

5 ANON. "Editor Anderson at Play." New York Times (29 August), p. 20.
Anderson's country journalism is an improvement in creativity over typical small-town newspaper writing.

6 BAIR, FRED. "Notes from a Roving Correspondent: Sherwood Anderson's Unintentional Jest." Haldeman-Julius Monthly, 7 (April), 3-16, 114.
An interview with Anderson reveals that this famous writer had not embarked on any great experiment when he began editing his rural Virginia newspapers. Anderson spoke of his literary friends and evaluated them.

7 BERGE, ANDRÉ. "Sherwood Anderson.--Un Conteur Se Raconte: I. Mon Père et Moi." La Revue Nouvelle (October), pp. 171-72.
The typical French author of memoirs would not write the disorganized book A Story Teller's Story; yet the reader senses power and life behind Anderson's words about his parents.

*8 BOLANDER, CARL-AUGUST. "Sherwood Anderson." Dagens Nyheter (7, 8 June).
Cited: 1957.B1.

9 _____. "Sherwood Anderson." Ismer och Dikt. Stockholm: Albert Bonniers Förlag, pp. 125-36.
As with Tore Svennberg, Anderson lives life fully and writes from his own experiences, as A Story Teller's Story demonstrates. Anderson chose not to become a standardized American author; instead, he portrays daily life realistically but also psychologically. His later work is more the poetically mystical expression of inner freedom.

10 CESTRE, C. "Sherwood Anderson: A New Testament." Revue Anglo-Américaine, 5 (August), 580-81.
Using the real world of facts as only a vehicle for his meditations in A New Testament, Anderson transports the reader into a re-created transcendant world.

1928

11 CESTRE, C. "Sherwood Anderson. Tar, a Mid-West Childhood." Revue Anglo-Américaine, 5 (April), 400-401.
When Anderson the adult reconstructs childhood in Tar, he is a realist, a psychologist, and a poet. Interested in the child's growing aware of and into society, he gives little plot or sentimentality.

12 COSTER, DIRK. "Amerikaansche Litteratuur." Stem, 8 (December), 894-99.
Poor White is not so realistic as Anderson's earlier works, being instead a poetic thesis on the effects of American industrialization on lives; yet in trying hardest to present spirits, Anderson has lost psychological authenticity.

13 CROSS, WILBUR L. The Modern English Novel: An Address Before the American Academy of Arts and Letters. New Haven: Yale University Press, pp. 28, 40.
The reader who would cultivate an interest in sex may read Many Marriages, although Winesburg, Ohio, The Triumph of the Egg, and Dark Laughter must be listed among noteworthy modern works.

14 DICKINSON, L. R. "Smyth County Items." Outlook, 148 (11 April), 581-83.
Residents of Marion, Virginia, have begun adjusting to having Anderson the famous novelist as editor of their local newspapers.

*15 ELGSTRÖM, ANNA LENAH. "Tre Gula." Social-Demokraten (18 December).
Cited: 1957.B1.

16 ERNST, MORRIS L. and WILLIAM SEAGLE. To the Pure: A Study of Obscenity and the Censor. New York: Viking Press, pp. 46, 246, 248, 295.
The nude scene in Many Marriages "led in America to many travesties and a good deal of banter." Among Anderson's banned books are Many Marriages and Dark Laughter.

17 FADIMAN, CLIFTON P. "Sherwood Anderson." Nation, 126 (15 February), 189.
In The Phenomenon of Sherwood Anderson, Fagin overpraises Anderson for his naiveté and bewilderment at modern life; Chase in Sherwood Anderson examines Anderson's weaknesses and observes that the author hates modern life. Whereas Fagin's work is "excited and perspiring affirmative," Chase's study is "admirably honest and invigorating."

Recent publication of A New Testament--an "absurd collection of Zarathusthrian aphorisms"--proves Chase correct.

18 FAŸ, BERNARD. "Vue Cavalière de la Littérature Américaine Contemporaine." La Revue Hebdomadaire (19 May), pp. 288-89.
As Anderson tries to free America from Puritanism, he mixes amorality with nationalism. While his novels lack good structure, his short stories shine with genius and show at their best an "American" art.

19 FISCHER, WALTHER. "Sherwood Anderson, Dark Laughter." Anglia Beiblatt, 39 (1928), 23-26.
Dark Laughter is Anderson's post-War novel about the need to lose repressions and clichés--in short, about the "lost" generation. Anderson hangs his novel on the inner development of the hero, all action being current or flash-backs. The reader must manufacture a vision of unity, of a possibly honest America.

20 FREEMAN, JOSEPH. "Notes on American Literature." Communist, 7 (August), 513, 516.
Anderson writes material scarcely known by the masses and has despaired over reforming industrial problems and retreated to rural Virginia to edit local newspapers. His earlier books "depicted the social and psychological tragedies of American petit-bourgeois life under the pressure of monopoly capital; his later books struggled with machine cultures; and his autobiographies long for a past golden age."

21 GOSS, MARIAN MAXWELL. "Chicagoans: Tennessee Mitchell Anderson." Chicagoan, 6 (3 November), 19, 23.
After a difficult girlhood, Tennessee Mitchell became a piano tuner in Chicago. Then she became Mrs. Sherwood Anderson. Now Tennessee Anderson is interested in sculpture and writing.

22 GREEN, ELIZABETH LAY. The Negro in Contemporary American Literature. Chapel Hill: University of North Carolina Press, pp. 43, 45, 52, 63.
Anderson uses Negroes as minor figures in Dark Laughter to serve as a raucous chorus; and Jean Toomer's Cane has been influenced by Anderson's works.

*23 GULLBERG, HJALMAR. "Amerikansk och Fransk Exotism." Sydvenska Dagbladet Snäll Posten (18 June).
Cited: 1957.B1.

1928

24 HUDDLESTON, SISLEY. Paris Salons, Cafés, Studios . . . Being Social, Artistic, and Literary Memories. New York: Blue Ribbon Books, pp. 78-82.
In attitude toward life and in prose style, Anderson is more English and European than American, for he "consciously aims at being an artist" in an environment publicly hostile to art. In Paris Anderson is respected, but a modern American young woman avoided the boredom of meeting her famous compatriot.

25 JARNÉS, BENJAMÍN. "Sherwood Anderson." Revista de Occidente, 29 (June), 349-57.
Both optimist and pessimist, Anderson vibrates to the fine tunings of characters and measures the gap between art and life. In A Story Teller's Story he describes his early poverty, his years in business, and his growth toward writing lyrically of grotesque lives. In emotional life is all his vitality.

26 JESSUP, MARY E. "A Checklist of the Writings of Sherwood Anderson." American Collector, 5 (January), 157-58.
[Brief descriptions of fifteen books by Anderson, from Windy McPherson's Son through A New Testament]

27 JOLAS, EUGÈNE. "Transatlantic Letter." transition (Summer), p. 275.
Given power to destroy all governments, Anderson once told Jolas, he would not do so.

*28 KARSNER, DAVID. Review of Chase, Sherwood Anderson. New York World (4 March), M, p. 11.
Cited: Book Review Digest 1928, p. 144.

29 _____. "Sherwood Anderson." Sixteen Authors to One. New York: Copeland, pp. 45-63.
Reprint of 1926.B49.

*30 LANDQUIST, JOHN. "Sherwood Anderson." Aftonbladet (5 August).
Cited: 1957.B1.

31 LEITICH, ALBERT. "Der Erzähler Erzählt Sein Leben." Die Literatur, 30 (October 1927-September), 391-92.
A Story Teller's Story introduces imagination to American literature and brings Anderson's incredible sensitivity to life's hurts to bear on common people's sufferings.

32 LEWIS, WYNDHAM. "Sherwood Anderson." Enemy, No. 2 (September), 26-27.

Whether his writings are good or bad, Anderson--a celebrated "child" of Whitman--has been very influential on American writers. The Anderson "school" is romantic, although Hemingway is far less romantic than Anderson.

*33 LUNDKVIST, ARTUR. "Mörkt Skratt." Arbetaren (20 June). Cited: 1957.B1.

34 MacDONALD, DWIGHT. "Sherwood Anderson." Yale Literary Magazine, 93 (July), 209-43.

The unfortunate recent loss of distinction between prose and poetry is not shown in Anderson's works. Anderson's primary subject is the common human understood emotionally. At his best, Anderson fuses objective description with personal feeling, giving perfect tone to his stories; but in his novels his mastery disintegrates into blurred confusion.

35 MACY, JOHN. "The Short Story." Saturday Review of Literature, 4 (14 January), 517.

"The Man's Story" again proves that Anderson has lost his original sharp ability to tell stories well. Formerly he had power to break through life's wall to find "pathos, tragedy, humanity, and perchance a bit of beauty."

36 MARBLE, ANNIE RUSSELL. "Sherwood Anderson." A Study of the Modern Novel, British and American, Since 1900. New York: D. Appleton and Co., pp. 372-77.

Anderson still has "the feverish, prurient desire to expose every scandalous secret, to satirize every confusing element in modern life"; and Winesburg, Ohio, "seen through the eyes of a prurient newspaper reporter, shows the sordidness and sewerage of a village that, in the opinion of its narrator, had become 'grotesque' by its very inhibitions."

37 MICHAUD, RÉGIS. The American Novel Today. Boston: Little, Brown and Co., pp. 22, 31, 53, 57, 154-99.

Translation of 1926.B55.

38 MORE, PAUL ELMER. The Demon of the Absolute. Princeton: Princeton University Press, pp. 70-72.

Because Anderson denies that any moral law governs life and should dictate literature, none of his books will be recalled in twenty years. He writes of subjects best repressed into nightmares and in a style close to fevered sleeping. Reprinted in part from 1928.B39.

1928

39 MORE, PAUL ELMER. "The Modern Current in American Literature." Forum, 79 (January), 131, 132, 134-35.

Lewis, much more highly educated than such Midwestern realists as Anderson, is ironically the crudest of the school. The autobiographies of Dreiser and Anderson may excel any other works by Midwestern realists. In narrative style, Anderson shows Stein's circular influence; and, regarding Anderson's at first clean attitude toward sex, this author presents his thoughts unwholesomely. Reprinted in part: 1928.B38.

40 MUNSON, GORHAM B. Destinations: A Canvass of American Literature Since 1900. New York: J. H. Sears & Co., pp. 2-3, 9-10, 101, 164, 179, 185, 208.

Anderson is one of the respected "Middle Generation" of American writers since 1905, although he has failed to develop beyond his first books; and such writers as Hart Crane and Jean Toomer have been influenced by him, for Anderson carried his youthful heroes to rebellion against amoral materialism.

*41 ÖSTERLING, ANDERS. "Sherwood Anderson." Svenska Dagbladet (25 March).

Cited: 1957.B1.

*42 P., FR. "Mörkt Skratt." Folklets Dagblad (9 June).

Cited: 1957.B1.

*43 RABENIUS, OLOF. "Amerikanst." Stockholms-Tidningen (16 June).

Cited: 1957.B1.

44 ROCHER, MARGUERITE L. "Sherwood Anderson: Un Païen de l'Ohio." Revue Anglo-Américaine, 6 (October), 87.

In Winesburg, Ohio Anderson gives brutal sympathy and lyric freshness as he writes of humble people hurt by fate and mediocre people facing discontent and rebellion.

45 ROMAINS, JULES. "Inquiry among European Writers into the Spirit of America." transition (Summer), p. 254.

Although Anderson has not yet influenced French authors, his influence may soon appear.

46 ROSENFELD, PAUL. By Way of Art: Criticisms of Music, Literature, Painting, Sculpture, and the Dance. New York: Coward-McCann, pp. 111, 125, 160, 162.

Such writers as Anderson have proved Stein right in her unreal use of words, for Anderson has always led others' acknowledgements of her influence. Hemingway has learned from Stein and Anderson the effects used in his stories.

47 SMERTENKO, JOHAN. "Anderson, the Writer." Saturday Review of Literature, 4 (25 February), 632.
In Sherwood Anderson Cleveland Chase shows neither sympathy nor understanding of Anderson; worse, Chase is arbitrary and contradictory.

*48 SÖDERHIELM, HENNING. "En Amerikansk Roman." Göteborgs Handels och Sjöfarts-Tidning (6 July).
Cited: 1957.B1.

49 SPIVAK, AARÓN. "Risa Negra." Síntesis, 1, No. 10 (March), 75-93.
Upset with staid city life, the hero of Dark Laughter becomes a vagabond searching for meaning. He learns to hear the dark chorus of Negro laughter at civilized life and responds to primitive urges. The heroine, who has been in Europe, responds to her own urges toward liberation. Perhaps their union represents the coming North American of native and European culture.

50 WARREN, C. HENRY. "Sherwood Anderson." Bookman [London], 74 (April), 22-24.
Anderson's best works are his short stories and his autobiographies; yet Dark Laughter is his best single book.

51 WARREN, ROBERT PENN. "Hawthorne, Anderson and Frost." New Republic, 54 (16 May), 400-401.
Chase's Sherwood Anderson, an "unambitious biography," presents Anderson soundly as always in danger of writing cheap sentimentality; and Fagin's The Phenomenon of Sherwood Anderson, ignoring the European background of American culture, glorifies the very tendencies that urge Anderson to write sentimentally.

52 WEAVER, RAYMOND W. "A Complete Handbook of Opinion: Being a Compendium of Ten Famous People's Evaluations of the Great Old and New." Vanity Fair, 30 (April), 68-69, 114.
Scoring 6.4 of 25.0 on a "recognition scale," Anderson as one of the evaluating critics is "the foremost American story-teller, of, by and for the people. . . ."

53 WEST, REBECCA. "Sherwood Anderson, Poet." The Strange Necessity: Essays and Reviews. London: Jonathan Cape, pp. 281-90.
Reprint of 1926.B72.

54 WHIPPLE, T. K. Spokesmen: Modern Writers and American Life. New York: D. Appleton, pp. 70, 76, 115-38, 158, 170, 176,

(WHIPPLE, T. K.)
177, 227, 237, 238, 254, 255, 257, 260, 262, 265, 267, 270.

Anderson presents an imaginative understanding of the American life he has known intimately. Suggesting a conclusion to problems he raises, Anderson is "the most instructive of our contemporaries." The world he pictures lacks provision for humanistic values; his mystic answer is development of the imaginative life to parallel or replace wrong societal emphases. Reprinted in part: 1947.B34. Reprinted: 1974.A3.

55 YOSHIDA, KINETARO. "Anderson from the Working Class." Bunsho Kurabu [Shinchosha] (September), pp. 88-91.

Anderson's legend is deeply connected with the distress of America at the nation coming-of-age. Anderson is not a leftist writer, but he is a writer from the working class. He is seeking the truth of life through the modern American culture. [Takashi Kodaira] Reprint in part of 1927.B65.

56 _____. "Anderson Today." Jiji Shinpo (28 May), p. 6; (29 May), p. 8; (30 May), p. 12; (31 May), p. 8; (1 June), p. 12.

"Nearer the Grass Roots" explains why Anderson became the editor and the publisher of the Smyth County News and the Marion Democrat. Japanese writers need bitter advice, for they tend to think that they cannot write without becoming "gentlemen writers on the European plan." [Takashi Kodaira]

1929 A BOOKS - NONE

1929 B SHORTER WRITINGS

1 ADAMS, MILDRED. "A Small-Town Editor Airs His Mind." New York Times Magazine (22 September), pp. 3, 20.

Anderson has made a personal success of his editorship of two small-town Virginia newspapers.

2 ANON. "Anderson Is Expelled on Rumanian Trip." New York Times (9 March), p. 6.

For aiding Rumanian Hungarians Anderson has been asked to leave Rumania.

3 ANON. "Rumania Welcomes Writers." New York Times (20 March), p. 28.

The Minister of Rumania asserts that Rumania "is glad to welcome the intellectuals of the world, including Sherwood Anderson."

4 ANON. "Sherwood Anderson and the Small Town." Minneapolis Journal (28 April), p. 4.
Even readers who have disliked Anderson's fiction can love Hello Towns!, his picture of small-town America. This work teaches that Lewis tells no truths in comparison to Anderson.

5 ANON. "Suburban Weeklies." New York Times (2 May), p. 26.
Some suburban newspapers are more attractive than rural weeklies, contrary to Anderson's belief.

6 ANON. Review of Hello Towns! Canton News [OH] (5 May).
Anderson's new novel--Hello Towns!--is accurate reporting of his experiences as an editor in a rural area.

7 ANON. "Tennessee Gives Another Type." Columbia State [SC] (5 May), p. 4.
Anderson's observations of the waste of industry in Elizabethton, Tennessee--in the Nation for May 1, 1929--may help prevent such situations in future industry.

8 ANON. "Hello Towns Is Revealing Book." Raleigh Observer (5 May).
While Hello Towns! answers questions about Anderson's attitude toward country journalism, it does not answer what his readers think of him.

9 ANON. Review of Hello Towns! Reading News-Times [PA] (6 May).
Anderson's rural newspapers are exotic and amusing, and Hello Towns! gives Anderson the chance to show his talent again.

10 ANON. "Sherwood Anderson: A 'Main Street' Philosopher." St. Louis Times (9 May).
Hello Towns! proves that both Anderson and the country town are alive.

11 ANON. "Hello Towns." Patterson Call [NJ] (11 May).
Little that Anderson has published before Hello Towns! should survive, and almost all of the present book should be forgotten.

12 ANON. "Old Editor is the Cracker Box Philosopher in His 'Hello Towns.'" Anderson Mail [SC] (12 May).

1929

(ANON.)
Hello Towns! is bare of almost all aspects of modern life, being too picturesque to be true.

13 ANON. "Novelist Now Turns Rural Journalism Into Literature." Birmingham News [AL] (12 May).
Hello Towns! is sensationally successful, for in it Anderson feels the pulse of small-town life, much as Thoreau felt that of the New England woods.

14 ANON. Review of Hello Towns! Durham Herald [NC] (12 May).
There is too little of Anderson in Hello Towns! to justify its publication.

15 ANON. "Anderson Says 'Hello Towns.'" Toledo Times (12 May).
In Hello Towns! Anderson shows how threads of separate lives can be woven to form patterns of literature.

16 ANON. "Sherwood Anderson's Much Liked New Job." Chicago Journal of Commerce (18 May).
Hello Towns! is valuable Americana, picturing often bypassed people.

17 ANON. "Sherwood Anderson Looks at Life in a Small Town." Kansas City Star (18 May).
Hello Towns! combines small-town reporting with Anderson's imaginative reworking of journalism.

*18 ANON. Review of Hello Towns! St. Louis Library Bulletin, 27 (June), 205.
Cited: Book Review Digest 1929, p. 21.

19 ANON. "Sherwood Anderson's Small Town." Cincinnati Enquirer (1 June).
Not significant as literature, Hello Towns! is still a flavorful book.

20 ANON. Review of Hello Towns! Asheville Times [NC] (2 June).
Hello Towns! is a remarkable book of news stories and editorial reflections upon them.

21 ANON. Review of Hello Towns! Cleveland News (2 June).
Hello Towns! shows Anderson as such a perfect country editor that the picture may be faked.

22 ANON. Review of Hello Towns! Manchester Union [MA] (3 June).
Hello Towns! is the intimate study of Anderson's latest adventure--as rural Virginia journalist.

23 ANON. Review of Hello Towns! Philadelphia Record (18 June).
Hello Towns! could nominate Anderson as the "Grand Old Man of Literature."

24 ANON. "Crystal Gazing." Springfield Register [IL] (9 June).
In Hello Towns! Anderson describes small-town America with understanding, in contrast to Lewis' bitter attacks on the same kind of place.

25 ANON. "Philosophy." Miami Herald [FL] (16 June).
Hello Towns! records Anderson's writings for his country newspapers and is built around cycles of continuing stories.

26 ANON. Review of Hello Towns! Hastings Tribune [NB] (22 June).
Hello Towns! gives the picture of a mature, gentle, non-obscene Sherwood Anderson.

27 ANON. "Literature." Booklist, 25 (July), 385.
In the "direct and simple" style of Anderson's novels, Hello Towns! has appeal beyond the author's own small Virginia town.

28 ANON. Review of Hello Towns! Jacksonville Times-Union [FL] (9 July).
Compared to Winesburg, Ohio, Hello Towns! shows Anderson's pitiful decline.

29 ANON. "Weekly Book Review." Jackson Clarion-Ledger [MS] (21 July).
Hello Towns! shows Anderson cured of "professionalism" and writing again in tune with common Americans.

30 ANON. Speech by Anderson. New York Times (13 August), p. 8.
Anderson recently delivered a speech on the possibilities of rural journalism.

31 ANON. "Noted Writers Aid Textile Workers." New York Times (19 August), p. 39.
Anderson and other famous writers have joined to raise money to support southern mill workers on strike.

32 ANON. "Sherwood Anderson As Country Editor." Oakland Tribune [CA] (25 August).
Nearer the Grass Roots is handsomely printed and bound; it presents Anderson "at his happiest and best."

33 ANON. "Anderson Returns to Small Towns." Wheeling Register (15 September).

(ANON.)
Hello Towns! presents town news as art because Anderson reacts to events described.

34 ANON. Review of Hello Towns! Atlanta Journal (29 September).
In Hello Towns! Anderson is unique in chronicling small-town events.

35 ANON. "Contemporary Artists Of America to Show at Telfair Academy." Savannah Press (2 November).
Karl Anderson shares his brother's memories of their boyhood; their later lives have driven them apart artistically.

36 ANON. "Hello Towns." Pittsburgh Sun-Telegram (17 November).
Hello Towns! is interesting and dull, tragic and funny, important and trivial--as life in all places must be.

37 ANON. "Anderson in Florida." Chicago Tribune (27 December), p. 5.
Newspaper reporters in Florida informed Anderson of the death of his former wife, and the "noted novelist" was "shocked."

38 ANON. "Divorced Wife of Novelist Is Found Dead." Chicago Tribune (27 December), p. 5.
Tennessee Mitchell Anderson--writer, painter, and sculptor--was found dead of apparent lung hemorrhaging in her studio on December 26, 1929.

39 ANON. "Ex-Wife of Anderson, Novelist, Found Dead." New York Times (27 December), p. 12.
Tennessee Mitchell Anderson died asleep of lung hemorrhaging. Anderson divorced her in 1924 "on the ground of unjustifiable desertion."

40 ASHLEY, SCHUYLER. "Dark Laughter" and "Tar: A Midwest Childhood." Essay Reviews. Introduction by Rose Adelaide Witham. Kansas City: Lowell Press, pp. 112-14, 163-65.
Dark Laughter lacks pity and irony and thus wastes Anderson's dim view of human nature, leaving Anderson to grope and fumble. Tar, although about childhood, is certainly not for children to read.

41 BROOKS, WALTER R. "Picked at Random." Outlook, 152 (8 May), 78.
Hello Towns! shows much of Anderson and his adopted mountain village, but much of the book is painfully fake.

42 BUCHANAN, ANNABEL MORRIS. "Sherwood Anderson: Country Editor." World Today, 53 (February), 249-53.
People in Marion, Virginia, are accepting their famous newspaper editor and beginning even to read Anderson's books.

43 CHAMBERLIN, JOSEPH EDGAR. "At Ripshin Farm and Around There." Boston Transcript (27 February).
Anderson spent one year having "Ripshin," his home in rural Virginia, built, doing much of the work himself, feeling in building a house as he feels while writing a novel.

44 DINAMOV, S. "Šervud Anderson." Literaturnaja énciklopedija, 1. Moscow, 152-53.
Anderson's literary evolution mirrors both the development of American literature in the twentieth century and that of the movement of the radical intelligentsia. [James F. Cradler]

45 DiROBILANT, IRENE. Vita Americana (Stati Uniti del Nord-America). Turin: Fratelli Bocca, Editore, pp. 46, 50, 55, 309, 311.
Anderson represents the second era of Midwestern pioneers, telling stories comparable to those of Twain and showing the degeneration of pioneers from intellectual concerns to material obsessions.

46 EDGETT, EDWIN FRANCIS. "'Hello Towns'--Sherwood Anderson." Boston Transcript (27 April), Books, p. 3.
Hello Towns! documents Anderson's year as editor of two country-town newspapers in Smyth County, Virginia.

*47 ESPINOZA, ENRIQUE. "Era una Editorial Francesa la que Nos Revelaba a Teodoro Dreiser y Sherwood Anderson." La Vida Literaria, No. 14, p. 8.
Cited: 1966.B10.

48 FINGERIT, JULIO. "Das Ei Triumphiert, Amerikanische Novellen." Síntesis, No. 29, pp. 238-39.
In The Triumph of the Egg Anderson tells stories of escape. These are subjective stories of unpleasant, unhappy souls motivated by sex.

*49 _____. "Dos Novelistas Norteamericanos: En Traducciones Alemanas." Síntesis, No. 29, p. 236.
Cited: 1966.B10.

1929

50 FRANK, WALDO. The Re-Discovery of America: An Introduction to a Philosophy of American Life. New York: Charles Scribner's Sons, pp. 4, 134-35, 317, 318.
When Anderson philosophizes, he follows Rousseau, drawing "luminous portraits, more musical than plastic, of the childish consciousness of the American soul" in search of elemental truths.

51 FREEMAN, JOSEPH. "Sherwood Anderson's Confusion." New Masses, 4 (February), 6.
Anderson's writings are basically autobiographical, and the author seems unable to progress beyond the consistent confusion he admits to in the face of life. In the largest sense, Anderson represents the artist caught between capitalism and proletariat.

52 GALLISHAW, JOHN. Twenty Problems of the Fiction Writer: A Series of Lectures on the Craftsmanship of the Modern Short Story. New York: G. P. Putnam's Sons, pp. 89, 91, 92, 94, 96, 97-101.
Good use of first-person narration shows in "I'm a Fool." Seemingly the hero-narrator feels all but can express little.

53 GANNETT, LEWIS. "The Cracker Box Philosopher." New York Herald Tribune Books (5 May), p. 3.
Hello Towns! tells of a Virginia town curiously premodern, probably unsure of its newspaper editor, and soon to drive Anderson back to city life.

54 GROS, LÉON-GABRIEL. "Je Suis un Homme." Cahiers du Sud (May), pp. 319-20.
The second volume of A Story Teller's Story is Anderson's "testimony of human feeling," in which the author unites his ideas of the imagination and the so-called American "self-made man."

55 HAARDT, SARA. "Small Town." Saturday Review of Literature, 5 (4 May), 974.
Anderson has in Hello Towns! anthologized much of Southern small-town life--beauty, violence, mystery, pathos, poverty, and comedy.

56 HANSEN, HARRY. "The First Reader." New York World (18 April), p. 15.
By no means should a reader miss Hello Towns! This Anderson book is even more an event than usual.

1929

57 HEFLING, HELEN and EVA RICHARDS. "Anderson, Sherwood." Index to Contemporary Biography and Criticism. Boston: F. W. Faxon Co., p. 23.
[References to Anderson in 18 books of criticism]

58 HELLMAN, GEOFFREY T. "Hello, Sherwood." New Republic, 58 (15 May), 365.
Anderson is surely a charming country editor, as proved by Hello Towns!; but as a reporter he falls below the level of the New York Times, and he is missed as a storyteller.

59 HIERONYMUS, FAITH. "Under the Reading Lamp." Tulsa World (12 May).
Comparable to a newspaper diary, Hello Towns! is personal, small-town journalism that can "stimulate the imagination, nourish human relationships and speed the achievement."

60 HUTCHINSON, PERCY. "The Village Oracle Speaks." New York Times Book Review (28 April), p. 1.
Enhanced by personal essays and sketches of Virginia mountaineers, Hello Towns! rises above journalism to become part of Anderson's literary legacy.

61 JOHNSON, A. THEODORE. "Realism In Contemporary American Literature: Notes on Dreiser, Anderson, Lewis." Southwestern Bulletin, New Series 16 (December), 3-16.
Offering no philosophy in his books, Anderson creates autobiographical characters to illustrate his ideas of inner lives of common people. In technique, Anderson avoids "plot" stories and the fixed dénouement.

62 JOHNSON, MERLE. "Sherwood Anderson." High Spots of American Literature. [n.p.]: Bennett Book Studios, pp. 14-15.
[Brief bibliographical descriptions of Winesburg, Ohio, The Triumph of the Egg, and A Story Teller's Story]

63 JUSTESEN, VIGGO. "Fundamentally Honest." Des Moines Register (11 August).
Hello Towns! shows in its pictures and news items that Anderson is "honest and sympathetic."

64 KONOITZ, LORNA BALL. "Recent Books." Roanoke World News [VA] (22 May).
Hello Towns! shows again that Anderson is a truthful writer, accepting people as found.

1929

65 LEISY, ERNEST ERWIN. American Literature: An Interpretative Survey. New York: Thomas Y. Crowell Co., pp. 216-17.
Winesburg, Ohio, "a collection of naturalistic tales," shows "revolt against all those things which deny the spirit of man"--for example, received ideas and industrialism. Anderson writes with "more poetry and less wit than Lewis."

66 LEVINSON, ANDRÉ. "Sherwood Anderson et le Dilemme Américaine." Figures Américaines: Dix-huit Études sur les Écrivains de ce Temps. Paris: Editions Victor Attinger, pp. 20-28.
Anderson has written of nothing but himself, specifically of his imaginative life, which is the subject of Tar. Anderson represents the social movement of rebellion against businessmen and Puritans, combining in his stories the examples of great Russian authors and theories of Freud and his followers. He considers America at the impasse between idyllic Negro life and industry, between "the abolition of intelligence and its degradation." Reprint of 1927.B52.

67 LEWIS, JOHN FREDERICK, JR. "Sherwood Anderson Records Experiences as Small Town Editor." Philadelphia Record (20 April), p. 4.
Hello Towns! shows that Anderson has the talent of amusing rural newspaper readers--and any lover of humanity anywhere.

68 LEWIS, WYNDHAM. Paleface: The Philosophy of the 'Melting-Pot'. London: Chatto and Windus, pp. 95, 97, 116-17, 126, 139, 144-47, 151, 153, 187, 192-93, 237, 240, 247-49, 252, 264, 268.
With The Torrents of Spring Hemingway shows promise of leaving behind such romanticism as Anderson's. As with Lawrence, Anderson tries to educate civilized whites to adopt styles of life from primitives; yet Anderson is less intelligent about issues than Lawrence.

69 LEWISOHN, LUDWIG. Mid-Channel: An American Chronicle. New York: Harper & Brothers, pp. 11, 12-13, 182.
Anderson has probably suffered under Puritanism, unlike Lewis and Mencken. One cannot predict how Anderson's reformist works will be judged a century hence. In conversation Anderson belies cynicism with gentle, placid appearance, for he embodies "an ultimate inner desperateness. . . ."

70 McCOLE, CAMILLE. "Sherwood Anderson--Congenital Freudian." Catholic World, 130 (November), 129-33.

Few American writers have seemingly so enjoyed their art as Anderson, but "he carries this worship of the word and of the sheet to the point where he frequently disregards the idea," caring more for sound in his prose than ideas. So intense is the writer's devotion to Freud that expertise in psychology is prerequisite to interest in Anderson. Reprinted: 1937.B37.

71 MENCKEN, H. L. "Experiments by Old Hands." American Mercury, 17 (June), 253-54.
Hello Towns! is mostly about the surface of small-town life in Virginia, but no one has ever before tried Anderson's experiment.

72 MUNSON, GORHAM B. Style and Form in American Prose. Garden City: Doubleday, Doran & Co., p. 295.
Anderson's "loose wandering daydreams" are in American fiction in contrast to the "concentrated imaginative plots of Poe. . . ."

73 N., R. W. "Anderson, Editor." Springfield Republican (12 May), E, p. 7.
Probably no author or book ever quite resembled Anderson and Hello Towns! No other country journalism could remain readable a year after publication.

74 O'BRIEN, EDWARD J. The Dance of the Machine: The American Short Story and the Industrial Age. New York: Macaulay Co., pp. 236-40, 262.
Of current short story writers, Anderson and Hemingway may endure. All of Anderson's books are "the record of a drawn battle between a man and an oppressive environment." Now that Anderson has been found by lack of national appreciation unworthy of accolades, he has retreated to small-town life in Virginia.

75 OVERTON, GRANT. An Hour of the American Novel. Philadelphia: J. B. Lippincott Co., pp. 141-45.
Anderson would merit little discussion as a novelist, but as a story writer he merits great attention and credit. In the tradition of Midwestern realists, Anderson uses "lovely and powerful prose with its Old Testamental simplicities of diction" to tell always new stories.

76 PATTERSON, ISABEL. "Books and Other Things." New York Herald Tribune (23 April), p. 21.
Effective when Anderson is direct and a failure when he affects naive simplicity, Hello Towns! somehow resembles Hemingway's telegraphic style.

1929

77 RASCOE, BURTON. A Bookman's Daybook. Edited by C. Hartley Grattan. New York: Horace Liveright, pp. 4, 21, 26, 42-43, 53, 54-55, 65, 82, 129, 136, 139, 146, 151-52, 158, 215, 250, 253.

There is no urge now to deify Anderson by this writer who led the procession years ago. Anderson is sincere when he praises Stein's influence on his own work. Anderson's poems are better read by the author than printed by him. Anderson's favorite reported phrase is "Take it all in all. . . ," and some of his best tales are told, not written. Maugham praised Winesburg, Ohio and deplored Many Marriages. Sandburg used to use Winesburg, Ohio as a standard for describing motion pictures.

78 SCHMITZ, MARIE. "Sherwood Anderson, Arme Blanke." Niewe Rotterdamsche Courant (3 April).

Poor White seems dated, for it describes America in the nineteenth century; but at least the novel is emotional, passionate narrative--but flat monotony rules.

79 SCHURZ, FRANKLIN D. "Hello Towns." South Bend Tribune (12 May).

Hello Towns! shows Anderson getting stories from the oral tradition around him in a small town.

80 SHERMAN, STUART P. Life and Letters of Stuart P. Sherman, 2. Edited by Jacob Zeitlin and Homer Woodbridge. New York: Farrar & Rinehart, 690, 702, 711.

Sherman tried to get Anderson elected to the American Academy of Arts and Letters, and Anderson wrote him his appreciation of all of Sherman's criticism.

81 SMITH, H. ALLEN. "Anderson's New Book Is a Group of Short Stories." Denver Morning Post (5 May).

Hello Towns! again shows Anderson best at writing of himself, for he is eccentric and fascinating; but this new book about a small town is more boredom than artistry.

82 SMITH, RACHEL. "Sherwood Anderson: Some Entirely Arbitrary Reactions." Sewanee Review, 37 (April), 159-63.

Each year makes Anderson seem more and more the passé author, for he has never had a central message that could bear repeating, and he reaches no conclusions beyond puzzlement. Able to help end "plot" tradition in short stories, Anderson cannot handle novel-length narrative.

83 STAFFORD, BOB. "Books and Bookman." _Akron Times_ (22 December).
Akron's latest published novelist is Ward H. Parry, whose literary hero is Anderson.

84 T., C. "Hello Towns! by Anderson, Is an Event." _Tulsa Tribune_ (2 June).
Hello Towns! is "a study in tranquility"--literature "as quiet and as engaging without being blatant as anything that has come from Mr. Anderson's pen."

85 TER BRAAK, MENNO. "Twee Methoden--Theodore Dreiser: An American Tragedy; Sherwood Anderson: Dark Laughter." _Vrije Bladen_, 6 (April), 97-110.
In _Dark Laughter_ Anderson lets loose his romantic, intuitive, symbolic inclinations, as compared to Dreiser's stricter realism in _An American Tragedy_. However, both writers unmask the false world of conventions and facades.

86 WHITE, WILLIAM ALLEN. "The Country Editor Speaks." _Nation_, 128 (12 June), 714.
Anderson reflected the post-War mood of pessimistic determinism; now he reflects humanitarianism, editing his Virginia newspapers. Compared to professional country-town editors, Anderson shows no distinction in _Hello Towns!_

87 WICKHAM, HARVEY. "Laughter and Sherwood Anderson." _The Impuritans_. New York: L. MacVeagh, pp. 268-82.
Unable to bring a humorous view to bear upon his characters or themes in _Windy McPherson's Son_, _Dark Laughter_, and _Tar_, Anderson "transposes to America the Englishman's doubt of his right to live."

88 WULLICH, VÍCTOR MAX. "_Pobre Blanco_, Novela de Sherwood Anderson." _Nosotros_, 66 (December), 432-33.
Poor White, a novel on the effects of industrialism on common lives, is Anderson's prose epic about the growth of the modern United States of America.

89 YOSHIDA, KINETARO, "Sherwood Anderson and I." _Bugaku Jidai_ (December), pp. 68-70.
In 1924 Anderson permitted Yoshida to translate some short stories into Japanese. Anderson supposed that _Poor White_ would be to Yoshida's liking. His works had already been translated into German, Swedish, French, and Russian; and Anderson would be expecting royalties from Japan. Anderson expressed regret that the Federal Immigration Act has passed the House of Representatives and later permitted

1929

(YOSHIDA, KINETARO)
Yoshida to translate any of his works without paying royalties. [Takashi Kodaira]

90 ZORN, GREMIN. "The Book Parade." Jamaica Press [NY] (11 May).
With a Shavian attitude toward the world and support for Communist causes, Anderson may be lying about being apolitical in his newspapers. It is doubtful that the Anderson of Hello Towns! can remain peacefully in his village.

1930 A BOOKS - NONE

1930 B SHORTER WRITINGS

1 ANDERSON, MARGARET. My Thirty Years' War: The Autobiography, Beginnings and Battles to 1930. New York: Covici, Friede, pp. 38-39, 44, 49, 50, 52, 91, 141, 142, 216, 249.
When Anderson met with literary people in Chicago, he preferred to tell stories instead of discussing esthetics. When a friend's story was "reworked" by Anderson for publication, original traces were lost. When Anderson read Windy McPherson's Son from manuscript, Dell "was passionate about it" far more than Margaret Anderson was. Anderson has, after all, not grown beyond a ten-year-old's romanticism.

2 ANON. "Anderson, Sherwood." National Cyclopaedia of American Biography: Current. New York: James T. White & Co., p. 68.
Careless of form and taste, Anderson "adopted authorship as a relief from the strain and tedium of commercial occupations"--and he retains a tie to advertising and writers of the Chicago Renaissance.

3 ANON. "Woburn Books Again." Times Literary Supplement (2 January), p. 10.
In Alice and the Lost Novel Anderson's stories are written in a style "as bare and simple as a clean pocket handkerchief."

4 ANON. "Laud Work of Harris As Southern Editor." New York Times (19 January), p. 25.
Anderson praised Julia and Julian Harris for perpetuating southern charm in their Columbus, Georgia, newspaper.

5 ANON. "Book Collectors Start Quarterly." New York Times (24 February), p. 12.

In The Colophon Anderson writes of the creation and publication of "The Rabbit-Pen," his first story.

6 ANON. "Not Unmixed Realism." New York Times (17 May), p. 16.
Even a tough, crude, realistic writer such as Anderson can become sentimental, as when he reviews a book of Lawrence's essays.

7 ANON. Publicity Item. Macon Telegraph [GA] (29 June).
Covici-Friede is publishing as a free pamphlet Anderson's review of Margaret Anderson's My Thirty Years' War.

8 ANON. Note on Winesburg, Ohio. Monroeville Spectator [OH] (13 August).
Every Ohio villager should read Winesburg, Ohio, for Anderson has written of the citizens' "hopes and fears, their lusts and ambitions, their frustrations and eccentricities portrayed with subtle sympathy and understanding."

9 ANON. "Sherwood Anderson Pleads for Small Town." Columbus Dispatch [OH] (14 September).
In "Cotton Mill" Anderson attacks realists like Lewis and asks for more tolerance toward small-town America.

10 ANON. "Dr. Ransom Charges Barr's 'Regulated' Industrialism Would End in Communism." Richmond Times-Dispatch (15 November), pp. 1, 2.
Presiding over the Ransom-Barr debate, Anderson defended farmers and small-town citizens. Anderson deplored Lewis' Nobel Prize because Lewis hates small-town America; Dreiser deserved this prize instead of Lewis.

11 ANON. "Champions Mill Strikes." New York Times (17 November), p. 19.
In addressing textile workers on strike in Danville, Virginia, Anderson hoped for their victory.

12 BRUNS, FRIEDRICH. "Sherwood Anderson." Die Amerikanische Dichtung der Gegenwart. Leipzig: Verlag und Druck von B. G. Teubner, pp. 34-40.
Anderson's autobiographical A Story Teller's Story is written as fantasy, emphasizing always the inner life. Life becomes unpleasant for Anderson's characters as they become factual, business-oriented; the writer himself excels in lyrical prose, especially as written in Winesburg, Ohio.

1930

13 CABELL, JAMES BRANCH. Some of Us. New York: Robert M. McBride, pp. 77-80, 84-85.

Anderson and Dreiser have become famous enough to be censored by the Watch and Ward Society--to their advantage, naturally. Especially rebuked is Many Marriages for its nude-father scene; yet Anderson is merely honest, tolerant, and frank.

14 CAIRNS, WILLIAM B. A History of American Literature. Revised edition. New York: Oxford University Press, pp. 490, 526-27.

Anderson "is ranked by many readers among the foremost of writers who devote themselves to psychoanalytic studies of characters, sometimes of the perverse and the erratic."

15 CANBY, HENRY SEIDEL. "Sherwood Anderson's 'Many Marriages.'" Modern Writers at Work. Edited by Josephine K. Piercy. New York: Macmillan Co., pp. 495-98.

Reprint of 1924.B12.

16 ELIASON, NORMAN E. "Midwestern Writers: Sherwood Anderson." Prairie Schooner, 4 (Winter), 52-59.

Anderson, a "mystic novelist," having dramatically abandoned business, has achieved critical but not popular success from his writing. Afraid of conventions, Anderson makes his heroes "unsuccessful" in any traditional terms, for they mirror their creator. His two themes are sex-in-life and "the tragedy of the inarticulate."

17 FOERSTER, NORMAN, ed. Humanism and America: Essays on the Outlook of Modern Civilisation. New York: Farrar and Rinehart, pp. 135, 192-94, 204, 232.

Alan Thompson considers Anderson "softer" and thus less "cruel" than Lawrence in writing of sex; Harry Clark exemplifies the industrialization of America with Poor White; Gorham Munson places Anderson with so-called "renaissance" writers.

18 FORD, COREY. "Hello Yourself, Sherwood." The John Riddell Murder Case, a Philo Vance Parody. New York: Charles Scribner's Sons, pp. 102-22.

Anderson would help a detective and a police officer solve a crime; but, as the telephone service to Marion, Virginia, is disrupted, a reading of Anderson's country-journalism book substitutes.

19 FOSTER, RICHARD ALLEN. The School in American Literature. Baltimore: Warwick and York, pp. 192-93.

Although Anderson "may stigmatize the reputed idealism of the schoolmistress in America," other writers shall come to her deserved defense.

20 GARRISON, C. S. "Publicity Department, American Federation [of] Labor Southern Organization Campaign." Textile Worker, 18 (November), 462.
Anderson, while in Danville, Virginia, to write about labor, told striking workers, "I hope to God you win."

*21 GORMAN, FRANCIS J. "To the Editor of the Textile Worker." Textile Worker, 18 (November), 463-64.
Cited: 1966.A1.

22 GRATTAN, C. HARTLEY, ed. The Critique of Humanism: A Symposium. New York: Brewer & Warren, pp. 124, 264-65, 266-67, 275-76.
Burton Rascoe says that, while such writers as Anderson were silent, so-called "humanists" attacked modern writing; John Chamberlain says that in the early 1920's, Anderson was "our most sensitive, poetic and humane writer," then in a "definitely escapist mood."

*23 LETTENBAUR, J. A. "Sinclair Lewis und die Neuen in Amerika." Hochland, 27, No. 2, pp. 317-28.
Cited: Price, L. M. The Reputation of United States Literature in Germany. Chapel Hill: University of North Carolina Press, 1966, p. 220.

24 MUNSON, GORHAM. The Dilemma of the Liberated: An Interpretation of Twentieth Century Humanism. New York: Coward, McCann, p. 70.
In 1920 intellectual liberation through revolt became popular, and Poor White made the time exciting.

25 OPPENHEIM, JAMES. "The Story of the Seven Arts." American Mercury, 20 (June), 161.
Several of Anderson's Winesburg, Ohio stories that appeared in The Seven Arts impressed Oppenheim and made Anderson's career. Anderson demanded more pay for future stories; the editors declined.

26 PARRINGTON, V. L. The Beginnings of Critical Realism in America, 1860-1920. New York: Harcourt, Brace and Co., pp. xv, 241, 319, 324, 325, 326, 331, 361, 370-71, 373, 377, 393, 399.
Anderson, unlike earlier naturalistic writers, concerns himself with the inner life more than with external

1930

(PARRINGTON, V. L.)
environment; he accepts "determinism, distortion, pessimism" and his "symbolisms are obscure and puzzling." With one theme--"the disastrous effect of frustrations and repressions that create grotesques"--Anderson is "one of the three or four most important men now writing fiction in America."

27 PATTEE, FRED LEWIS. The New American Literature, 1890-1930. New York: Century Co., pp. 23, 35, 69, 92, 177, 181, 281, 321, 329-30, 332-37.
Because Anderson is totally self-centered, his early books are completely autobiographical. From his own adventures with life, Anderson wrote realistically. Freud gave Anderson answers to questions about post-frontier Americans, and Anderson centered his fiction around Freudian motivations. Being one who merely raises questions, Anderson will likely not be of permanent importance.

28 PIERARD, LOUIS. "La Vague de Pudeur en Amérique." Les Nouvelles Littéraires (19 April), p. 5.
Although only a few words in Dark Laughter are of dubious taste, Anderson is a businessman of pornography.

29 [RIDDELL, JOHN].
See FORD, COREY. 1930.B18.

30 SAYLOR, OLIVER M. Revolt in the Arts: A Survey of the Creation, Distribution and Appreciation of Art in America. New York: Brentano's, pp. 50, 62, 64, 82, 105, 109.
Anderson, himself hampered by taste-makers, challenges American business to aid in creation and distribution of art. Sometimes Anderson misreads facts of American life, but he is there interpreting for others in often crudely formed ways.

31 SCHYBERG, FREDERIK. Moderne Amerikansk Litteratur, 1900-1930. Copenhagen: Gyldendalske Boghandel-Nordisk Forlag, pp. 10, 15, 25, 31, 44, 45, 51, 57, 63-71, 72, 73, 76, 77, 78, 79, 81, 84, 87, 91, 93, 95, 110, 115, 117, 122, 123, 126, 137, 138, 139, 142, 148, 157, 158, 170, 181.
Not a satirist as is Lewis, Anderson preached freedom and fulfillment in the 1920's. Starting with misfits in small towns, then moving to unhappy industrialists, Anderson presented primitivistic, poetic answers to repression and oppression.

32 SMITH, ARTHUR H. "A Few Side Notes." An Authentic History of Winesburg Holmes County, Ohio Including a Winesburg "Who's Who." [n.p.: n.p.], p. 70.
Anderson's Winesburg, Ohio ("a burlesque"), which some have thought slander on Winesburg, Ohio, is really based on no specific Ohio town, according to the author. The imaginary town is larger and is served by a railroad.

33 WILLIAMS, STANLEY T. and NELSON F. ADKINS, eds. Course of Reading in American Literature with Bibliographies. New York: Harcourt, Brace and Co., pp. 143, 150-60.
[Brief six-item checklist of secondary criticism and four primary sources]

1931 A BOOKS

1 DAVIS, PHILIP RICHARD. A Country Editor Comes to Town. Chicago: Peacock Press, 12 pp.
On Saturday, April 25, 1931, Anderson ate at Schlogl's with Henry Justin Smith, Howard Vincent O'Brien, Lloyd Lewis, the author, Lew Sarett. Anderson praised the Chicago skyline, country living, small-town journalism, and women as saviors.

1931 B SHORTER WRITINGS

1 ADAMS, JOHN R. "Perhaps Women." San Diego Sun (20 December).
As impressionistic sketches, Perhaps Women succeeds, yet Anderson is not an optimist as mankind faces machines.

2 ANON. "Harrington and Lutz Speak to Georgia Editors on Increasing Responsibility of Newspapers." Atlanta Journal (20 February), p. 1.
Anderson will be one of the speakers at the University of Georgia journalism conferences.

3 ANON. "Fiction in Fancy Dress." New York Times Book Review (22 March), p. 29.
An American County Fair is written in Anderson's highly cultivated simple style, and the author evokes the men-and-horses tone of his subject.

4 ANON. "Noted Writer Here Monday." Clyde Enterprise [OH] (30 April), pp. 1, 8.
Anderson visited Herman Hurd in the latter's grocery store and home. The writer now gives talks on newspapers and idealizes small-town life.

1931

5 ANON. Review of Perhaps Women. El Paso Times (23 August).
Anderson is so honorably serious in Perhaps Women that the reader is ashamed to gag at the style, thought, and title of the work.

6 ANON. "Masculine Defeatism." San Francisco Argonaut (12 September).
Anderson should now abandon the repetitive, muddled style used again in Perhaps Women and return to clear thinking.

7 ANON. "Today's Author." New York World-Telegram (15 September).
Anderson writes fiction by "encouraging his memory," and he is "soft-spoken, gentle, generous, sympathetic to the underdog," likes rural cooking and long walks on country roads.

8 ANON. "Turning New Pages." Portsmouth Times [OH] (27 September).
Part verse, part prose, Perhaps Women is Anderson's "turning and returning of his problem, through many lights and mediums."

9 ANON. "We Recommend." World Tomorrow, 14 (October), 331.
Perhaps Women is a disturbing sketch of mill-village life drawn with "tragic vividness."

10 ANON. "Goodbye Men!" Darien Review [CT] (1 October).
A poetic sort like Anderson could not say how his women are to solve the problems posed in Perhaps Women.

11 ANON. Review of Perhaps Women. Wilkes-Barre Independent (4 October).
Often Anderson's controversial books, such as Perhaps Women, may not be so serious as most folk believe.

12 ANON. "Sees American Men Subdued By Women." New York Times (31 October), p. 31.
Believing in family integrity, Anderson thinks that industrialism has unmanned American males.

13 ANON. Review of Perhaps Women. Forum, 86 (November), vi, viii.
Perhaps Women is marred by lapses in Anderson's reasoning, his use of the English language, and his inability to structure his work.

14 ANON. "Abolition of Family Debated by Authors." New York Times (2 November), p. 19.
In the debate over child-rearing with Bertrand Russell, Anderson emphatically preferred the humanity of mothers over the sterile, scientific approach of behaviorists.

15 ANON. "Pre-Industrial Edens." New York Times (2 November), p. 20.
Usually sound in opinion, Anderson has wrongly blamed industrialism with current problems; his nostalgia for pre-industrial days is not wise.

16 ANON. "Machine Child-Rearing." New York Times (8 November), 9, p. 2.
At the Mecca Temple, sponsored by the Discussion Guild of New York, Anderson spoke ironically of mechanizing the nurture of children.

17 ANON. Review of Perhaps Women. Long Beach Press-Telegram (23 November).
Perhaps Women is important for warning of machinery's damage to the human and for acknowledging that women can rule life.

18 ANON. "Heading for Matriarchy." New York Times (23 November), p. 18.
Anderson prefers not to address women's clubs, for his current interests are newspapers and machinery.

19 ANON. "Shall the Home Be Abolished?" Literary Digest, 111 (28 November), 25-26.
In his debate over child-rearing with Bertrand Russell, Anderson favored emotional rather than philosophical principles, fearing some Freudian concepts, standardization of life, and misuse of eugenics.

20 ANON. "Is Our America A Matriarchy?" Patterson Call [NJ] (5 December).
Anderson broods in Perhaps Women and produces a poetic idea about mechanization.

21 ANON. "Anderson Decries Our 'Speakeasy Era.'" New York Times (7 December), p. 24.
Anderson spoke to three thousand listeners about southern labor troubles, blaming American officialdom and intellectuals for keeping silent in a "speakeasy" manner.

1931

22 ANON. Review of Perhaps Women. Santa Ana Register (27 December).
As Perhaps Women merely restates Anderson's fear of industry, his answer of possible female salvation is comparable to the mountain making a molehill.

23 BARRON, MARK. "A Man Learns." Tulsa World (13 December).
Anderson talked to reporters of the new women's freedom to have divorce without alimony and of politics and country journalism.

24 BLANKENSHIP, RUSSELL. American Literature as an Expression of the National Mind. New York: Henry Holt and Co., pp. 517, 611, 630, 656, 665-72.
Unlike Sinclair Lewis's satiric reportage style, Anderson's approach to village characters is to love them and understand their minds. Anderson is a psychological naturalist with an added mysticism. He faces life reverently; and at his best he is a significant figure in the world's literature.

*25 BOLANDER, CARL-AUGUST. "Redaktör Anderson, U. S. A." Dagens Nyheter (2 February).
Cited: 1957.B1.

26 CANBY, HENRY SEIDEL. "Machine-Made Men." Saturday Review of Literature, 8 (10 October), 183.
Sharing Lawrence's attitude toward mechanization as destructive of sexuality, Anderson in Perhaps Women uses a Whitman-Stein style to call for the redemption of sensibility.

27 CORSON, J. J. "Sherwood Anderson and Machines." Richmond News-Leader (17 September).
Perhaps Women--"told partly in blank verse and partly in story form"--is good writing and poor social observation.

28 DAVIS, ELRICK B. "World Ripe for Rule By Women, Says Anderson." Cleveland Press (15 September).
Anderson supports his theory of machinery in Perhaps Women "with some of the very finest writing he has ever done."

29 DREWRY, JOHN E. "New Book News." Columbus Enquirer-Sun [GA] (11 October).
Perhaps Women is as interesting for Anderson's poetic prose style as for its theory of machinery and humanity.

30 FAŸ, BERNARD. "Sherwood Anderson." Les Romanciers Américains. Edited by V. Llona. Paris: Denoël et Steele, pp. 7-14.
Truly a poetic author of the American Midwest, Anderson in his novels creates "poems" to express modern life. His prose is musical, his topic love and youth, his purpose is to penetrate others' lives even briefly, and his muse is his sirene--to understand "the American personality."

31 FELD, ROSE C. "Mr. Anderson's Vision of a Machine Age Matriarchy." New York Times Book Review (27 September), p. 2.
Perhaps Women is narrative, essay, poem, threnody, invocation, and challenge--all with a message that Anderson escapes telling clearly.

32 FITZGERALD, F. SCOTT. "Echoes of the Jazz Age." Scribner's Magazine, 90 (November), 461.
In Winesburg, Ohio Anderson proved that the world contains much sexual activity, if people would look carefully about them.

33 G., D. F. "Sherwood Anderson On the Woman's Era." Boston Transcript (17 October), p. 1.
In often Biblical poetry, Perhaps Women is "an unusual but somewhat irritating study of the mechanical spirit of America. . . ."

34 GANNETT, LEWIS. "Books and Things." New York Herald Tribune (15 September), p. 17.
Now that Anderson does not want all machines destroyed but instead understood, he invents in Perhaps Woman a quasi-religious idea compounded of machinery and females.

35 GODWIN, MURRAY. "Scant Tether." New Republic, 69 (18 November), 24-25.
In Perhaps Women Anderson is repetitive and dull, and his anthropological-sociological ideas about humans and machines are ridiculous.

36 GRAFTON, SAMUEL. "'Perhaps Women' Will Save Age, Says Anderson." Philadelphia Record (20 September).
Anderson is totally humorless in Perhaps Women; and his style is "bubble, bellow, thought and observation mixed, a formless miasma of condemnation and hope."

37 GREGORY, HORACE. "Perhaps Anderson." Nation, 133 (14 October), 401-402.

(GREGORY, HORACE)
Perhaps Women is "a poem written in essay form about women and machines," by "an American business man turned inside out"--who should return to story-writing.

38 HANSEN, HARRY. "The First Reader." New York World-Telegram (15 September), p. 25.
The poetry of Perhaps Women is so cadenced that the reader almost too late realizes that poetry does not help solve the problem of industrialism.

39 _____. "The First Reader." New York World-Telegram (28 December).
Philip Davis' Christmas card is a booklet, A Country Editor Comes to Town, about Anderson's visit to Chicago.

40 KNIGHT, GRANT C. The Novel in English. New York: Richard R. Smith, pp. 361-63.
Anderson's manner of writing is to use a deliberated simplicity to agonize over his characters, and his confused result comes from this manner instead of from his subjects. All of his characters crave escape into freedom; Anderson's works are flawed by lack of humor.

41 KNOX, VIC. Review of A Country Editor Comes to Town. Chicago Evening Post (26 December).
A Country Editor Comes to Town "will be an honored denizen of my bookshelf and promises, in time, to be a valuable Anderson item."

42 KRUEGER, JESS. "Looping the Loop." Chicago American (24 December).
A Country Editor Comes to Town has been published in an autographed, limited edition.

43 KUNITZ, STANLEY J. "Sherwood Anderson." Living Authors: A Book of Biographies. New York: H. W. Wilson Co., pp. 7-9.
A self-taught writer, Anderson came from a gypsy-like family, abandoned his business career while dictating a letter, endured a nervous breakdown in 1916, won slow success with Winesburg, Ohio, and now lives above his printshop in Marion, Virginia.

44 McMURRY, G. H. "Perhaps Women." San Jose Mercury-Herald (11 October).
Perhaps Women is more satisfactory as a prose poem than as sociology.

45 MACY, JOHN, ed. American Writers on American Literature: By Thirty-Seven Contemporary Writers. New York: Horace Liveright, pp. 490-91.
As do other Midwestern writers, says Llewellyn Jones, Anderson chooses for his heroes small-town boys who mature into oddity; after fictionalizing his own youth, Anderson has had trouble inventing mature situations for his characters.

46 O'BRIEN, HOWARD VINCENT. "Footnotes." Chicago Daily News (22 December).
Davis' privately printed A Country Editor Comes to Town contains a description of Anderson telling small-town tales at Schlogl's.

47 ÖSTERLING, ANDERS. "Sherwood Anderson." Dagens Gärning, Tredje Samlingen: Essayer och Kritiker, 1927-1931. Stockholm: Albert Bonniers Förlag, pp. 108-18.
Anderson's "groping" toward answers makes him interesting, for he expresses America with "dazed apprehension" as progressing through national puberty. In panoramic scope and profound depth, Anderson analyzes the homeless, thwarted American. Mystic and rebel, he questions the complacency and hypocrisy of his countrymen. Perhaps his emphasis on sex and autobiography will be his permanent weakness.

48 PAVESE, CESARE. "Sherwood Anderson." Cultura, 10 (April), 400-407.
Writing always of repressed people, Anderson in his early books presented the sad and tragic stories of American life; after 1923, he wrote more autobiographical stories of escape from such lives into freedom of creativity. In style, Anderson superbly creates living American speech. Reprinted: 1951.B29.

49 ROBINSON, JOSEPH. "Anderson on the Machine." Gastonia Gazette (10 September).
Anderson's dubious machine thesis in Perhaps Women is forgotten in his "Menad song of machines shrilling through it. . . ."

50 ROSS, MARY. "Men, Women, and Machines." New York Herald Tribune Books (20 September), p. 5.
Perhaps Women--"partly in broken verse, partly in story and prose opinion"--is Anderson's hope that humans will master machines and remaster themselves.

1931

51 ROURKE, CONSTANCE M. American Humor: A Study of the National Character. Garden City: Doubleday & Co., p. 230.
Although Anderson's stories are valuable for recapturing native phrasing with human warmth, the author intrudes in monologue-form. These stories restore humor and colloquial style to the American tradition of fiction.

52 S., A. W. "Anderson's Book Worth Reading and Keeping." Evanston News-Index (21 October).
Perhaps intoxicated by the machine sounds he has heard, Anderson in Perhaps Women is "garrulous and poetic."

53 SALPETER, HARRY. "The Week's Reading." Outlook and Independent, 159 (7 October), 184.
Without diatribe or knowledge of economics, Anderson philosophizes in Perhaps Women, admitting his own success in writing stories of failure. Here perhaps can be seen the author's own failure.

54 SMITH, SAMUEL STEPHENSON. The Craft of the Critic. New York: Thomas Y. Crowell Co., pp. 21-22, 194, 200.
Anderson exemplifies the novelist without a sense of the past, eternally romantic in spite of his subjects of poverty, disappointment, and suffering; his "boyish sense of the wonder and mystery of life" cannot be escaped.

55 STALLINGS, LAURENCE. "The Book of the Day." Milwaukee Sentinel (19 September).
Anderson does not listen to critics who think his Winesburg, Ohio classic and his later books, such as Perhaps Women, ridiculous.

56 TANTE, DILLY.
See KUNITZ, STANLEY J. 1931.B43.

57 TIPPETT, TOM. When Southern Labor Stirs. New York: Jonathan Cape & Harrison Smith, pp. 249-53.
Anderson's address to striking workers in Danville, Virginia, packed the auditorium; and Anderson spoke emotionally to the strikers of their need to use machinery to free themselves from poverty.

58 TORREY, WARE. "A Few New Books." Pasedena Post (26 September).
Perhaps Women is stronger for being stated in Anderson's "characteristic style."

59 TYLER, ERIC E. "Women Rule Anderson's Forecast." Albany Knickerbocker Press (8 November).

Perhaps humanity is too late in fearing machinery, as Anderson in Perhaps Women warns; but the writer's driving style is convincing of a problem.

60 WEBB, WALTER PRESCOTT. Great Plains. New York: Ginn and Co., pp. 473, 477-78.
In A Story Teller's Story Anderson writes of Midwestern poverty along with love for the legends of the West.

61 WILDES, HARRY EMERSON. "'Of Making Many Books--.'" Philadelphia Public Ledger (15 September).
Anderson's worship of both women and handcraft is medieval, as is the religion that he presents in Perhaps Women; he now praises the machines that he used to hate.

62 WILLIAMS, ROBERT. "Buck Fever." Varsity Review, 8 (November), 9-11.
With his two rural Virginia newspapers to publish, Anderson is reliving some of the hero's life from Winesburg, Ohio; and Anderson's fictional reporter creates hilarity for readers of the papers.

63 WILSON, EDMUND. Axel's Castle: A Study in the Imaginative Literature of 1870-1930. New York: Charles Scribner's Sons, pp. 238-39, 252-53, 287-88.
From Stein, Anderson learned the repetition and simplicity of his style--perhaps even his interest in Negro characters; yet Ohio factories--not New Orleans streets--are Anderson's setting.

1932 A BOOKS - NONE

1932 B SHORTER WRITINGS

1 ADAMIC, LOUIS. Laughing in the Jungle: The Autobiography of an Immigrant in America. New York: Harper & Brothers, p. 264.
The work of Anderson helped this immigrant to learn of the United States.

2 ANON. "Son Buys Sherwood Anderson Out." New York Times (1 January), p. 30.
Robert L. Anderson has assumed controlling interest in his father's Marion, Virginia, newspapers.

3 ANON. "Newspaper Change at Marion." Roanoke Times [VA] (1 January).

1932

(ANON.)
Robert Lane Anderson has assumed responsibility for publishing his father's country newspapers, for Sherwood Anderson's current interests are elsewhere than Marion; and the writer has not operated the papers for two years. The elder Anderson will now roam over America to speak, write, and think.

4 ANON. "Sherwood Anderson." Jersey City Journal (16 January).
Anderson recently spoke on journalism at the Brooklyn Institute of Fine Arts.

5 ANON. Review of Tar. New Haven Journal-Courier (18 January).
Republication of Tar shows Anderson "sombre, meditative, photographic, preoccupied with the inner wells of motivation that make the human animal go."

6 ANON. "Sherwood Anderson in City; Would Sell Useless Studio." Chicago Daily Times (18 March).
Anderson wants to sell "Ripshin," his country home, because he cannot write well there. In Chicago to speak on journalism, Anderson thinks that machinery will become a literary subject and that young writers should do factory work to meet truly important individuals.

7 ANON. "Sherwood Anderson ou l'Amérique Secrète." Le Mois (1 April--1 May), pp. 165-68.
Writing always of the interior lives of Americans, Anderson is even in prose the greatest American poet since Whitman. In Tar the author describes poetically a childhood of vicissitudes and vagabondage.

8 ANON. "Anderson Gets Into Hot Water." Waterbury Republican [CT] (3 April).
Anderson spoke recently to the Advertising Council in Chicago to urge rich people to finance youthful country journalists.

9 ANON. Review of Perhaps Women. Greensboro News (23 April).
Anderson's dogmatic conclusion in Perhaps Women is damaging to his poetic premises.

10 ANON. "Sherwood Anderson's Offer." Mountain Missionary, 2 (July), 2.
Anderson has decided to sell his country home in Virginia and has suggested that the Mountain Mission Association use it as a health center. Built at a cost of $25,000, "Ripshin" is for sale at $5,000. If some rich donor would give help, the house would be a home for mountain nurses.

11 ANON. "To 'Challenge' Hoover On Ejecting Veterans." New York Times (9 August), p. 4.
Anderson will lead a delegation of writers, sponsored by the National Committee for the Defense of Political Prisoners, to question Herbert Hoover's use of militia against protesting ex-soldiers.

12 ANON. "Challenge To Hoover Planned By Writers." New York Times (10 August), p. 2.
Anderson says that his group of protesting writers will ask Hoover whether his military action against ex-soldiers will become procedural against the unemployed poor.

13 ANON. "President Too Busy For Bonus Protest." New York Times (11 August), p. 2.
Hoover being too busy to discuss the Bonus Army with the group of writers joined by Anderson, the press secretary would not let Anderson read a prepared statement. Instead, he lectured the writers to begin telling the truth.

14 ANON. "Writers Are Bitter At Hoover Rebuff." New York Times (12 August), p. 17.
The group of liberal writers protesting Hoover's military action against ex-soldiers were denied an audience with the President.

15 ANON. "Men Useless to Women, Sherwood Anderson Says." New York World-Telegram (16 September).
Anderson says that one theme of Beyond Desire is men's worship of machinery contrasted to women's ability to rule human affairs.

16 ANON. "Sherwood Anderson Disappoints." Cleveland Plain Dealer (25 September).
Beyond Desire is as disappointing as most Anderson novels are and is not "an artistic achievement."

17 ANON. "Sherwood Anderson Stands Puzzled." Cincinnati Post (30 September).
Dealing with economic facts, Beyond Desire dramatizes the wilderness of the Depression.

18 ANON. "When Are Authors Insulted?" Bookman, 75 (October), 565.
Now that Anderson has turned to politics, one remembers sadly his contributions to American literature.

19 ANON. "Sherwood Anderson's Newest Book Is Beautifully Moving." Birmingham Post [AL] (1 October).

(ANON.)
In Beyond Desire Anderson's characters act "in the perplexing and chaotic drama which incarnates the perplexity and chaos of America itself."

20 ANON. "One Corner of the Canvas." Chicago Herald-Examiner (1 October).
Beyond Desire is Anderson's portrait of one small part of the American scene--in dim colors but clear lines.

21 ANON. "Mill South." Cleveland Press (1 October).
Beyond Desire reflects Anderson's new social conscience but is in his "characteristic style."

22 ANON. "Humanity's Woe Is Plumbed in Anderson Book." Davenport Times [IA] (1 October).
Without aligning himself politically, Anderson has in Beyond Desire pictured a part of American society suffering from economic woe.

23 ANON. Review of Beyond Desire. Augusta Chronicle [GA] (9 October).
Although the style rambles in Beyond Desire, Anderson's characters are memorably etched.

24 ANON. "Sherwood Anderson Looking 'Beyond Desire.'" Chicago Daily News (12 October).
The South of Beyond Desire is "torn by its resistance to change."

25 ANON. "Šervud Anderson o svoem novom romane k priezdu v SSSR." Literaturnaja gazeta (23 October), p. 1.
Anderson says that his story is always the same, for Beyond Desire transports the downtrodden people of Winesburg, Ohio into a more modern context. Presenting the worker's factual story, he asserts, is a more effective revolutionary activity--for writers with talent--than writing direct propaganda. [James F. Cradler]

26 ANON. "Book Reviews." Culver City Star-News (2 November).
In Beyond Desire Anderson shows that social and personal problems must be solved before confusion can end.

27 ANON. "Beyond Desire." Caldwell Progress [NJ] (11 November).
The women in Beyond Desire remain sexually psychotic; the hero finds fulfillment beyond sex. Anderson here is a "finished groper"--"a distinctive label of artistic style."

28 ANON. Review of Beyond Desire. Washington Post (11 December).
Not a propaganda novel, Beyond Desire shows the southern struggle between conservatism and Communism.

29 ANON. "Beyond Desire." San Diego Union (18 December).
In Beyond Desire Anderson presents his typical confused wanderer--this time before an industrial setting.

30 BABBITT, IRVING. On Being Creative and Other Essays. Boston: Houghton Mifflin Co., pp. 218-19.
Anderson argues that literature must be crude to reflect a crude people, and he probably contains enough to supplement the world's possible lack of crudity.

31 BEACH, JOSEPH W. The Twentieth Century Novel: Studies in Technique. New York: Century Co., pp. 107, 268, 275, 276, 278, 281, 309, 516, 531, 540.
Dark Laughter is narrated through the hero's memories; Many Marriages generally follows the same technique and occurs mostly on one night. Anderson's recent novels all use this point of view and time-span, making the heroes actually speakers for Anderson.

32 BERND, A. B. "Beyond Desire." Macon Telegraph (9 October).
As the characters in Beyond Desire are human, Anderson has not yet put his pen to political propaganda.

33 BOSWELL, JR. "Books." Fort Wayne Journal-Gazette (19 March).
In Beyond Desire "confusion" is the keynote of Anderson's purpose. Perhaps only in death does he allow an answer for his hero.

34 BUCKALTER, HELEN. "Confusion in Industrial South Pictured in New Anderson Novel." Washington News (8 October).
In Beyond Desire Anderson presents the irony of destroyed hope and life amid industrialism.

35 CALVERTON, V. F. The Liberation of American Literature. New York: Charles Scribner's Sons, pp. 35, 274, 406, 408, 424-30, 433, 453.
Having escaped business for literature, Anderson keeps as his main theme the effects of the industrialization of America, especially the effects on his characters' minds. One must note, however, that Anderson's nostalgia for a lost golden age (purely mythical) may flaw his work against anything new.

1932

36 CESTRE, C. "Sherwood Anderson: Perhaps Women." Revue Anglo-Américaine, 9 (February), 269.
Now writing in Perhaps Women of machines instead of his usual topics, Anderson still emerges the storyteller and champion of love over oppression.

37 CHAMBERLAIN, JOHN. "Mr. Anderson's 'Labor' Novel." New York Times Book Review (25 September), p. 6.
Beyond Desire demonstrates that Anderson has investigated and pondered over the labor problem of the South--even if he reaches no conclusions or makes no predictions about chaos.

38 D., N. C. "Sherwood Anderson in a Town in Georgia." Boston Transcript (26 November), p. 1.
Inferior to Zola, Anderson could have created a more unified novel in Beyond Desire, for his sympathies are well displayed.

39 DAWSON, MARGARET CHEYNEY. "Anderson Up To Date." New York Herald Tribune Books (25 September), p. 7.
Even without the subjects of sex and social class, Beyond Desire is "a wise and fascinating story."

40 DICKINSON, THOMAS H. The Making of American Literature. New York: D. Appleton-Century Co., pp. 668, 678-79.
Convinced that mankind suffers from democracy and technology, Anderson "studies derelicts, sorry specimens who even in being twisted into strange shapes keep some flavor of primitive passion and feeling."

41 DRURY, JOHN. "Grub Street Shavings." Economy Spectator, 3, No. 1.
Davis omits one item about Anderson's visit in A Country Editor Comes to Town--the "moment when Sherwood Anderson became so enthusiastic in what he was saying about women that he lost his balance and fell off the chair." Anderson did not interrupt his speech.

42 DUDLEY, DOROTHY. Forgotten Frontiers: Dreiser and the Land of the Free. New York: Harrison Smith, pp. 13, 59, 71, 159, 254, 277, 318, 337, 347, 351, 365-66, 374, 403, 426, 427-28, 429-30, 431-32, 433, 434, 439, 443, 449-50, 461.
Dreiser deserved Anderson's praise in Horses and Men, for Anderson did follow the literary steps taken by Dreiser. Their careers are alike in waves of critical acclaim and disapprobation, for they share goals and moods.

43 EDGERTON, JAY. "Anderson in a Mill Town." Minneapolis Journal (2 October).
Anderson began his writing career by rebelling against middle-class existence; he now praises the machine society which makes that existence possible. Beyond Desire presents almost lyrically the New South with its cotton mill. In this novel Anderson creates ambiguity over his preference--machine or individual.

44 ELY-ESTORICK, ERIC. "Beyond Desire." Contempo, 3 (15 December), 2.
In Beyond Desire Anderson retains characters' psychological differentiations while writing of class struggles and industrialism. The author incorporates "somewhat naive essays charged with good humanitarian intentions, and a terrible unideological earnestness."

45 FADIMAN, CLIFTON. "Sherwood Anderson: The Search for Salvation." Nation, 135 (9 November), 454-56.
Before Anderson's dramatic escape from business midway in his life, his existence was unimportant; and his so-called sex obsession is no more than "re-emerged adolescence." On the other hand, his confusion or bewilderment in writing reflects middle-aged thought. Because Anderson has tried to find salvation from nada, his searches into nostalgia, into class struggle, and into labor--all fail while escape into boyhood is successful.

46 _____. "Still Groping." Nation, 135 (2 November), 432-33.
None of Anderson's novels is sound; and, now that he has added class struggle to sex and quality of life, his works reach embarrassment in Beyond Desire.

47 GANNETT, LEWIS. "Books and Things." New York Herald Tribune (19 September), p. 11.
Not naturally politically revolutionary, Anderson in Beyond Desire shows flashes of good storytelling; but the author does not fully believe his own propaganda.

48 GRAFTON, SAMUEL. "Anderson Hero Finds Content 'Beyond Desire.'" Philadelphia Record (25 September).
Whereas Upton Sinclair could have written a tract about the plot of Beyond Desire, Anderson has written a sex novel.

49 HANSEN, HARRY. "The First Reader." New York World-Telegram (19 September), p. 23.
In his sympathy for less-favored people, Anderson is not patrician but humanitarian. Avoiding in Beyond Desire the

1932

(HANSEN, HARRY)
rules of character observation, Anderson maintains his groping, naive style; but he uses too much of Stein's technique and his own sex emphasis.

50 HAZEN, DAVID W. "Editor, Novelist and Poet in City on Lecture Tour." Morning Oregonian (16 April).
The public not having been impressed with Anderson's poetry and non-fiction prose, the author has tried to encourage country journalism and expects authors to become politically involved now in national problems.

51 HERRING, HARRIET. "Southern Problems in Story." Journal of Social Forces, 11 (December), 295-98.
Hitting only high spots of southern life in Beyond Desire, Anderson writes of a middle-class young man wanting meaning and a mountain girl wanting success.

52 HICKS, GRANVILLE. "Red Pilgrimage." New Republic, 73 (21 December), 168-69.
Beyond Desire is important because the novel shows Anderson--always caught creatively in bewilderment at life--sensing and expressing the nation's discontent.

53 KNIGHT, GRANT C. American Literature and Culture. New York: Ray Long & Richard R. Smith, pp. 450-53.
A Story Teller's Story may eventually outrate all of Anderson's other writings, for it shows most clearly his love for human beings. Sometimes overdoing his conscious simplicity, best in writing short stories, Anderson has retired to rural Virginia to escape a literary milieu in which he no longer fitted.

54 KREYMBORG, ALFRED. The Little World: 1914 and After. New York: Coward-McCann, p. 152.
A poem for "S. A.": "Ohio was naught / but Ohio once / until his warm art / found words for the dunce."

55 LEWISOHN, LUDWIG. Expression in America. New York: Harper & Brothers, pp. 280, 370, 482-88.
Truly obsessed by sex, Anderson has written--ironic fact--almost Puritan literature. His works contain only misery and troubles; in them is no success or respite or peace: "His art is the half-articulate cry of tormented souls in a self-made inferno."

56 LUNDKVIST, ARTUR. "Anderson Sökaren." Atlantvind. Stockholm: Albert Bonniers Förlag, pp. 29-43.

Although not always autobiographical, Anderson's works reveal facets of the author, giving direct emotions and penetrating analyses. From a proletarian background, Anderson fought against becoming a standardized middle-class American; in Winesburg, Ohio he avoided satire and bitterness to call for psychological health and liberation. His novels are personalized escapes into freedom, often mystical instead of realistic. Always a seeker, Anderson reconciled the individual rebellion with the common good, achieving contentment with self and acceptance of all humanity.

57 M., C. "The Passing of Sherwood Anderson." Jacksonville Times-Union (9 October).

Beyond Desire is a contrived novel, showing Anderson as old and weary.

58 MEADE, EVERARD. "Sherwood Anderson's First Novel Since 'Dark Laughter.'" Richmond Times-Dispatch (25 September).

Beyond Desire presents through very human characters Anderson's social theories of sterile tradition and individual need for passion.

59 MEARS, HELEN. "There Is Confusion." Survey, 68 (1 November), 565.

Always first and among the best to make raw material of life available to literature, Anderson in Beyond Desire describes modern industrial chaos and leaves future novelists to present solutions.

60 MONROE, HARRIET. A Poet's Life: Seventy Years in a Changing World. New York: Macmillan Co., p. 390.

Sandburg's use of his rural youth in "Prairie" served as model for Anderson in Mid-American Chants.

61 NELSON, JOHN C. "Women May Win." Survey, 67 (1 February), 498-99.

Anderson has directly observed the American factory system and has poetically described its dehumanizing effects in Perhaps Women.

62 N[IEBUHR], R[EINHOLD]. "Still on Probation." World Tomorrow, 15 (30 November), 525-26.

More about the decay of old, middle-class order than the birth of a new, proletarian society, Beyond Desire is not orthodox enough to move Anderson into the Communist canon.

1932

63 PAUL, ELLIOT. "Farthest North: A Study of James Joyce." Bookman, 75 (May), 158.
Anderson and Joyce had previously met at the home of Victor Lohnase; in 1926-27 they met at a Paris restaurant and Joyce ordered oysters for Anderson, who hated French oysters. The uncomfortable dinner over without literary talk, "each man left the table somewhat baffled and covertly annoyed."

64 PERDECK, A. "Amerikaansche Letteren." Niewe Rotterdamsche Courant (10 November).
Formerly thought to be primarily a Freudian writer, Anderson in Beyond Desire shows that interest in the community outweighs interest in individual lives, and that social concerns overwhelm inner problems of the psyche. In a recent personal interview, while on his way to Russia, Anderson said that his hopes for literature after social revolution were dim.

65 SCHRIFTGIESSER, KARL. Review of Beyond Desire. Boston Transcript (30 November), p. 1.
Poorly constructed, Anderson's Beyond Desire admirably exploits Southern mill workers.

66 SCHUTTE, ALICE MAUDE. "Beyond Desire." San Jose Mercury-Herald (20 November).
While Beyond Desire may study Communism, no one place (or book) could hold so many depraved characters, not one of whom gets beyond desire.

67 SEAVER, EDWIN. "American Writers and Kentucky." New Masses, 7 (June), 9.
For Anderson to join in defending Dreiser's actions with Kentucky miners should not be surprising, for Anderson has been moving toward a new sensitivity about the class struggle for some time.

68 _____. "Beyond Desire." Modern Monthly, 7 (1932), 58-59.
All of Anderson's works are images of himself; yet no comparable author has reflected American concerns better. Thus, in spite of flaws in mood, form, and character types, Beyond Desire is a vital document about industry and conflict in the modern South.

69 SOSKIN, WILLIAM. "Reading and Writing." New York Evening Post (20 September).
Still sincerely groping in bewilderment, Anderson can now be thought "the Harold Bell Wright of the proletarian

literary movement," for Beyond Desire is melodramatic propaganda.

70 STALLINGS, LAURENCE. "The Book of the Day." New York Sun (20 September).

Beyond Desire moved Anderson from "Winesburg, Ohio," to Gastonia, North Carolina; and this book fulfils all of one's hopes that the author would again succeed in his chosen, free-style technique.

71 STEIN, HANNAH. "My Conception of Beauty." Philadelphia Public Ledger (2 May).

To Anderson, beauty is finding the unexpected in people, nature, and writing. In Perhaps Women Anderson shows the beauty of machines.

72 STONE, GEOFFREY. "Beyond Desire." Bookman, 75 (October), 642-43.

Beyond Desire, too imitative of Stein's style, tries to discuss sex as pleasure-pain, factories as oppressive institutions, and machines as beauty; but Anderson neither creates believable characters nor tells a worthwhile story.

73 THOMSON, WILLIAM S. "'Beyond Desire.'" Atlanta Journal (23 October).

Beyond Desire is a "chaos of thoughts and wonderings, from which the reader emerges confused and unsatisfied."

74 TYLER, ERIC E. "Turmoil of Spirit Shown by Anderson." Albany Knickerbocker Press (30 October).

Readers of Beyond Desire will again find Anderson thinking about American life; someday he will find the answer in his groping way.

75 W., J., JR. "Fiction." Dallas Times-Herald (15 January).

Without theme or structure, Beyond Desire is a failure.

76 WARD, A. C. American Literature, 1880-1930. New York: Dial Press, pp. 111-13, 120-33.

Anderson, Lewis, and Dreiser are realists; but their only common feature is challenge of romantic American myths: "Dreiser is pained; Anderson puzzled; Lewis hilarious. . . ." All three are seemingly overconcerned with sex, but only naturally so. In Poor White Anderson is interested in the national change from agrarian to urban society; in Winesburg, Ohio he somehow fails in social purpose through overemphasis on grotesque characters.

1932

77 WHIPPLE, T. K. "Sherwood Anderson." Saturday Review of Literature, 9 (10 December), 305.

The shining literary movement between 1915 and 1925 died, and Anderson too has died in literature. Having in his earlier work written "a sharp and bitter epitaph for the old world that was perishing, and a curse for the new world being born," Anderson in Beyond Desire proves that the world has passed him by.

1933 A BOOKS

1 MOSES, W. R. "Sherwood Anderson: His Life, His Philosophy, His Books and What Has Been Said About Him." Master's thesis, Vanderbilt University, 145 pp.

Critics of Anderson--selected randomly and as available--praised the author before 1924; after 1927 critics tended to be unfavorable to him. Writing for release from himself, Anderson has written autobiographically more often than not; and he has too willingly accepted Lawrence and Stein as models for his later works. At his best, Anderson brilliantly fuses character-reactions and psychological understanding.

1933 B SHORTER WRITINGS

1 ANON. Review of Death in the Woods. Middletown Journal [OH] (30 March).

Returning to reading Anderson can be like returning to one's home town. Death in the Woods may be as good as the early Anderson.

2 ANON. "Anderson and English." Cleveland Press (15 April).

Even if readers remember Anderson's stories from their periodical publication, reading them in Death in the Woods shows Anderson still the old master of immortal tales.

3 ANON. "The Triumph of a Literary Egg." Chicago News (19 April).

Death in the Woods proves again that without Anderson there would be no Faulkner or Hemingway--or modern short stories.

4 ANON. "'A Writer Should Be Poor.'" New York Times (20 April), p. 15.

Anderson thinks that having too much money could ruin authors. The author has just toured the Midwest to study the effects of the Depression on common people, and he found basic optimism among ordinary Americans.

5 ANON. "Death in the Woods." Philadelphia Ledger (22 April).
In Death in the Woods Anderson shows that as story teller he is "supreme; as prober into the dark psychologies of beaten peoples, he is unmatched."

6 ANON. "Stories by Sherwood Anderson." Cleveland Plain Dealer (23 April).
While no other than the title story of Death in the Woods can help Anderson's reputation, each story has some merit.

7 ANON. "Death in the Woods." Springfield Sun [OH] (23 April).
Of simple truths, in simple terms, Death in the Woods is authentic Sherwood Anderson.

8 ANON. "Death in the Woods." Madison Times (30 April).
When Anderson lets his attention to detail and sincerity override his pretended sympathy, his Death in the Woods stories are superb.

9 ANON. "Sherwood Anderson's Despair of Letters." Literary Digest, 115 (13 May), 15.
Anderson has decided that he--and aspiring young writers--should consider writing motion picture scripts instead of traditional literary genres.

10 ANON. "Current Books." Mobile Register (14 May).
In Death in the Woods Anderson balances his usual realism and frustration with humor and light.

11 ANON. "Death in the Woods." Washington Post (14 May).
The stories in Death in the Woods reveal Anderson sometimes matching his earlier stories on horse racing; unlike his novels, these new stories are clear and skillful.

12 ANON. "'Death in the Woods' Both Good and Bad." Sacramento Union (21 May).
Having missed Anderson's books of stories for ten years, the reader welcomes the mostly good stories of Death in the Woods.

13 ANON. "Books for Your Library." Scribner's Magazine, 93 (June), ii.
Death in the Woods, containing some of Anderson's best work, proves that the author should write no other genre.

1933

*14 ANON. "Death in the Woods." American Mercury, 29 (July). Unlocatable (clipping as source). The title story of Death in the Woods, originally published in The American Mercury, "is, indeed, one of the finest short stories ever written in English." Two other stories--"The Return" and "Brother Death"--are "brilliant pieces of work."

15 ANON. "Book Notes." New York Times (20 September), p. 19. Hemingway--now published by Scribner's--was dropped by Liveright because of The Torrents of Spring; now Anderson's books will be published by Scribner's.

16 ANON. "Book Notes." New York Times (9 October), p. 15. Anderson shames censors of Whitman's poetry in his introduction to Whitman, scheduled for publication October 10.

17 ANON. "Book Notes." New York Times (12 October), p. 23. Anderson has joined O'Neill, Dreiser, Boyd, Nathan, and Cabell as an editor of The American Spectator and his first contribution will be in the December issue.

18 ANON. "Editorial." American Spectator, 2 (December), 1. For Anderson to become an editor of The American Spectator is to provide another distinguished writer's expertise for the magazine.

19 BERND, A. B. "Anderson Masterly." Macon Telegraph (30 April). Death in the Woods contains five stories of sixteen that are of enough exceptional merit to enter American literature.

20 BOAS, RALPH PHILIP and KATHERINE BURTON. Social Backgrounds of American Literature. Boston: Little, Brown and Co., pp. 255, 258-59.

In his early novels Anderson showed Dreiser's influence, but his later work has become subjective. However, whereas Dreiser seeks reasons, Anderson seeks psychological effects of characters who want "escape sought in vain in civilized society." Anderson ultimately denies the possibility of escape.

21 BUSSE, A. "Amerikanischer Brief." Die Literatur, 35 (October 1932-September), 403.

In Beyond Desire, based on the American Depression, Anderson narrates a character's descent from the middle class to the laboring class. The hero must face both poverty and Communist agitation--a theme fitting into Anderson's pattern of disinheritance in America.

22 BUZBY, GEORGE C. "No Heroes in S. Anderson's Tales of the South." Philadelphia Record (23 April).
About tortured, frustrated beings, Death in the Woods has no heroics, no conventional plots, no raving or whining at injustice--and, best of all, no conclusive endings.

*23 CALVO, NOVÁS. Review of Beyond Desire. Revista de Occidente (January), p. 93.
Cited: 1966.B10.

24 CARSON, SAUL. "In Reply to Sherwood Anderson." Modern Monthly, 7 (July), 347, 351.
Unlike Anderson, Dreiser should learn that there is enough unemployment and poverty to lead to revolution. Anderson's observation of Americans is limited because he is sentimental.

25 CATEL, JEAN. "Lettres Anglo-Américaines." Mercure de France (1 October), pp. 218-20.
Reflecting life cyclically and disorderedly, Beyond Desire discusses dreamily the new Southern generation that wants "an absurd liberty."

26 CHAMBERLAIN, JOHN. Farewell to Reform: Being a History of the Rise, Life and Decay of the Progressive Mind in America. Second edition. New York: Liveright, p. 164.
D. G. Phillips' writings about sex might have prepared the American milieu for Winesburg, Ohio--Anderson's "ingrown romance."

27 _____. "A Story Teller Returns." Saturday Review of Literature, 9 (29 April), 561.
Death in the Woods shows Anderson still "incapable of irony, of satire, of a studied view of the human comedy"--capable, after all, of only a great sense of wonder and thus making his writing formless. Some of these stories are journalistic, but the best of them are "spurts of heightened consciousness that are universally experienced."

28 COLLINS, NORMAN. The Facts of Fiction. New York: E. P. Dutton & Co., p. 305.
Jung and Freud provide ammunition for Anderson, whose novels are "unattractively designed to resemble the halting utterances of a halfwit child who has been brought up in country places."

29 CRAWFORD, BRUCE. "A Night in Atlanta." Crawford's Weekly (17 May), p. 4.

1933

(CRAWFORD, BRUCE)
Anderson once told Julian Harris of a hometown barber who would not cut Anderson's hair until he denied having written books.

30 DANIEL, FRANK. "Death in the Woods." Atlanta Journal (21 May).
In Death in the Woods Anderson has again recovered his excellence in short stories; unless his style is flawless, it becomes trickery.

31 DELL, FLOYD. Homecoming: An Autobiography. New York: Farrar & Rinehart, pp. 236-37, 253-54, 256, 274, 290, 343.
Dell met Anderson at Margery Currey's party and admired the manuscript version of Windy McPherson's Son enough to help get it published, for this work had Midwestern and Dostoevskian qualities of "soul-questioning." But Dell secretly excised the last page of the manuscript for verisimilitude. Later Anderson tried to influence Dell's fiction to resemble his own, and the friendship ended when Anderson wrote to Dell of the latter's conceit.

*32 DINAMOV, S. "O Tvorcheste Shervuda Andersona." Literaturnaya Gazeta (29 September).
Cited: 1969.B29.

33 _____. "Sherwood Anderson: American Writer." International Literature, No. 4 (October), pp. 84-91.
To understand Anderson, it is necessary to read Marching Men as an anti-capitalist work, condemning workers who refuse to join class-struggles; but Anderson's idea of non-violent revolution is dangerous. In his short stories, Anderson pictures grotesque characters; but he does not go toward calling for destruction of the anti-human forces surrounding and behind these unhappy lives. But with publication of the class-conscious Beyond Desire, "Sherwood Anderson is on the right road."

34 EDGAR, PELHAM. "Four American Writers: Anderson, Hemingway, Dos Passos, Faulkner." The Art of the Novel: From 1700 to the Present Time. New York: Macmillan Co., pp. 338-51.
No other second-rank American writer has had so much influence as Anderson, for he has mastered under-statement, is only mildly rebellious, excels in short story form, and is "the poet of a shirt-sleeve civilization with none of the amenities of life to compensate its rigors. . . ."

35 GANNETT, LEWIS. "Books and Things." New York Herald Tribune (13 April), p. 15.

Now that Anderson is in his mid-fifties, his stories--as in Death in the Woods--are mellower and more serene.

36 GRAY, JAMES. "New York Theater Hunts Material for Serious Drama." St. Paul Dispatch (9 November).

When creating new writing style with Winesburg, Ohio, Anderson probably was not being deliberately psychoanalytical; Winesburg, Ohio is so superior to Main Street that Lewis' Nobel Prize should be half Anderson's.

37 HANSEN, HARRY. "The First Reader." New York World-Telegram (15 April), p. 13.

Death in the Woods contains some of both Anderson's best and worst stories, at best minor studies. Some years ago Anderson knocked Dos Passos and Sinclair for pretending to be workmen rather than literary artists.

38 HICKS, GRANVILLE. "American Fiction: The Major Trend." New Republic, 74 (12 April), 240-41.

Anderson would be dishonest to write perfectly formed novels, for the current world around him is chaotic. Anderson tries to write of a modern life repellent to him, as in Beyond Desire; but "it is doubtful if he can ever free his imagination from its burden of doubt and bewilderment."

39 _____. The Great Tradition: An Interpretation of American Literature Since the Civil War. New York: Macmillan Co., pp. 210, 211-12, 229-30, 231, 232-34, 236-37, 257.

When Anderson succeeds in his work, one feels the "lightning flash" of a life revealed instantly; yet Anderson does not always flash out of his bewilderment into revelation. After writing of small-town life as the destructive force in Winesburg, Ohio, Anderson later moved to industrialism as the external force that warps lives. Unfortunately, he "cannot achieve proportion and order in the larger narrative."

40 _____. "Problems of American Fellow Travelers." International Literature, 3 (1933), 107.

In Beyond Desire Anderson still shows his obsession with sex and mysticism; and this novel "makes a very poor model for revolutionary writers," for Anderson does not concentrate strongly enough on Communism.

1933

41 JACKSON, FREDERICK. "Short Stories Of Distinction Are Collected." Lexington Leader [KY] (23 April).

Death in the Woods demonstrates Anderson's "distinction, the troubled, patient, vigilant honesty and the shrewd, sensitive power of observation seen in his earlier works."

42 KANTOROVICH, HAIM. "Proletarian Literature in America." American Socialist Quarterly, 2 (Winter), 5-7.

Beyond Desire illustrates what happens when an author tries to write about something not "in his blood," for Anderson knows almost nothing of Marxism. Half of Beyond Desire is the writer's "usual erotic and neurotic personages," and the other half is unbelieveable Communist shadows.

43 KRONENBERGER, LOUIS. "Sherwood Anderson's Story-Telling Art." New York Times Book Review (23 April), p. 6.

In a few short stories--some of them in Death in the Woods--Anderson is an outstanding writer, having long paid his debt to Chekhov.

44 LEVIDOV, M. "Po tu storonu Želanija." Literaturnaja gazeta (18 February).

Beyond Desire is in essence an examination, a powerful socio-psychological record, an x-ray of a small Georgia town. [James F. Cradler]

45 MARSH, FRED T. "The Story Teller's Return." New York Herald Tribune Books (16 April), p. 4.

The residue of Anderson's work--after the failures are discounted--is literature, and Death in the Woods affirms the author's place among the passing generation of storytellers.

46 MATTHEWS, T. S. "Novels, Stories and Prophecy." New Republic, 75 (7 June), 105-106.

Death in the Woods confirms Anderson's pretentious awkwardness, showing that we should no longer overrate his accomplishments.

47 MELLQUIST, JEROME. "Sherwood Anderson Returns." Commonweal, 18 (7 July), 273.

Death in the Woods proves again that Anderson must use materials from his own youth to create successful stories.

48 NEEDHAM, WILBUR. "Sherwood Anderson Again Measures Up to Standard." Los Angeles Times (21 May).

Death in the Woods is the return of the old Sherwood Anderson with the old story teller's fire.

49 NELSON, JOHN HERBERT. Contemporary Trends: American Literature Since 1914. New York: Macmillan Co., pp. 480-81.
A "self-educated man, the author of fiction showing a rich subjective vein," Anderson in his writing is "uneven, most of it being crude and unformed by a disciplined mind of sure tastes; but a number of his short stories bear on them the stamp of an unusual narrative talent."

50 NEMEROVSKAYA, O. "Novy roman Šervuda Andersona." Literaturnyj kritik, No. 4, pp. 199-203.
The death scene in Beyond Desire is the best moment, from both artistic and ideational standpoint. [James F. Cradler]

51 PETITT, BEN. "Sixteen Short Stories From Mr. Anderson's Typewriter." Richmond Times-Dispatch (23 April), p. 10.
Death in the Woods contains stories lacking plot but filled with the crucial moment observed--moment of forces affecting lives briefly but deeply.

52 PIERCE, BESSIE LOUISE and JOE L. NORRIS, eds. As Others See Chicago: Impressions of Visitors, 1673-1933. Chicago: University of Chicago Press, p. 377.
Anderson and other authors have established Chicago as a literary center, one tracing its beginnings back to the Columbian Exposition.

53 SELDES, GILBERT. The Years of the Locust (America, 1929-1932). Boston: Little, Brown and Co., p. 332.
For Anderson to ally himself to the Communist Party, along with Dreiser, is newsworthy.

54 SMITH, W. BRADFORD. "Sherwood Anderson." Rikkyo Review, Art and Letters (March), pp. 2-11.
Modern industrial life and the quest of the bewildered individual are the bases of understanding Anderson. He is a realist in the presentation of the former, while he is a romanticist in trying to understand the latter. In style, Anderson admits the bounds beyond which understanding and the art of the novelist cannot go. If his method is vague, it is because he writes of something which can be expressed only through a sympathetic and suggestive art. Anderson adopts his rhythm to the tempo of modern industrial and farm life, through colloquialisms and a familiar war of expression. [Takashi Kodaira]

55 SPEARMAN, WALTER. "Sherwood Anderson Writes New Stories." Charlotte News (23 April).

1933

(SPEARMAN, WALTER)

With scarcely any plot or clarity, Anderson's stories in Death in the Woods reveal intuition, puzzlement, and character interpretation.

56 STARTSEV, A. "Po etu storonu barikad." Khudozhestvennaya Literatura, No. 1, pp. 34-37.

In Beyond Desire Anderson calls to social protest those crippled by capitalism. Sex and ambiguity toward machines are understandable but regrettable features of the writer's art and politics. [James F. Cradler]

57 STEIN, GERTRUDE. The Autobiography of Alice B. Toklas. New York: Harcourt, Brace and Co., pp. 241-42, 260-61, 265-66, 268, 271, 300, 302-304.

When Sylvia Beach brought Anderson to meet Stein, the great gift was Anderson's simple praise for Stein's writing. Later Hemingway came with Anderson's letter of introduction, but Stein and Anderson were afterwards to agree that Hemingway is very different from his legend. When Hemingway disliked Anderson's "taste," Stein defended Anderson as a great prose writer. Someday Stein and Anderson may collaboratively write about U. S. Grant. Reprinted in part in Sherwood Anderson / Gertrude Stein: Correspondence and Personal Essays. Edited by Ray Lewis White. Chapel Hill: University of North Carolina Press, 1972, pp. 72-75.

58 STEIN, HANNAH. "No Nests-Birds!--Sherwood Anderson." Philadelphia Public Ledger (10 September).

Anderson says that machinery, movies, and automobiles take women away from their homes now; but he worries that mankind may someday serve machinery, and maybe women could save men from this fate.

59 SUGIKI, TAKASHI. "On Anderson's Poems." Study of English (July), 82-85.

What is a poet or a poem to Anderson? What is the external or internal motive and the meaning of producing a poem? These questions may be answered by studying the forewords from Mid-American Chants and A New Testament. [Takashi Kodaira]

60 SULLIVAN, MARK. Our Times: 1900-1925. V. Over Here, 1914-1918. New York: Charles Scribner's Sons, pp. 626, 641, 649.

Among events during the war years was the appearance of Windy McPherson's Son, Marching Men, and Mid-American Chants.

61 TAKAGAKI, MATSUO. "Sherwood Anderson." Study of English (July), pp. 73-76.

Anderson's sentences are written in the words of common people. Comparing The Triumph of the Egg with Death in the Woods reveals that his sentences tend to become shorter, for the author realizes that his readers demand simple and plain expression. The colloquial style fits Anderson's social class, and the reading public among that class is growing in numbers. [Takashi Kodaira] Reprinted revised: 1934.B39; 1946.B17.

62 TROY, WILLIAM. "'Fragmentary Ends.'" Nation, 136 (3 May), 508.

Death in the Woods shows Anderson regressing in story-telling ability to thinness of character, non-social concerns, and fascination with ordinary people. Perhaps his early achievements were merely accidents.

63 TYLER, ERIC E. "Short Tales By Anderson Please." Albany Knickerbocker Press (25 June).

Some of Anderson's stories in Death in the Woods are "hopelessly bad"; other stories are full of zest and commentary in Anderson's loose, wandering style.

64 VAN SCHAIK-WILLING, JEANNE. "Amerikaansche Letteren: Sherwood Anderson, Een Speling der Cultuur." Gids, 1 (March), 477-82.

Anderson presents the former, abandoned world of the natural, in contrast to the present world of the sophisticated, the "cultured." Anderson writes well of characters and scenes almost dreamlike, making imaginative fables of his versions of reality. This writer is guileless and honest and wise in knowing intuitively of the buried life.

65 W., R. M. "Sherwood Anderson as a Short-Story Writer." Boston Transcript (29 April), p. 1.

Anderson's characters in Death in the Woods resemble Hemingway's characters in being "intellectual morons," motivated solely by emotions.

66 WILLIAMS, STANLEY T. American Literature. Philadelphia: J. B. Lippincott Co., pp. 144, 146, 147, 149.

As a modern author, Anderson is best able to "strike fire" from use of his own geographical area in fiction. Modern realism "triumphs in Sherwood Anderson's weavil-like descent into the subconscious mind," post-war bewilderment confirming his "previous futilitarian utterances."

1933

67 YLISTRATOVA, A. "Literatura SASŠ." Literaturnaja gazeta (29 November).
Anderson is a writer of the emotions. The rational and logical is always subordinate to the emotional and the irrational in his works. The plight of the hero of Beyond Desire is essentially that of the author as well. [James F. Cradler]

68 YOSHIDA, KINETARO. "Sherwood Anderson's Winesburg, Ohio." Eigo Eibungaku Koza, 5. Tokyo: Newer Spirit in British and American Literature Society, pp. 69-94.
Awareness of Anderson's biography and writings is necessary to understand Winesburg, Ohio--a work misunderstood by the critic Burton Rascoe. The success of this book is due mainly to its authenticity, its dealing with the subject and events of the grotesque, and the expression of all life through these studies of the grotesques. Anderson has the ability of writing coarsely but closely. [Takashi Kodaira]

1934 A BOOKS

1 McNICOL, ELINORE C. "The American Scene as Sherwood Anderson Depicts It." Master's thesis, University of Colorado, 80 pp.
Anderson sees and pictures life as "frustrated and inhibited," the machine age having driven individuals to seek money and power or sex and craftsmanship.

1934 B SHORTER WRITINGS

1 ANON. "'The Cheerfulest City.'" Knoxville Sentinel (4 February), p. 2.
Visiting T.V.A. dams, Anderson stayed in Knoxville, Tennessee, where he appeared to be a "big, gray-haired, tweed-suited, friendly-looking man."

2 ANON. "Sherwood Anderson." Knoxville Sunday Journal (4 February).
Anderson has emerged from publishing his Virginia newspapers to reenter the world. His work has good style but far more brutality than the works of Faulkner and Stribling.

*3 ANON. Review of Winesburg, Ohio Drama. Philadelphia Daily News (2 July).
Cited: 1960.B30.

*4 ANON. Review of Winesburg, Ohio Drama. Philadelphia Evening Bulletin (2 July).
Cited: 1960.B30.

*5 ANON. Review of Winesburg, Ohio Drama. Philadelphia Evening Ledger (2 July).
Cited: 1960.B30.

*6 ANON. Review of Winesburg, Ohio Drama. Philadelphia Inquirer (2 July).
Cited: 1960.B30.

*7 ANON. Review of Winesburg, Ohio Drama. Philadelphia Record (2 July).
Cited: 1960.B30.

8 ANON. "We Present a Southwest Virginia Woodcut." Marion Democrat [VA] (24 July), p. 3.
Wharton Esherick, who contributed the woodcut of "Buck Fever," has recently contributed a woodcut of horseracing.

9 ANON. Notice of Winesburg, Ohio. Lorain Journal [OH] (19 November).
Anderson passed through Camden and Elyria, Ohio, recently while gathering material on the Midwest. He seemed surprised at the poor Communist showing in recent elections. Winesburg, Ohio "contains some of the most graphic and revealing pen-portraits of modern literature."

10 ANON. "Books and Authors." New York Times Book Review (25 November), p. 14.
When No Swank is published on December 3, it will include Anderson's commentaries on Lawrence, Lardner, Stein, Henry Wallace, and Dreiser, among others.

11 BENÉT, WILLIAM ROSE. "A Story Teller's Story." Designed for Reading: An Anthology Drawn from The Saturday Review of Literature, 1924-1934. New York: Macmillan Co., pp. 293-97.
Reprint of 1924.B6.

12 BREWSTER, DOROTHY and ANGUS BURRELL. Modern Fiction. New York: Columbia University Press, p. 391.
A Story Teller's Story creates the problem of delineating fact and fiction.

*13 CHRISMER, LESLIE. "Books and Authors." Chester Times [PA] (15 August).
Cited: 1960.B30.

1934

14 DILLING, ELIZABETH. "Anderson, Sherwood." The Red Notebook: A "Who's Who" and Handbook of Radicalism for Patriots. Chicago: Elizabeth Dilling, p. 262.

Member of the John Reed Club, Communist League of Professional Groups, the American Committee for Struggle Against War, the National Student League, and the National Committee for the Defense of Political Prisoners--among other Leftist groups--Anderson has published in The New Masses and The Student Review.

*15 ELISTRATOVA, A. "Po tu storonu zhelaniia." Internatsional'naia Literatura, No. 2 (1934), pp. 115-19.

Cited: 1969.B29.

16 FAŸ, BERNARD. "Portrait de Sherwood Anderson Américain." Revue de Paris, 41 (15 October), 886-901.

Anderson is more highly regarded in Europe than in America. He capitalizes on Americans' nostalgia; life in "moments"; and the ugliness of materialism. Even detractors in America have to admit Anderson's abilities, for he has invented the short-story form that is based on the momentary flashes of insight into buried lives.

17 GARLAND, ROBERT. "Small Town Realism Marks 'Winesburg, O.'" New York World-Telegram (20 August), p. 10.

When Arthur Barton's adaptation of Winesburg, Ohio was performed in Moylan-Rose Valley at Jasper Deeter's playhouse, several local residents walked out in disgust over the offensive action and dialogue; and this realistic play is not pleasant.

18 HALLECK, REUBEN POST. The Romance of American Literature. New York: American Book Co., pp. 328-31, 348.

Himself romantic and mystic, Anderson creates characters that need to escape routine. Windy McPherson's Son--which ultimately fails because of sentimentality--was modeled on Dreiser's Cowperwood novels; both Marching Men and Poor White protest indignities of the industrial age. In the stories in Horses and Men and The Triumph of the Egg Anderson uses unconventional plotting and frequent first-person narration. Winesburg, Ohio, "an unpleasant book, shows good technique in its drab sketches of morbid eccentrics, crushed by ugly, cramped surroundings."

19 HARTWICK, HARRY. The Foreground of American Fiction. New York: American Book Co., pp. 43, 85-86, 111-42, 151, 152, 157, 158, 161, 163, 164, 166, 170, 174, 185, 307, 308, 367, 398.

Anderson is a would-be naturalist who "works inwardly," his books conjoining Freud and the "subconscious," the writer himself fleeing a world beyond his understanding. He is "Dreiser with the backbone removed," "a Whitman gone to seed," a "bacchic St. Francis of Assisi"--and yet no one has been more influential on modern literature.

20 HILLQUIT, MORRIS. Loose Leaves from a Busy Life. New York: Macmillan Co., p. 224.

Sherwood Anderson was later a famous writer who had started his career by publishing in The Masses, a magazine on trial for hindering the American effort in the World War.

21 JOHNS, ORRICK. "American Spectator--A Nazi Sheet." New Masses, 13 (16 October), 23.

Anderson has become an editor of The American Spectator and hence has fallen for pro-Nazi propaganda. He also vilifies the working class by writing for magazines that support Roosevelt. Anderson will find no middle point between "the potential Fascist assassins of The Spectator" and "the rising revolutionary movement in America."

22 LEWIS, WYNDHAM. Men Without Art. London: Cassell, pp. 42-48.

William Faulkner may be "composed in equal measure of Sherwood Anderson and of Powys," for Faulkner perpetuates many of Anderson's stylistic gaucheries.

23 LOTH, DAVID. "Young in Literary Spirit, Sherwood Anderson Is 58." New York Post (13 September), p. 26.

The quality of youth in Anderson's stories keeps the author young. When Anderson left business for literature, "He had just realized there were only eight steps between his desk and freedom." His hometown hunting him, Anderson sat in a cold Chicago tenement creating short stories.

24 LOVETT, ROBERT MORSS. "The Promise of Sherwood Anderson." Literary Opinion in America. Edited by Morton Dauwen Zabel. New York: Harper, pp. 327-32.

Reprint of 1922.B35.

25 LUCCOCK, HALFORD E. Contemporary American Literature and Religion. Chicago: Willett, Clark & Co., pp. 28, 56, 59, 68-71, 170, 211.

Anderson is already of historical importance, his work lately being of far worse quality than his early pieces. The writer is important for seeking buried lives, affected by industrialism; but he is repetitious, obsessed with sex, and often more mystical than realistic.

1934

*26 MINGULINA, A. "Po To Storonu Zhelaniia." Khudozhestvennia Literatura, No. 5, pp. 7-9.
Cited: 1969.B29.

27 MOHRMANN, HERMANN. "Industrialismus und Puritanismus als Formende Kräfte des Modernen Amerikanischen Lebens: Sherwood Anderson." Kultur- und Gesellschaftsprobleme des Amerikanischen Romanes der Nachkriegzeit (1920-1927). Düsseldorf: G. H. Nolte, pp. 76-88.
Whereas Lewis satirizes American life as it is, Anderson writes of how it became as it is--through Puritanism and mechanization. Anderson's characters seek meaningful lives, to be in contact with some force beyond themselves, to transcend isolation by way of love.

28 OZAKI, SHIRO. "Anderson." Bungakukai [Bunpodo] (June), pp. 183-88.
Ozaki draws his experience with a geisha in the gay quarters and with a sad clarinet player in a band of musical sandwich men in Anderson's style. Having belonged to an Anderson society headed by Kinetaro Yoshida, he knew Yoshida to translate some stories from The Triumph of the Egg into Japanese for publication with Shinchosha. The two then asked Anderson to contribute to Jiji Shinpo; and Anderson's "The Future of Japanese and American Writing" was serially published in that newspaper. Having spent Anderson's contribution fee for amusement, they frankly apologized to him and he generously forgave them and added that he was sorry he could not have spent the money for amusement with them. [Takashi Kodaira]

29 PAVESE, CESARE. "Faulkner, Cottivo Allievo di Anderson." La Cultura (April).
Anderson's influence on William Faulkner shows in Sanctuary, for Faulkner presents a bewildered Southern character analyzing himself, making common details magical and common situations tense--all in almost "slow motion" but without boredom. Reprinted: 1951.B29.

30 R., G. "'Winesburg' Debut Quiet." New York World-Telegram (2 July).
Boredom relieved by intermissions describes the premiere of Winesburg, Ohio, for the weather was hot, the play was long, and drama was minimal.

31 ROSENE, M. R. "The Five Best American Books Published Since 1900." Writer, 46 (October), 370.

Although Anderson's emotional self-indulgences are irritating, Winesburg, Ohio made the first improvements in the American short story since Crane.

32 SAKUMA, GEN. "Sherwood Anderson." Studies in American Novels. Tokyo: Kenkyusha, pp. 379-89.
Anderson is literary heir in the direct line of naturalism. Of course, there are differences among Norris, Crane, London, Dreiser, and Anderson. Anderson is more suitable at the short story form than the novel--and he writes best of all in autobiographies, having a hobo soul. [Takashi Kodaira]

33 SMITH, HENRY JUSTIN. "The Midwest's Literary Background." Midwest, 1 (September), 3, 11.
Anderson's first publication developed from his readings to friends in Chicago. The simplicity of Anderson's style combines with "dreaminess, a note of experimentation, a groping, which gives to Anderson's work both charm and difficulty."

34 SOUPAULT, PHILIPPE. "La Nouvelle Littérature Américaine." Europe (15 October), p. 273.
The novels of Anderson describe sex naively but publicize related problems; yet this author, who led younger writers into freedom, has become passé, in favor of Joyce, Lawrence, Hemingway, Cummings, and Dos Passos.

35 STEWART, POWELL and MICHAEL BRADSHAW, JR., et al. A Goodly Company: A Guide to Parallel Reading. New York: American Book Co., p. 270.
Surely no town in America could contain all of the "sordidness and frustration and unhappiness" found in Winesburg, Ohio, for Anderson has ignored the wholesome aspects of life. Winesburg, Ohio--"these gloomy tales of sex-starvation, of religious mania, of strange obsessions"--excited morbid curiosity.

36 STIRLING, PETER. "'Winesburg, Ohio' Given at Hedgerow." Philadelphia Record (2 July).
Winesburg, Ohio--a fine novel--has become poor drama, lacking coherence and sense.

*37 STOLETOV, A. "Po Tu Storonu Zhelaniia." Pod'em [Voronezh], No. 4-5, pp. 165-66.
Cited: 1969.B29.

1934

38 TAKAGAKI, MATSUO. "Sherwood Anderson." Contemporary American Literature. Tokyo: Kenbunsha, pp. 316-29.
Reprint with revisions of 1925.B45. [Takashi Kodaira] Reprinted: 1941.B96.

39 _____. "Sherwood Anderson's Technique." Contemporary American Literature. Tokyo: Kenbunsha, pp. 330-37.
Reprint with revisions of 1933.B61. [Takashi Kodaira] Reprinted: 1948.B31.

40 YOSHIDA, KINETARO. "An Old Story: On Reading Shiro Ozaki's 'Anderson.'" Bungakukai [Bunpodo] (July), pp. 108-11.
Having spent Anderson's contribution fee for amusement with friends, Yoshida sent Anderson money later. When he apologized for being late in payment, Anderson forgave him. Yoshida quotes letters from Anderson. [Takashi Kodaira]

1935 A BOOKS - NONE

1935 B SHORTER WRITINGS

1 ADAMIC, LOUIS. "A Puzzled American." Saturday Review of Literature, 11 (13 April), 621.
The title Puzzled America fits Anderson's book, for this writer has always been confused about everything since he became an author, unable to contribute any solutions to anything.

2 ANON. "Anderson Talks on 'Experiments at Group Theater.'" New Orleans Times-Picayune (16 January).
Not essentially political, Anderson now says he could be called a Socialist. Now that writers have entered political affairs, there may be a second Renaissance in America. Even at the cost of being commercial, any theater should be self-supporting.

3 ANON. "Author Returns to Favorite City After Vacation." New Orleans Times-Picayune (24 February), p. 4.
Fresh from a vacation in Mexico, Anderson expects Puzzled America to appear in April. In visiting twenty states, Anderson found little Communism among Americans--as well as little Socialism or Fascism.

*4 ANON. Review of Puzzled America. Cleveland Open Shelf (March), p. 7.
Cited: Book Review Digest 1935, p. 22.

5 ANON. Review of Puzzled America. New York Mirror (24 March).
Puzzled America catches America off guard and "made brilliantly visible."

6 ANON. "Anderson on America, Depressions, Etc." New York Post (29 March).
Anderson concludes in Puzzled America that the greatest need in our nation is "a rebirth of faith."

7 ANON. Review of Puzzled America. New York American (30 March).
Anderson's Puzzled America is too romantic, too soft, and "slightly dreamy."

8 ANON. Review of Puzzled America. New York Mirror (30 March).
In Puzzled America Anderson "cuts clean through the pitiful dry-rot of the New Deal decadence" to argue against the status quo.

*9 ANON. Review of Puzzled America. Springfield Republican (4 April), p. 12.
Cited: Book Review Digest 1935, p. 22.

10 ANON. "Puzzled Writer Has Book About Puzzled America." Davenport Times [IA] (6 April).
Anderson plainly states in Puzzled America that he found neither Fascism nor Communism overtaking traditional government in America.

11 ANON. "Among the Outstanding Books." Literary Digest, 119 (6 April), 26.
Puzzled America reveals the author's observations of his troubled countrymen--observations that give him undirected optimism for the future.

12 ANON. "Between the Lines." Miami Herald (6 April).
In Puzzled America Anderson finds Americans less bitter than eager to work, more confused than hopeless.

13 ANON. "'Puzzled America' Tinged with Pink." Memphis Commercial Appeal (7 April).
Not romantic until its conclusion, Puzzled America shows Anderson "only faintly pink" and arouses only "a proper sort of patriotism."

14 ANON. Review of Puzzled America. Rutland Herald [VT] (9 April).
Puzzled America shows Anderson less radical as reporter than as novelist.

1935

15 ANON. "Taking the U. S. Apart to See How It Works." _Chicago Journal-Commerce_ (13 April).
Perhaps Anderson would have given a different picture in _Puzzled America_ if he had visited cities instead of rural areas.

16 ANON. "Little Reviews." _Newsweek_, 5 (13 April), 40.
Puzzled America is "a literary newsreel of the depression" about the common people in whom Anderson has always been interested. The old problems are freshened by "the rural novelist's stout homespun language."

17 ANON. "Sherwood Anderson Turns Reporter to Take Inventory of Puzzled America." _Milwaukee Journal_ (14 April).
Of use to future historians, _Puzzled America_ is "an important social document without being in the least documentary."

18 ANON. "Books To Own." _Bristol Herald-Courier_ [VA] (15 April).
Pretending to know little about writing well has always ruined Anderson for literature. However, _Puzzled America_ is good social observation.

19 ANON. "America's Bewildered People." _Atlanta Georgian_ (21 April).
What the poor need is cash instead of sympathy from Anderson in _Puzzled America_.

20 ANON. Review of _Puzzled America_. _High Point Enterprise_ [NC] (21 April).
Southerners especially will find _Puzzled America_ "food for thought."

21 ANON. "Depression Types." _Newark News_ (25 April).
The point to Anderson's studies of Southerners and Midwesterners in _Puzzled America_ is that Americans deserve better conditions than surround them.

22 ANON. "Problems Test Faith." _Keene Sentinel_ [NH] (27 April).
Reporting well on his observations of common Americans, Anderson in _Puzzled America_ "records his findings bluntly, the waste, the extravagance, and the folly of the past, but with a note of hope in them."

23 ANON. "Sherwood Anderson Depicts A Nation of Puzzled Men." _Richmond News_ (28 April).
Without answers or pessimism, _Puzzled America_ is stimulating and "elusively American."

24 ANON. "Literature." Wisconsin Library Bulletin, 31 (May), 68.
In Puzzled America Anderson reports "on what the common people of America are thinking," and the book "is all written with so much of the born story-teller's charm that it is very readable."

25 ANON. "Sherwood Anderson Writes of America of This Puzzled Period." Charlotte Observer (5 May).
Puzzled America conveys Anderson's hope for answers to the nation's social problems and his faith that democracy will somehow solve common problems: "This is Sherwood Anderson at his best."

26 ANON. "Books. . . ." Ronceverte News [WV] (11 May).
In Puzzled America Anderson shows his reporting by picturing every American as meek and bewildered; where are the radicals?

27 ANON. "The Inquiring Reporter." San Francisco Argonaut (17 May).
Having no economic solutions in Puzzled America, Anderson contributes confusion to the problem.

28 ANON. Review of Puzzled America. Santa Ana Journal (21 May).
The nation presented by Sherwood Anderson in Puzzled America is fraternal, Whitmanesque, and full of "positive optimism."

29 ANON. "Books in Brief." Christian Century, 52 (29 May), 731-32.
Puzzled America is Anderson's record of his wanderings among common people to investigate the Depression's effects, and the title of the book summarizes Anderson's discoveries.

30 ANON. "Description and Travel." Booklist, 31 (June), 339.
Puzzled America describes Anderson's observations of non-urban America and finds confusion and hope.

31 ANON. "Publications of Special Interest." Special Libraries, 26 (July-August), 189.
Puzzled America is of help "in understanding the essential value of a program for social security."

32 ANON. "Book Reviews." Santa Ana Register (24 August).
In Puzzled America Anderson proves himself one of our foremost writers and also one of our most sensitive social critics.

1935

33 ANON. "Nazis Evoke World Protest." New York Daily Worker (19 December), pp. 1, 2.

As a member of the Executive of the World Committee Against War and Fascism, Anderson laments the Nazi beheading of Rudolph Claus of the German International Labor Defense.

34 ARVIN, NEWTON. "Fiction Mirrors America." Current History, 42 (April-September), 612, 613.

Most of the characters in Anderson's works are isolated individuals, in revolt against the conventions and forces that make them frustrated isolates. When Anderson describes them, these characters grope toward community as the author gropes toward meaning.

35 BASSO, HAMILTON. "Anderson in America." New Republic, 82 (1 May), 348.

Contrary to critical descriptions of Puzzled America as "puzzled Anderson," this book is not an economic thesis or sociological study; it is what a sensitive artist saw in his nation.

36 BATES, ERNEST SUTHERLAND. "The American Countryman." New York Herald Tribune Books (7 April), p. 5.

Now that Anderson is mellower and past his affair with Communism, Puzzled America shows that he was always "fundamentally a simple, honest country man who happens to have been endowed with a share of literary genius and intuitive insight into the workings of individual psychology."

37 BOHENBERGER, CARL. "A New Birth of Belief." Jacksonville Times-Union [FL] (28 April).

Puzzled America documents American poverty and calls for united action to have "One strong land."

38 CARLOSS, BILLY. "Puzzled America." New Orleans Times-Picayune (21 June).

In Puzzled America Anderson proves his literary independence and warns against influences "seeking to destroy our beloved country."

39 CATTON, BRUCE. "Sherwood Anderson Says We Need A Cause To Follow." Gastonia Gazette (27 April).

Although Puzzled America will not rally Americans to action, it is written from close observation and with charm.

40 CLAY, CHARLES. "Beware Dictators and Bureaucracies." Winnipeg Free Press (15 June), p. 16.

In Puzzled America Anderson reports his observations of the average Americans among whom he has traveled. The work combines humor, tragedy, and wistfulness.

41 [CHRICHTON, KYLE].
See FORSYTHE, ROBERT. 1935.B51.

42 CURRIE, GEORGE. "Passed in Review." Brooklyn Daily Eagle (11 April).
With too many stories to tell about Depression America, Anderson in Puzzled America tells some very good ones very kindly.

43 DAVIDSON, DONALD. "The Innocent at Home." American Review, 5 (May), 234-38.
Puzzled America shows Anderson's affinity for New Dealers, the author now thinking that suffering people should be helped. Not people he interviews but Anderson himself comes out puzzled over the existence of poverty amid national wealth.

*44 DINAMOV, S. "Tvorcheskiye Prizaniya Shervuda Andersona." Internatsionalnaya Literatura, No. 10, pp. 129-36.
Cited: 1969.B29.

*45 _____. "Zhianennyiput' Shervuda Andersona." Internatsional'naia Literatura, No. 11, pp. 115-18.
Cited: 1969.B29.

46 DREWRY, JOHN E. "New Book News." Dalton News [GA] (22 August).
Puzzled America shows as much common people trusting their stories to Anderson as Anderson diagnosing social ills.

47 DUFFUS, R. L. "A View of Our America Today." New York Times Book Review (7 April), pp. 1, 16.
Having deepened in sympathies and having lost his "struggling expression" phase, Anderson reports interestingly and accurately in Puzzled America.

48 EFFELBERGER, HANS. "Sherwood Anderson: Puzzled America." Die Neueren Sprachen, 43 (1935), 576-77.
In all of life Anderson seeks for wonder, for emotional renewal; more photographic than literary, Puzzled America is Anderson's attempt to describe the fairly optimistic mood of his countrymen.

1935

49 ELLIOTT, DOROTHY. "'Puzzled America' Is Graphic Sketch of Present Times." Appleton Post (11 May).

Written for the common people enduring economic troubles, Puzzled America provides the observations needed by Americans unable to travel and talk as Anderson has done.

50 FINN, LOUISE. "These Troubled Times." New York News (31 March).

Puzzled America is Anderson's "interesting and touching picture of the times."

51 FORSYTHE, ROBERT. Redder Than the Rose. New York: Covici, Friede, p. 46.

Ernest Hemingway likes only critics who unstintingly praise him; other critics he attacks as he attacked Anderson in The Torrents of Spring, "a devastating burlesque."

52 GANNETT, LEWIS. "Books and Things." New York Herald Tribune (30 March), p. 9.

Although Anderson makes no predictions in Puzzled America, his homespun ideas and clear observations are important.

53 H., B. K. "The American Workingman Seen by Sherwood Anderson." Providence Journal (7 April).

No longer radical but old and sentimental, Anderson in Puzzled America is more bewildered than cynical, now "very anxious to help."

54 HAIGHT, ANNE LYON. "Anderson, Sherwood." Banned Books: Informal Notes on Some Books Banned for Various Reasons at Various Times and in Various Places. New York: R. R. Bowker, p. 69.

In 1923 Many Marriages was censored in England; in 1930 Dark Laughter "was put on the black list"; in 1931 Horses and Men was banned in Ireland.

55 HARDY, BETH. "What Ails World Told By Sherwood Anderson." Salt Lake City Deseret News (24 August).

Someday, Anderson believes, the current vogue for economic explanations of every issue will be considered medieval. He hopes for a new leader, "a new Lincoln."

56 HART, HENRY, ed. The American Writers' Congress. New York: International Publishers, pp. 60, 107, 108.

Beyond Desire, says Malcolm Cowley, is a failure because, in trying to write about Communists, Anderson "sentimentalized and priapified them, made them smell of sex." Thus,

Anderson quickly abandoned the revolutionary movement. James T. Farrell uses Windy McPherson's Son to illustrate the modern novel's reversal of theme: here success leads to discontent. Many authors have imitated Anderson--enough to form the "I-Am-Dumb" school of short story writers.

57 HART, JAMES S. "Sherwood Anderson Is Puzzled by Ugliness and Want in U. S." Providence Bulletin (17 April).

Anderson would have brotherhood, honesty, and altruism solve problems described in Puzzled America.

58 HATCHER, HARLAN. Creating the Modern American Novel. New York: Farrar & Rinehart, pp. 31, 32, 60, 72, 91, 101, 113, 114, 155-71, 173, 176, 179, 181, 192, 193, 212, 230, 235, 236, 287.

Anderson's dramatic rejection of a career in business marks the change in American values from the pre-War to modern times. No other writer about small-town characters can surpass Anderson with his Freudian psychology; Anderson's idea of character is that past moments mold future broodings and behaviors. Hence, Anderson dwells in and upon the silent, internalized world of his people.

59 HEMINGWAY, ERNEST. "Remembering Shooting-Flying: A Key West Letter." Esquire, 3 (February), 21.

Hemingway calls Winesburg, Ohio one of "the best of the books," one he "would rather read again for the first time . . . than have an assured income of a million dollars a year. . . ."

60 HIGH, FRED. "Solving Our Big American X-Word Puzzle." Green County Record [PA] (17 May), pp. 1, 4; (24 May), pp. 1, 4.

With his nation desperate under the Depression, Anderson has abandoned for documentary reporting in Puzzled America the writing of fiction.

61 HUXLEY, JULIAN. "The Analysis of Fame." Saturday Review of Literature, 12 (11 May), 12, 13.

The 1935 Who's Who is uneven in its entries, including Anderson but not Stark Young.

62 JACKSON, JOSEPH HENRY. "A Bookman's Notebook." San Francisco Chronicle (19 April).

In Puzzled America Anderson combines reportage with personal feeling; the reporting is better than the sentimentality.

1935

63 LOCKRIDGE, RICHARD. "A Puzzled Author." New York Sun (30 March).
Not doctrinaire, Puzzled America is as much the investigations of Sherwood Anderson by Sherwood Anderson as of America by a reporter.

64 M., J. T. "Anderson Finds U. S. Still Land of Opportunity." Knoxville Sentinel (31 March).
Knoxville, Tennessee, readers will recognize their area and activities in Puzzled America.

65 McALISTER, COLEMAN. "Puzzled America." Churchman, 149 (15 July), 18.
Puzzled America is "full of the ferment that was in America as the New Deal got well into its stride--the ferment and the puzzlement too." Now social programs have ended this optimism.

66 MacCAMPBELL, DONALD. "Puzzled America." Atlantic Monthly, 156 (August), 10.
Anderson has looked at the ordinary people he has known so intimately, and in Puzzled America he finds some optimism prevalent.

67 MAHANEY, FRANCIS J. "Sherwood Anderson's Puzzled U. S. A." Boston Transcript (6 April), p. 4.
Anderson finds very little bitterness and almost no Fascism in America, and Puzzled America shows this novelist's enduring love for the strange in life.

68 MAILLARD, DENYSE. L'Enfant Américain dans le Roman du Middle-West. Paris: Nizet, pp. 20, 22, 23, 35, 50, 51, 56, 63, 65, 73, 87, 99, 120, 124, 131, 141, 142, 155, 156, 166, 168, 170, 179, 181, 204, 210, 245, 247, 249, 252.
In Tar the author joins fact and fancy to present the childhood of a rural boy in a typical American family; in Poor White the hero is taught as a child by a mother figure. As an adult the hero of Tar sees Europe as small in comparison to the Midwest, this book being a mixture of feelings and impressions from youth and mellow age.

69 MARTIN, W. A. Review of Puzzled America. Buffalo Evening News (13 April).
While no person can challenge Anderson's sympathies in Puzzled America, droves can challenge his credentials as a social philosopher.

70 MYRICK, SUSAN. Review of Puzzled America. Macon Telegraph (5 April).

As Puzzled America is "far the best writing Sherwood Anderson has done in a long time," Anderson gives promise of a future time without humans wasted.

71 NEEDHAM, WILBUR. "Books." Saturday Night (27 April).

Rich with Anderson's empathy, Puzzled America is "a series of stories, all factual, about American working men and their families, as he has observed them during the years of the depression."

*72 NEMEROVSKAYA, OLGA. "Subda Amerikanskoi Novelly." Literaturnaya Uchyoba, No. 5, p. 98.

Cited: 1962.B6.

73 NORTH, STERLING. "Sherwood Anderson Stages a Comeback." Chicago Daily News (3 April), p. 16.

Publication of Puzzled America will recall fame to the sometimes forgotten author of Winesburg, Ohio and Dark Laughter. Anderson here is as good as any other reporter in America, for he deals with "the source of all American literature--the American people."

74 O'NEILL, JAMES M. "Gullible's Travels." Camden Courier [NJ] (13 April).

In Puzzled America Anderson is honest and sympathetic, fair and hopeful, although "there is much bitterness in his cup."

75 PERRY, ANNE. "My Country 'Tis of Thee." Brooklyn Citizen (17 May).

Without thesis or solution, Anderson in Puzzled America provides description and sympathy.

76 PRESTON, JOHN HYDE. "A Conversation." Atlantic Monthly, 156 (August), 190.

Anderson has been unjustly unpraised by younger writers, for he can "be one of the very few Americans who has achieved that perfect freshness of creation and passion, as simple as rain falling on a page, and rain that fell from him and was there miraculously and was all his." Thus spoke Gertrude Stein of Sherwood Anderson.

77 RAMOS, JOSE ANTONIA. Panorama de la Literatura Norteamericana 1600-1935). Mexico, D. F.: Ediciones Botas, pp. 5, 112, 170, 194, 195, 201, 202, 203, 214, 215, 218.

Anderson reveals his own inhibitions in his works, seeming juvenile, Freudian, and unable to mature beyond

1935

(RAMOS, JOSE ANTONIA)
Winesburg, Ohio. In stasis in technique and inspiration, Anderson is more the artist than Theodore Dreiser in recording the earlier generation's atmosphere and interests.

78 RUSSELL, PHILLIPS. "Literary Lantern." Charlotte Observer (14 April).
Anderson's poor, defeated people in Puzzled America are wistfully hopeful but not radically bitter.

79 SHEPARDE, JONATHAN. "Puzzled America." New Haven Journal-Courier (10 April).
Enough books have analyzed the Depression; in Puzzled America Anderson simply describes what is.

80 SPENCER, SHIRLEY. "Handwriting Reveals Character." New York Daily News (27 July).
Anderson's script shows him to be impulsive, lusty, sensitive, inquiring, indifferent to details, and emotional and analytical.

81 STEIN, GERTRUDE. "Gertrude Stein Reviews New Anderson Book." Chicago Daily Tribune (1 May), p. 14.
America is puzzled, but Anderson is not puzzled, and the nation is not really puzzled. Puzzled America is among Anderson's best books. Reprinted: Sherwood Anderson / Gertrude Stein: Correspondence and Personal Essays. Edited by Ray Lewis White. Chapel Hill: University of North Carolina Press, pp. 96-97.

82 SULLIVAN, MARK. Our Times: 1900-1925 VI. The Twenties. New York: Charles Scribner's Sons, pp. 397, 548, 565-66, 652.
In Winesburg, Ohio Anderson "in all earnestness and sincerity recorded the life of an American middlewestern village as he believed it to be, its inhabitants pre-occupied either consciously or unconsciously with sex."

83 T., J. "Puzzled America." Nashville Tennessean (14 April).
Anderson has lost the storyteller's magic and in Puzzled America is "more puzzled than the people of whom he writes."

84 THORNBERRY, ETHEL. Review of Puzzled America. Madison Times (11 May).
Puzzled America does show confusion in Sherwood Anderson, but the confusion is more rhetorical than real, for he simply records and sorrows over common people's sufferings.

85 TUPPER, SAMUEL, JR. "'Puzzled America.'" Atlanta Journal (5 May).

Sentimental to the practical, poetic to the sensitive, Puzzled America appeals quietly and indirectly.

86 TYLER, A. RANGER. "Human Sides of Depression." Albany Knickerbocker Press (14 April).

Puzzled America gives the human effects of the Depression--matters usually buried as statistics in objective works.

87 VALLELY, MRS. JACK. "Book Stuff." Beverly Hills Script (25 May).

Anderson maintains in Puzzled America that if America is entering a new stage, there are no old rules that apply. The author is obviously puzzled, too.

88 WATSON, LATIMER. "Sherwood Anderson Writes Story of America Today In Latest Book." Columbus Enquirer [OH] (6 May).

Puzzled America shows Anderson as the keen observer and wise sayer of people's economic suffering.

89 WORTH, ROBERT. "Sherwood Anderson Takes Look At Modern 'Puzzled America.'" Charlotte News (14 April).

Anderson turned from literature as art to writing as cause, and in Puzzled America he finds ultimate hope in democracy; yet the reader longs still for Anderson the storyteller.

1936 A BOOKS

*1 HAUGHT, VIVA ELIZABETH. "The Influence of Walt Whitman on Sherwood Anderson and Carl Sandburg." Master's thesis, Duke University, 147 pp.

Cited: 1960.A2.

1936 B SHORTER WRITINGS

1 ANON. "Anderson's Position as a Writer." Trenton Times (5 January).

Anderson is cynical and depressed enough to think that his work will be forgotten.

2 ANON. "Anderson Hails Improved Press." Richmond Times-Dispatch (17 January).

In a speech the previous day Anderson complimented youths who chose journalism for careers, as Anderson's son Robert had replaced him on the Virginia newspapers.

1936

3 ANON. "Finds Quality of Loneliness Americans' Distinctive Mark." Baltimore Sun (18 January).
In Baltimore to lecture at The Johns Hopkins University, Anderson linked his hope for the little theater movement to the loneliness of Americans, who lack common origins. Because of all artists actors do not have to work alone, drama is the most important art.

4 ANON. "Novelist Speaks: Anderson in City." Chicago Herald-Examiner (24 January).
"America's wandering novelist" loves Chicago's excitement but not its cold weather. Having lectured on "Puzzled America" at Northwestern University, Anderson praised current Midwestern writing as often as good as that of Mark Twain.

5 ANON. "Photos Bring Back Memories of Ripshin Days." Squib (8 June), p. 6.
Local college girls enjoyed an outing at Anderson's country house.

6 ANON. "Shervuda Anderson." Literaturnaja gazeta (26 September).
Despite the feelings of frustration and impotence Anderson has expressed through his autobiographically-inspired heroes, he has not become reconciled to the realities of a society that oppresses the honest little man. [James F. Cradler]

7 ANON. Review of Kit Brandon. New York American (9 October).
Anderson brings the heroine and secondary characters to life in Kit Brandon.

8 ANON. "The New Books." Philadelphia Ledger (9 October).
Melodramatic but observant, Anderson in Kit Brandon writes his usual "interludes of mad fantasy."

9 ANON. Review of Kit Brandon. Washington Star (10 October).
Kit Brandon becomes "a record of character worth noticing," for Anderson has abandoned description of social groups to return to description of individuals.

10 ANON. Review of Kit Brandon. Buffalo Courier-Express (11 October).
Kit Brandon is superior to Anderson's earlier novels in being more objective and contemporary.

11 ANON. "Odyssey of Mountain Girl Presented by Anderson." Buffalo Times (11 October).

The heroine's odyssey in Kit Brandon re-creates an American epoch broadly and sympathetically.

12 ANON. "'Kit Brandon' Written From Real Incidents." Oakland Tribune (11 October).
Anderson made himself a gentle character in Kit Brandon, based on Virginia trials that he attended.

13 ANON. "Living Women." Time, 28 (12 October), 87.
Anderson adds a new ingredient to his traditional tales of isolated grotesqueness, for Kit Brandon contains "melodramatic fire and smoke."

14 ANON. "Picaresque Weds Proletarian: The United Front in Fiction." Chicago Daily News (14 October).
In Kit Brandon Anderson has written his most readable and important novel--and the first readable proletarian novel in America.

15 ANON. Review of Kit Brandon. Newsweek, 8 (17 October), 31.
In Kit Brandon "The teller of the Winesburg tales stages an abortive comeback with a rankly sentimental novel. . . ."

16 ANON. Review of Kit Brandon. Portland Express [ME] (17 October).
Anderson and his readers will emerge from Kit Brandon into the confusion of "an economic labyrinth."

17 ANON. Review of Kit Brandon. New Haven Register (18 October).
Kit Brandon is "an exciting novel, sensational in subject, but well done."

18 ANON. Review of Kit Brandon. Southbridge News [MA] (20 October).
Kit Brandon uses an exploited subject to allow Anderson to write honestly and personally about an interesting American heroine.

19 ANON. "Power Found in Prose Volume By Anderson." Oakland Tribune (25 October).
Anderson records Kit Brandon in oral, colloquial style; but his real interest is the lost, defeated little souls enmeshed in the heroine's autobiography.

20 ANON. "Anderson's Bootleg Queen." Albany Times-Union [NY] (29 October).

1936

(ANON.)
Anderson gives bizarre but interesting life to his heroine in Kit Brandon, but excessive use of flashbacks serves no purpose.

21 ANON. Review of Kit Brandon. Fort Wayne Journal-Gazette (3 November).
The special details carefully used in Kit Brandon raise the work from easy-reading level to literature.

22 ANON. "Sherwood Anderson Speaker." New York Times (8 November), 2, p. 10.
Anderson spoke at a book fair about authors who draw closer to humanity through drawing close to their characters.

23 ANON. "Puzzled Sherwood Anderson." Santa Monica Outlook (12 November).
In Kit Brandon Anderson forgets to tell a story and tells instead of his own feelings.

24 ANON. Review of Kit Brandon. Darien Review [CT] (19 November).
Anderson has the heroine of Kit Brandon realize that brotherhood is more desirable than lust for power and money.

25 ANON. "'Kit Brandon.'" Philadelphia Inquirer (21 November).
Sociologically weak, Kit Brandon is fictionally "first rate."

26 ANON. Review of Kit Brandon. Athens Banner-Herald [GA] (22 November).
Kit Brandon exploits immorality and corruption for royalties; Anderson gives only a partial view of a basically wholesome nation.

27 ANON. Review of Kit Brandon. New York News (22 November).
Anderson should avoid writing adventures such as Kit Brandon and return to writing "Americana" such as Winesburg, Ohio.

28 ANON. "Fiction." Booklist, 33 (December), 121.
In Kit Brandon, the "indirectness of Anderson's style is suitable to this theme [of confused values] and to the groping for a meaning."

29 ANON. Review of Kit Brandon. New Haven Journal-Courier (1 December).

Kit Brandon has so much charm that Anderson's subtle attacks on economic wrongs may be overlooked.

30 ANON. "To Retain Needy Artists." New York Times (22 December), p. 33.
Harry Hopkins has assured Anderson that deserving art projects will continue to be funded by Federal Government relief agencies.

31 ANON. "New Fiction." Book Buyer, New Series 2 (Christmas), 9.
Kit Brandon "reveals America as no other novel has ever done" and is "a book of revelation for the America of today."

32 ANON. Review of Kit Brandon. Cincinnati Enquirer (26 December).
In Kit Brandon Anderson hints that energy spent breaking laws could have been used to dominate "industry, commerce and public life."

33 BASSO, HAMILTON. "Two Mid-American Novelists." New Republic, 88 (21 October), 318.
Using poetic method to tell Kit Brandon, Anderson leaves a superb story to search for the Grails of Woman's essential truth and America's ultimate meaning.

34 BENDER, NAOMI. "The Book World." Akron Beacon-Journal (24 October).
Written in "ultra-modern style," Kit Brandon never convinces the reader that Anderson understands his plot and characters.

35 BERRY, LEE. "This World of Books." Milwaukee Sentinel (18 October).
While Anderson's social ideas in Kit Brandon may be distasteful, his heroine is fascinating.

36 BOYNTON, PERCY H. Literature and American Life for Students of American Literature. Boston: Ginn and Co., pp. 679, 759, 761-62, 767-69, 792-94, 816-17, 862, 875.
Anderson wrote well only when he moved from novels about social forces to fiction about individual characters, as in Winesburg, Ohio.

37 BRICKELL, HERSCHEL. "Sherwood Anderson's New Novel, 'Kit Brandon,' Story of Wet Era, Is Also About Puzzled America." New York Post (9 October).

(BRICKELL, HERSCHEL)
The rum-running adventures in Kit Brandon seem incredible, but Anderson's social commentaries are interesting.

38 C., R. J. "Along Borderline of Civilization." Springfield Union and Republican [MA] (18 October), E, p. 7.
Kit Brandon proves again that Anderson does not react intellectually to life and that his talent is bound up in inarticulateness.

39 CAMERON, MAY. "Sherwood Anderson Sees Hope Of New Era of Good Feeling as a Result of Presidential Election." New York Post (14 November).
The recent election having given Americans a clear choice for President, Anderson hopes for a new age of cooperation, preferring mass decisions in America to dictatorship by Hitler. Anderson calls Kit Brandon, just published, "a novel, half written."

40 CANBY, HENRY SEIDEL. Seven Years' Harvest: Notes on Contemporary Literature. New York: Holt, Rinehart and Winston, pp. 15, 253.
Anderson is one of the few American writers of discontent--"the most American literature we have."

41 CATTON, BRUCE. Review of Kit Brandon. Lafayette Advertiser [LA] (8 October).
Kit Brandon is Anderson's latest observation of the American scene--the scene fascinating to him since 1916.

42 COOPER, NAOMI. "The Bookshelf." Columbus Ledger [GA] (12 October).
Kit Brandon is realistic but, further, it is hopeful.

43 CORNISH, RICHARD V. "Lessons Learned." Camden Post [NJ] (10 October).
Please God the Prohibition era described in Kit Brandon never return to haunt America!

44 CURRIE, GEORGE. "Passed in Review." Brooklyn Daily Eagle (17 October).
Kit Brandon is possibly about the need for implementation of a better society than the current one.

45 CURRIER, ISABEL R. A. "Anderson Paints Regional Picture." Worcester Telegram [MA] (11 October).
Similar in setting to John Fox, Jr.'s The Trail of the Lonesome Pine, Anderson's Kit Brandon shows how far

American literature has come in style and morality--and taste.

46 DANIEL, FRANK. "'Kit Brandon' a Portrait." Atlanta Journal (18 October).
Kit Brandon contains fascinating prose and heroine.

47 DARROW, MARY B. "Bound To Be Read." Glendale News-Press (23 October).
Kit Brandon is authoritative, for Anderson has seen the life of which he writes.

48 DeVOTO, BERNARD. Forays and Rebuttals. Boston: Little, Brown, p. 222.
Winesburg, Ohio and Main Street produced "a suspension of critical intelligence" in appealing to revolters against villages.

49 DORAIS, LEON. "More Groping By Sherwood Anderson." San Francisco Chronicle (8 November).
If Anderson would stop pretending to be unable to tell a story well, he could have told a good story in Kit Brandon.

50 EISHISKINA, N. "Strantovaniye v mire fantazii faktov." Literaturnaya gazeta (10 May).
A Story Teller's Story illuminates the origins of Anderson's utopian vision, his passive melancholy, and his "denouement-less" psychological short-story form. [James F. Cradler]

51 FREEMAN, JOSEPH. An American Testament: A Narrative of Rebels and Romantics. New York: Farrar & Rinehart, pp. 114, 233-34, 378, 380, 638.
Floyd Dell gave early praise to Anderson's novels; Anderson advised a poet named Oscar to write novels; and The Masses published Anderson's stories. However, Anderson in his fiction is "still mumbling prayers before the ancient phallic gods."

52 G., A. "Anderson of 1936." New Orleans Times-Picayune (18 October).
In Kit Brandon Anderson returns to "the impressive moods he revealed in 'Winesburg'"--but here with social reform added.

53 GANNETT, LEWIS. "Books and Things." New York Herald Tribune (9 October), p. 21.

1936

(GANNETT, LEWIS)
Having embraced and rejected several philosophies since he began writing, Anderson in Kit Brandon gives "his best-rounded story in a decade, and perhaps his sharpest criticism."

54 GILES, HARRY. "Books." Columbus State-Journal [OH] (14 October).
The social observation in Kit Brandon is that people are still good in America but that their institutions are all wrong.

55 GRAINGER, PAUL. "Kit Brandon." Minneapolis Journal (11 October).
In Kit Brandon Anderson creates living characters, but his style is more pointless and oblique than ever.

56 H., W. E. "Sherwood Anderson." Boston Transcript (10 October), p. 8.
Kit Brandon reveals Anderson adding the new psychology and sociology to the old story of moonshining.

57 HENDERSON, PHILIP. The Novel Today: Studies in Contemporary Attitudes. London: John Lane, pp. 130-31, 147.
Anderson's naturalism is chaotic, even though he first taught Hemingway how to write.

58 HERRON, LAWRENCE. "Sherwood Anderson Heroine Stands Puzzled and Isolated." Dayton Journal (31 October).
The heroine of Kit Brandon resembles Hawthorne's character in The Scarlet Letter; Anderson's woman might as well wear the scarlet question mark.

59 HOLLIS, E. E. "Portrait of Youth." Salt Lake City Tribune (13 December).
Amid the confusion in Kit Brandon, Anderson could be saying that self-respect and brotherhood could salvage human life.

60 HONIG, EDWIN. "Puzzled Anderson." Madison Journal (8 November).
Anderson's purpose in Kit Brandon is not new; it is the observation of a part of the American scene.

61 IMBS, BRAVIG. Confessions of Another Young Man. New York: Henkle-Yewdale House, pp. 119, 172, 177-78, 179, 181-82, 187.
Stein announced Anderson's comment at Mrs. Jolas' dinner--that were he rich he should have nightly fresh

pajamas and a new wife after each three-year period; when Anderson lunched with Joyce the latter failed to understand Anderson, who was not Irish but who asked about Ireland. At Stein's party Anderson was monopolized by Stein but spoke forcefully as a natural raconteur. Anderson claimed to be most comfortable among the common workers, whom he did not resemble. John Anderson became Imbs' friend after Sherwood Anderson left Paris.

62 JONES, HOWARD MUMFORD. "Many Andersons." Saturday Review of Literature, 14 (10 October), p. 13.
Three Andersons wrote Kit Brandon: the describer of character, the revolutionary, and the new author of adventure-romances.

63 KAZIN, ALFRED. "Sherwood Anderson, Still Shuffling Along." New York Herald Tribune Books (11 October), pp. 1-2.
The artistry of Kit Brandon, "so subtle that it appears imperceptible," reveals Anderson again shuffling the pieces of his novel before the reader's eyes, puzzling humanely over the sense of the lost in American life.

64 KHMEL'NITSKAIA, T. "Istorija rasskazčika." Literaturnyi sovremennik, No. 9, pp. 213-15.
Flight being the essential element of Anderson's art, joie de vivre pervades A Story Teller's Story, along with freshness, humor, realistic portrayals, and clarification of the author's relationship to the world and to art. [James F. Cradler]

65 KHOKHLOV, G. "Istorija rasskazčika." Literaturnoe obozrenie, No. 3, pp. 23-24.
Anderson's childhood provides the most complete and vivid episodes of A Story Teller's Story. Perhaps love of craft, artistic expression, and life may lead the writer from his current social cul-de-sac. [James F. Cradler]

66 KIMBALL, FREDERICK H. "Authors and Books." Adams Journal [NY] (14 October).
In Kit Brandon Anderson calls for the willing cooperation of all people to save the human race.

67 LAWRENCE, D. H. Phoenix: The Posthumous Papers of D. H. Lawrence. Edited by Edward D. McDonald. New York: Viking Press, p. 272.
"The tragedian, like Theodore Dreiser and Sherwood Anderson, still dramatizes his defeat and is in love with himself in his defeated role."

1936

68 LOVETT, ROBERT MORSS. "Sherwood Anderson." New Republic, 89 (25 November), 103-105.

In Winesburg, Ohio Anderson proved his mastery of writing about the mystery of life--the essence behind mere existence. In his novels the writer makes his work more realistic and loses the sense of imminence. Reprinted: 1937.B21.

69 LOWE, ORTON. Our Land and Its Literature. New York: Harper & Brothers, pp. 56, 101, 112, 115.

When Winesburg, Ohio was published in 1919, a "new type of material and treatment" entered the American short story. In Dark Laughter Anderson poetically pictures river life in the United States. When Anderson chooses characters, he looks in "neglected layers of society."

70 MASTERS, EDGAR LEE. Across Spoon River. New York: Farrar & Rinehart, pp. 295-315.

[The character "Deirdre" has been identified as Tennessee Mitchell, the second Mrs. Sherwood Anderson.] Of Deirdre, Masters says: "I see her now as a cold, uncanny, farsighted mind, with a sort of congenital nymphomania." Further, "She married a few years after we separated. Her husband turned upon her bitterly after a few years, and they were divorced. Later she committed suicide."

71 MILLER, MAX. "Sherwood Anderson's Power As Writer Again Revealed." San Diego Union (15 November).

Kit Brandon, published by Anderson after many years without a novel, is "his most spell-binding novel to date."

72 MOUTOUX, JOHN T. "Week-Ending with Sherwood Anderson." Knoxville News Sentinel (30 August), Magazine, p. 1.

Having written somberly of individuals facing social forces, Anderson now lives as a country squire in Virginia. The writer claims to put themes instead of plots into his books and never to read critics, for they review past works instead of new writing.

73 MYRICK, SUSAN. "Today's Book." Macon Telegraph (9 October).

Kit Brandon is as romantic about Prohibition as any adventure novel of pirate-infested seas.

74 NEEDHAM, WILBUR. "Moonshiner's Daughter Turns Into Rum-Runner." Los Angeles Times (25 October).

Anderson's apparent defects are deliberate techniques, and in Kit Brandon he writes an authentic story in the oral style and from the mentality of the people involved.

75 P., A. S. "Carolina Portrait." Raleigh Observer (25 October).
New in subject, more confused than even Anderson's other novels, Kit Brandon wastes good literary materials.

76 PRESCOTT, JOSEPH. "Sex in Literature." English Leaflet, 35 (May), 68-69.
Compared to Manhattan Transfer, Winesburg, Ohio handles psychology more delicately. Unlike Main Street, Winesburg, Ohio is "simple, imaginative, and poignant with human drama." Many high-school students resemble the central Winesburg character; they are blind to experience surrounding them.

77 QUINN, ARTHUR HOBSON. American Fiction: An Historical and Critical Survey. New York: D. Appleton-Century, pp. 644, 656-60, 669, 714.
The great flaw in Anderson's novels is his lack of technical ability, for these undirected works "proceed by a series of spirals, where progress becomes a lost art, and the story finally fades away into thin air." Anderson's characters are unrealistic, being "monsters of lust, of perversion, of frustration," and this writer should never have been given serious consideration.

78 ROBINSON, TED. "Sherwood Anderson's New Novel Interprets Springs of America's Restlessness." Cleveland Plain Dealer (11 October).
Except in exploring the typical American's desire to have success and bigness, Kit Brandon is the typical Anderson novel--"an exercise in prose in which the writer continually parodies and burlesques his own style."

79 RORTY, JAMES. "Heaven Won't Protect the Working Girl." Advance (November), pp. 25-26.
Kit Brandon is a novel "as fresh and clean and supple as the performance of a twenty-year-old athlete," even though Anderson gropes in "politico-aesthetic apple sauce" theory, but here Anderson has actually written proletarian fiction.

80 RUSSELL, PHILLIPS. "The Literary Lantern." Charlotte Observer (20 December).
Anderson has experimented in writing about non-heroic people, especially in Winesburg, Ohio.

81 _____. Review of Kit Brandon. Charlotte Observer (8 November).
The minor characters in Kit Brandon illustrate Anderson's ideas on industry and labor; the heroine is unsatisfactory.

1936

82 S., F. M. "Anderson Novel, a Portrait of a Milltown Girl." Milwaukee Journal (18 October).

Kit Brandon joins Anderson's 1930's books in being more labor sermon than poetic song.

83 SELDES, GILBERT. Mainland. New York: Charles Scribner's Sons, pp. 13, 48.

Anderson's emotionalism contributed to the anti-American tone of literature from 1914 to 1929. Writers take vengeance on inventors of hated modern life.

84 SERGEL, ROGER. "Of Sherwood Anderson and 'Kit Brandon.'" Book Buyer, Fourth Series 2 (November), 2-4.

Although Kit Brandon shows occasionally Anderson's uncouth style, this novel is a great work of storytelling, now adventure, now social commentary.

85 SHIPP, CAMERON. "Kit Brandon, Bootleg Girl." Charlotte News (11 October).

Kit Brandon is "the worst book of the year" in style, plot, and excessive sex.

86 STONE, GEOFFREY. "Rather Bewildered." Commonweal, 25 (20 October), 109-110.

Being aware of the nation's economic breakdown does not clarify Anderson's bewilderment at life and fiction-writing. In Kit Brandon he merely directs his lack of clear intelligence toward Moscow.

87 TAYLOR, WALTER F. A History of American Letters. New York: American Book Co., pp. 376-80.

Anderson's naturalism is based on Freudian views of human behavior, combined with his personal qualities of "sensuality, morbidness, love of beauty, naiveté, and mysticism." Anderson studies people in moments of crisis in order to fathom their inner lives.

88 THOMPSON, RALPH. "Books of the Times." New York Times (14 October), p. 23.

In treatment and style, Kit Brandon shows Anderson able to use an exploited subject and an interesting first-person narrator.

89 TOBIAS, ROWENA WILSON. "Books and People." Charleston Evening Post [SC] (17 October).

While Kit Brandon has Anderson's usual repetitive style, sympathy, indignation, and confusion, this novel offers something new--a tentative answer in spiritual faith.

90 VAN DOREN, CARL. Three Worlds. New York: Harper & Brothers, pp. 154, 196-97, 251, 287.

Lewis objected that Masters' influence on Anderson and on himself was probably not direct but possibly by way of literary milieu. Century published many of Anderson's stories; and, at a New York lunch for Anderson, Mencken refused to meet S. P. Sherman. Earlier Van Doren had explored New Orleans accompanied by Anderson.

91 VAN DOREN, MARK. "Still Groping." Nation, 143 (17 October), 452-53.

In broken sentences and unfinished thoughts, Anderson proves in Kit Brandon that writing twenty books does not give ability. Reprinted: 1942.B109.

92 [WRIGHT, DONALD M.] "A Mid-western Ad Man Remembers: Sherwood Anderson, Advertising Man." Advertising and Selling, 28 (17 December), 35, 68.

When Anderson worked in advertising, he both wrote and sold copy, becoming a more subtle salesman with experience. The man's gift was intuition, as evidenced in advertising copy as in later fiction, and humor, known mostly in his office jokes.

93 YOUNG, STANLEY. "Mr. Anderson's Salute to Youth." New York Times Book Review (11 October), p. 3.

In Kit Brandon Anderson writes poetically of realistic materials, but this time he provides an answer to the eternal problem of loneliness--"to make 'a real partnership in living.'"

1937 A BOOKS

1 DAVENPORT, KENNETH. "Sherwood Anderson: An Appreciation of His Life and Fiction." Master's thesis, Fort Hayes Kansas State College, 55 pp.

Belonging to the period when naturalism was becoming passé, Anderson has complained of the end of an American frontier and has written from his Midwestern curiosity about people to implant hope of community. Should society change from hypocrisy and repression, Anderson's characters could have rounded, integrated lives.

1937

1937 B SHORTER WRITINGS

1 ANON. "Southern Writers Honored in Selection." Richmond Times-Dispatch (22 January).
Douglas S. Freeman, Wolfe, and Anderson have been elected to membership in the National Institute of Arts and Letters.

2 ANON. "Roaming the Rural Routes: The Story of Camden." Dayton Daily News (29 February), p. 3.
Now a rich author of books that attack his father, Anderson edits papers in Virginia. Elderly Mrs. Pierce now lives in the house in Camden, Ohio, where Anderson was born.

3 ANON. "Anderson Praises Exposé of Slums." Chattanooga Times (20 March).
The campaign against slums is a credit to the Chattanooga Times. The South must solve its tenant-farmer problem; Roosevelt's attempt to pack the Supreme Court is not wrong or harmful, as Anderson observes.

4 ANON. "Kit Brandon." Times Literary Supplement (3 April), p. 256.
Kit Brandon, made technically difficult for the reader, contains "a penetrating study of American sociological conditions."

5 ANON. "Who's Who at the Conference." University of Colorado Bulletin, 37 (May), 7.
As an advisor at the conference of writers from July 26 through August 13, Anderson will conduct workshops and lecture twice each evening.

6 ANON. Review of Plays, Winesburg and Others. Boston Herald (11 September).
Anderson's Plays, Winesburg and Others are as striking as his prose versions of the same material.

7 ANON. Review of Plays, Winesburg and Others. Portland Express [ME] (18 September).
The title play in Anderson's collection Plays, Winesburg and Others ignores the theme but holds the spirit of the novel.

8 ANON. "Sherwood Anderson In Playwright's Role." Hartford Courant (26 September).
Plays, Winesburg and Others will be of interest primarily to students of recent American drama.

9 ANON. "Plays, Winesburg and Others." Theatre Arts Monthly, 21 (October), 824-25.

Dramatic structure and attempted realism defeat Anderson in Plays, Winesburg and Others. While the short dramas are worth attention, the title play replaces the gentle charm of fiction with dramatic excesses.

10 ANON. "Winesburg and Other Plays." Durham Herald [NC] (24 October).

Plays, Winesburg and Others proves Anderson's versatility and his stature "with America's outstanding literary figures."

*11 ANON. Review of Plays, Winesburg and Others. Cleveland Open Shelf (November), p. 23.

Cited: Book Review Digest 1937, p. 24.

12 ANON. "Classified Books." Booklist, 34 (15 November), 99.

Anderson has dramatized Winesburg, Ohio in nine scenes. The three short pieces in Plays, Winesburg and Others are of limited use because of their "stark realism and frank treatment."

13 ANON. "Winesburg and Other Plays." New Haven Journal-Courant (22 November).

The play version of Anderson's novel in Plays, Winesburg and Others improves upon the fiction by eliminating diffusion.

14 ANON. "Middle Western Scenes." San Francisco Argonaut (26 November).

Anderson's dramas in Plays, Winesburg and Others are effective plots with technical interest.

15 BAILEY, HOWARD. "Small Town Life." Raleigh Observer (10 October).

Plays, Winesburg and Others is worth adding to one's library, for Anderson has retained the excellence of his fiction in dramatized form.

16 BARISH, MILDRED. "Sherwood Anderson Does a Book of Plays." Los Angeles Times (19 September).

Anderson's Midwestern dramas in Plays, Winesburg and Others view people by fluoroscope rather than telescope, but the works are better prose than theater.

17 BRODIN, PIERRE. Le Roman Régionaliste Américain. Preface by Maurice-Edgar Coindreau. Paris: Librairie G.-P. Maisonneuve, pp. 36-38, 40.

1937

(BRODIN, PIERRE)
In Poor White Anderson shows troubles that industrialization brings to a growing Ohio town--a topic which he knows from his own Midwestern youth. Anderson is preoccupied with being sincere and does not hesitate to show realistic details. In all of his works Anderson evokes the romantic shadows and opportunism of the Midwest.

18 BROWN, STERLING. The Negro in American Fiction. Washington, D. C.: Associates in Negro Folk Education, p. 151.
When Anderson writes of Negro characters--as in Dark Laughter--he is more interested in the supposed eroticism of the race than in shocking facts of Negro life.

19 BURNS, GEORGE R. "Average Man? Sherwood Anderson!" Philadelphia Record (13 November).
Now that the Horatio Alger idealism has been lost, Anderson thinks that young people should devote their idealism to "some human thing." The author has abandoned politics, admitting that "During the height of the Depression I got rather excited and very red. . . ."

20 CLEATON, IRENE and ALLEN CLEATON. Books & Battles: American Literature, 1920-1930. Boston: Houghton Mifflin Co., pp. xviii, 22, 35, 36, 42, 63-64, 74, 99, 100, 119, 121, 129, 134, 153, 160, 179-83, 187, 190, 207, 239, 248.
When Anderson joined the Chicago Renaissance group, he wrote "strange, half-articulate stories of the secret, shabby dreams of lonely and beaten men." Later, whenever Anderson lectured, he always prefaced his speeches with the claim of being still a businessman. Now he operates country newspapers in Virginia.

21 COWLEY, MALCOLM, ed. After the Genteel Tradition: American Writers Since 1910. New York: W. W. Norton Co., pp. 15, 16, 17, 35, 82, 88-99, 108, 113, 141, 192, 216, 217, 222, 225, 239, 241, 245, 251, 255, 256, 260.
Part of the generation of writers that broke the Victorian tradition, Anderson shows influence from Dreiser and on later writers such as Hemingway. Anderson transferred his interests from small-town life to modern problems of industry and standardization, becoming along the way a less definite writer. Reprint of 1936.B68.

22 DICKINSON, ASA DON. Best Books of the Decade 1926-1935: A Later Clue to the Literary Labyrinth. New York: H. W. Wilson Co., p. 21.
Tar is "the imaginative re-creation of an American boyhood from four to adolescence" by the "American fictionist and autobiographer."

23 DUNCAN, C. WILLIAM. "Sherwood Anderson Lives on Farm and Likes It." Philadelphia Evening Ledger (18 November).
Anderson has found contentment living in rural Virginia, where people are less money-minded and life is simpler than in cities.

24 EATON, WALTER PRICHARD. "'Our Country! Right or--.'" New York Herald Tribune Books (31 October), p. 22.
In Plays, Winesburg and Others, Anderson proves that he cannot rewrite Winesburg, Ohio in dramatic form.

25 FIELD, FREDERICK. "Andersoniana." Washington Post (3 October).
Using sex as the vortex, Anderson creates powerful drama in Plays, Winesburg and Others.

*26 FILIPS, U. "'Kit Brendon' Shervuda Andersona." Internatsional'naia Literatura, No. 1, pp. 211-12.
Cited: 1969.B29.

27 FRANK, WALDO. In the American Jungle (1925-1936). New York: Farrar and Rinehart, pp. 93-96, 99, 214.
Anderson's work is an attempt to form religious values for the present age; one must "live through Anderson in order to grow beyond our childhood" nationally.

28 HART, HARRY, ed. The Writer in a Changing World. [n.p.: Equinox Cooperative Press, pp. 18, 43, 97.
Joseph Freeman feels unable to separate Anderson's writings from the politics of the World War era, for the pathos of Winesburg, Ohio reflected the crush of monopolistic forces upon small people. Carlton Beales finds Winesburg, Ohio less entertaining and informative than recent Latin American writing.

29 HORTON, PHILIP. Hart Crane: The Life of an American Poet. New York: Viking Press, pp. 75-76, 85-86, 97, 101, 112.
After Crane praised Winesburg, Ohio, Anderson suggested that Crane read and consider works about "the national consciousness"; and Crane described Anderson as "crowd-bound, with a smell of the sod about him, uncouth." Anderson showed Crane's paintings to artistic friends.

30 HUEBSCH, BENJAMIN W. "Footnotes to a Publisher's Life." Colophon, New Series 2 (Summer), 415-17.
The John Lane Company found Anderson's Winesburg, Ohio "too gloomy" to publish, and B. W. Huebsch accepted the

1937

(HUEBSCH, BENJAMIN W.)
book at Francis Hackett's urging. As Anderson did not care about titles, Huebsch entitled Winesburg, Ohio and published the work. Of Anderson's books, published by Huebsch, only Many Marriages (which deserved "best-seller" status) sold well. At Huebsch's party on the publication of A Story Teller's Story, Mencken and Sherman even "ate in the same room." Lawrence responded to a free copy of Winesburg, Ohio by disliking Anderson's characters.

31 JACK, PETER MONRO. "Sherwood Anderson Turns to the Stage." New York Times Book Review (14 November), p. 9.
Plays, Winesburg and Others contains uneven work, the author being unable to create a successful, moving drama.

32 JOHNS, ORRICK. Time of Our Lives: The Story of Father and Myself. New York: Stackpole Press, pp. 245, 291, 309.
In the Renaissance years in America, Anderson's stories "had a powerful native ring of sourness and sweetness"; his novels concerned people escaping from "environments but not from themselves." Anderson visited Lincoln Steffens in Carmel, California.

33 L., M. "Sherwood Anderson's Plays." Richmond Times-Dispatch (19 September).
The stage version of Anderson's novel in Plays, Winesburg and Others does not sacrifice its spirit.

34 LITTLE, HERBERT. "Sherwood Anderson Says He's Glad Celebrity Days Are Over." Washington Daily News (1 May), p. 16.
Anderson thinks that Plays, Winesburg and Others will sell eighteen copies and that American literature is in good condition with another Anderson book soon to be published. The author's preferred subjects now are mountain stories told by common people.

35 LOGGINS, VERNON. I Hear America: Literature in the United States Since 1900. New York: Thomas Y. Crowell Co., pp. 11, 110-11, 146, 147, 151-59, 170, 178, 291, 324.
Anderson met Faulkner and shared an apartment with him in New Orleans. All of Anderson's characters are shadows of the writer himself, for Anderson is among "the most subjective of writers," and the heroes want to break free from convention and live out hitherto repressed urges. Dreiser encouraged Anderson to read Lawrence, who led Anderson into Freudian thought--an influence that controls Winesburg, Ohio.

36 M., M. "Dramatized Stories." San Diego Union (17 October). Anderson has been lucky to have the Hedgerow Theater perform some of his Plays, Winesburg and Others.

37 McCOLE, C. JOHN. Lucifer at Large. London: Longmans, Green, pp. 32, 110, 115, 125-50, 151, 153, 162-63, 178, 206, 217, 244, 248, 293, 298.
Anderson has written "the most influential Freudian novels America has yet produced." Extreme use of Freudian psychology renders Anderson's work disgusting, and his admitted confusions render questionable his few valid points about life. Reprint in part of 1929.B70.

38 MULLER, HERBERT J. Modern Fiction: A Study in Values. New York: Funk & Wagnalls, pp. 51, 245-46, 275, 303, 396, 397, 414.
Whereas Lawrence probes deeply into the unconscious, Anderson can "remain on the surface only to watch what comes up out of the depths and to picture the havoc wrought upon conventional designs for living." Anderson has popularized the primitive in behavior and the plotless in fiction; both Hemingway and Wolfe have learned from him.

39 MYRICK, SUSAN. "Today's Book." Macon Telegraph (10 November). Local citizens who enjoyed Anderson's several talks will delight in Plays, Winesburg and Others.

40 P., M. "Printed Plays." Worcester Telegram [MA] (12 September).
In Plays, Winesburg and Others Anderson is unable to construct drama clear in message and character.

41 RAILO, EINO. Yleisen Kirjallisunden Historia, 6. Porvoo, Helsinki, p. 128.
Anderson's works "are weighty psychological documents, devoid of beauty of form and high spirits, but there is a serious attempt to listen to the deepest voices of the human heart and to disclose the ultimate motives of human actions. It is an attempt which is bound to inspire respect." [Tauno Mustanoja]

42 RASCO, BURTON. Before I Forget. Garden City: Doubleday, Doran and Co., pp. 237, 321, 344-45, 355, 358, 365-66, 368, 427-34.
Rascoe entertained Sherwood Anderson and Tennessee Anderson in Chicago; and Anderson accused Rascoe of intellectualizing life, Anderson preferring to believe that two plus two do not necessarily equal four. Anderson was then

1937

(RASCO, BURTON)
poetic and religious; later easterners lionized him and hurt his simple style. Anderson's best oral tale was his extended joke about Mama Geighan. Reprint of 1924.B38.

43 _____. The Joys of Reading: Life's Greatest Pleasure. Garden City: Nelson Doubleday Co., pp. 11, 22-23, 183.
As with Anderson's writing, public taste can parallel classic good taste in books. To come upon "Hands" thrilled Rascoe, for Anderson was an important part of the old Chicago Renaissance.

44 SIMONS, W. J. "Anderson's Plays Issued in Book Form." San Francisco Chronicle (5 September).
In Plays, Winesburg and Others Anderson the dramatist is like Anderson the storyteller in embracing frustration and shadows.

45 SNELLING, PAULA. "Sherwood Anderson . . . A Composite Picture." Pseudopodia, 1 (Winter), 1-2, 18.
Kit Brandon, according to Anderson, returns his work to his pre-sociological days--and Anderson's later work has not deserved praise. Anderson writes from his mental suffering; and at his best he writes with feeling and cadence. Kit Brandon fails because Anderson is writing about the South, an area not native to him. Reprinted: 1972.B30.

46 STEIN, GERTRUDE. Everybody's Autobiography. New York: Random House, pp. 222-23, 256, 257, 270, 271-72.
Stein and Anderson met as planned in Minnesota while she was touring America in 1934-35 and while he was traveling to gather material for Puzzled America. In New Orleans Anderson brought oranges and guided Stein about the city. Stein and Anderson may yet collaborate in writing about General Grant. Reprinted: Sherwood Anderson / Gertrude Stein: Correspondence and Personal Essays. Chapel Hill: University of North Carolina Press, 1972, pp. 102-105.

47 TUPPER, SAMUEL, JR. "Sherwood Anderson's Plays." Atlanta Journal (19 September).
Publication of Plays, Winesburg and Others creates amazement that Anderson could dramatize his famous novel successfully; he has created dramas of the inarticulate.

48 WILENSKY, HARRY. "Sherwood Anderson in Atlanta: Novelist Just Over Siege of Flu." Atlanta Journal (18 March), pp. 1, 2.

On his way from Texas to Virginia, Anderson--"a rugged giant of American prose" and "one of the foremost biographers of small town life"--is currently writing an autobiography and a novel.

1938 A BOOKS - NONE

1938 B SHORTER WRITINGS

1 ANON. "Plays From Sherwood Anderson's Stories." Springfield Republican (2 January), E, p. 7.
Plays, Winesburg and Others is Anderson's attempt to dramatize scenes or characters from his novels and stories.

2 CHONEZ, CLAUDINE. "Du Middle-West à Greenwich Village: Avec Sherwood Anderson, Européen d'Amérique." Les Nouvelles Littéraires (26 March), p. 6.
Awaiting Chonez for an interview in New York City in February, Anderson mistakenly sat with the wrong woman. He thinks The Triumph of the Egg his most successful work, but he personally likes the anti-materialism theme of A Story Teller's Story. Not mystical but imaginative, Anderson claims to be ignorant of Freud and God.

3 House of Representatives. Hearings Before a Special Committee on Un-American Activities, Seventy-Fifth Congress, Third Session, on H. Res. 282. Washington: United States Government Printing Office, 557, 558, 6218, 6234.
Anderson in 1930 belonged to the John Reed Club's Emergency Committee for Southern Political Prisoners; he signed that year a public statement to protest the "red scare." Later Anderson attended in Amsterdam a meeting of the World Congress Against War; in the August, 1933, issue of Struggle Against War he called for a New York City congress against war.

4 MacDONALD, DWIGHT. Fascism and the American Scene. [New York]: Pioneer Publishers, p. 10.
Many Marriages is "a novel whose mysticism is peculiarly American" and which quotes a version of Byron's "Every Man a King!"

5 MONROE, HARRIET. A Poet's Life: Seventy Years in a Changing World. New York: Macmillan Co., p. 390.
Sandburg's poems about his rural youth in "Prairie" led the way for Anderson's Mid-American Chants.

1938

6 STEARNS, HAROLD, ed. America Now: An Inquiry into Civilization in the United States. New York: Charles Scribner's Sons, pp. 36, 37, 47.
As the Depression approached, novels such as Dark Laughter served as escapist reading. In the 1930's Anderson wrote mediocre books or fell behind social progress completely.

7 TIETJENS, EUNICE. The World at My Shoulder. New York: Macmillan Co., p. 21.
Anderson was an occasional poet associated with Tietjens in the Chicago Renaissance soon after 1912.

1939 A BOOKS

1 DINSMOOR, MARY HELEN. "An Inquiry into the Life of Sherwood Anderson as Reflected in His Literary Works." Master's thesis, Ohio University, 74 pp.
Anderson began writing after he was a man and began trying to understand himself as more than a part of an industrialized nation. To tell his own story, Anderson created several characters under names other than his own.

2 RISLEY, EDWARD H., JR. "Sherwood Anderson: The Philosophy of Failure." Honors thesis, Harvard University, 30 pp.
Anderson's escape from business is the key to understanding the man's career as a writer, for the escape led to need for self-discovery and later for expressing understanding of other people. In failure is new, honest puzzlement, out of which comes sensitive expression.

1939 B SHORTER WRITINGS

1 ANON. "Sherwood Anderson Welcomed as Campus Lecturer." Olivet College Echo, 49 (11 January), 1.
Anderson now follows Ford M. Ford as this year's lecturer at Olivet College. Anderson's writings of plain Americans have told Americans their qualities, and his short stories "have been ranked by the critics as among the best in our language."

2 ANON. "Appears in Lecture." Olivet Optic [MI] (19 January).
Having spent a month teaching creative writing at Olivet College, Anderson will now deliver a public lecture.

3 ANON. "An Informal Introduction to Literature at Wells College." New York Herald Tribune (17 December).

Students enjoy a conversation with the novelist Sherwood Anderson.

4 ANON. "El Cuente Norteamericano." La Nacion (24 December), p. 8.
Anderson has written "Unforgotten" for La Nacion. He fathered the great North American writers Faulkner, Hemingway, and Caldwell.

*5 ARNAVON, CYRILLE. "Sherwood Anderson et la Connaissance de Peuple." Cahiers de Paris (May), pp. 143-47.
Cited: 1971.A1.

6 BOMBAL, MARÍA LUISA. "En Nueva York con Sherwood Anderson." La Nacion (8 October), 2, p. 3.
Bombal planned to ask very pompous questions of Anderson, but the polite author was interested in the Latin American interest in his works.

7 BURNETT, WHIT. The Literary Life and the Hell with It. New York: Harper & Brothers, pp. 148-49, 205, 215, 221, 222.
Anderson offended the family maid at Burnett's house through rough talk; he was visiting with John Emerson and Anita Loos. Anderson's writings have been motivated by his need for self-understanding, not by prior reading of writers such as Chekhov or Stein.

8 FILLER, LOUIS. Crusaders for American Liberalism. Yellow Springs [OH]: Antioch Press, p. 377.
When Upton Sinclair could find no audience for writing as muckraker, he turned to literary gossip and gave his opinion of Anderson in Money Writes!

9 FRIEDERICH, WERNER P. Werden und Wachsen der U. S. A. in 300 Jahren: Politische und Literarische Charakerköffe von Virginia Dare bis Roosevelt. Bern: Verlag A. Francke, pp. 238-39, 251.
Anderson and other "new naturalists" had tones of muckraking in their works of rebellion against nineteenth-century esthetics. Longfellow would not have approved of Anderson, O'Neill, Sandburg, and Masters.

10 HAGER, R. M. "Sherwood Anderson Finds Literary Road Bumpy." Daily Princetonian (20 October).
"Easily mistaken for a college football coach," Anderson spoke yesterday on "Man and His Imagination."

1939

11 HANEY, JOHN LOUIS. The Story of Our Literature: An Interpretation of the American Spirit. Revised edition. New York: Charles Scribner's Sons, pp. 265-66, 368.
Anderson added sentiment to his realism, "hoping that some betterment might eventually be achieved." Before 1920 Anderson's novels were less sentimental; after 1920 he added a mystical tone to his fiction.

12 HERRON, IMA HONAKER. The Small Town in American Literature. Durham: Duke University Press, pp. xvi, 21, 71-72, 121, 188, 353-54, 369-77, 390, 419, 422, 432.
"A dreamer and so-called cornfed mystic," Anderson broods over human behavior and sees the artist as free to express his truths about the psychology of his characters. Anderson rebels against literary reticence and emphasizes character instead of plot. In all of his fiction about small-town life, Anderson "wanted to search out the passions, the veiled tragedies, the bitter futilities of existence." His flaw is "preoccupation with Freudian obsessions and frustrations."

13 HOEL, SIGURD. "Sherwood Anderson." 50 Gule. Oslo: Gyldendal Norsk Forlag, pp. 37-40.
Windy McPherson's Son proved a total failure, and Anderson achieved success first with Winesburg, Ohio. From then through Dark Laughter he wrote of a rather primitive America with a strong environmental influence. In Dark Laughter especially Anderson rebels against repression of instincts natural to humans.

*14 LeBRETON, M. "Tendances du Roman Américain d'Aujourd'hui." Cahiers de Paris (May), pp. 122-27.
Cited: 1971.A1.

15 LUNDKVIST, ARTUR. "Sherwood Anderson." Tre Amerikaner: Dreiser--Lewis--Anderson. Stockholm: Albert Bonniers Förlag, pp. 46-63.
Winesburg, Ohio revealed Anderson as a psychological writer in rebellion against small-town America. All of his works reflect the disjunction between sexual instincts and internal hindrances, for Anderson wrote intuitively, and even his psychology is informal and often mystical. Knowledge of the author's life aids in understanding his fiction.

16 RAHV, PHILIP. "Paleface and Redskin." Kenyon Review, 1 (Summer), 253-55.
Anderson wrote against conventions already being abandoned by American society, his "redskin" faults being

part of the national crudity and thus dating his work prematurely.

17 SHIPP, CAMERON. "Reading and Writing." Charlotte News (9 April).
In town with Eleanor Anderson, Sherwood would not discuss his new fiction project or play the literary giant.

18 _____. "Sherwood Anderson Works On New Book While Here." Charlotte News (9 April).
Mrs. Anderson in town to address working women, her husband played recluse and finally talked of his country newspapers in Virginia.

19 SMITH, BERNARD. Forces in American Criticism: A Study in the History of American Literary Thought. New York: Harcourt, Brace and Co., pp. 159, 297-98, 307, 314.
Admirers of Howells disliked Anderson's crudity. Dell praised Anderson's early work simply because he liked realism. Mencken admired Anderson for showing "the meanness and cruelty of rural and small-town life."

20 UNTERMEYER, LOUIS. From Another World: The Autobiography of Louis Untermeyer. New York: Harcourt, Brace and Co., pp. 84, 87, 314.
Waldo Frank introduced Anderson's stories in The Seven Arts. When Secession began publication, its program was to advance beyond Anderson and Lewis. Before Anderson became victim of his simplicity, he "pioneered in a celebration of people whom his predecessors had considered 'unliterary' if not illiterate."

21 VAN DOREN, CARL and MARK VAN DOREN. American and British Literature Since 1890. Revised edition. New York: Appleton-Century Co., pp. 98-100.
Most of Anderson's writings deal with the hero who rebels against conformity and then does not know how to use his freedom to have happiness. Anderson is mystified by life and writes wistfully of bewilderment, whereas Lewis satirizes the cramped lives he dislikes. Anderson would have converted American work toward artistic and psychological fulfillment.

1940

1940 A BOOKS - NONE

1940 B SHORTER WRITINGS

1 ANON. Review of Home Town. Rockland Courier-Gazette [ME] (17 September).
Anderson's text in Home Town results from his years of exploring America's thousands of villages.

2 ANON. Review of Home Town. Buffalo Courier-Express (27 October).
Winesburg, Ohio made Anderson "the best writer in America on life in the small town." Home Town is the author's best book.

3 ANON. Review of Home Town. Cleveland Plain Dealer (27 October).
Home Town is "a vivid story of the small town--not an inquiry, not a study, but rather a memory, though the scenes are all contemporary."

4 ANON. Review of Home Town. Greensboro News (27 October).
Home Town proves Anderson's lasting affection for small-town life.

5 ANON. "Mellowed Mystery." Time, 36 (28 October), 60-61.
In Home Town Anderson is still fascinated with small-town America, but here "the musings are less those of a rebel paint manufacturer, fed up with it all, than those of a small-town editor, himself jest folks."

6 ANON. "Home Town." New Yorker, 16 (2 November), 87.
Home Town is a "Nostalgic text-and-picture book that catches the tone of American small-town life from Vermont to Alabama."

7 ANON. Review of Home Town. Toledo Blade (2 November).
Home Town is "a nostalgic, amiable, informative treatise on American small town life, coupled with more than 150 magnificent photographs dealing with the same subject."

8 ANON. "Anderson At 64 Scoffs At Fame; Finds It A Joke." Akron Beacon-Journal (3 November).
Now broke and lecturing, Anderson has revealed in Home Town a new tolerance and wisdom alien to him earlier.

9 ANON. "Sherwood Anderson and FSA Together Picture Small Town." Dallas News (3 November).

Simply having written Winesburg, Ohio would qualify Anderson to write the text for Home Town to accompany the Farm Security Administration photographs.

10 ANON. "Safety Valves of America." New York News (3 November).
Only in surface appearance have small towns changed, Anderson says in Home Town.

11 ANON. "'Home Town' Latest Book By Anderson." San Francisco News (9 November).
Anderson writes Home Town in "a lean pungent style."

12 ANON. Review of Home Town. Charlotte News (10 November).
Without too much nostalgia or over-eulogizing of his subject, Anderson writes faithfully of his topic in Home Town.

13 ANON. "Anderson Apotheosizes the Small Town." Hartford Courant (10 November).
Perhaps small-town life is not so unpleasant as Anderson shows in Home Town--all the while thinking he presents an attractive description.

14 ANON. "Stringfellow Barr and John Crowe Ransom Will Debate Merits of Agrarianism Versus Industrialism in South at City Auditorium." Richmond Times-Dispatch (14 November), pp. 1, 3.
Anderson, "the distinguished author and editor," will introduce the two debators.

15 ANON. Review of Home Town. New Orleans Times-Picayune (17 November).
Anderson's "characteristic wit" in Home Town is outdone by the photographs.

16 ANON. "Bookshelf." Atlantic Monthly, 166 (December), n.p.
In Home Town Anderson's mellow prose combines with the Farm Security photographs to produce a book worth keeping or bestowing.

17 ANON. "Photographic Review of the Week." Advertising Age (9 December), p. 31.
Anderson told copywriters about writing his first story on company time in Chicago's Critchfield & Company.

18 ANON. "Mansfield's Enterprise." Ft. Worth Star Telegram (11 December).

1940

(ANON.)
Home Town is written by an "exponent of the small American town who has supported his beliefs by making his home in a Virginia village. . . ."

19 ANON. Review of Home Town. Philadelphia Record (15 December).
Nostalgic friends would appreciate Home Town for Christmas--"Sherwood Anderson's folksy, photographic gem."

20 ARCHER, WARD. "Small Towns Shown Here." Memphis Commercial Appeal (3 November).
Home Town is by an author less thoughtful about small-town life than in Winesburg, Ohio.

21 BABBITT, IRVING. The Spanish Character and Other Essays. Edited by Frederick Manchester, Rachael Giese, and William F. Giese. Boston: Houghton Mifflin Co., p. 218.
Mechanization is now being considered a dehumanizing force in the nation: "Even a Sherwood Anderson has enough wit to perceive that all is not well with the present standardized America."

22 BERTI, LUIGI. "Ulissismo di Sherwood Andersón." Boccaporto. Florence: Parenti, pp. 133-39.
A "primitive" author in technique, Anderson is lyrical and poetic, a quality perhaps derived from Chekhov. He heightens reality by including psychology to show his characters' desire for joy in life, the author seeing his people clearly and maturely and openly. Winesburg, Ohio concerns the townspeople who are hungry for life.

23 BOYNTON, PERCY H. "Sherwood Anderson." America in Contemporary Fiction. Chicago: University of Chicago Press, pp. 113-30.
Reprint of 1927.B25.

24 BREYER, F. A. "Sherwood Anderson Does Text For Small-Town Reflector." Cincinnati Enquirer (9 November).
Anderson's Home Town is a mirror of village life.

25 CORT, JOHN C. "Contemporary Social Problems." Commonweal, 33 (20 December), 233.
With knowledge of the importance of little things, Anderson has given in Home Town "a really beautiful book of pictures and essays on the American small town and the very interesting people who live there."

26 CRANDELL, RICHARD F. "Cheerful Chekhov of America's Whistle Stops." New York Herald Tribune Books (27 October), p. 5.
Now less the reformer or liberator, Anderson in Home Town documents the American villager's life and charm--and distrust of the outside world.

27 [DISRAELI, ROBERT]. "S. R. L. Photographer at P. E. N. Dinner." Saturday Review of Literature, 21 (6 April), 19.
Anderson sat with Margaret Widdemer and told of the mason initialing the mantel stonework of Anderson's country home.

28 DUFFUS, R. L. "The Small Towns of America." New York Times Book Review (27 October), pp. 1, 30.
Home Town is Anderson's memories of "Winesburg" but here his attitude is loving and genial.

29 GANNETT, LEWIS. "Books and Things." New York Herald Tribune (23 October), p. 27.
Knowing and loving the American small town, Anderson in Home Town creates a nostalgic panorama.

30 GETZ, ELEANOR. "The Heart of America." San Francisco Chronicle (1 December).
Home Town will appeal to urbanites foreign to small towns and to villagers nostalgic over their past.

31 GRAHAME, ROBERTA MARGARET. "A Study of the Cross-Section Novel Written in English Since 1915." Dissertation, University of Minnesota, pp. 35, 36, 37, 96, 104, 127.
Winesburg, Ohio may be a novel or a collection of short stories unified by "the iron repression of the small town" but damaged by Anderson's wilful confusion of past and present.

32 HANSEN, HARRY. "The First Reader." New York World-Telegram (26 October), p. 15.
Interest in small-town life--spurred by the Depression--continues to grow. In Home Town Anderson gives an "excellent summation of the changing face of rural America."

33 KELLOGG, FLORENCE LOEB. "Back Home." Survey Graphic, 29 (December), 635, 637.
Home Town "ought to be bound in red plush and have a large gilt clasp. For here is truly the family album of the American small town."

1940

34 KIHSS, PETER. "Sherwood Anderson Fooled in One of His Protests." New York World-Telegram (22 May).

Reacting in the early 1930's to poverty, Anderson joined several liberal causes that he might now regret; one petition in French he innocently signed to aid the League Against War and Fascism. Anderson backs the Allies now in the World War.

35 LENROW, ELBERT. Reader's Guide to Prose Fiction. New York: D. Appleton-Century Co., pp. 75, 96, 110, 122, 188, 195, 224, 225, 237, 245, 284, 299.

Dark Laughter is told by "indirect narration"; Tar reveals "the psychology and sociology of childhood"; Kit Brandon tries "to suggest possible solutions to perplexities that beset young people of today"; Winesburg, Ohio is "preoccupied with primitive instinct" yet poetically truthful; and Poor White chronicles effects of industrialization.

36 M., M. "Country and City Life Mingled." Los Angeles Times (1 December).

Home Town will help Americans realize that their national wealth comes from small towns.

37 _____. "Pleasant Photos[,] Innocuous Text in 'Home Town.'" Hartford Times (2 November).

Home Town "has little to offer except a lot of pictures and serenely innocuous text."

38 MACE, JED. "Roots of U. S. Democracy." Dallas Times-Herald (3 November).

Writing pastorally in Home Town, Anderson has produced a sane and poignant "escape biography of America's common denominator."

39 MELZER, BEN. "Home Town." San Jose Mercury-Herald (10 November).

Anderson's Home Town describes the background of most great Americans and "why this country is so beloved by its inhabitants and should be fought for desperately."

40 MILLETT, FRED BENJAMIN. Contemporary American Authors: A Critical Survey and 219 Bio-Bibliographies. New York: Harcourt, Brace, pp. 32-33, 46, 95, 221-25.

Anderson goes beyond naturalism by penetrating the surface reality of his characters in order to show their buried passions. He uses few characters, frequent digressions, and the colloquial style heightened by poetic repetition and rhythm. His heroes rebel against their ordinary lives to grope for meaning in freedom. Anderson learned some of his techniques from Stein as he sought non-traditional narrative styles; and Winesburg, Ohio is "one of the most searchingly American creations of its time."

41 MOODY, MINNIE HITE. "'Home Town.'" Atlanta Journal (29 December).

Anderson's wise philosophy of "thinking small" permeates Home Town.

42 ORIANS, G. HARRISON. A Short History of American Literature: Analyzed by Decades. New York: F. S. Crofts, p. 302.

Winesburg, Ohio with its simple style "admirably reflected the bewildered thought of [Anderson's] moody adolescents and frustrated adults." Dark Laughter shows the influence of Freud and Stein.

43 P., R. "Book Takes You Back To Those Grass Roots." New York PM (20 October).

In Home Town Anderson has traced American civilization back to its historic roots.

44 PLAYER, WILLIAM O., JR. "Sherwood Anderson Hopes--and Wonders." New York Post (27 November).

While traveling over America to collect material for Home Town, Anderson learned that F. D. Roosevelt would win the Presidency and perhaps unite Americans. While writing his memoirs, Anderson is learning Spanish before visiting South America.

45 SELBY, JOHN. "'Home Town' Shows Rural American Life." Youngstown Vindicator (3 November).

Anderson's flaw in Home Town is having still no articulated philosophy beyond simple observation of life.

46 T., A. R. Review of Home Town. Albany Knickerbocker News (15 November).

In Home Town Anderson captures the value of small-town life.

47 THOMPSON, RALPH. "Books of the Times." New York Times (22 October), p. 21.

In Home Town Anderson "rambles on about life in American small towns without saying much of anything new or getting anywhere in particular, but he says it amiably and characteristically."

1940

48 VAN DOREN, CARL. The American Novel, 1789-1939. Revised edition. New York: Macmillan Co., pp. 296-98, 303, 324, 340, 341, 379.

In his very first novels Anderson's heroes leave towns for cities but not for contentment; in Winesburg, Ohio Anderson looked at "the buried life" of the village with sympathy, whereas Masters had looked at village life cynically.

1941 A BOOKS - NONE

1941 B SHORTER WRITINGS

*1 [ABRAMOV, A.]. "Smert' Sherwood Andersona." Internatsional'naia Literatura, No. 3, p. 186.

Cited: 1969.B29.

2 A.[NDERSON], R.[OBERT] L.[ANE]. "As His Home Town Knew Him." Smyth County News (13 March), pp. 1, 6.

Anderson's great virtue was his consuming interest in people. When young he sold papers in bars, lived with a doctor, cared for a captain's cow in the 1898 war, and vacationed in the Ozarks because of a breakdown. Some other writers he influenced regretted that influence. Wherever he wandered, Anderson always came back to the Marion village he loved.

3 ANON. "Anderson, Sherwood." Current Biography (1941), pp. 25-26.

Most productive from 1919 to 1926, Anderson was associated with such writers as Lewis, Dreiser, O'Neill, Cather and Mencken. With his best book (Winesburg, Ohio) and his theme ("escape from reality"), he influenced many authors of his time.

4 ANON. "New Non-Fiction." Greenwich Press [CT] (9 January).

Home Town warns the young not to leave their home villages so eagerly.

5 ANON. Review of Home Town. Lansing Journal (19 January).

In Home Town Anderson tries to regain popularity lost because of his "somber and unpleasant" works.

6 ANON. News Item. Jacksonville Times-Union (2 February).

Via South America comes an Italian publisher's request to consider publication of Home Town in Italian.

7 ANON. Comment on Home Town. New York Herald Tribune Books (2 February).
An Italian publisher may bring out Home Town--just what Italian soldiers are thinking of.

8 ANON. "Sherwood Anderson Ill." New York Times (6 March), p. 23.
When removed from a ship today in the Canal Zone, Anderson "appeared to be suffering from an abdominal malady."

9 ANON. "Anderson Has Peritonitis." New York Times (7 March), p. 13.
According to health officials in the Canal Zone, Anderson has developed peritonitis from his intestinal malady.

10 ANON. "Sherwood Anderson, 64, Dies; Author was Former Ohioian." Cincinnati Enquirer (9 March).
Known for writing of Middle West life, Anderson led in the post-War school of realistic writers.

11 ANON. "Off for South America." New York Herald Tribune (9 March).
With Eleanor Anderson, Sherwood Anderson left on the Santa Lucia to visit South America.

12 ANON. "Anderson Dead of Peritonitis." New York Herald Tribune (9 March), p. 34.
When he escaped from business, Anderson took $8.00 and the desire to write from his own life the stories of little people's lives. In gloomy tones Anderson caught the moments of human unawareness.

13 ANON. "Anderson Is Dead; Noted Author, 64." New York Times (9 March), p. 41.
Dead of peritonitis, Anderson was famous for walking out of his Ohio business and into striving for fame in the literary world.

14 ANON. "Sherwood Anderson, Former Elyria Manufacturer[,] Dies." Elyria Chronicle-Telegram [OH] (10 March), pp. 1, 8.
A famous novelist who at one time made paint in Elyria, Anderson "found the call of the literary world more attractive than business." A photographer remembers Anderson and his brother running the paint factory while Sherwood wrote magazine pieces.

1941

15 ANON. "Sherwood Anderson." New York Times (10 March), p. 16.
Never a city man, Anderson loved American village life and returned to it as editor of two small-town weekly papers. At his best in writing short stories, Anderson "understood the American scene, its toil, its sweat, its troubles and its triumphs, as few have done."

16 ANON. "Prophet of the Small Town." Roanoke Times [VA] (11 March).
At his best describing small-town Americans, Anderson "wrote understandingly of the passions and emotions that cause people to act as individuals."

17 ANON. "Sherwood Anderson." Winston-Salem Journal (12 March).
Anderson wrote from the experiences he crowded into an adventurous life. His first preoccupation was the theme of escape, the search for the true America; and he was always more the interpreter than the reformer.

18 ANON. "Two Americans." Person County Times [NC] (13 March).
Anderson and the sculptor Gutzon Borglum have both died. Both loved Americans, both were dreamers, both planned more than they finished. Although Winesburg, Ohio seemed shocking in 1919, Anderson's genius was more "turned to Whitmanque nobility and love of the common man."

19 ANON. "Sherwood Anderson, Noted Author and Native of Camden, Died Saturday." Preble County News [OH] (13 March), p. 1.
Wandering over America gave Anderson his understanding of the common people on whom his stories are based. Few local people could recall Anderson but he visited Camden after becoming famous.

20 ANON. "Industry to Art." Miami Herald [FL] (15 March), A, p. 6.
When Anderson left paint manufacturing, he took up the manufacturing of words, writing from his experience instead of from his imagination.

21 ANON. Obituary. Nation, 152 (15 March), 284.
At his recent death, Anderson had accepted a small Virginia town as his home, long after his early rebellion against the village of his youth and the town of his paint factory.

22 ANON. "Sherwood Anderson." Publishers' Weekly, 139 (15 March), 1212.
In spite of difficulties Anderson was an established writer by 1925; since then, he had lived in Virginia and edited small-town newspapers.

23 ANON. "Small Townsman." New Republic, 104 (17 March), 357.
In Winesburg, Ohio Anderson wrote new material of American small towns in a new style; and his masterpiece affected Caldwell, Faulkner, Steinbeck, and Hemingway.

24 ANON. "To Bury Anderson in Virginia." New York Times (19 March), p. 21.
Anderson's body left the Canal Zone on March 18 for burial in Marion, Virginia.

25 ANON. "Fallece Sherwood Anderson, un Amigo de los Pueblos Hispanos." Diaro de la Marino (23 March).
Always an admirer of Latin Americans, Anderson died on his way to study the poor of an Andean village.

26 ANON. "Sherwood Anderson is Buried in Round Hill." Marion Democrat (1 April).
On March 26, "while nature smiled," Anderson was buried after a service at "Rosemont." His casket was flag-draped, and tributes from Dreiser and Paul Posenfeld were read.

27 ANON. "Dark and Lonely." Time, 37 (7 April), 98.
Anderson had died as a creative artist before he died physically, but his literary achievement was secure; he had seen life as pessimistic and "On that lonely darkness he tried all his life to shed light."

28 ANON. "Explains Writer's Death." New York Times (10 April), p. 15.
An autopsy at Colón Hospital revealed that a wooden cocktail toothpick that Anderson had swallowed penetrated his intestine and caused peritonitis.

29 ANON. Review of Home Town. Vidalia Advance (10 April).
Home Town, Anderson's last book, "reflected his attachment for and understanding of his native America." The book is a kind of up-dated, factual, and illustrated sympathetic Main Street.

30 ANON. "Sherwood Anderson." Deutsche Rundschau, 267 (May), 99-100.
Anderson was a vagabond in life, taking pleasure in all he met. His stories were called formless by critics not understanding his higher idea of form; by example to such authors as Steinbeck, Wolfe, and Faulkner, Anderson changed the short story from reportage to character-study.

1941

31 ANON. Review of The Intent of the Artist. New York Sun (14 May).
Anderson's explanation of imagination in art is part of The Intent of the Artist.

32 ANON. "The Artist Talks It Over." Trenton Times (25 May).
In The Intent of the Artist Anderson calls for artistic integrity amid whatever confusion pervades the world.

33 ANON. "Books and Authors." New York Times (31 August), p. 10.
Story for September-October is to be a tribute to Anderson's achievement.

34 ANON. "Sherwood Anderson." Dallas News (7 September).
The Anderson memorial issue of Story will become a collector's item and is indispensable to short story enthusiasts.

35 BATES, H. E. The Modern Short Story: A Critical Survey. Boston: Writer, pp. 18, 23-24, 27, 34, 35, 52, 71, 90, 133-34, 161-62, 163-67, 178.
Anderson's stories, of much compressed detail, are earth-bound as were those of Gogol. Winesburg, Ohio is as important to short-story development as The Sportsman's Sketches. Between the stories of Stephen Crane and Anderson is only the desert of O'Henry and his imitators. Part of Anderson's contribution was to insist on the realism of description of his Middle West, however depressing and drab it might appear. He observes hitherto untold lives with buried secrets of frustration and bewilderment: "Winesburg, Ohio is the first directional signpost of the contemporary American short story. . . ."

36 BEISWANGER, GEORGE. "Artists' Symposium." Theatre Arts, 15 (July), 553-54.
Perhaps Anderson has lost control of imagination when he ill defines creativity in The Intent of the Artist.

37 BENNETT, WHITMAN. A Practical Guide to American Book Collecting (1663-1940). New York: Bennett Book Studios, pp. 216-17.
Having thought only New England authors could create small-town tragedy, shocked readers reacted negatively to Winesburg, Ohio in 1919. [Bibliographical description of first printing of Winesburg, Ohio]

38 BERCOVICI, KONRAD. It's the Gypsy in Me: The Autobiography of Konrad Bercovici. New York: Prentice-Hall Co., pp. 176, 204-205.
In Spain Bercovici met Perez D'Ayala, who liked Anderson's short stories; and in Passy, he met Anderson at a party given by some Peruvian poet. Anderson there sat on the floor.

39 BIRNEY, EARLE. "Sherwood Anderson: A Memory." Canadian Forum, 21 (June), 82-83.
When Anderson lectured around 1931 in Salt Lake City, Birney and other young men "abducted" the writer from his fashionable hosts in order to talk and drink intimately with him.

40 BLAND, WINIFRED. "Through a College Window." Story, 19 (September-October), 82-86.
[Written in 1933 at the publication of Death in the Woods, this publication in memory of Anderson praises him for stories of joyful plotlessness and honesty.] Reprinted: 1970.A1.

41 Both Barrels. "Sherwood Anderson, Our Friend and Neighbor." Smyth County News (13 March), p. 2.
People who knew Anderson personally saw him as warm friend more than famous author.

42 BOYD, JAMES. "A Man in Town." Story, 19 (September-October), 88-91.
Being a small-town man, Anderson fitted into Boyd's home town of Southern Pines, N. C. Anderson accepted all sides of human nature, for this author knew his own integrity. Reprinted: 1970.A1.

43 BROOKS, VAN WYCK. The Opinions of Oliver Allston. New York: E. P. Dutton & Co., pp. 120, 278.
Concerning Thomas Wolfe, the hero notes that in family life in Anderson's works the father is weak; the mother "strong and even heroic." Anderson's genius was the ability to be surprised by new things.

44 BUCHLER, JUSTUS. "A Symposium on the Intent of the Creative Artist." New York Times Book Review (28 October), p. 27.
Anderson likes to let imagination play over private small worlds, and his philosophy of creative art thus becomes diffuse and unfocussed in The Intent of the Artist.

1941

45 BURNETT, WHIT, MARTHA FOLEY, and KURT M. SEMON. "To Sherwood Anderson." Story, 19 (September-October), 1.

The September-October issue of Story is the first issue dedicated to and written about one person--"the greatest contemporary short story writer."

46 C.[ANBY], H.[ENRY] S.[EIDEL]. "Home Town." Saturday Review of Literature, 23 (11 January), 21.

Home Town is presented as a townsman would see the American small town and is thus beautifully unpretentious.

47 _____. "Sherwood Anderson." Saturday Review of Literature, 23 (22 October), 10.

Being self-educated--"trained by experience"--Anderson cared more for life than for literature; and he won modest achievement and some contentment, becoming a writer, a memoirist, a journalist, and finally an editor.

48 CARGILL, OSCAR. Intellectual America: Ideas on the March. New York: Macmillan Co., pp. 322-31, 335, 351, 352, 358, 370, 372, 387, 388, 393, 397, 591, 674, 676-85, 763.

Anderson was one of the first writers to understand Stein's purposes in her experiments; but his first novel, Windy McPherson's Son, is less primitivism than "sentimental naturalism," as is Marching Men. Three Lives inspired Winesburg, Ohio in both crafted simplicity and theme of the ways of love surrounded by frustration. Poor White fails through overemphasis on the technical problems of sex, whereas The Triumph of the Egg, Horses and Men and Many Marriages incorporate "psychoanalysis and a modified primitivism." Dark Laughter deliberately attempts primitivitism but fails, and Tar needs subtlety along with simplicity. Although Death in the Woods is primitivistic, Kit Brandon imitates Fitzgerald. Anderson's failures result from pretense to less intelligence than he possessed.

49 CARR, LEW. "The Little Tin Box." Columbus Journal-Herald Spotlight [OH] (21 December).

Known as "the modern Walt Whitman" and as the "Poet of the Buckeye Country," Anderson influenced Lewis and wrote many things including Whitman-like poetry.

50 COAN, OTIS W. and RICHARD G. LILLARD. America in Fiction: An Annotated List of Novels that Interpret Aspects of Life in the United States. Stanford: Stanford University Press, pp. 30, 56, 65, 74, 111.

Winesburg, Ohio is an attack on "the hypocrisies and the pharisaic code of villagers"; The Triumph of the Egg imitates Spoon River Anthology to show "the ugliness, emptiness, and misery of some futile lives of people with repressed emotions, petty desires, and thwarted instincts"; Marching Men is "sentimental"; Kit Brandon is "poorly written"; Windy McPherson's Son concerns "the utter futility of America's present ideals."

51 DREISER, THEODORE. "Sherwood Anderson." Clipper, 2 (May), 5.
Anderson wandered all his days in quest of all of life, a quest to which he brought unlimited acceptance and tenderness. Reprinted: 1941.B52; 1970.A1.

52 _____. "Sherwood Anderson." Story, 19 (September-October), 4.
Reprint of 1941.B51.

53 EIKENBERRY, E. C. "Sherwood Anderson." Preble County News [OH] (13 March), pp. 1, 4.
After he had in Tar created an ideal Camden, Ohio, Anderson finally visited his real birthplace.

54 FRANK, WALDO. "Winesburg, Ohio After Twenty Years." Story, 19 (September-October), 29-33.
The classic Winesburg, Ohio has form: character-mood leads to actions on the background of the town. The form is lyrical; the subject is the decay of traditions and search for new expression. Reprinted: 1966.A3; 1966.A7; 1970.A1.

55 FRIEND, JULIUS W. "The Philosophy of Sherwood Anderson." Story, 19 (September-October), 37-41.
Anderson's thought was more intuitive than logical, more mystical than rational. His concern was meaning in human relationships--an "acceptance of all that was affirmative. . . ." Reprinted: 1970.A1.

56 _____. "Sherwood Anderson: An Appreciation." New Orleans Times-Picayune (16 March), p. 11.
Anderson did not sink to writing mere psychoanalysis in the 1920's nor economics in the 1930's. Always favoring intuition over reason, Anderson liked Whitman but did not invent the proletarian novel. His writings convey best of all the adventure of human life.

57 FRYE, DOROTHY. "New Books." Lynn Item [MA] (15 March).
The former paint manufacturer who became a writer will become again alive as his books are read.

1941

58 GALANTIÈRE, LEWIS. "French Reminiscence." Story, 19 (September-October), 64-67.
Anderson fitted easily into Paris in 1921 because he was like that city's poor people, he was gloomy, and he loved life. Proud of being an artist, Anderson represented the best qualities of Americans. Reprinted: 1970.A1.

59 GOLD, MICHAEL. The Hollow Men. New York: International Publishers, pp. 21, 69-72, 77, 78, 79.
The World War killed the blossoming democracy in the works of such writers as Anderson. Winesburg, Ohio, still Anderson's most accomplished work, is "a social portrait of the American petty-bourgeois and his family" always crushed by monopolists. However, when Anderson is successful he writes with a neo-Fascist tone full of hatred of workers. Then, in the 1930's Anderson tried to be a proletarian writer and failed.

60 GOLDSTEIN, ALBERT. Obituary. New Orleans Times-Picayune (16 March).
When Anderson's home was New Orleans, he used to sit after work on his Vieux Carré balcony or walk to meet people and listen to people who knew how to play.

61 HANSEN, HARRY. "Anderson in Chicago." Story, 19 (September-October), 34-36.
Being part of the Chicago Renaissance was stimulating to Anderson, but he already had his materials and purpose firmly in mind when he arrived. The writer hungered to know the secret lives of common people, and his fiction shows this desire and life-like formlessness. Reprinted: 1970.A1.

62 _____. "The First Reader." New York World-Telegram (11 March).
Hansen was the first to write Anderson's life in a book, for Anderson was of contemporary American writers the most concerned with craft. Like Whitman, Anderson wrote subjectively of his society and his creatures. The best of Anderson's stories will survive any competition.

*63 HARNACK-FISH, MILDRED. "Die Entwicklung der Amerikanischen Literatur der Gegenwart in Einigen Vertretern des Romans und der Kurzgeschichte." Dissertation, University of Giessen.
Cited: 1960.B24.

64 HARTLEY, MARSDEN. "Spring, 1941." Story, 19 (September-October), 97-98.

Lamenting the death of Anderson from swallowing a toothpick, Hartley bids the author "so long" instead of "good-bye" and appends a poetic "Postscript." Reprinted: 1970.A1.

65 HECHT, BEN. "Go Scholar--Gypsy!" Story, 19 (September-October), 92-93.

Anderson was the leader of writers in the Chicago Renaissance, reading his ungrammatical manuscripts aloud and seducing women and searching for something lost in his own and other men's lives. Reprinted: 1970.A1.

66 KIRCHWEY, FREDA. "Sherwood Anderson." Nation, 152 (22 March), 313-14.

Anderson became ill at sea, suffered violent pain, remained cheerful, and probably knew he was dying as he left the ship in Panama.

67 KOMROFF, MANUEL. "Procession in the Rain." Story, 19 (September-October), 94-95.

People walked and carried Anderson's coffin in the rain--this man who fathered characters and knew all people before they were born. Anderson gave liberation to American literature. Reprinted: 1970.A1.

68 KOUWENHOVEN, JOHN A. The Arts in Modern American Civilization. Introduction by Mark Van Doren. New York: W. W. Norton Co., pp. 201-202.

Being alone among crowds of unthinking creative people, Anderson wondered in Perhaps Women whether new values would replace old destroyed values.

69 L., S. L. "Artists Let Down Their Hair." Nashville Tennessean (22 June).

Presenting Anderson's discussion of fiction-writing, The Intent of the Artist tries to differentiate "what is honest effort and what is outright rascality."

70 LEWIS, GORDON. "Sherwood Anderson, Greatest of Storytellers, Was Writer's Writer." Durham Herald-Sun [NC] (30 March), 2, pp. 3, 5.

A friend since 1922, Anderson helped rid America of the sterility in its literature. Leaving his business and $6,000 annual income, Anderson went to Chicago to become an author and became "probably the best American storyteller we've had."

1941

71 LOVETT, ROBERT MORSS. "Sherwood Anderson, American." Virginia Quarterly Review, 17 (Summer), 379-88.

When Anderson began writing, realism was being modified by symbolism; and Winesburg, Ohio demonstrated his ability to get at poetic truth beneath surface reality. Anderson was full of Midwestern acceptance of life and found inspiration in life's plenitude. Reprinted: 1951.B25.

72 LUCCOCK, HALFORD E. American Mirror: Social, Ethical and Religious Aspects of American Literature, 1930-1940. New York: Macmillan Co., pp. 7, 41.

E. W. Howe foreshadowed Anderson "in discovering and revealing the devilishness of the small town and country." The social upheaval of the 1930's made Anderson's work dated.

73 LYONS, EUGENE. The Red Decade: The Stalinist Penetration of America. Indianapolis: Bobbs-Merrill Co., pp. 129, 144.

Anderson was one of the talented writers who fell for Stalinist propaganda, taking his principles from The New Masses.

74 MacDOUGALL, KENNETH. "Rooted." Boston Transcript (4 January), p. 2.

In Home Town Anderson advises young people to stay in small-town America, a scene that he sketches ably.

75 MALLEA, EDUARDO. El Sayal y la Púrpura. Buenos Aires: Editorial Losada, p. 198.

An important representative soul from the United States has died in Panama. Sherwood Anderson's most typical works were Winesburg, Ohio and Dark Laughter. He wrote inconclusively about life in the colloquial style descended from Twain.

76 MATHER, FRANK JEWETT, JR. "Anderson and the Institute." Saturday Review of Literature, 23 (5 April), 11.

The author and Stuart Sherman and Paul Elmer More nominated Anderson for his 1937 membership in the National Institute of Arts and Letters.

77 MEJÍA NÍETO, ARTURO. "El Realismo Poetico de Sherwood Anderson." La Nacion (6 April), p. 2.

Anderson's poetic realism derives from his experiences, his love of the psychological, American values, and his understanding of common people.

78 MILLER, HENRY. "Anderson the Storyteller." Story, 19 (September-October), 70-74.

Scarcely knowing Anderson personally, Miller liked this writer who admitted taking his stories from the lives of common people; and Anderson's stories are great for being causally yet beautifully told us around a drinking-table. Reprinted: 1962.B26; 1970.A1.

79 _____. The Colossus of Maroussi. Norfolk, Ct.: New Directions, pp. 34-35.

Always fond of Many Marriages, Miller tried to encourage Europeans to know Anderson's works. Anderson was "the one American writer of our times who has walked the streets of our American cities as a genuine poet."

80 MOSELY, SETH. "Author Anderson Offers Six-Point Program." Richmond Times-Dispatch (23 February).

Planning to visit a small Chilean town to gather materials for fiction, Anderson suggests six practical ways the novice can become an author.

81 MULDER, ARNOLD. "Mulder Sums Up Anderson." Green Bay Press-Gazette (22 March).

"Puzzled" should always have been a complimentary adjective for Anderson, for his interest in humanity and his distrust of final answers were admirable.

82 _____. "Puzzled Mr. Anderson." Ann Arbor News (2 April).

When Anderson called himself "puzzled," he referred to the complexity of life; but he was fascinated always by the motivation of behavior.

83 NUHN, FERNER. "Auction Day in Missouri." Story, 19 (September-October), 96.

The author walked among country people at an auction in Missouri and considered them Anderson's people. Reprinted: 1970.A1.

84 OLIVER, MARÍA ROSA. "Sherwood Anderson." Sur, No. 78 (March), 80-82.

In Winesburg, Ohio Anderson wrote the first book of the new school of daring and cynical works after the World War. Anderson saw little beauty in the Midwestern life he knew and analyzed. His characters endure the anguish of solitude.

85 PANHUIJSEN, JOS. "Sherwood Anderson." Boekenschouw, 35 (15 May), 14-19.

1941

(PANHUIJSEN, JOS.)

Only Poor White has been translated into Dutch; but Europeans know of Anderson as an American realist who wrote of the modernization of Midwestern America. Dark Laughter weakens Anderson's vision into almost obscurity and no ending. Not a traditional novelist, Anderson transmutes his own experiences into fiction; and he shows the usual American fascination with sex. His best stories reflect the emptiness of life, but his Notebook will outlast all of his fiction.

86 PATCHEN, KENNETH. "We're All Fools (for Sherwood Anderson)." Story, 19 (September-October), 87.

"O men of little faith, salute one whose life was a flame; / May the gentle flowers of heaven fall on his upturned face." Reprinted: 1970.A1.

87 RASPAILLAIRE, JEANNE. "The Use of the Oral Idiom in the Modern American Novel." Master's thesis, Ohio State University, 105 pp.

Anderson does not use literary language but writes colloquially as though he were in a friendly conversation. When Anderson learned to imitate Joyce, he tried to reproduce the blurred consciousness of characters.

88 ROSENFELD, PAUL. "The Man of Good Will." Story, 19 (September-October), 5-10.

From first meeting Anderson in 1917, Rosenfeld felt power and acuity in the "peasant-like and highly civilized being"--power soon displayed in Winesburg, Ohio. Above all full of benevolence, Anderson embraced life wholly and passionately. Reprinted: 1970.A1.

89 ROSKOLENKO, HARRY. "Hello Towns." Story, 19 (September-October), 36.

"The world weeps itself in the chain of the mist; / it lowers a curtain, a faltering fountain. . . ." Reprinted: 1970.A1.

90 RUKEYSER, MURIEL. "Sherwood Anderson." Decision, 4 (April), 12-13.

Anderson cared for people more than plot in his stories, his works being records of sudden communications, sudden touches by life. Anderson's writings are never cynical or pompous; they are "candid and general, very clear."

91 S., ALEX. "Home Town Photographs." Fort Worth Telegram (12 January).

In Home Town Anderson tells the small-town story "simply and compactly."

92 SAROYAN, WILLIAM. "His Collaborators." Story, 19 (September-October), 75-76.
Anderson's story (and stories) is lonely, spare, full of the wonder of life. His death (and much of his writing) was undramatic, but his death leaves grief to his silent collaborators at fiction (and life). Reprinted: 1970.A1.

93 SILLEN, SAMUEL. "Sherwood Anderson." New Masses, 39 (25 March), 23-26.
However optimistic Anderson may have become, he never ceased struggling to understand modern problems. Most of Anderson's ideas and works refer to his life before his escape from business into creativity. Thus his critique of recent life was by an out-dated, pre-monopolistic optimist. His ultimate failure was to separate workers and artists as categories of humanity.

94 STEIN, GERTRUDE. "Sherwood's Sweetness." Story, 19 (September-October), 63.
In New Orleans Anderson brought Stein fresh sweet oranges, and Stein remembers Anderson as sweet. Reprinted: Sherwood Anderson / Gertrude Stein: Correspondence and Personal Essays. Edited by Ray Lewis White. Chapel Hill: University of North Carolina Press, 1972, pp. 114-15; 1970.A1.

95 SUSMAN, MILTON K. "As I See It." Jewish Times (21 March).
Anderson's death is mourned by "all lovers of the stout word," for his books combined hard rhetoric and rich, colorful imagination.

96 TAKAGAKI, MATSUO. "Sherwood Anderson." Comments on American Literature. Tokyo: Kenkyusha, pp. 330-47.
Reprint of 1934.B38.

97 TRILLING, LIONEL. "Sherwood Anderson." Kenyon Review, 3 (Summer), 293-302.
Anderson emphasized so much his dramatic escape from business into art that he never adapted to newer themes, preferring to think that his legend would protect him. He appeals to readers at his own level--adolescent emotionalism--but America has grown beyond Anderson's own limited but valuable development. Reprinted revised: 1950.B16.

1941

98 WEBSTER, DAN. "Anderson's Camden." Dayton Daily (15 March), M, p. 15.
A Camden, Ohio, banker recalled Anderson's father as "a genial, hard-working provider for his rather numerous brood." Other people in Camden recalled the father's cornet-playing and church-school teaching.

99 WHITE, WILLIAM ALLEN. "Home Town." Book-of-the-Month Club News (January).
Home Town is "one of the most perfect pictures of American country town life that has ever been made."

100 WINCHELL, WALTER. "Walter Winchell on Broadway." Columbus Enquirer [GA] (1 April).
"People were drawn to Sherwood Anderson as to an open fire. . . ."

101 WOLFE, THOMAS. "A Letter from Thomas Wolfe." Story, 19 (September-October), 68-69.
On September 22, 1937, Wolfe wrote Anderson to express his need to complete any writing simply to have lived (or relived) through the experience of intense creativity. Only by enriching life has Anderson influenced Wolfe, for Anderson too saw the nation as a poet should. Reprinted: 1970.A1.

102 YOUNT, DAVID LEROY. "Portraits in Verse: Sherwood Anderson." Greensburg Morning Review [PA] (17 March).
"Sherwood Anderson the writer / Died today at sixty-four / So a torch which made earth brighter / Shines upon another shore."

103 Z., A. J. "Passing Parade." Springfield News [MA] (14 March).
Although Anderson wrote of an America long past, he never despaired of present life.

1942 A BOOKS

1 KINTNER, EVELYN. "Sherwood Anderson: Small Town Man, A Study of the Growth, Revolt, and Reconciliation of a Small Town Man." Master's thesis, Bowling Green State University, 161 pp.
In his early work, Anderson presented the small town as a place that warps its citizens into grotesques; even after his later reconciliation, Anderson did not reflect blind love for Midwestern towns. The one small-town virtue supreme in this author is his absorbing, consuming interest

in other people's lives. Thus Anderson has more tales than he could tell, and his plotless stories may result from too much material. Anderson's books until 1926 are autobiographical recastings of his own youth in Ohio towns; after 1926 Anderson used his life in Virginia small towns to reflect upon urban problems. At the end of his life, Anderson knew that not small towns but some human forces were his early antagonists in small-town life.

1942 B SHORTER WRITINGS

1 ADAMS, EUGENE T. *et al*. *The American Idea*. New York: Harper & Brothers, p. 170.
Whereas Stephen Crane handles convincingly the naturalistic forces in *The Red Badge of Courage*, Anderson produces questionable work when using these same forces.

2 ANON. News Item. *Sidney Record* [NY] (28 March).
In Mexico, Anderson says in his *Memoirs*, he was flatteringly introduced by someone who had forgotten all of Anderson's books' titles.

3 ANON. "Sherwood Anderson's Memoirs." *Bulletin of Virginia Kirkus' Bookshop Service* (1 April).
The "honest attempt to write his last testament," Anderson's *Memoirs* are "sordid and earthy and primitive."

4 ANON. "New Book Appraisals." *Library Journal*, 67 (1 April), 320.
Anderson's *Memoirs* is a "Direct personal statement of his life and his understanding of his country."

5 ANON. "General." *New Yorker*, 18 (11 April), 87.
Sherwood Anderson's Memoirs "contains little that is not to be found in his other books, except a few rather pointless literary reminiscences and some odd, vague stories of his early sexual life."

6 ANON. "Personal History." *Pittsburgh Post Gazette* (11 April).
The prose in the *Memoirs* confirms the author's "almost legendary reputation."

7 ANON. "Sherwood Anderson Limns Self-Portrait." *Springfield News* [OH] (12 April).
The reader can learn about Anderson most easily from *Windy McPherson's Son*, his first novel, and the *Memoirs*, his last book.

1942

8 ANON. "Sherwood Anderson's Life." Springfield Republican (12 April), E., p. 7.
The Memoirs are "a magnificent case-history of a literary master in the making."

9 ANON. "Sherwood Anderson Leaves His Memoirs." NEA Service (14 April).
Anderson presents in his Memoirs a surprising view of the writers who helped destroy the Victorian hold on American literature by writing of life as they knew it. This author's main interest was the forgotten "little people" of the earth.

10 ANON. Review of Sherwood Anderson's Memoirs. Hempstead Newsday (17 April).
The Memoirs is the "Revealing, absorbing autobiography of a literary pioneer."

11 ANON. "Today's Books." St. Louis Globe-Democrat (18 April).
The "Terrence of yesterday," Anderson in his Memoirs is penetrating and inarticulate and human. Anderson groped toward exactitude in his style and became a Midwest voice against Eastern sterility.

12 ANON. "The Memoirs of Ohio's Anderson." Akron Beacon-Journal (19 April).
The Memoirs add little now to knowledge of the author. The discussions of the interesting unknown little people shine as well as stories of the literati of Chicago and New York.

13 ANON. Review of Sherwood Anderson's Memoirs. Buffalo Courier-Express (19 April).
Being his own Boswell, Anderson in his Memoirs proves that at one time he wrote well and lived independently.

14 ANON. "Check and Double Check." Chelsea Evening Record [MA] (20 April).
The Memoirs contains Anderson's great story of being the great author of some forgotten work.

15 ANON. Review of Sherwood Anderson's Memoirs. Cincinnati Post (20 April).
Sherwood Anderson's Memoirs is best when Anderson describes the contentment he found as his life neared its end.

16 ANON. "Album for a Classic." _Time_, 39 (20 April), 90.
The _Memoirs_ "contains some of the gentlest, most beautiful writing about American living that has ever been done."

17 ANON. Review of _Sherwood Anderson's Memoirs_. _Easton Express_ [PA] (23 April).
The unconventionally written _Memoirs_ is a view into Anderson's consciousness.

18 ANON. Review of Sherwood Anderson's _Memoirs_. _Promenade_ (May).
The _Memoirs_ show the high yearning of Anderson for unity with nature and people.

19 ANON. Review of _Sherwood Anderson's Memoirs_. _Virginia Spectator_ (May), p. 24.
The _Memoirs_ show Anderson's main concern to have been "to delve deeply into the innermost depths of the great ticking machine that is the heart of America."

20 ANON. "Biography." _Wisconsin Library Bulletin_, 38 (May), 84.
Of interest to devotees of recent literary history, Anderson's _Memoirs_ retell his life story in the style of his fiction.

21 ANON. "Biography." _Booklist_, 38 (1 May), 329.
Anderson's last book, his _Memoirs_, is "an impressionistic record of a literary career rather than a formal biography."

22 ANON. Review of _Sherwood Anderson's Memoirs_. _Atlanta Constitution_ (3 May).
Sherwood Anderson's Memoirs confirms the suspicion raised by Anderson's other works--that he never grew beyond emotional boyhood.

23 ANON. "Father of American Realism As Revealed in His Memoirs." _Daily Oklahoman_ (17 May), C., p. 10.
Containing perhaps ten dates, Anderson's _Memoirs_ concern the author's growth as a human and writer. Frank, mystical, and realistic, the _Memoirs_ supplement Anderson's autobiographical novels.

24 ANON. "Notes on Current Books." _Virginia Quarterly Review_, 18 (Summer), liv.
In his _Memoirs_ Anderson retells his life in poetic, humorous, and unsentimental terms.

1942

25 ANON. "Selected Non-Fiction." Glamour (June).
Whenever Anderson calls himself a minor writer, each page of his Memoirs belies that appellation.

26 ANON. "Sherwood Anderson's Memoirs." English Journal, 31 (June), 518-19.
The Memoirs is "an excellent study of a man who drank deeply of life and earnestly tried to share his convictions with others."

27 ANON. "Household Suggests Reading." Household Magazine (June), p. 31.
Sherwood Anderson's Memoirs is "the best autobiography that has appeared in years."

28 ANON. "So Long, Sherwood Anderson." Kapustan (June), pp. 26-27.
All people could learn to live fully from reading these Memoirs.

29 ANON. "The Writer's Library." Writer (June), p. 181.
Study of Anderson's Memoirs can be useful to aspiring authors, for this writer "was naturally and instinctively an artist."

30 ANON. "Sherwood Anderson's Memoirs." Scholastic (July).
Anderson's Memoirs should be read by every college student who aspires to write.

31 ANON. "Art." Pratt Institute Quarterly (December), p. 4.
Augusto Centeno provides in The Intent of the Artist a long introduction to essays on creativity by Anderson, Wilder, Sessions, and Lescaze.

32 ANON. "Biography." Pratt Institute Quarterly (December), p. 5.
Sherwood Anderson's Memoirs is the "Intimate life story of a great literary artist."

33 APPLEBY, JOHN T. "Anderson: The Lonely Narcissus." Washington Post (19 April).
These Memoirs confirm that Anderson was too self-centered to distance himself from his characters--hence, also, the writer's vast loneliness. Anderson never liked being an adult and thus wrote much of his childhood with its appealing irresponsibility.

34 BARKER, RUSSELL H. "The Storyteller Role." College English, 3 (February), 433-42.

His novels generally considered failures, Anderson always assumed the role of storyteller, the pose of the intimate oral raconteur. Perhaps his yoking of this role to psychological subjects explains his frequent artistic failures, for sequential plots, assumed naiveté, and authorial intrusions mix badly. Finally, in the single theme of frustration and technique of inarticulation lies Anderson's limit of range.

35 BATES, GLADYS GRAHAM. "Sherwood Anderson's Memoirs." *Book-of-the-Month Club News* (May), p. 11.

The *Memoirs* are Anderson's stories of experiencing life, struggling to express conclusions, and returning for new experiences; and this book belongs "with other great personal impressions of individuals who have considered questioning more important than glib answering."

36 BERMAN, HERSCHEL. "Sherwood Anderson Has Left Another Literary Landmark." *Memphis Commercial Appeal* (26 April).

His *Memoirs* reveal Anderson as time-bound in subject and style, having contributed little to literature.

37 BIRCHFIELD, JAMES. "Anderson's Memoirs." *Richmond Times-Dispatch* (19 April).

While providing information useful to literary historians, Anderson's *Memoirs* are chiefly about famous and obscure people whom he knew.

38 BRADSHAW, MICHAEL. "Facts of Life Blared in Anderson's Memoirs." *Dayton Journal-Herald* (3 May).

Dreiser, Lewis, and Anderson "had the idea that mud and filth and disease were exclusively mid-western prerogatives"; and, like little boys, they wrote to shock little girls. Anderson's so-called "wisdom"--his *Memoirs* show--came from ignorance of literary traditions; and some of his memories and stories "are as cheap and tawdry, not to say humdrum and ordinary, as the mud and filth and disease out of which they were contrived."

39 BUTCHER, FANNY. "As Author Sees Himself." *Chicago Tribune* (15 April), p. 21.

In his *Memoirs* Anderson gives "a comprehensive set of vital literary statistics if not emotional data."

40 C., E. B. "Posthumous Autobiography." *Durham Herald-Sun* (27 April).

Anderson's *Memoirs* mix fancy and fact and thus reveal little of the artist.

1942

41 CHAMBERLAIN, JOHN. "Books of the Times." New York Times (9 April), p. 17.
Totally nostalgic for a simpler America, Anderson's Memoirs contain very little new matter but retell "a story of shining mists and elusive overtones."

42 CHURCH, ELEANOR B. "Anderson, by Himself." Chattanooga Times (3 May).
The Memoirs tell more of Anderson as a man than as an author.

43 CLOUGH, F. GARDNER. "Books." Orange County Post (8 May), p. 8.
Never a great stylist, his stories plotless, Anderson reveals in his Memoirs his poetic record of living with and observing other people's hearts.

44 DELL, FLOYD. "How Sherwood Anderson Became an Author." New York Herald Tribune Books (12 April), pp. 1-2.
Having helped arrange publication of Anderson's first novel and having known him well, Dell was surprised to learn later that Anderson was not modernly cynical but instead "full of doubts, fears and dark suspicions." Essentially, however, these Memoirs "must be taken as a book of fiction."

45 DERLETH, AUGUST. "The New Books." Madison Capital Times (19 April), p. 15.
An important and impressionistic record of a writer's life, Anderson's Memoirs is also the life record of a leader of Midwestern literature in America.

46 DUFFUS, R. L. "Sherwood Anderson's Last Book Is a Revealing Memoir." New York Times Book Review (12 April), p. 3.
The Memoirs reveal all of Anderson's acknowledged contradictions, but they explain finally the basis and growth of the school of Midwestern realistic writers.

47 E., B. "Bookends And Odds." Macon Telegraph (31 May).
The Memoirs show that Anderson's handicaps gave him the understanding necessary to drive formalism from American literature.

48 FAGIN, BRYLLION. "Sherwood Anderson's Last Story." New Leader (25 July), pp. 3, 7.
In his Memoirs Anderson is a valuably typical common American except in deserting and exposing the flaws in American capitalism--"a social system which drained all

beauty out of the lives of people and made creative expansion for the individual impossible."

*49 FARRELL, JAMES T. "Of Books and Men: An Author's Autobiography." Northwestern University on the Air, 1 (18 April).
Cited: Branch, Edgar. A Bibliography of James T. Farrell's Writings. Philadelphia: University of Pennsylvania Press, 1959, p. 72.

50 _____. "James T. Farrell Writes a Tribute to Sherwood Anderson." Chicago Daily News (1 July), p. 18.
The example of Anderson is of a writer struggling with the problem of identity, and Anderson influenced Farrell through inspiration much more than did Dreiser. When Anderson wrote short stories, he was "unmatched in modern American literature." Reprinted: 1946.B8.

51 F.[EIBLEMAN], J.[AMES] W. "Anderson's Own Story Reveals Rich Personality." New Orleans Times-Picayune (19 April).
Continuing beyond A Story Teller's Story and Tar, Anderson's Memoirs is a rich final book.

52 GANNETT, LEWIS. "Books and Things." New York Herald Tribune (9 April).
Always writing from guilt and against repression, Anderson shows in his Memoirs his love of the lonely, defeated people of the earth.

53 GARLIN, SENDER. "Constant Reader." New York Daily Worker (10 April).
Anderson's Memoirs shows again that the author's rich gift for fabricating autobiography does not negate his excellence as a story writer.

54 GARRISON, MAXINE. "Memoirs Of Author Published." Pittsburgh Press (19 April).
Almost formless and frequently repetitious, Anderson's Memoirs are unique writing by a famous ex-businessman.

55 GEISMAR, MAXWELL. "Babbitt on Pegasus." Yale Review, New Series 32 (Autumn), 183-85.
Having had "the ill luck, as was T. S. Eliot's lot also, to become an ancestor before he became mature," Anderson achieves in his Memoirs answers to charges of puzzlement, confusion, and naiveté.

1942

56 GEISMAR, MAXWELL. Writers in Crisis: The American Novel, 1925-1940. Boston: Houghton Mifflin Co., pp. 148, 249, 282.
In early tributes and in the dedication of Sartoris Faulkner paid homage to Anderson's techniques. As with Steinbeck, Anderson can write "neo-pagan literature" and thus apply his ability "to a tepid use." Sheer revolt in the 1920's--as in some of Anderson's works--can be "as unproductive as the tribal tabus it defied."

57 GEROULD, GORDON HALL. The Patterns of English and American Fiction: A History. Boston: Little, Brown and Co., p. 483.
Winesburg, Ohio, Anderson's stories of town and country life, is indebted to Mark Twain.

58 GISSEN, MAX. "Back to Winesburg." New Republic, 106 (20 April), 548-49.
His growth in artistry stopped in 1925, Anderson never adjusted to twentieth-century life; and his Memoirs distill all of his writings into one book of disappointment.

59 GOHDES, CLARENCE. "Three Books for the Student of America." South Atlantic Quarterly, 41 (July), 335.
Filled with "a super-impressionistic psychological insight," Anderson's Memoirs are "a series of snapshot recollections of his own career."

60 GRAY, JAMES. "The Story of a Writer's Tireless Quest for Honesty." St. Paul Dispatch (10 April).
Avoiding the traps of success in America, Anderson has made himself a success in his Memoirs, being honest about an honest literary life.

61 GROSSMAN, MAX. "The Strange Case of a Man Who Offers No Apologies." Boston Post (12 April).
Anderson provides reasons for his continual escapes into freedom, but in his Memoirs he gives no apologies.

62 H., E. "Sherwood Anderson Wrote Autobiography in His Fiction." Dayton News (19 April).
The Memoirs are so repetitive of Anderson's earlier work that they could be simply re-editings. Good in describing his youthful years, Anderson seems to have resisted maturity.

63 HANSEN, HARRY. "The First Reader." New York World Telegram (9 April).

The "original revolving doorman of literature," Anderson retold and retold his feelings and his adventures. These _Memoirs_ contain such stories as the drink in Paris with Hemingway, Dreiser's naked lawn shower, and Dreiser's rudeness to Fitzgerald.

64 _____. "The First Reader." _New York World-Telegram_ (14 April).

Carl Van Vechten disputes the _Memoirs_ story of Dreiser's rudeness to Fitzgerald; Dreiser actually welcomed Boyd, Fitzgerald, and Van Vechten.

65 _____. "The First Reader." _Norfolk Pilot_ (21 April).

Some readers of Anderson's _Memoirs_ think that he was not present at the time of Dreiser's alleged insult of Fitzgerald, for Dreiser served no drinks; also, Dreiser likely bathed nude only in his own pool.

66 _____. "Sherwood Anderson's Story." _Saturday Review of Literature_, 25 (11 April), 5-6.

Thematically based on the eternal artist-society struggle, Anderson's _Memoirs_ retell more factually stories used in his fiction.

67 HARDWICKE, HALLIE READ. Review of _Sherwood Anderson's Memoirs_. _Fort Worth Star-Telegram_ (19 April).

The _Memoirs_ reveal that "in spite of his unevenness, crudeness and his preoccupation with dirt and cesspools," Anderson's power was felt in American writing.

68 HATCHER, HARLAN. "Harlan Hatcher Says." _Columbus Citizen_ [OH] (12 April).

Instead of retelling Anderson's earlier books, the _Memoirs_ freshen and gather up the essence of the author's other works, of which only _Winesburg, Ohio_ has become classic.

69 HEIMER, MEL. "Authors Are That Way." _New York World-Telegram_ (4 September), p. 21.

Returning to Chicago from the Ozark Mountains, Anderson threw from his train a completed novel.

70 HOWDEN, BENJAMIN. "Confusion Reigns in Memoirs." _Los Angeles Times_ (19 April).

When Howden attacked Anderson before Dreiser, the latter called Anderson "greatly gifted"; and these _Memoirs_ elicit agreement with Dreiser. Whether consciously or not, Anderson was a great artist--one who seemed bewildered but imaginative.

1942

71 HUBBELL, ALBERT. "The Unconventional Autobiography of a Great Literary Pioneer." Chicago Sun (11 April), p. 14.

Interested in humanity and obsessed with himself, Anderson in his Memoirs presents "a research into past time, nimbly skipping in and out of chronological sequence, lighting now on one tiny remembered incident, now on another, sandwiching in stories of people known and loved and hated--in brief a hodge-podge."

72 ISHERWOOD, CHRISTOPHER. "An American Life." Partisan Review, 9 (July-August), 341-42.

Made appealing by "disingenuousness, this gay unabashed trickiness," Anderson in his Memoirs is self-consciously and totally the typical American.

73 JACKSON, JOSEPH HENRY. "A Bookman's Notebook." San Francisco Chronicle (15 April), p. 14.

About writing and about life, Anderson's Memoirs reveal the author's ability to see aspects of himself in all of his works. Containing little gossip, this book shows Anderson's bravery and suffering.

74 JOHNSON, MERLE D. American First Editions. Fourth Edition. Revised by Jacob Blanck. New York: R. R. Bowker Co., pp. 25-27.

[Brief bibliography of primary and secondary materials]

75 J.[OSEPHSON], B. E. "Sherwood Anderson's Memoirs." Ohio Archaeological and Historical Quarterly, 51 (Third quarter), 249.

Remembering that Anderson best told his life story through his characters, the reader will find the Memoirs to be otherwise "a typical collection of memoirs."

76 KAPUSTKA, BRUCE. "So Long, Sherwood Anderson." Polish Daily Zgoda (8 July).

Knowing how to use his loneliness to push toward and write from a full life, Anderson in his Memoirs records his experiences with humanity.

77 KAZIN, ALFRED. On Native Grounds: An Interpretation of American Prose Literature. New York: Harcourt, Brace and Co., pp. 19-20, 166, 172, 175, 192, 193, 194, 197, 200, 205-18, 229, 231, 247, 249, 257, 269, 312-13, 331-32, 367, 394, 398, 454, 457, 498.

Winesburg, Ohio and Main Street announced the new realism in American literature, inspired by post-war liberation instead of 1880's realism. Perhaps alone of the new realists, Anderson cared about perfecting the technique of his realism. His great theme was the need for personal freedom, and his myths of this quest seldom acknowledged surface reality. Asking unanswered questions about life, Anderson told and retold his own escape stories, creating "moments" of revelation and relation. Reprinted in part: 1966.A3.

78 KENDRICK, ALEXANDER. "Frank Self-Revelation By Sherwood Anderson." Philadelphia Inquirer (8 April).
The record of Anderson's mind, the Memoirs rank with those of Lincoln Steffens and Henry Adams.

79 KIRSCHTEN, ERNEST. "Shd And's [sic] Memoirs, Souvenirs of the Good Old Days." St. Louis Post-Dispatch (8 May).
The Memoirs shows Anderson's ability to shape facts to his purposes. He pictures the American corruption of which he was part. Never a fully integrated personality, Anderson remained yet human.

80 KOHLER, DAYTON. "Sherwood Anderson's Memoirs." Southern Literary Messenger (August), pp. 370-71.
Covering the transition years of modern American life, Sherwood Anderson's Memoirs will remain more important to social than to literary history.

81 KRISTENSEN, SVEN MØLLER. Amerikansk Literatur: 1920-1940. Copenhagen: Athenaeum, pp. 18-21, 24, 27, 36, 59, 78, 94, 107, 133, 185, 220, 221, 223, 224, 227.
Anderson rebelled against the idyl of the American small town, joining Masters and Lewis in questioning this myth, creating his own fictional legends of dissatisfied people who rebel against convention. Anderson belongs in the subjective-naturalist group of authors who opposed Dreiser's documentary technique.

82 KUNITZ, STANLEY J. and HOWARD HAYCROFT. "Anderson, Sherwood." Twentieth-Century Authors: A Biographical Dictionary of Modern Literature. New York: H. W. Wilson Co., pp. 24-26.
Anderson claims to have reconstructed his father's oral tales into short stories, after he feigned mental illness to escape from a business life. Although accused of writing of only sex, Anderson wrote against all repressive forces in modern life. After editing his country newspapers, Anderson praised motion-picture writing but did none of that work. Thoroughly Midwestern, Anderson at first cultivated the epithet "bewildered" so often applied to his literary failures.

1942

83 LEWIS, JAY. "Books and Authors." Norfolk Ledger-Dispatch (10 April).
Anderson's Memoirs are a "prose poem as realistic as anything in Piers Plowman" and "an epic with all the details of a saga, told by a poet who snatches the stars from the sky and displays them as dust in his hands."

84 LUNDKVIST, ARTUR. "Sherwood Anderson." Diktare och Avslöjare i Amerikas Moderna Litteratur. Stockholm: Kooperativa Förbundets Bokforlag, pp. 87-97.
Anderson is the foremost predecessor of the psychological naturalism that flowered after the World War. Personal and subjective in his writing, Anderson broods over his stories and gropes for meaning through psychoanalytic understanding of repressed and buried lives. His later works study the effects of modern life on individuals.

85 McGEE, SIDNEY L. "A Born Story Teller." Nashville Banner (15 April).
The Memoirs show Anderson as a story teller, proletarian sympathizer, egoist, vague thinker, and lyrical prose writer.

86 McLAUGHLIN, RICHARD. "Anderson Memoirs Round Out Life of Great Writer." Cleveland Press (9 April).
The Memoirs concern Anderson's mind and imagination more than his personal life. Seldom at peace, Anderson created from his frustrations.

87 MARSHALL, MARGARET. "Notes by the Way." Nation, 154 (16 May), 574.
Considered a Midwestern Lawrence for writing of sex, Anderson denounced all factors that suppress natural life. When Anderson considered creating fiction a magic gift, he lost responsibility and self-control over his style, as his Memoirs demonstrate.

88 MOLLOY, ROBERT. "The Book of the Day." New York Sun (10 April), p. 29.
The Memoirs reveal Anderson's character as that of a humorous man who wrote without humor, a poetic man who wrote best in ordinary words.

89 MOODY, MINNIE HITE. "'Sherwood Anderson's Memoirs.'" Atlanta Journal (12 April).
Anderson's Memoirs are written by a man involved with life to the fullest extent.

90 NORTH, STERLING. "Sherwood Anderson's Life Is the American Dream--With Nightmares." New York Post (15 April).
Full of poetic if not factual truth, Anderson's Memoirs reflect his eternal complexity over himself and his artistic struggle with human life.

91 PATTERSON, ALICIA. "Book of the Week." Washington Times-Herald (12 April).
Understanding the Anderson of the Memoirs is better understanding of his other books.

92 PAULDING, J. K. "Sherwood Anderson's Memoirs." Commonweal, 36 (24 April), 19-20.
Publication of Sherwood Anderson's Memoirs confirms that the author was more interesting than his unrealistic, anti-Victorian works.

93 PRESCOTT, ORVILLE. "Current Books of Note." Cue (25 April), p. 7.
Anderson's books were always autobiographical and always fictional, and his Memoirs contain little new material. His work is still confused, rhapsodic, and full of ego and sex.

94 R., R. P. "Anderson On Himself." Hartford Courant (12 April).
Lyrical, serious, common, and humorous, the Memoirs show Anderson's compromise in all except his writing.

95 REDDIG, W. M. "Sherwood Anderson Closed His Career in Triumph." Kansas City Star (11 April), p. 14.
Knowing the unhappy loneliness of typical Americans, Anderson wrote of himself in his Memoirs.

96 ROBERTS, MARY-CARTER. "Sherwood Anderson's Life Story Is Skillfully Written." Washington Star (12 April).
Again Anderson has retold his past, but these Memoirs are dull and pathetic.

97 ROBINSON, TED. "Sherwood Anderson's Memoirs Disclose An Interesting Life." Cleveland Plain Dealer (12 April).
A poet at heart, operating from feeling rather than intellect, Anderson in his Memoirs is naive, vain, and honest.

98 ROGERS, CHARLES E. "Sherwood Anderson's Memoirs." Journalism Quarterly, 19 (September), 312-13.
Anderson's Memoirs, confusing fact and fancy, has little value for journalists except as all journalists are would-be storytellers.

1942

99 ROSENFELD, PAUL. "The Conflict in Anderson." Nation, 154 (23 May), 611.

Contrary to Margaret Marshall's allegations, Anderson's Memoirs are controlled in style and subject. Anderson's subject is conflict between idealism and opportunism as the creative artist must choose; and the author's style is rambling and digressive but deliberately so.

100 ROSKOLENKO, HARRY. "Ballad: For Sherwood Anderson." Poetry, 59 (February), 243.

"He wrote some books, looked up from a word, / And the deaf could hear and the mute could speak, / And they told of their vision and told of their lives. / He wrote up the saga of American towns."

101 S., J. K. "Sherwood Anderson's Memoirs." Minneapolis Star-Tribune (26 April).

The Memoirs show Anderson's good and bad qualities honestly and with puzzlement.

102 SCHERER, JAMES A. B. "Sherwood Anderson's Pungent Book." Pasadena Star-News (7 May).

The Memoirs show Anderson's honesty and work in his writing; for he was "the most original and most direct American writer of our time."

103 SCOTT, W. T. "Sherwood Anderson's Life, Story-Telling to the End." Providence Journal (12 April).

Fascinated by American life, Anderson tells in his Memoirs of searching for meaning.

104 SELBY, JOHN. "Sherwood Anderson's Memoirs." Arizona Daily Star (12 April).

According to his Memoirs, Anderson suffered a psychic shock as he entered adulthood--hence, his life-long confusion about himself and society.

105 SUTTON, WILLIAM A. "Sherwood Anderson's Memoirs." Historical Society of Northwestern Ohio Quarterly Bulletin, 14 (July), 109-111.

As historical documents, Anderson's Memoirs fail through the author's admitted re-creation of facts and through his ignoring certain lengthy episodes of his life in Ohio.

106 T., M. "Anderson's Boy Sherwood, the Eternal Groper." Milwaukee Journal (26 April).

All of Anderson's fiction is autobiographical but not factual. The Memoirs show his groping toward unanswerable questions.

107 TEMPLE, LUCY CURTIS. "Books." Knoxville News-Sentinel (19 April), C, p. 6.

Anderson never outgrew bitterness toward people and America, for he was ashamed of his boyhood poverty. These Memoirs explain Anderson's choice of subjects--"the hopes, fears, betrayals, cowardice, blunders, embarrassments that most persons successfully bury in the sub-conscious."

108 TOBIAS, ROWENA W. "Story Teller's Memoirs." Charleston News & Courier [SC] (15 April).

Able to ignore ordinary affinities but sensitive to the imagination, Anderson makes his Memoirs a record of his "wandering, physically, emotionally and artistically."

109 VAN DOREN, MARK. "Still Groping." Private Reader. New York: Henry Holt and Co., pp. 247-51.

Reprint of 1936.B91.

110 W. "Memoirs: Anderson Wrote About the Novel." Greensboro Daily News (19 April).

Anderson's leaving his factory for literature has served the American novel, although his Memoirs are more about others than about himself.

111 WAGNER, CHARLES A. "Books." New York Mirror (10 April).

Written in common language, Anderson's Memoirs are the "diary-like tales of an immortal Chicagoan."

112 WEEKS, EDWARD. "First Person Singular." Atlantic Monthly, 169 (May), Bookshelf.

Much like notes for unfinished compositions, the Memoirs are "the source material of the autobiography of a man who was openhanded, egotistical, candid to the point of embarrassment, humorless in his writings, yet humble and deeply responsive to the simple life."

113 WORTHY, PAULINE. "Sherwood Anderson's Memoirs." Raleigh News & Observer (31 May).

Showing his worst facets in these Memoirs, Anderson seems honest--embarrassingly honest--about his voyage from confusion to serenity.

114 WYNGAARD, JOHN. "Memoirs of Author Told." Green Bay Press-Gazette (9 May).

Sherwood Anderson's Memoirs reveal mostly the author's own "glorious ego."

1943

1943 A BOOKS

1 SUTTON, WILLIAM A. "Sherwood Anderson's Formative Years (1876-1913)." Dissertation, Ohio State University, 237 pp.
[Described below as published in periodicals and revised form] Partially published as 1947.B28; 1948.B30; 1950.B13-14. Revised, expanded, and published as 1972.A2.

1943 B SHORTER WRITINGS

1 BAIWIR, ALBERT. "Sherwood Anderson." Le Déclin de l'Individualisme chez les Romanciers Américains Contemporains. Paris: Librairie E. Droz, pp. 199-216.
Anderson's theme is the individual's troubles in remaining whole in an impersonal world. Sex is unfulfilling, for people fear their own repressions; his characters need free, instinctual union--and Anderson presents no answers or method. Besides conventions, industrialism hurts personality development. Not a destroyer, Anderson would remake society for individuals.

2 BARBOSA, A. ROLMES. Escritores Norte-Americanos e Outros. Pôrto Alegro: Edicão da Livraria do Globo, pp. 128-34, 155.
Anderson abandoned business for the telling of stories of common people. He was a "lyrical impressionist" in prose, creating Winesburg, Ohio as his masterwork. "Good night, Sherwood Anderson."

3 CROY, HOMER. Country Cured. New York: Harper & Brothers, p. 182.
When West of the Water Tower appeared, some critics assumed that Anderson instead of Croy was the author.

4 GEISMAR, MAXWELL. "Maxwell Geismar Writes of Anderson's 'Winesburg.'" New York Times Book Review (18 July), p. 4.
Winesburg, Ohio apparently first brought to literature the grotesques of American villages, presented in honest if grim realism. Much as Anderson does concern himself with sex, his ultimate concern is loneliness in isolation; and his approach and answer are love.

5 S., M. Review of Dark Laughter. Suomen Sosialidemokraatti (19 December).
Dark Laughter is more positive than Anderson's other books, reflecting individuals as products of society. Few writers as well understand the human soul as Anderson. [Tauno Mustanoja]

6 SILVEIRA, BRENNO. "Sherwood Anderson." Pequena Historia da Literatura Norte-Americana. Sao Paulo: Livraria Martins, pp. 194-98.

Anderson hates the evil effects of the industrialization and standardization of the United States, which prohibit the individual's living free from restraints. Unlike Lewis, Anderson is interested in his characters' minds, using psychology to reveal essence.

7 STOVALL, FLOYD. American Idealism. Norman: University of Oklahoma Press, p. 138.

Anderson in his social rebellion was "less a naturalist than a frustrated idealist turned primitive who attributed to the objective world the vague restlessness and dislocation that existed within himself."

8 WHIPPLE, T. K. Study Out the Land: Essays. Introduction by Edmund Wilson. Berkeley: University of California Press, pp. xviii, 71, 72, 74-75, 76.

Anderson's social criticism comes from an author born into an age which he hated, from one who writes of an age even more despised. Anderson has not adjusted well to the post-agrarian age; yet this fact does not lessen the worth of Winesburg, Ohio.

1944 A BOOKS - NONE

1944 B SHORTER WRITINGS

1 ADAMS, J. DONALD. The Shape of Books to Come. New York: Viking Press, pp. 69-73.

Unlike Dreiser in his ability to present life with no possibility of answers, Anderson never ceased questioning his own and others' assumptions, for Anderson's writing is more subjective naturalism than Dreiser's. Only Hawthorne and James before Anderson had so deeply studied the psychology of their characters, for Freud had influenced Anderson's concern over buried, inner life. Obsessed with his theme of freedom from standardization, Anderson influenced all younger rebels of the 1920's.

2 ANON. "Black Winesburg." Time, 43 (21 February), 99.

Canape-Vert by Philippe Thoby-Marcelin and Pierre Marcelin is "a Winesburg, Ohio of the Republic of Haiti."

3 ANSERMOZ-DUBOIS, FÉLIX. L'Interpretation Francaise de la Litterature Américaine l'entre-Deux-Guerres (1919-1939). Lausanne: Imprimerie La Concorde, pp. 39, 42, 48, 53, 57,

1944

(ANSERMOZ-DUBOIS, FÉLIX)
59, 60, 63, 76, 87, 94, 100, 112, 117, 143, 153, 155-62, 164, 166, 171, 172, 176, 185, 187.
[Annotated, discursive lists of French commentaries on Anderson and translations of his works into French]

4 DeCAPITE, MICHAEL. No Bright Banner: A Novel. New York: John Day, pp. 86-87.
The fictional hero of this novel reads Anderson's work in Claremont, first finding in "I Want to Know Why" a "moment of beauty" and then in Anderson's novels "the puzzling elegiac sadness of Americans."

5 FAGIN, BRYLLION. "Sherwood Anderson." South Atlantic Quarterly, 43 (July), 256-62.
Anderson never understood vagaries of literary fame. As he aged, his controlling sense of wonder either deserted him or destroyed the outlines of his characters. He discussed his bafflement in letters to and conversations with Fagin.

6 _____. "Sherwood Anderson's Memoirs." American Literature, 15 (January), 434-36.
Anderson's Memoirs contain stories as good as any he wrote and answers to his reasons for eternal fascination with himself and with all people.

7 LIBEN, MEYER. "From 'Structures of Our Behavior.'" New Directions, No. 8, pp. 71-73.
When Anderson left his factory to become an author, he lost the possible tension between greed and morality.

8 PALOLA, EINO. Review of Dark Laughter. Helsingin Sanomat (18 April).
Dark Laughter is now of historical importance in Finnish translation. [Tauno Mustanoja]

9 PEKKANEN, TOIVO. Review of Dark Laughter. Suomalainen Suomi (1944), pp. 341-42.
Dark Laughter, Anderson's first work to be translated into Finnish, is a disappointment, for the issues that Anderson discusses are outdated. [Tauno Mustanoja]

10 TAIPALE, A. K. M. "Sherwood Anderson." Nykyajan Amerikkalaisia Kirjailijoita. Helsinki: Kustannusosakeyhtiö Otava, pp. 58-80.
In the short stories comprising Winesburg, Ohio, The Triumph of the Egg, and Horses and Men, Anderson uses

modern psychology to present inner reality. In his various novels Anderson presents autobiographical heroes in rebellion against social restraints.

11 VERHO, URHO. Review of Dark Laughter. Turun Sanomat (27 February).
Dark Laughter presents Anderson at his best, wrapping his points in a cobweb of refined and sensitive poetry. [Tauno Mustanoja]

1945 A BOOKS - NONE

1945 B SHORTER WRITINGS

1 ALMY, ROBERT F. "Sherwood Anderson--The Non-Conforming Rediscoverer." Saturday Review of Literature, 28 (6 January), 17-18.
Anderson's best writing is his stories and memories of the Midwest, for in his democratic ordinariness combined with Whitmanesque purposes he formed his own legend.

2 ANON. "Anderson, Sherwood." Schweizer Lexikon, 1. Zurich: Encyclios-Verlag, 351.
Anderson writes of individuals out of phase with their societies; his works show lyrical, mystical tendencies in basic naturalism.

3 ANON. "A Gift for Soviet Libraries." New York Times (11 November), p. 17.
Mrs. Eleanor Anderson is giving several of her late husband's books to Soviet libraries destroyed by Nazis.

4 COWLEY, MALCOLM. "The Middle American Style: D. Crockett to E. Hemingway." New York Times Book Review (15 July), pp. 3, 14.
The Hemingway style--supposedly learned from Anderson and Stein--actually predates the twentieth century and is found in Adventures of Huckleberry Finn.

5 FITZGERALD, F. SCOTT. The Crack-Up. Edited by Edmund Wilson. New York: New Directions, pp. 16-17, 256, 316.
Winesburg, Ohio taught the prevalence of sex, The Triumph of the Egg is "a wonderful title," and Fitzgerald was invited to visit Anderson from Oteen, N. C., with Thomas Wolfe.

6 MILLER, HENRY. The Air-Conditioned Nightmare. New York: New Directions, p. 32.

1945

(MILLER, HENRY)
Ohio has given Anderson and Kenneth Patchen, "the one looking for poetry everywhere and the other driven almost mad by the evil and ugliness everywhere. The one walks the streets at night in solitude and tells us of the imaginary life going on behind closed doors"; the other is hurt and disgusted.

7 REVOL, E. L. "Sherwood Anderson." _Panorama de la Literatura Norteamericana Actual_. Córdoba: Editorial Assandri, pp. 54-56.
With mystic vitalism Anderson wrote of the evolution of the United States of America from small-town to city life. Resembling Lawrence in philosophy and Stein in style, Anderson recorded the authentic experiences of emotional lives.

8 SCHIRMER, WALTER F. _Kurze Geschichte der Englishen Literatur von den Anfangen bis zur Gegenwart_. Halle/Salle: Max Niemeyer Verlag, p. 294.
While Anderson's stories are well written, his novels are flawed, confused, and ill-proportioned. When Anderson tries to imitate Lawrence, he writes trivia and caricature.

9 VAUCHER-ZANANIRI, NELLY. "Sherwood Anderson et la Besoin d'Evasion." _Voix d'Amérique: Études sur la Littérature Américaine d'Aujourd'hui_. Cairo: R. Schindler, pp. 11-15.
Anderson peoples his works with malcontents, unstable misfits and dreamers and tries to create their daily, dull lives. His style attempts to capture the inarticulate hopes and incomplete acts of his heroes caught by fate.

1946 A BOOKS

1 CARR, EDWARD F. "Sherwood Anderson, Champion of Women." Master's thesis, University of Pittsburgh, 66 pp.
Anderson idealized women and unconsciously dedicated all of his writings to women, for he was woman-obsessed more than sex-obsessed. He idealized his mother, had contempt for men as brutes, gave sexual drives to men only, and saw women as beyond materialism and possessiveness.

2 LOWREY, BURLING HUNT. "A Study of Sherwood Anderson's Short Stories." Master's thesis, Cornell University, 67 pp.
Anderson abandoned traditional plot and style to obtain truth in his stories. Fascinated by all human lives, Anderson developed a colloquial style to tell human stories.

His characters conflict with society, the universe, or their own natures.

3 THURSTON, JARVIS A. "Sherwood Anderson: A Critical Study." Dissertation, State University of Iowa, 274 pp.
All of Anderson's novels are failures because they resemble daydreams, mirror-images of Anderson's own character and autobiography. Because Anderson's emotional growth stopped in adolescence, he never knew the discipline essential to art; and his characters often are more "slick" than real.

1946 B SHORTER WRITINGS

*1 ANON. "Molti Matrimoni." La Civiltà Cattolica, 97 (20 April), 149.
Cited: 1969.B3.

2 ANON. "Winesburg, Ohio." New York Post (25 April).
When Anderson published Winesburg, Ohio in 1919, he created new style and subject--"the crudities and frustrations of small-town life in the midwest."

*3 ANON. "Molti Matrimoni." Letture (June), pp. 9-10.
Cited: 1969.B3.

4 ANON. "Winesburg, Ohio: A Life Artist Visits Sherwood Anderson's Town." Life, 20 (10 June), 74-79.
The imaginary Winesburg, Ohio, has become "a classic symbol of a U. S. small town." David Fredenthal has drawn scenes from Anderson's home town of Clyde, Ohio, showing how closely Anderson copied from his memories for background but how inventive he was of "grotesque" characters.

5 BAIWIR, ALBERT. Abrégé de l'Histoire du Roman Américain. Brussels: Éditions Lumière, pp. 16, 49-52, 99.
Champion of people stifled by materialism and Puritanism, Anderson in his first two novels reflected social preoccupations. In Winesburg, Ohio and The Triumph of the Egg he interested himself in the buried life--a subject to dominate his work for several years. At the close of his career, Anderson combined social concerns with individual isolation.

6 BURLINGAME, ROGER. Of Making Many Books: A Hundred Years of Reading, Writing and Publishing. New York: Charles Scribner's Sons, pp. 10, 13, 34.

1946

(BURLINGAME, ROGER)
Anderson told Max Perkins that he never discussed any novel while he was completing it. Anderson wanted to read Van Gogh's letters while writing a novel, choosing to mix his reading and his composing. He once claimed to write long paragraphs to avoid being called a "prose-poet."

7 COINDREAU, MAURICE-EDGARD. Apercus de Littérature Américaine. Fifth edition. Paris: Librairie Gallimard, pp. 15, 23, 24, 26, 76, 78, 92, 104, 111, 138, 179.
Anderson fathered recent psychological novelists, such as Faulkner. Sometimes Anderson wrote quickly and superficially, as in Kit Brandon; but his best writing illuminates his characters' minds, demonstrating their inability to communicate.

8 FARRELL, JAMES T. "Tributo a Sherwood Anderson." Babel: Revista Bimestral de Arte Critica, 8 (March-April), 59-61.
Translation of 1942.B50.

9 FONTANET, G. "Quelque Thèmes Essentiels de Sherwood Anderson." Romanciers Américains Contemporains. Paris: Didier, pp. 87-113.
While writing realistically of Midwesterners, Anderson probes beneath surface reality into their souls. Study of Tar reveals Anderson's development to 1926, because in this book Anderson discusses the matter-spirit, instinct-fancy problem in life. When matter ordinarily wins, Anderson is pessimistic.

10 GRAY, JAMES. On Second Thought. Minneapolis: University of Minnesota Press, pp. 19-20.
In Arrowsmith Lewis was influenced by Mencken's satiric voice and Anderson's psychological fiction.

11 HOFFMAN, FREDERICK J., CHARLES ALLEN, and CAROLYN F. ULRICH. The Little Magazine: A History and A Bibliography. Princeton: Princeton University Press, pp. 1, 37, 60, 65, 90-91, 245, 250, 257, 261, 262, 266, 270-71, 274, 278, 279, 284, 300, 304, 322, 338, 339, 358, 374.
The little magazines of America led literary recognition of Anderson through publication of works by and about him. He contributed to The Little Review, The Seven Arts, Playboy, Broom, The Double Dealer, Laughing Horse, Phantasmus, The Oracle--among others.

*12 MILLER, HENRY. "Anderson the Storyteller." Selected Writing No. 4. Edited by Reginald Moore. London: Nicholson & Watson.
Reprint of 1941.B78.

13 ROSENFELD, PAUL. "Sherwood Anderson's Work." Anglica, 1 (April-June), 66-88.

Anderson's fascination with all of life gave him scope and depth to create his own fictional world. Primarily a naturalist, Anderson in style is often lyrical; and his characters are often representative people, even if they are mythically drawn. Reprinted: The Sherwood Anderson Reader. Edited by Paul Rosenfeld. Boston: Houghton Mifflin Co., 1947, pp. viii-xxvi.

14 SANDS, MAURICE. "Sherwood Anderson." An Outline of [the] American Novel. Boston: Student Outlines, pp. 50-54.

By going more psychologically into naturalism than Dreiser, Anderson tried to express inarticulate springs of action. Anderson's grotesque characters find life a trap, the author mystically hoping that articulation will bring joy; using symbolism and colloquial language is Anderson's contribution to the novel.

15 SHIPLEY, JOSEPH T., ed. Encyclopedia of Literature, 2. New York: Philosophical Library, 987, 1059.

An expressionistic writer, Anderson was in style "probably the most influential prose writer of the period" after the World War, rebelled against repression and standardization.

16 SOMMA, LUIGI. Storia della Letteratura Americana. Rome: Casa Editrice Libraria Corso, pp. 196, 197, 198, 199, 200-201.

Anderson's fictional world of suffering characters may lack relation to readers. The author was sincere, lyrical, and psychological; and his credo was not esthetic separatism. One who saw life as gray, Anderson was forgotten by his contemporaries; now he seems dignified and brooding.

17 SUGIKI, TAKASHI. "On Sherwood Anderson's Poems." Essays on American Literature: American Literature Today. Tokyo: Taikosha, pp. 157-69.

Reprint of 1933.B61. [Takashi Kodaira]

1947 A BOOKS

1 FELDMAN, EUGENE. "The Isolation of the Individual as Seen by Sherwood Anderson." Master's thesis, Columbia University, 46 pp.

As a child, Anderson was estranged from his parents and his community. All of his works result from his realization of individual isolation and despair, but this writer

1947

(FELDMAN, EUGENE)
provides no real escape for the isolated. Marching Men suggests "totalitarian discipline"; Dark Laughter and Many Marriages "simple repudiation"; Beyond Desire class struggle and Communism. Anderson starts his characters toward community; then he abandons them.

2 GOZZI, RAYMOND D. "A Descriptive Bibliography of Sherwood Anderson's Contributions to Periodicals." Master's thesis, Columbia University, 213 pp.
[Summary of Anderson's life, psychological orientation, role as storyteller; annotated, chronological list of 254 periodical publications by Anderson]

3 MUELLER, FRANCES HACKATHORNE. "The American Scene in Sherwood Anderson's Novels." Master's thesis, Columbia University, 57 pp.
The main character in each of Anderson's novels spends his time and life trying to find community, to "belong." America--damaged by industrialism--cannot provide the community; and Anderson presents troubled souls without answers except escape. Weak in direct social criticism, Anderson at his best presents studies of troubled characters.

1947 B SHORTER WRITINGS

*1 ANON. Review of The Sherwood Anderson Reader. Bulletin of Virginia Kirkus' Bookshop Service, 15 (1 July), 346.
Cited: Book Review Digest 1947, p. 20.

*2 ANON. "Le Memorie di un Narratore che ha Inventato se Stesso." Il Popolo di Milano (24 August), p. 3.
Cited: 1969.B3.

*3 ANON. Review of The Sherwood Anderson Reader. New Yorker, 23 (15 November), 129.
Cited: 1962.B44.

4 ANON. "Literature." Booklist, 44 (15 December), 148.
The Sherwood Anderson Reader makes available parts of sixteen books, reprints 11 articles and stories, and publishes nine new items.

5 BAILEY, ROBESON. "'Life's Core of Sweetness.'" Saturday Review of Literature, 30 (6 December), 52.
The legend and the facts of Anderson's life being as important as his writing to full understanding, The

<u>Sherwood Anderson Reader</u> merely confirms that author and reader share confused wonder at life.

6 BARTLETT, GEORGE A. <u>Is Marriage Necessary: Memoirs of a Reno Judge</u>. Revised edition. Preface by Margaret Bartlett. New York: Penguin Books, pp. viii, ix.
Margaret Bartlett recalls "quarrels" over Anderson's identity and ancestry; on Sunday Anderson served popovers to breakfast guests. In Reno to complete <u>A Story Teller's Story</u> and divorce Tennessee Mitchell, Anderson wore peculiar socks and cuffed George Bartlett's pants on a sewing machine. Anderson last visited the cynical, elderly judge in 1940.

7 BASSO, HAMILTON. "A Sherwood Anderson Anthology." <u>New Yorker</u>, 23 (15 November), 117-18.
<u>The Sherwood Anderson Reader</u> shows that Anderson is a better writer than Lewis or Dreiser because he was more interested in psychology than in naturalistic reportage.

*8 BIGIARETTI, LIBERO. "Anderson e lo Specchio." <u>La Fiera Letteraria</u> (1 May), p. 8.
Cited: 1969.B3.

9 BRODIN, PIERRE. "Sherwood Anderson." <u>Les Écrivains Américains du Vingtième Siècle</u>. Paris: Horizons de France, pp. 47-58.
A common man, a vagabond among American writers, Anderson was essentially a free author, for his works have little plot and the man wrote as he pleased of interior life of the person and the societal life of the nation. Anderson's poetic spirit made him the best at creating life of the naturalistic novelists.

10 BROOKHOUSER, FRANK. <u>Request for Sherwood Anderson and Other Stories</u>. Denver: Alan Swallow, pp. 170-76.
A soldier on leave in France tells of a French woman whose hand had been mutilated by Germans. He concludes, "What we need, pal, is Sherwood Anderson--he always knew how to write about people who were all mixed up inside--we need Sherwood Anderson and he isn't around to help us."

11 BURGUM, EDWIN BERRY. <u>The Novel and the World's Dilemma</u>. New York: Oxford University Press, pp. 148, 157, 158, 159, 160, 164, 223-24, 246, 275, 292.
Anderson's mysticism avoided both Puritanism and sophisticated vulgarity. Although Anderson may have learned some elements of style from Stein, he is by far the better writer of psychology; yet his message was less worth saying than Dreiser's.

1947

12 CANBY, HENRY SEIDEL. American Memoir. Boston: Houghton Mifflin Co., pp. 263, 266, 298, 321-22, 325.

Although Winesburg, Ohio excited New York City in the early 1920's, the book was really part of "the ripe and vigorous end and summary of the latter nineteenth century." Many Marriages was Anderson's statement of the conflict of artist and plutocrat.

13 COWLEY, MALCOLM. "Sherwood Anderson, Still Fresh and New." New York Herald Tribune Weekly Book Review (9 November), pp. 1-2.

The Sherwood Anderson Reader proves that Anderson's best work is timeless, that he gave "final expression" to certain parts of American life, that he appealed to other writers more than to the public at large. Anderson wrote by instinct essentially plotless stories in the oral tradition.

14 DEDMON, EMMETT. "Sherwood Anderson's Voyage of Discovery." Chicago Sun Book Week (23 November), p. 6.

The Sherwood Anderson Reader proves again that Anderson wrote of the buried lives of others to understand his own buried life.

15 GEISMAR, MAXWELL. The Last of the Provincials: The American Novel, 1915-1925. Boston: Houghton Mifflin Co., pp. 31, 93, 122, 146, 156, 223-84, 324, 337, 342, 356, 360-62, 367, 369, 370, 374, 377.

Anderson became "pioneer and prophet" almost before he matured artistically. Instead of being the bewildered, confused figure critics have made him, Anderson was "perhaps the most balanced, communal, and sympathetic American writer of two decades"--one who first wrote of industrialism in nineteenth-century America and who ended his life writing of industrialism and loss of community in small towns of the 1930's. Reprinted in part: 1966.A3.

*16 GIGLI, LORENZO. "Leggenda del Medio Ovest." La Gazzetta del Popolo [Turin] (8 May), p. 3.

Cited: 1969.B3.

17 GURKO, LEO. The Angry Decade. New York: Dodd, Mead and Co., pp. 91-92, 109, 270, 276.

Some writers--such as Anderson--begin life as businessmen. Some optimistic writers of the 1930's avoided "the sexually maladjusted, spiritually frustrated creatures of Sherwood Anderson and Edgar Lee Masters." Wolfe's characters may fulfill Anderson's call for natural, unmechanized humans.

18 HELLESNES, NILS. "Sherwood Anderson, den einsame amerikanaren." Syn og Seyn, 53 (November), 433-39.

A Romantic mystic, Anderson was also the first great psychological writer in American literature. After learning to write Dreiserian naturalism, Anderson moved on to write symbolic romances about repression and the need for sexual and personal freedom. He was more successful in story forms, because with stories he could "tell" instead of "plot."

19 LOSH, B. J. "Memorial Volume Deserves High Place in Library." Dayton News (30 November).

Publication of The Sherwood Anderson Reader shows again that Anderson was not a good novelist. His great ability was to pose problems in stories and leave them unsolved.

*20 MEI, FRANCESCO. "Ieri e Oggi il Romanzo." Il Popolo [Rome] (28 December), p. 3.

Cited: 1969.B3.

21 MILLER, HENRY. "Sherwood Anderson--Der Erzähler." Die Fahre, 2 (November).

Reprint of 1941.B78.

22 MORRIS, LLOYD R. "Babbitt Strikes Out." Postscript to Yesterday. New York: Random House, pp. 145-48.

Offended readers in 1919 would hardly have expected Winesburg, Ohio to be called a classic in the 1940's. All of Anderson's books are the search for the meaning of his life--"the experience of a Babbitt at odds with his environment." Leaving his factory was Anderson's "most explicit criticism of his environment," and in his books he set forth counter values to those of modern society.

23 PAVESE, CESARE. "Un Libro Utile." L'Unita [Turin] (9 March).

A Story Teller's Story shows Anderson aware that literature eventually equals civilization, that he had to break his own ties to American society 1890-1914 in order to live and write in a new age. Reprinted: 1951.B29.

24 PUTNAM, SAMUEL. Paris Was Our Mistress: Memoirs of a Lost & Found Generation. New York: Viking Press, pp. 15, 20, 21, 25, 35, 38, 103-104, 236.

World War I caused writers such as Anderson to question received attitudes and values. Such new writers came, as did Anderson, from the Midwest. The Dial became less radical and gave Anderson $2,000 for his literary achievement and promise. Anderson did not associate with Putnam's crowd when in Paris.

1947

25 RASCOE, BURTON. *We Were Interrupted*. Garden City: Doubleday, pp. 26, 28, 32, 104, 122, 127, 142, 151, 154, 187-88, 242, 296-97.

Anderson broke tabus in literature and traveled from New York to Birmingham to New Orleans to Paris to Marion to Panama. Academic critics failed to see Anderson's merit. Rascoe found Stein to look, as Anderson described, "like the wife of an Iowa corn doctor"; but she dismissed Anderson's work, which she may never have read.

*26 RISI, NELO. "Un Poeta della Propria Vita." *Tempo* [Milan] (10-17 May), p. 21.

Cited: 1969.B3.

27 SNELL, GEORGE. *The Shapers of American Fiction, 1798-1947*. New York: E. P. Dutton & Co., pp. 160, 243.

Hemingway was influenced by Anderson, Stein, Pound, and Eliot. Anderson's Midwest realism was in "his halting, tentative stories of escape."

28 SUTTON, WILLIAM A. "Sherwood Anderson: The Clyde Years, 1884-1896." *Northwest Ohio Quarterly*, 19 (July), 99-114.

The Anderson family was poor but never destitute in Clyde, Ohio; and young Sherwood Anderson knew hard work and ordinary family and social life. He quit school, enjoyed horse races, investigated sex, joined the militia, and longed to escape the small town for a city. Reprinted: 1972.A2.

29 TRILLING, LIONEL. "The World of Sherwood Anderson." *New York Times Book Review* (9 November), pp. 1, 67-69.

What Anderson wrote in the early 1920's seemed to become irrelevant as he kept writing and readers matured. *The Sherwood Anderson Reader* cannot revive Anderson's reputation, for he still has the effect of "limiting our faculties and diminishing our world," of developing beyond such "moments" as escaping from constraints.

30 VAN KRANENDONK, A. G. *Geschiedenis van de Amerikaanse Literatur*, 2. Amsterdam: G. A. van Oorschot Uitgever, 183, 193, 198-203, 216, 217, 225, 251, 285, 313.

Anderson used his escape from the paint factory in several of his novels. Better at stories than novels, Anderson continually worried that standardization and industrialism were crushing romantic, poetic tendencies out of Americans. With *Winesburg, Ohio* Anderson became one of the first writers to probe the unconscious.

31 WAGENKNECHT, EDWARD. "Anderson's Attempts to Startle Us." Chicago Tribune Magazine of Books (16 November), p. 4.
The Sherwood Anderson Reader may start a revival of interest in this author of stories about lonely people seeking the communion of essentially naked humanity.

32 WALKER, DON DEVERE. "Anderson, Hemingway, Faulkner: Three Studies in Mytho-Symbolism in American Literature." Master's thesis, University of Utah. 127 pp.
Anderson's naturalism went beyond recording of experience into subjective interpretation of subconscious motives and feelings. He dramatizes the isolation of the individual in the fantasy of "reasserting the primeval, egoless forces of life and communion"--symbolized by "perceptual life, manual labor and craft, and natural acceptance of the flesh."

33 WARREN, ROBERT PENN. "Paul Rosenfeld: Prompter of Fiction." Commonweal, 46 (15 August), 424.
Rosenfeld told of walking with Anderson in New York City and disliking a policeman, while Anderson noticed the policeman's limp.

34 WHIPPLE, T. K. "Sherwood Anderson." Berkeley, No. 1, pp. 3-4, 7.
Reprint in part of 1928.B54.

35 WITHAM, W. TASKER. Panorama of American Literature. [n.p.]: Stephen Daye Press, pp. 246, 250, 251-53, 256, 264, 322.
Stein's experiments with language influenced Anderson and Hemingway. Winesburg, Ohio portrays psychologically "the more sensitive and eccentric inhabitants of an imaginary small town, who are motivated by the same restless search for truth as the author," and Dark Laughter is semi-autobiographical.

1948 A BOOKS

1 HARVEY, CYRUS I. "Sherwood Anderson's Natural History of Winesburg." Undergraduate thesis, Harvard University, 75 pp.
Not a work of social protest, Winesburg, Ohio is Anderson's illumination of moments of beauty in village lives. The book is imaginative, not a "technician's" work but instead a relating of man and environment.

2 POPPE, HANS WOLFGANG. "Psychological Motivations in the Writings of Sherwood Anderson." Master's thesis, University of Southern California, Los Angeles, 138 pp.

In his early books Anderson wrote to expurgate unpleasant experiences in his early life. Later heroes in the novels follow Anderson's own need for escape and freedom; yet the Anderson hero retains social responsibilities. Anderson wrote to solve psychological problems of value and image for himself.

3 SANDERSON, ARTHUR MARSHALL. "Sherwood Anderson's Philosophy of Life as Shown by the Actions of Characters in His Novels." Master's thesis, Montana State University, 196 pp.

Anderson's writings are examined for answers to three problems--profession, social responsibility, and love. The central characters in Anderson's novels come to hate the effects of standardization and mechanization and to realize their need for community and love.

4 STROHL, DONA RUTH. "Materials for the Literary Pen: The Life of Sherwood Anderson Prior to the Literary Career." Master's thesis, University of Illinois, 156 pp.

Seeking to order the events of Anderson's life chronologically, terminating the study of Anderson when he started writing, it is shown that Anderson's boyhood days of emotional struggle led to the awareness of artistic ambition and that these years constitute the material for most of Anderson's writings.

1948 B SHORTER WRITINGS

1 AAMOT, PER. _Streiftog: Essays_. Oslo: Dreyers Forlag, pp. 71-72, 116-17, 121, 122.

Hemingway's _The Torrents of Spring_ parodies _Dark Laughter_. Anderson wandered around Greenwich Village, unknown and with long hair and with romantic praise for bohemia, before that locale made him an immediate success.

2 ANDERSON, KARL JAMES. "My Brother, Sherwood Anderson." _Saturday Review of Literature_, 31 (4 September), 6-7, 26-27.

Sherwood Anderson was "the exuberant one" of the children, working hard to get ahead in spite of not being well-educated. The escape from the paint factory was probably both deliberate and unconscious mental breakdown. When working at advertising, "he composed stories in his mind during business hours, made notes on his cuffs, and wrote by night." Clyde, Ohio, suggested both geography and characters for Winesburg, Ohio; but Anderson invented the plots. Perhaps Earl Anderson inspired some tales. Reprinted: 1957.B2.

3 ANON. "Anderson Letters Given To Chicago Library." Hobbies, 53 (April), 147.
Eleanor Copenhaver Anderson has given about ten thousand of her husband's letters and papers to The Newberry Library.

4 ANON. "The Sherwood Anderson Papers." Newberry Library Bulletin, Series 2, No. 2 (December), pp. 64-70.
Anderson's correspondence at The Newberry Library comes mostly from his years as an author--3,000 letters to others and 7,000 letters to Anderson.

5 BASLER, ROY P. Sex, Symbolism, and Psychology in Literature. New Brunswick: Rutgers University Press, pp. 8-9.
Any understanding of Anderson's life and work must take account of "sex, the unconscious, and the nonrational logic of dream imagery"--the influence of Freud and Jung.

6 BISHOP, JOHN PEALE. Collected Essays. New York: Charles Scribner's Sons, pp. 233-40.
Reprint of 1921.B14.

7 BUTCHER, FANNY. "The Literary Spotlight." Chicago Tribune Magazine of Books (1 February), p. 4.
The Newberry Library is collecting all letters to and from Anderson. With 10,000 letters already, the collection reveals Anderson's loneliness and use of letter-writing as "warm-up" exercise to literature.

8 DAUGHERTY, GEORGE H. "Anderson, Advertising Man." Newberry Library Bulletin, Series 2, No. 2 (December), pp. 30-38.
Daugherty and Anderson met in Springfield, Ohio, in 1899, when they attended Wittenberg College. Daugherty knew Anderson again in Chicago until 1906. Anderson was a clever and ambitious writer and seller of copy. When he came back to Chicago in 1913 he wrote novels as well as copy. Eventually Anderson had his own clients and office.

9 DUPEE, F. W. "Anderson's Legacy." Nation, 166 (3 January), 20.
The Sherwood Anderson Reader contains too many pieces that demonstrate Anderson's failure in all but brief fiction. His disciples have simply out-written him.

1948

*10 FRANCIOSA, MASSIMO. "Anderson." Il Popolo [Rome] (14 February), p. 3.
Cited: 1969.B3.

11 FRANK, WALDO. "Sherwood Anderson: A Personal Note." Newberry Library Bulletin, Series 2, No. 2 (December), pp. 39-43.
Frank received "The Untold Lie" for The Seven Arts and noted erratic punctuation. Frank thought Anderson epitomized the new Midwest, and Anderson respected Frank as representing the East; later Frank grew beyond Anderson's lyric sentimentality.

12 FRIEDE, DONALD. The Mechanical Angel: His Adventures and Enterprises in the Glittering 1920's. New York: Alfred A. Knopf, pp. 26, 27-29, 233.
Friede arranged a dinner for Anderson, Dreiser, and O'Neill; Anderson told a ghost story that he later published.

*13 GIGLI, LORENZO. "Segreti di Anderson." Il Giornale dell'Emelia (4 August), p. 3.
Cited: 1969.B3.

14 GLOSTER, HUGH M. Negro Voices in American Fiction. Chapel Hill: University of North Carolina Press, pp. 108, 130, 164.
Dark Laughter is Anderson's glorification and generalization of the amoral, instinctive Negro. Winesburg, Ohio influenced some parts of Toomer's Cane; and a character in McKay's Home to Harlem reads works by Anderson.

15 GOZZI, RAYMOND D. "A Bibliography of Sherwood Anderson's Contributions to Periodicals: 1914-1946." Newberry Library Bulletin, Series 2, No. 2 (December), pp. 71-82.
[Unannotated list of 256 items, condensed from 1947.A2.]

16 GUYOT, CHARLY. Les Romanciers Américains d'Aujourd'hui. Paris: Éditions Labergerie, pp. 7, 22-28, 46.
More interested in internal reality than external facts, Anderson influenced writers such as Hemingway and Steinbeck between the World Wars. Kinder than Main Street, Winesburg, Ohio is Anderson's best book. Whereas Lewis resembles Flaubert, Anderson is like Chekhov.

17 HANSEN, HARRY. "Sherwood Anderson Reminiscences." Chicago Tribune Magazine of Books (16 May), p. 5.
Anderson's brother Karl read a paper about the author at the Westport Library, emphasizing their boyhood and Sherwood's final years in Virginia.

18 HOFFMAN, FREDERICK J. Review of The Sherwood Anderson Reader. American Literature, 20 (March), 73-74.

Publication of The Sherwood Anderson Reader confirms again that Anderson's best genre was the short story, for Anderson was "a muddled writer, and usually a very bad one." He never matured beyond sympathy for his characters.

19 HOFFMAN, HESTER R., ed. Bessie Graham's Bookman's Manual: A Guide to Literature. Sixth edition. New York: R. R. Bowker Co., p. 673.

More important as influence on other writers than for his own work, Anderson wrote "nostalgic and realistic re-creations of the towns of his father's generation. He was among the first of the story-tellers to use the unconscious and the psychology of sex. His style is often involved and obscure."

20 HOWE, IRVING. "Sherwood Anderson: The Unavailable Self." Partisan Review, 15 (April), 492-96, 498-99.

The Sherwood Anderson Reader forces recognition that Anderson never organized his response to the chaos of modern life, for he never could separate himself from his characters nor could he "integrate narrative and symbol."

21 KEMPTON, KENNETH PAYSON. The Short Story. Cambridge: Harvard University Press, pp. 91, 99.

In "I Want to Know Why" Anderson uses the puzzled narrator for ironic effect; the narrator must differ from the author.

22 LOVETT, ROBERT MORSS. All Our Years: The Autobiography of Robert Morss Lovett. New York: Viking Press, pp. 6, 202-203, 246.

Lovett met Anderson in Chicago, later praised his stories and knocked his novels, and all in all wrote more about Anderson than any other contemporary. In 1937 both Lovett and Anderson worked in a Colorado writers' workshop.

23 ORVIS, MARY BURCHARD. The Art of Writing Fiction. New York: Prentice-Hall Co., pp. 88, 177, 189-94, 211.

In "I Want to Know Why" Anderson begins near the end and then completes the earliest part of the story. Some critics think that Freud and Dostoevski influenced Anderson's use of psychology. Winesburg, Ohio best illustrates how an author uses social forces in his stories. A Story Teller's Story is recommended for every aspiring writer.

1948

24 PARGELLIS, STANLEY. "Foreword." _Newberry Library Bulletin_, Series 2, No. 2 (December), p. 29.
"The Sherwood Anderson Memorial Number" of _The Newberry Library Bulletin_ announces the opening of Anderson's papers for scholarly use.

25 PEARSON, NORMAN HOLMES. "Anderson and the New Puritanism." _Newberry Library Bulletin_, Series 2, No. 2 (December), pp. 52-63.
Winesburg, Ohio rebelled against Puritanism, which equalled materialism and false ethics; yet Anderson was essentially optimistic and moral in honest Midwestern fashion.

26 RAGAN, SAM. "Author Anecdotes." _Raleigh News & Observer_ (11 July).
In his _Memoirs_ Anderson tells of Faulkner's storing nine gallons of moonshine whiskey in Anderson's apartment in New Orleans.

27 ROGERS, W. G. _When This You See, Remember Me: Gertrude Stein in Person_. New York: Rinehart, pp. 43, 56-57, 244, 246.
Anderson likened Stein's short hair to a monk's; he had earlier admitted his indebtedness to her. The three writers whom Stein met early and continued to care for were Anderson, Hemingway, and Fitzgerald.

28 SERGEL, ROGER. "The Man and the Memory." _Newberry Library Bulletin_, Series 2, No. 2 (December), pp. 44-51.
Sergel met Anderson in the mid-1920's and loved the writer's dream-like wonderment at life and character. Though inwardly melancholy, Anderson remained curious and sweet until he died.

29 STEVENSON, LIONEL. Review of _The Sherwood Anderson Reader_. _Personalist_, 29 (October), 426-27.
The Sherwood Anderson Reader shows that Anderson failed to change in style or mood from his first writing to his memoirs.

30 SUTTON, WILLIAM A. "Sherwood Anderson: The Spanish-American War Year." _Northwest Ohio Quarterly_, 20 (January), 20-36.
Anderson enlisted in the American forces to escape heroically from manual labor in Chicago. After uneventful service in Cuba, he was discharged and later wrote little of the war year. Reprinted: 1972.A2.

31 TAKAGAKI, MATSUO. "Sherwood Anderson's Technique." Essays on Contemporary American Literature. Tokyo: Genrisha, pp. 89-96.
Reprint of 1934.B39. [Takashi Kodaira]

32 WEBER, BROM. Hart Crane: A Biographical and Critical Study. New York: Bodley Press, pp. 42-43, 57-58, 62, 63, 77, 88, 105, 120-23, 124, 125, 130, 134-35, 141-42, 164, 165, 169, 189, 239.
Crane's review of Winesburg, Ohio marked the poet's awareness that creation excelled photography; and Anderson warmly encouraged Crane over the next years. But Crane lost faith in Anderson after 1921 because of Anderson's essentially uncontrolled prose. Reprint of 1919.B11; 1921.B20.

33 WOOLF, VIRGINIA. "American Fiction." The Moment and Other Essays. New York: Harcourt, Brace and Co., pp. 113-27.
Reprint of 1925.B67.

34 YOUNG, STARK. "A Marginal Note." Paul Rosenfeld: Voyager in the Arts. Edited by Jerome Mellquist and Lucie Wiese. New York: Creative Age Press, pp. 195-97.
In Anderson truth and lie, fact and fiction mixed magically and naturally. Paul Rosenfeld was the friend Anderson most admired for both "culture and style."

1949 A BOOKS

*1 GRONNA, ANNE T. M. "Analysis of Two Stories by Sherwood Anderson." Master's thesis, State University of Iowa, 66 pp.
Cited: 1960.A3.

2 McINTYRE, RALPH E. "The Short Stories of Sherwood Anderson." Master's thesis, Columbia University, 211 pp.
Anderson's best work is the short stories in Winesburg, Ohio, The Triumph of the Egg, and Horses and Men. Anderson could write well of the buried lives of frustrated, inarticulate, grotesque people; but he never had a full view of life or a total philosophy integrating the "moments" which he illuminated.

3 PHILLIPS, WILLIAM LOUIS. "Sherwood Anderson's Winesburg, Ohio: Its Origins, Composition, Technique, and Reception." Dissertation, University of Chicago, 218 pp.

1949

(PHILLIPS, WILLIAM LOUIS)
Winesburg, Ohio was written in Chicago but geographically based on Anderson's boyhood home town of Clyde, Ohio; the characters are based on little, forgotten people whom Anderson knew in Chicago; the inspiration was Spoon River Anthology; Anderson drafted the stories once and made several revisions; the book was admired but sold poorly.

4 SMITH, SARA FRANCIS. "Poe and Anderson: A Study in the Tradition of the Short Story." Master's thesis, Alabama Polytechnic Institute, 89 pp.
Poe had given purpose and rule to the short story; Anderson demanded freedom from plot requirements in order to follow life. Anderson "stressed the subjective, individualistic approach to the short story. Also, he demanded that the language of the story truly express the people of the story."

1949 B SHORTER WRITINGS

1 ANON. "Tribute to Anderson Paid at Library Fete." New York Times (15 January), p. 15.
Anderson's papers were formally opened for scholarly use at The Newberry Library.

2 ANON. "Midwestern Primitive." Time, 53 (28 February), 96, 98, 100.
Although his later work is failure, Anderson "was a great writer and. . . Winesburg, Ohio is a great book."

3 ANON. Publication of The Portable Sherwood Anderson. Booklist, 45 (1 March), 226.
[Item soon to be published]

4 ANON. "Story-teller for America." Chicago Sun-Times Book Week (3 April), X, p. 8.
The Portable Sherwood Anderson is a "valuable addition to the shelf of American literature in anyone's library."

*5 ANON. "Un Povero Bianco." Letture, 4 (May), 164.
Cited: 1969.B3.

*6 ANON. "L'Uomo che Diventò Donna." Il Mondo [Rome] (19 November), p. 8.
Cited: 1969.B3.

7 BERNARD, HARRY. Le Roman Régionaliste aux États-Unis (1913-1940). Montreal: Fides, pp. 18, 26, 79, 111, 175, 179-80, 195, 196.
Anderson more than any other writer contributed to Ohio literature in the early twentieth century. Inspired by Freud and resembling Spoon River Anthology, Winesburg, Ohio reveals the unknown and strange citizens of a village. Poor White discusses the failure of a town to develop intellect and art along with industry.

*8 BIGIARETTI, LIBERO. "Lo Scrittore allo Specchio." Il Giornale [Naples] (13 May), p. 3.
Cited: 1969.B3.

*9 _____. "Lo Scrittore e lo Specchio." Progresso d'Italia (3 August), p. 3.
Cited: 1969.B3.

10 BREIT, HARVEY. "Repeat Performance Appraised." New York Times Book Review (17 April), p. 19.
Publication of The Portable Sherwood Anderson now allows debate with Trilling's school, who think that Anderson is passé, and Gregory's school, who believe that Anderson's worth continues.

11 BUTCHER, FANNY. "The Literary Spotlight." Chicago Tribune Magazine of Books (30 January), p. 4.
James T. Farrell praised Anderson at a celebration held by The Newberry Library in honor of the opening of Anderson's papers for scholars to use. Farrell claimed to have read Anderson and been influenced by the older writer's questioning of all aspects of life.

12 FRAHNE, KARL HEINRICH. Von Franklin bis Hemingway: Eine Einführung in die Literatur Nordamerikas. Hamburg: J. P. Toth, pp. 10, 114, 121, 122, 143, 145, 176, 186-87, 215, 291.
Anderson pioneered subjective naturalism, using his own experience and learning from Freud and Stein to develop the personal emotions rather than outward detail.

13 GUIDO, AUGUSTO. "Cavalli da Corsa e Uomini dell'Ohio." La Fiera Letteraria, No. 43 (23 October), p. 5.
Horses and Men contains stories dealing with the troubles and delusions of adolescents, the misanthropy of eccentrics, and the beauties of horses and races. Anderson avoids sentimental romanticism but presents lyrical truth.

1949

14 HOWE, IRVING. "Sherwood Anderson and the American Myth of Power." Tomorrow, 8 (August), 52-54.

Poor White is the novel in which Anderson tries to use all of American society. Influenced by Twain, Anderson is best when describing the hero's youth along the Mississippi. After the hero becomes a successful inventor, Poor White declines into an unsatisfactory work, missing the needed tragic ending. Reprinted with revision: 1951.A1.

15 KLEIN, ALEXANDER. "Sherwood Anderson in Retrospect." New Republic, 121 (15 August), 18-19.

Once important for freeing American writing from Victorian gentility, Anderson never grew beyond his awakening from business to writing. The Portable Sherwood Anderson confirms his failure to mature beyond sentiment toward intellect.

16 LANE, ROBERT R. "Old Books for New." Newark News (23 January).

Rereading Winesburg, Ohio thirty years later proves that the book holds its appeal and merits never having been out of print.

17 MORRIS, LLOYD. "Heritage of a Generation of Novelists: Anderson and Dreiser, Hemingway, Faulkner, Farrell and Steinbeck." New York Herald Tribune Book Review (25 September), pp. 12-13, 74.

Having rejected materialism himself, Anderson spoke to younger writers of the 1920's about finding artistic and individual meaning in America, never doubting that life had meaning to be found.

18 RAHV, PHILIP. Image and Idea: Fourteen Essays on Literary Themes. Norfolk, Ct.: New Directions, pp. 3, 4-5, 8, 15-16, 29-30, 64, 163.

Anderson exemplifies writers who value their experiences over their intellects. The heroines of Many Marriages and Dark Laughter are mythic females who exude sexuality.

19 REDMAN, BEN RAY. "New Editions." Saturday Review of Literature, 32 (23 April), 40.

The Portable Sherwood Anderson conserves the best of Anderson's stories--his best genre--and reprints Poor White.

*20 TERRA, DINO. "I Narratori Americani Giocano a Tennis con la Luna." Il Popolo [Rome], Il Popolo di Milano (23 October), p. 3.

Cited: 1969.B3.

21 WECHTER, DIXON, et al., eds. Changing Patterns in American Civilization. Philadelphia: University of Pennsylvania Press, pp. 38, 39, 56-57.

F. O. Matthiessen believes that Winesburg, Ohio might teach values for living. Lewis had caricatured the small-town lives; Anderson looked into them with love. To recapture Anderson's possibility of love through understanding, democracy must become true and writers must lose alienation. Thus, private absorptions of writers will be replaced by belief in common life.

1950 A BOOKS

1 HILTON, EARL RAYMOND. "The Purpose and Method of Sherwood Anderson." Dissertation, University of Minnesota, 205 pp.

Anderson's fictional world is unique and valuable for the study of creative writing, for the writer's temperament is reflected in his "tone." Anderson's few stories of true merit are carefully crafted and developed from his years at college and in advertising and were written from 1916 to 1923. Afterwards, Anderson was basically a competent reporter.

2 TAYLOR, WILLIAM E. "Sherwood Anderson: His Social Creed." Master's thesis, Vanderbilt University, 114 pp.

Anderson could not take his characters beyond a conflict or "conversion"--symbolically, Anderson's own conversion in 1912. The writer's interest in individual lives prevented him from writing Communistic fiction.

1950 B SHORTER WRITINGS

1 CAHEN, JACQUES-FERNAND. La Littérature Américaine. Paris: Presses Universitaires de France, pp. 86-88.

While Lewis wrote of social forces, Anderson wrote of interior troubles that cause frustration, being more careful artistically than Lewis. Influenced by Freud, Winesburg, Ohio deals with socially and morally repressed villagers. Anderson never seemed to understand what he was saying.

2 COMMAGER, HENRY STEELE. The American Mind: An Interpretation of American Thought and Character Since the 1880's. New Haven: Yale University Press, pp. 125, 127.

Anderson in Many Marriages and Dark Laughter tries to follow the primitivists, who preferred emotion to thought,

1950

(COMMAGER, HENRY STEELE)
the body to the mind. Tender Buttons to Anderson was Stein's try to write the ineffable.

3 DeVOTO, BERNARD. The World of Fiction. Boston: Houghton Mifflin Co., pp. 260-61.
Anderson's later novels contain passages that are offensive to readers by being "Whitmanesque soliloquies" on several "vague but passionately developed themes." These emotional passages are dull and bothersome because the emotion is the author's and not the characters'.

4 FLANAGAN, JOHN T. "The Permanence of Sherwood Anderson." Southwest Review, 35 (Summer), 170-77.
Opening Anderson's papers at The Newberry Library or publishing anthologies from his works will likely not aid in reestablishing a major reputation for this writer, but Anderson's perception of and treatment of character assure him a place in literary history.

5 HOWE, IRVING. "Sherwood Anderson and D. H. Lawrence." Furioso, 5 (Fall), 21-33.
Freud being too mechanistic and Joyce being too intellectual, Anderson read Lawrence as the great novelist of sexuality. In Many Marriages and Dark Laughter Anderson tried unsuccessfully to imitate Lawrence's primitivism. Reprinted: 1951.A1.

6 _____. "Sherwood Anderson and the Power Urge: A Note on Populism in American Literature." Commentary, 10 (July), 78-80.
Marching Men is not about Anderson's worship of totalitarian dictators but instead concerns the author's own forced choice between order and disorder in his life that climaxed in his 1912 collapse. Reprinted: 1951.A1.

7 KAUFMAN, WOLFE. "Sherwood Anderson's Advice." Saturday Review of Literature, 33 (26 August), 21.
In Stein's apartment Anderson advised Kaufman that young writers should work in factories when broke rather than in journalism, for hack writing might dissipate their writing talent.

8 KRISTENSEN, SVEN MØLLER. Lidt om Amerikansk Litteratur. Copenhagen: Carit Andersons Forlag, pp. 17-18.
Anderson was among those Midwestern writers who developed realism after the World War. Dealing with despondent lives and disappointed destinies, Winesburg, Ohio

shows Anderson as one of those who call for honest relations and human contacts.

9 LEWIS, WYNDHAM. Rude Assignment: A Narrative of My Career Up-to-Date. London: Hutchinson, pp. 203-205.
Hemingway complimented Lewis' praise of The Torrents of Spring, saying that Lawrence had been "Anderson's god in the old days--and you can trace his effect all through A.[nderson]'s stuff after he commenced reading him."

10 PERKINS, MAXWELL. Editor to Author: The Letters of Maxwell Perkins. Edited by John Hall Wheelock. New York: Charles Scribner's Sons, pp. 165-68, 224, 273-74.
In August, 1940, Perkins encouraged Anderson to let Scribner's publish his memoirs. Later Perkins defended Van Wyck Brooks against Anderson's feeling that Brooks lacked strength to lead, and he praised Anderson's writing from experience.

11 SHIGA, MASARU. "Sherwood Anderson." The Realism Age of American Literature. Tokyo: Kenkyusha, pp. 88-92.
Anderson's most important characteristics are his psychological realism and his style, both influential on Hemingway and Faulkner. [Takashi Kodaira]

12 SIMON, JEAN. "Sherwood Anderson." Le Roman Américain au xxe Siècle. Paris: Boivin, pp. 56-64.
Avoiding Dreiser's objective realism, Winesburg, Ohio is poetic prose tales of the interior lives of repressed people. Anderson wrote immaturely before 1919 and declined after 1927, having shown how to use the subconscious in literature. For author and characters life is a poetic mystery. Anderson is the only realist to care about style.

13 SUTTON, WILLIAM A. "Sherwood Anderson: The Advertising Years, 1900-1906." Northwest Ohio Quarterly, 22 (Summer), 120-57.
Anderson's first publications were columns for advertising serials, written thoughtfully to show concern for the ethic and duty of a businessman. Occasionally Anderson wrote "characters" and semi-fictional essays about business. He and his first wife lived in a Chicago middle-class area. Reprinted: 1972.A2.

14 _____. "Sherwood Anderson: The Cleveland Year, 1906-1907." Northwest Ohio Quarterly, 22 (Winter 1949-50), 39-44.
Anderson left the advertising business in Chicago to become chief promoter for United Factories in Cleveland.

1950

(SUTTON, WILLIAM A.)
He wrote catalog copy, had a pleasant family life, and decided to create his own company. Reprinted: 1972.A2.

15 TAKIGAWA, MOTOO. "Sherwood Anderson's Thought: Chiefly on Winesburg, Ohio and Dark Laughter." Rising Generation (November), 17-19.
In Winesburg, Ohio Anderson regards the grotesques as people worthy of the name, who groan under the tyranny of civilization. In Dark Laughter he depicts what the positive image of true men is. Thus, Winesburg, Ohio and Dark Laughter expose both sides of Anderson's thought. [Takashi Kodaira]

16 TRILLING, LIONEL. "Sherwood Anderson." The Liberal Imagination: Essays on Literature and Society. New York: Viking Press, pp. 24-33.
Reprint with slight revision of 1941.B97. Reprinted: 1966.A3; 1966.A7; 1974.A1.

17 WILSON, EDMUND. Classics and Commercials: A Literary Chronicle of the Forties. New York: Farrar, Straus, pp. 76, 105, 107, 416, 462, 504-505, 506, 512.
Anderson's death seems premature, for he seemed ageless and still striving. Dark Laughter was probably Anderson's one book written solely for money. Wilson saw Anderson and Tennessee Anderson in New York before Rosenfeld took them to Europe.

18 ZABEL, MORTON DAUWEN. Historia de la Lateratura Norteamericana: Desde los Origenes hasta el Dia--Sua Maestros, Tradiciones y Problemas. Buenos Aires: Editorial Losada, pp. 354, 355, 360, 411-12, 416, 455, 543-44, 545, 549, 551.
Anderson wrote a new kind of realism, interested in describing typical lives of an American town. Anderson's realism in Winesburg, Ohio contrasts clearly with Lewis' satire in Main Street, for Anderson created poetic realism of character.

1951 A BOOKS

1 HOWE, IRVING. Sherwood Anderson. New York: William Sloane Associates, 271 pp.
Seeking to understand why Winesburg, Ohio is remembered with pleasant awe, one finds a remnant of Anderson's works worth preserving. Perhaps Anderson was too highly praised as he began writing. Perhaps his move to imitate Lawrence

and Stein was unwise. Perhaps he struggled to have ideas in conflict with his emotional approach to life. Whatever the reason, Anderson lived in deprivation or isolation from people or movements that he had been taught to admire; or, on the contrary, he sometimes created his own world of impossible innocence and then could not communicate that world clearly. Anderson will remain a minor writer for the few works that give expression to some few aspects of American life. Reprint of 1949.B14; 1950.B5; 1950.B6; 1951.B23; 1951.B24. Reprinted in part: 1966.A3; 1966.A7; 1974.A3. Reprinted: 1966.A4.

2 SCHEVILL, JAMES. Sherwood Anderson: His Life and Work. Denver: University of Denver Press, 360 pp.

The major theme in Anderson's work is that the imagination creates for the whole of life and that the imaginative life balances the outer reality of facts. Critics have emphasized Anderson's dramatic rejection of business and his creation of Winesburg, Ohio as moments of supreme importance, but understanding through imagination must explain the author's life and many books. In storytelling, in writing novels about freedom, in country journalism, in social action, and in eternal self-assessment, Anderson was seeking to fulfill his inner dream of communication, community, and love. Of the many books, Winesburg, Ohio and the Memoirs shall endure as classics, along with parts of A Story Teller's Story and some short stories. Reprinted in part: 1966.A7.

1951 B SHORTER WRITINGS

1 AARON, DANIEL. "Waiting for the Apocalypse." Hudson Review, 3 (Winter), 634-36.

West's The Day of the Locust resembles Anderson when characters become "suddenly seized and ridden by private demons"; and a country figure is "a botched re-working of Sherwood Anderson's grotesque in his story 'Hands.'"

2 ADAMS, SCOTT. Review of Howe, Sherwood Anderson. Library Journal, 76 (15 March), 511.

In Sherwood Anderson Howe satisfactorily interpets "an influential though minor figure in twentieth century American letters."

3 ANGOFF, CHARLES. "He Belongs with the Giants." Saturday Review, 34 (28 April), 17.

Howe has discussed Anderson as a product of the socioeconomy of nineteenth-century Ohio. The thesis is deceptive, and the author deserves a wiser critic.

1951

4 ANON. "General." New Yorker, 27 (14 April), 125-26.
Schevill's critical biography of Anderson is less interesting than Anderson's own legends; Howe's book is stern and didactic about Anderson's inability to continue growing artistically.

5 ANON. "The Writer as Victim." Time, 57 (16 April), 116, 118.
Because Anderson was never clear about himself or his writing, little of his work endures. Howe's study--"weighted though it is with psychoanalytical jargon and conjecture"--presents Anderson's failure as the fault of American culture; Schevill agrees that America prevented Anderson's maturing.

6 ANON. Review of Howe, Sherwood Anderson. Booklist, 47 (1 May), 309.
Howe's Sherwood Anderson is a "significant study of a much criticized American novelist, which probes the dark recesses of his thinking and registers an impartial verdict."

*7 ANON. Review of Schevill, Sherwood Anderson and Howe, Sherwood Anderson. Bookmark, 10 (May), 182.
Cited: Book Review Digest 1951, p. 425.

*8 ANON. Review of Howe, Sherwood Anderson. Wisconsin Library Bulletin, 47 (May), 120.
Cited: Book Review Digest 1951, p. 425.

9 ARVIN, NEWTON. "Sherwood Anderson's Brief Triumph." New York Times Book Review (8 April), pp. 5, 21.
Howe presents a personally responsive yet critically responsible view of Anderson, finding him truly productive only from 1919 to 1924.

10 BAB, JULIUS. Amerikas Dichter der Gegenwart. Berlin-Hamburg: Christian Verlag, pp. 19-21, 84.
Winesburg, Ohio lacks Lewis' journalistic descriptions of small-town life but does present character lyrically. Becoming entrapped by psychoanalytic models, Anderson never succeeded in his writing after 1924.

11 BEACH, J. W. "New Books in Review." Yale Review, New Series 40 (Summer), 749-50.
Howe is off the point of Poor White, he is very fine on Winesburg, Ohio, and overall Sherwood Anderson is "a just and discriminating account of the life and personality of Anderson. . . ."

12 BERLAND, ALWYN. "Sherwood Anderson and the Pathetic Grotesque." Western Review, 15 (Winter), 135-38.
In Winesburg, Ohio Anderson avoids sentimentality by juxtaposing "objective statement" and "pathetic insight." Anderson's characters--no matter how frustrated--retain some beautiful ideal of life.

13 BROSSARD, CHANDLER. "Sherwood Anderson: A Sweet Singer, 'A Smooth Son of a Bitch.'" American Mercury, 72 (May), 611-16.
Publication of Howe's Sherwood Anderson recalls amazement felt at first reading Winesburg, Ohio, for in that book Anderson returned to colloquial style. Such mastery of craft early in the writer's career makes doubly unfortunate his later failures.

14 CORCORAN, MARGUERITE PACE. Review of Schevill, Sherwood Anderson. Catholic World, 174 (October), 79.
Schevill's sympathetic Sherwood Anderson "is a tragic commentary on the life of a man who sought with fierce intensity and only partial success to find the sublimated meaning of life through art."

15 COWLEY, MALCOLM. Exile's Return: A Literary Odyssey of the 1920's. Revised edition. New York: Viking Press, pp. 8-9, 107, 180, 296.
Younger writers of the 1920's had life easier than Anderson, who was forty before he could write full-time. But the new exile generation owed to Anderson's generation the possibility of living and writing freely.

16 _____. "No Rules for What Sherwood Anderson Tried to Do." New York Herald Tribune Book Review (8 April), p. 3.
Howe is unable to respond well to Anderson, for this writer did not follow academic or intellectual rules; Anderson created by instinct. However, Howe's chapter on Winesburg, Ohio is the best such study to date.

*17 DAHLBERG, EDWARD. "My Friends Stieglitz, Anderson and Dreiser." Tomorrow, 10 (May), 22-27.
Reprinted: 1964.B9.

18 DEEGAN, DOROTHY YOST. The Stereotype of the Single Woman in American Novels: A Social Study with Implications for the Education of Women. New York: King's Crown Press, pp. 97, 115, 121, 156, 234.
The heroine of Poor White, a teacher, engages in a possibly homosexual relationship. Few single-women

1951

(DEEGAN, DOROTHY YOST)
characters are "more startling and memorable" than Kate Swift in Winesburg, Ohio.

19 DREISER, HELEN. My Life with Dreiser. Cleveland: World Publishing Co., pp. 218, 237, 279-80.
Dreiser enjoyed visiting with Anderson in the summer of 1931; later he asked Anderson to contribute to The American Spectator. At Anderson's funeral Stanley Young read Dreiser's tribute to Anderson.

20 FERGUSON, DELANCEY. Review of Schevill, Sherwood Anderson. New York Herald Tribune Book Review (16 September), p. 12.
The subject of Schevill's Sherwood Anderson is more pathetic than tragic, author of one good book and a very few good stories.

21 FORER, VALERIA. "A Note on Sherwood Anderson." Shenandoah, 2 (Summer), 8-9.
In "Death in the Woods" Anderson recalls a childhood memory which has helped form his adult personality.

22 HOFFMAN, FREDERICK J. The Modern Novel in America: 1900-1950. Chicago: Henry Regnery, pp. 77, 78, 80, 82-83, 106-10, 116, 154.
Hemingway learned much from knowing and reading Anderson and Stein; but Stein's own influence on Anderson was probably harmful. Anderson's heroes ceremonially leave conventional society for freedom, often finding grotesquerie their end. Always simplifying problems and answers, Anderson writes against repression and soulless societies.

23 HOWE, IRVING. "The Book of the Grotesque." Partisan Review, 18 (January-February), 32-40.
Not intended as realism, Winesburg, Ohio is lyrical drawings of characters--grotesques who once strived for meaning but now suppress desires for love. The recurring central figure centers and anchors their attempts again to have community and love. Reprinted: 1951.A1.

24 _____. "Sherwood Anderson: An American as Artist." Kenyon Review, 13 (Spring), 193-203.
Anderson felt isolated from American society and turned defensively inward for solace and inspiration. Without complex intellect or philosophy, Anderson responded emotionally, loving his characters instead of developing them--or himself beyond them. Reprinted: 1951.A1.

25 LOVETT, ROBERT MORSS. "Sherwood Anderson, American." Literary Opinion in America. Edited by Morton Dauwen Zabel. Revised edition. New York: Harper & Brothers, pp. 478-84.
Reprint of 1941.B71.

26 MANCHESTER, WILLIAM. Disturber of the Peace: The Life of H. L. Mencken. Introduction by Gerald W. Johnson. New York: Harper & Brothers, pp. 42, 78, 86, 189, 220.
Anderson submitted manuscripts when Mencken began editing The Smart Set. John Lane could not publish Winesburg, Ohio because the company had folded. Even Anderson's work was censored in Boston. When Mencken lost contact with such writers as Anderson, The American Mercury suffered.

27 MATTHIESSEN, F. O. Theodore Dreiser. New York: William Sloane Associates, pp. 7, 61, 96, 164, 169-70, 171, 187, 214, 238.
Whereas Anderson wrote much about rural Midwestern life, Dreiser set his fiction in cities. Anderson always praised Dreiser for writing of life exactly as observed, especially sexual aspects of life. Later Dreiser would disagree with Anderson's anti-industrial comments.

28 OZAKI, SHIRO. "My Literary Youth." Gunzo [Kodansha] (February), pp. 96-101.
[Retelling of 1934.B28.] [Takashi Kodaira]

29 PAVESE, CESARE. La Letteratura Americana e Altri Saggi. Turin: Giullio Einaudi Editore, pp. 6, 29, 31, 33-49, 66, 78, 113, 131, 148, 167, 169, 177, 184, 195, 293, 361, 362.
Reprint of 1931.B48; 1934.B29; 1947.B23. Translated: 1970.B28.

30 PHILLIPS, WILLIAM L. "How Sherwood Anderson Wrote Winesburg, Ohio." American Literature, 23 (March), 7-30.
Study of Anderson's manuscript of Winesburg, Ohio reveals that the author wrote one draft (often highly revised) of each story and determines (through verso page numberings) his general order of composition.
Reprinted: 1966.A6; 1966.A7; 1971.A2; 1974.A3.

31 POLICARDI, SILVIO. Breve Storia della Letteratura Americana. Milan: Varese Cisalpino, pp. 228, 231-32, 233.
Anderson's naturalism developed beyond that of Norris and Dreiser, for he had learned from Freud that psychoanalytic forces determine action as much as social forces. His writing is mystical and poetic; his subject, the inner life revealed in momentary insights.

1951

32 POORE, CHARLES. "American Realism and Mr. Anderson." New York Times Book Review (8 April), p. 21.
Scheville's study of Anderson presents views from detractors and advocates, suggesting the middle course of evaluating the writer's achievement.

33 PRAZ, MARIO. "Parodia di 'Risa Nero.'" Cronache Letterarie Anglosassoni, 2. Rome: Edizioni di Storia e Letteratura, pp. 190-95.
In The Torrents of Spring Hemingway parodied Anderson's simplicity in seeing heroic qualities in Negroes and other primitive peoples. Stylistically, Hemingway's parody is of monosyllables, repetitions, and tautologies.

34 QUINN, ARTHUR HOBSON, ed. The Literature of the American People: An Historical and Critical Survey. New York: Appleton-Century-Crofts, pp. 864, 871-73, 884, 958.
George F. Whicher believes that Winesburg, Ohio was not a satire but a "caress" of village life, for Anderson ignored conventional definitions of good and bad and retained fascination with inner lives. A "connoisseur of psychological grotesques," Anderson felt bardic urges to tell stories of small lives in moments of flowering understanding.

*35 REYNOLDS, HORACE. Review of Howe, Sherwood Anderson. Christian Science Monitor (18 April), p. 9.
Cited: Book Review Digest 1951, p. 425.

36 SCHLOSS, GEORGE. "Sherwood Anderson." Hudson Review, 4 (Autumn), 477-80.
Whereas Howe's study of Anderson is academic and exegetic, Schevill creates a dull, standard, and human book. Both writers reveal Anderson's life as interesting but extending until he had little to say.

37 SHIFFMAN, JOSEPH. "The Alienation of the Artist: Alfred Stieglitz." American Quarterly, 3 (Fall), 253-54.
Anderson prefaced the catalogue for a Stieglitz exhibit in 1925 and supplied literary confirmation of the photographer's dissatisfaction with modern life.

38 SMITH, HENRY NASH. "'The Liberated Artist.'" Nation, 172 (19 May), 472-73.
Schevill in Sherwood Anderson: His Life and Work presents a chronological approach; Howe in Sherwood Anderson focuses upon the author critically, finding a limited amount of writing to admire.

39 STRAUMANN, HEINRICH. _American Literature in the Twentieth Century_. New York: Hutchinson's University Library, pp. 52, 73, 79, 83-84, 85.

Using psychological approaches in his fiction, Anderson probes deeply into recessed lives, siding with expressed, vital instincts. Whereas _Winesburg, Ohio_ attacked sexual repressions, _Poor White_ attacked industry's effects on humans.

40 TRILLING, LIONEL. "Dreiser, Anderson, Lewis, And the Riddle of Society." _Reporter_, 5 (13 November), 37-40.

Regarding Anderson's alleged emphasis upon sexuality, the truth is that he handles sex poorly in fiction. Anderson lacked the ability to discuss individual-society conflicts intellectually, dropping into isolationist, mystical solutions.

41 WAGENKNECHT, EDWARD. "A Study of One of Our Most Puzzling Authors." _Chicago Tribune Books_ (15 April), p. 4.

Irving Howe's _Sherwood Anderson_ has presented an objective study to determine why the writer is no longer important.

42 WEAVER, ROBERT L. "Turning New Leaves." _Canadian Forum_, 31 (September), 134-35.

In _Sherwood Anderson_ Howe demonstrates that the author himself became artistically grotesque--believing that words and ideas must remain soft and fuzzy instead of "hard and bright."

43 WEBER, BROM. "Anderson and 'The Essence of Things.'" _Sewanee Review_, 59 (Autumn), 678-92.

Whereas Schevill admires Anderson and faithfully chronicles his life, Howe proves his bias against an admittedly non-intellectual writer. Anderson is actually a literary anarchist.

44 WINSTON, RICHARD. Review of Howe, _Sherwood Anderson_. _Tomorrow_, 10 (May), 58-59.

Anderson is not important to current writers, for he was always the intellectually avant-garde. Howe's study is objective, fair, reserving for Anderson a place as re-creator of a "sleepy nineteenth-century American midwest which was passing forever."

45 YOUNG, STARK. _The Pavilion: Of People and Times Remembered, Of Stories and Places_. New York: Charles Scribner's Sons, pp. 59-60.

1952

(YOUNG, STARK)

Young encouraged Elizabeth Prall to hire Faulkner for the bookstore that she managed; as Mrs. Sherwood Anderson, she introduced Faulkner to her husband and encouraged Anderson to help the younger writer to publish his first novel.

1952 A BOOKS

1 FIORAVANTI, JOSEPH A. "A Comparative Study of the Grotesques in Sherwood Anderson and Hawthorne." Master's thesis, New York University, 130 pp.

The actions of several Hawthorne characters in The Twice-Told Tales resemble those of characters in Winesburg, Ohio. Hawthorne first expressed loneliness as part of the national character; and Anderson writes of the nineteenth century--the age of Hawthorne himself. These writers shared the belief that a lack of love is life's central problem.

1952 B SHORTER WRITINGS

1 ALDRIDGE, JOHN W., ed. Critiques and Essays on Modern Fiction, 1920-1951. New York: Ronald Press, pp. 572-74.

[Secondary bibliography]

2 BRODBECK, MAY, JAMES GRAY, and WALTER METZGER. American Non-Fiction, 1900-1950. Chicago: Henry Regnery Co., pp. 115-16.

When Anderson could not fictionally say everything that he needed to say, he wrote autobiographies, "public confessions." The former journalist wanted to shock the bourgeoisie with his hatred of a materialistic society. In A Story Teller's Story Anderson combines the criticism with his optimism about positive American values.

3 BROOKS, VAN WYCK. The Confident Years, 1885-1915. New York: E. P. Dutton & Co., pp. 140, 189, 239-40, 325, 407, 409, 410-12, 413, 418, 419, 439-40, 500, 515, 526, 533, 545, 560, 566.

When Anderson wrote stories using sex frankly, he was wrongly accused of having been influenced by Freud and Lawrence, for the assumption was that no native could naturally write thus. The characters in Winesburg, Ohio developed from life-stories Anderson learned in Chicago. Influenced by Stein's work, Anderson should never have quit writing stories in favor of novels.

4 COURNOS, JOHN and SYBIL NORTON. Famous Modern American Novelists. New York: Dodd, Mead and Co., pp. 30, 112, 130, 173-74, 175.
Anderson valued writing for content and need for expression. Winesburg, Ohio expressed the inarticulate yearnings of unhappy Midwestern villagers and shocked complacent, hypocritical America. Anderson is distinguished "as a story teller, forthwright, warm and compassionate."

5 HARRIS, MARK. City of Discontent. Indianapolis: Bobbs-Merrill Co., pp. 195, 272, 319.
Only slowly would the common person realize the new power of such Midwestern Renaissance writers as Anderson. Winesburg, Ohio created a prototypical American town; later, teachers would perhaps read daringly in Anderson's work.

6 HILTON, EARL. "The Evolution of Sherwood Anderson's 'Brother Death.'" Northwest Ohio Quarterly, 24 (Summer), 125-30.
Realizing that the tone of a story develops as the work is being created, Anderson told "Brother Death" through completely, making few changes that would equal "revision," instead of "rewriting." Such changes in "Brother Death" affect point of view, details, and theme.

7 HORTON, ROD W. and HERBERT W. EDWARDS. Backgrounds of American Literary Thought. New York: Appleton-Century-Crofts, pp. 259, 321, 331, 355, 356-57.
Blix by Norris suggests in studying adolescence Anderson's works. In the 1920's, Anderson ironically referred to Freud's popularity in America; he had imitated Stein's "naive" style from "Melanctha." Winesburg, Ohio showed that Anderson wrote toward primitivism rather than Freudianism.

8 JONES, HOWARD MUMFORD. The Bright Medusa. Urbana: University of Illinois Press, pp. 6-8.
Howe's Sherwood Anderson most unsympathetically denigrates the Chicago Renaissance and Anderson's role in it.

9 LEWIS, SINCLAIR. From Main Street to Stockholm: Letters of Sinclair Lewis, 1919-1930. Edited by Harrison Smith. New York: Harcourt, Brace and Co., pp. 32, 48, 214, 299.
Lewis believed that he and Anderson saw the flaws of small-town life. Anderson's friend Lewis Galantière wanted Main Street translated into French; Anderson should receive a copy of Lewis' latest book, for Lewis admired Anderson's work.

10 MASON, FRANKLIN. "The American County Fair II." Prairie Schooner, 26 (Spring), 97-101.

A fine writer, Anderson described a county fair imaginatively.

11 NAGASAWA, TAKAKO. "'Loneliness': Man and Literature." Eibei Bungakukai Kaiho [Rikkyo Daigaku Eibei Bungakukai], 12 (February), 10-11.

"Loneliness" may answer the question of what literature is. Not only literature but also philosophy, religion, and such are nothing but creatures of the fancy by lonely people. Consciousness by mankind--loneliness--has made history until now. [Takashi Kodaira]

12 NISHIKAWA, MASAMI. "Some Characteristics of Sherwood Anderson's Style." Rising Generation (May), pp. 4-5.

It is true that Anderson's revisions of "Hands"--as described by Phillips--have something to do with the relation between author and audience, but it has much to do with the author's own nature. Anderson could not write broadly; he is an oral storyteller, often telling the end of a story and then giving a detailed account, as in "Adventure." [Takashi Kodaira]

13 PHILLIPS, WILLIAM L. "The First Printing of Sherwood Anderson's Winesburg, Ohio." Studies in Bibliography, 4 (1951-52), 211-13.

A reviewer's comment in 1919 about Anderson's poor grammar helps to differentiate the first and second printings of Winesburg, Ohio.

14 SAROYAN, WILLIAM. The Bicycle Rider in Beverly Hills. New York: Charles Scribner's Sons, pp. 120-21.

Saroyan's father--like Anderson's father--raised chickens to sell eggs, and his venture likewise failed.

15 SCHERMAN, DAVID E. and ROSEMARIE REDLICH. "Sherwood Anderson." Literary America: A Chronicle of American Writers from 1607-1952 with 173 Photographs of the American Scenes that Inspired Them. New York: Dodd, Mead and Co., pp. 118-19.

Based on Clyde, Ohio, Anderson's Winesburg, Ohio exaggerates tendencies in all people. Always as baffled as his characters, he positively influenced writers of the 1920's.

16 SISK, JOHN. "American Pastoral." Thought, 27 (Autumn), 372, 373.

In Winesburg, Ohio Anderson glorifies the misfit as a type of pastoral hero; yet Anderson never perfects the ideal world for his misfits.

17 TAKIGAWA, MOTOO. "On Winesburg, Ohio." Journal of the Literary Association of Kwansei Gakuin University (February), pp. 111-23.

The motif of Winesburg, Ohio is to draw the inside of a Middle Western small town broken down under capitalistic civilization. Its theme is the problem of the grotesques--different from "impotent" people but on the road to impotency. Grotesqueness results from lack of love. Once Anderson's thoughts and realism received the baptism of impressionism, it may well be that his works became either too subjective or too idealistic. His art cannot follow in the wake of his thought; but in Winesburg, Ohio is the unity of his original realism and his humanistic love toward the grotesque. Thus, Winesburg, Ohio is imperishable in the history of American literature. [Takashi Kodaira]

18 _____. "Sherwood Anderson's Sensuousness." Studies in English Literature [English Literary Society of Japan] (November), pp. 219-33.

Machines deprive men of independence and individuality and make men impotent. Women are less affected, for every woman has within herself love untouchable by machines. In the machine age men cannot love and satisfy women. Frustrated women, who cannot control their love, try to find satisfaction in Nature, as do men. Man is born in Nature and returns to Nature; the pursuit is pathetic because Nature is being hurt by the machine age. Anderson's writings are the tragic fruit of sensuousness of genius in the machine age. [Takashi Kodaira]

19 UEMURA, IKUO. "Anderson's Attitude and Style." Study of English (September), pp. 26-31.

Anderson says that what interests him is human life. He tried to recover real life by liberating sex. His sense of structure is so loose, as Kazin said, that he takes designs only from life. But to Anderson "the style of writing is a thing as subtle as women's clothes," and he recommends Borrow as a model for style. [Takashi Kodaira]

20 WAGENKNECHT, EDWARD. Cavalcade of the American Novel: From the Birth of the Nation to the Middle of the Twentieth Century. New York: Henry Holt and Co., pp. 311-18, 372, 391, 418, 539-41.

The American D. H. Lawrence, Anderson praised liberation from convention and mechanization; and his characters suffer from frustration and loneliness. Anderson thus influenced the American novel without being able to write a good novel.

1952

21 WALCUTT, CHARLES CHILD. "Sherwood Anderson: Impressionism and the Buried Life." Sewanee Review, 60 (Winter), 28-47.

Anderson "renders qualities of personality and dimensions of experience beyond anything in the work of Crane, Norris, London, or Dreiser"; his naturalism is concerned with inward, psychological motivation but restricted sometimes by lack of order and structure. Reprinted: 1956.B16; 1966.A3; 1966.A7.

22 *WEST, RAY B., JR. The Short Story in America: 1900-1950. Chicago: Henry Regnery Co., pp. 11, 24, 26, 30, 34, 36, 42, 43-45, 46-48, 49, 50-54, 115, 116, 119.

Six months with Anderson in New Orleans was Faulkner's most significant apprenticeship. Anderson's naturalism was more psychologically based than Dreiser's, for Anderson emphasized the individual more than society and saw natural life as redemptive of social ills. When Anderson tried social reforming, his fiction suffered.

23 WILSON, EDMUND. The Shores of Light: A Literary Chronicle of the Twenties and Thirties. New York: Farrar, Straus and Young, pp. 91-93, 95, 100, 117, 119, 125, 134-35, 154, 233-34, 236, 246, 370, 399, 422, 501, 577, 632, 656, 659.

O'Neill, like Anderson, emphasized the individual pitted against social norms. Hemingway denied imitating "I'm a Fool" or being inspired by Anderson, now "gone to hell." Although living by writing advertising, Anderson wrote stories to fix his fancy upon reality; writing from instinct instead of from rules, Anderson created some excellent fiction. Reprint of 1923.B63; 1924.B48; 1924.B49.

1953 A BOOKS

1 WELTZ, FRIEDRICH. "Vier amerikanische Erzählungszyklen: J. London: 'Tales of the Fish Patrol.' Sh. Anderson: 'Winesburg, Ohio.' J. Steinbeck: 'The Pastures of Heaven.' E. Hemingway, 'In Our Time.'" Dissertation, Ludwig-Maximilians-Universität zu München, 141 pp.

Wanting each story in Winesburg, Ohio to be an entity and yet form the element of a cycle, Anderson used his theory of moments to compose the work of equally important parts, not subordinate episodes. Anderson's theme is the maturing of the central character while in each story another character resists an unsympathetic milieu.

1953 B SHORTER WRITINGS

1 ANON. "Anderson, Sherwood." Der Grosse Herder, 1. Freiburg: Verlag Herder, 358.
Influential on the development of the short story, Anderson used psychological realism in his rhythmically, lyrically narrated work about small-town citizens.

*2 ANON. Review of Letters of Sherwood Anderson. Bulletin of Virginia Kirkus' Bookshop Service, 21 (1 March), 178.
Cited: Book Review Digest 1953, p. 14.

3 ANON. "Nonfiction." Bookmark, 12 (July), 225.
Anderson's Letters "reveal the preoccupation with his life and the many friendships of an important American writer."

4 ANON. Review of Letters of Sherwood Anderson. Wisconsin Library Bulletin, 49 (July), 172.
The Letters are "completely personal, and often brutally transparent" and "constitute a fairly full autobiography of the period [1916-1941]."

5 ANON. "Biography." Booklist, 49 (1 July), 356.
The Letters "strengthen Anderson's position as a writer who helped make possible the freedom of modern American fiction by uncovering the repressed life."

6 ANON. Review of Letters of Sherwood Anderson. New Yorker, 29 (8 August), 79-80.
The Letters show that Anderson had few ideas, much self-deception, and love of people and honesty.

7 ANON. Review of Letters of Sherwood Anderson. United States Quarterly Book Review, 9 (September), 259.
The Letters discuss Anderson's ideas on writing, psychology, industry, and social issues.

8 ARNAVON, CYRILLE. Histoire Littéraire des États-Unis. Paris: Librairie Hachette, pp. 182, 199, 262, 312, 321-23, 326, 330, 338, 343, 356, 411.
Unlike Lewis, Anderson is not caustic but instead nostalgic and troubled. He examines the secret aspects of individual lives, probing intuitively to unmask frustrations and despairs. Emotional rather than intellectual, Anderson writes of modern disorder from a too-romantic perspective, approaching writing as magical and spontaneous.

1953

9 BROOKS, VAN WYCK. The Writer in America. New York: E. P. Dutton & Co., pp. 64, 65, 82, 83.
American literature sometimes thought adolescent, Anderson's "adolescent gropings were matched by those of Thomas Wolfe, a writer of genius who never quite grew up"; or, as Howe said, Anderson never matched again the genius of his best early work. Perhaps Anderson got lost in Lawrence, Stein, or Joyce when he read them.

10 CARDWELL, GUY A. "Anderson, Sherwood." Der Amerikanische Roman (1850-1951). Vienna: United States Information Service, p. 41.
Not a satirist as was Lewis, Anderson brooded on life and tried to portray the emotional springs of his characters. Anderson could become sentimental over the lost innocence of small-town America.

11 DICKINSON, ASA DON. "Anderson, Sherwood." The World's Best Books: Homer to Hemingway. New York: H. W. Wilson Co., pp. 6-7.
[Six of Anderson's best books briefly described]

12 FAULKNER, WILLIAM. "Sherwood Anderson: An Appreciation." Atlantic, 191 (June), 27-29.
Anderson worked thoroughly and laboriously over each of his works, valuing expression above all. He taught Faulkner to do the same, accepting only satisfying work. Having helped Faulkner publish his first novel, Anderson was a giant, "even if he did make but the two or perhaps three gestures commensurate with gianthood." Reprinted: 1965.B8; 1966.A3; 1966.A7; 1974.A3.

13 FIELD, ARROW. "On 'Mother' in Winesburg, Ohio." Eibei Bungakukai Kaiho [Rikkyo Daigaku Eibei Bungakukai], 16 (December), 7-8.
Using such psychological terms as sexual dissatisfaction, perversion, and inferiority complex, the story "Mother" can be analyzed to determine Anderson's particular interest in the minds of his characters. [Takashi Kodaira]

14 FLANAGAN, JOHN T. "Anderson's Flashing Insight." Southwest Review, 38 (Autumn), xiv-xv, 350.
Although Anderson's Letters show frequent brilliant insights into art and life, they are full of "prolixity, repetition, fragmentation, abruptness, incompleteness, a certain mental disorderliness and incapacity for analysis."

15 GURKO, LEO. Heroes, Highbrows and the Popular Mind. Indianapolis: Bobbs-Merrill Co., pp. 47-48, 218.

Anderson's characters act on emotion and instinct, having scarcely any intellect, much as Anderson himself left his paint factory. Influenced by Ruskin and Lawrence, Anderson disliked the machine age and preferred primitivism.

16 H., R. F. "Author's Personal Views Voiced in Correspondence." Springfield Republican (12 July), D, p. 8.

Anderson may be the first totally American writer, his Letters show; but they add little new information about his life or importance.

17 HARDWICK, ELIZABETH. "Anderson, Crane and Millay in Their Letters." Partisan Review, 20 (November), 690-92.

Anderson's Letters reveal only his life as a writer, but that is painfully concentrated on self.

Reprinted: 1962.B15.

18 [HEAP, JANE.] "Words." The Little Review Anthology. New York: Hermitage House, pp. 284-85.

Reprint of 1922.B29.

19 HOWE, IRVING. "A Journey to Fame and Uncertainty." New York Times Book Review (14 June), pp. 1, 17.

Many of Anderson's Letters are irritatingly "folksy," but those dealing with his need to write or reacting to others' need to write are moving; his later letters show him bypassed by life.

20 JONES, HOWARD MUMFORD. "Portrait of a Mid-Westerner, Lonely but Happy, Simple but Complex." New York Herald Tribune Book Review (12 April), pp. 1, 19.

Even Anderson's letters are partly "fictional," as his fiction is partly autobiographical. Only Winesburg, Ohio and a few stories will survive as classics. Anderson swung from child to adult, from realist to mystic, from cheerfulness to despair--always dramatically and always reflected in his works. Reprinted in part as "Introduction." Letters of Sherwood Anderson. Edited by Howard Mumford Jones and Walter B. Rideout. Boston: Little, Brown and Co., 1953, pp. vii-xviii.

21 KAZIN, ALFRED. "Anderson's Letters: A Major Document of His Great Generation." New York Herald Tribune Book Review (7 June), pp. 1, 17.

Obsessed with the need to write rather than with a message, Anderson wrote more letters than anything else.

1953

(KAZIN, ALFRED)
The Letters document well the generation that truly created "American" literature. Reprinted: 1955.B13.

22 LEWIS, SINCLAIR. The Man from Main Street: A Sinclair Lewis Reader. Edited by Harry E. Maule, Melville Cane, and Philip Allan Freedman. New York: Random House, pp. 8-9, 11, 137, 158, 161, 165-68.
Had Anderson received the Nobel Prize, he would have been charged with "considering sex as important a force in life as fishing." Carl Van Doren could be wrong to say that Masters influenced Anderson, and DeVoto does not even mention Anderson as a writer of the 1920's.
Reprint of 1924.B26.

23 MILLER, PERRY. "A Curious Sense of Dirt." New Republic, 128 (22 June), 19-20.
The Letters reveal that Anderson's great concept was "cleansing" himself of business or family or society--all to escape from self and all described honestly.

24 MYKLEBOST, TOR. "Sherwood Anderson, Elskeren." Drømmen om Amerika: Den Amerikanske Roman Gjennom Femti År. Oslo: Gyldendal Norsk Forlag, pp. 74-80.
Only Anderson's last novel was the product of his fancy, the other major works being autobiographical. Winesburg, Ohio portends an era's end, while Poor White shows the village industrialized. Anderson went backward in time for the meaning of existence. Having perfect mastery over short stories, Anderson had trouble sustaining novel-length plots. Enemy of Puritanism, Anderson spoke for love and humanization of life.

25 PAULDING, GOUVENEUR. "Anderson." Reporter, 8 (23 June), 39.
Anderson's Letters reveal his acceptance of all life, his denial of arbitrary form, and his search for honesty in writing.

26 RAYMUND, BERNARD. Review of Letters of Sherwood Anderson. Arizona Quarterly, 9 (Winter), 357-59.
Anderson's Letters show him as cheerful, contrary to the picture in Schevill's biography. No one has written so much or so well about authorship as Anderson, and he maintained his imaginative faculty to the end.

27 REYNOLDS, HORACE. "Portrait of 'the Middle Western Man as Prophet.'" Christian Science Monitor (11 June), p. 11.
Anderson's Letters share the author's joy in creating literature and advice that writing must reflect life imaginatively.

*28 SCHEVILL, JAMES. Review of Letters of Sherwood Anderson. San Francisco Chronicle (14 June), p. 16.
Cited: 1962.B44.

29 THORP, WILLARD. "He Stuck to His Own Street." Nation, 176 (20 June), 526-28.
The Letters raise questions about Anderson's ability to handle facts even about himself; having few ideas, Anderson invented details. Some of his best letters deal with other authors.

30 WAGENKNECHT, EDWARD. "The 'Eternal Amateur' Who Loved Humanity." Chicago Tribune Magazine of Books (7 June), p. 3.
The Letters show Anderson's love of all people and of his self-confessed "amateur" status, for he influenced American literature more than he contributed to it.

31 WALBRIDGE, EARLE F. Review of Letters of Sherwood Anderson. Library Journal, 78 (1 June), 986.
Anderson's Letters show him "in turn naive, gross, mystical, practical, despairing, and piercingly observant."

32 WEBER, BROM. "A Torn, Noble Man." Saturday Review, 36 (20 June), 20.
Anderson's Letters amply show him to have been a success, for his novels even have good parts. Many letters are tenderly lyrical as is his best work.

1954 A BOOKS - NONE

1954 B SHORTER WRITINGS

1 ATHERTON, LEWIS. Main Street on the Middle Border. Bloomington: Indiana University Press, pp. 40, 88, 95-96, 97, 123, 182-83, 343.
Anderson has used livery stables as male meeting places in several stories. Obsessed with sex, Anderson "engaged in a series of tawdry sexual alliances" and "had trouble living a normal married life."

2 BROWN, GLENORA A. and DEMING B. BROWN. A Guide to Soviet Translations of American Literature. New York: King's Crown Press, pp. 20, 21, 33-34, 38-41, 45-47.
[Seventeen translations of Anderson's works into Russian]

1954

3 BROWN, JOHN. Panorama de la Littérature Contemporaine aux États-Unis: Introductions, Illustrations, Documents. Second edition. Paris: Librairie Gallimard, pp. 16, 21, 24, 26, 30, 32, 52, 75, 87, 89-92, 100, 107, 108, 112, 115, 158, 160, 185, 259.

There are three stages in Anderson's work: Winesburg, Ohio, the basis of his reputation; exploitation of this style in Horses and Men and The Triumph of the Egg; a turning toward psychological pretentions in Many Marriages. After 1919, Anderson tried to be the Ohio D. H. Lawrence, a move which limited his powers and confused his style. He liberated American literature from "plot stories," even if much of his work is of secondary importance.

4 CHAPMAN, ARNOLD. "Sherwood Anderson and Eduardo Mallea." Publications of the Modern Language Association of America, 69 (March), 34-45.

Both Anderson and Mallea use similar plots, symbols of isolation, and phrasing; they differ in treating the "action" of isolation and grotesquerie. They agree on sex, communication, love, and the role of the artist in society.

5 COX, NANCY. "Monument to Author Anderson, Ripshin." Richmond Times-Dispatch (18 April), p. 78.

Anderson's only home, "Ripshin," in Southwest Virginia, was built to provide isolation for the writer and a retreat for his creative friends. The house reflects the man's qualities of independence, realism, and unorthodoxy.

6 DUFFEY, BERNARD. The Chicago Renaissance in American Letters: A Critical History. East Lansing: Michigan State College Press, pp. 6, 90, 92, 131, 136, 137, 140, 189, 190, 191, 194-209, 212, 213, 221, 231, 237, 238, 247.

Anderson's abrupt rejection of business in Ohio in 1912 freed him to join the Chicago Renaissance in 1913, his first novels patterned on his own life. In all of his works, only love answers the problems of anomie. In Chicago Anderson had learned of Stein's prose experiments and had joined the liberation of vital Midwestern writers. In short, the Renaissance taught Anderson the value of imaginative work and living. Reprinted in part: 1966.A7.

7 _____. Review of Letters of Sherwood Anderson. American Literature, 26 (November), 640-41.

Anderson's subject in his Letters is always himself in search of self-identity.

8 FARRELL, JAMES T. "A Memoir on Sherwood Anderson." Perspective, 7 (Summer), 83-88.

Not Dreiser but Anderson most inspired Farrell, who read Anderson in 1927. Anderson's setting, tone, and personal bewilderment appealed to identical qualities in Farrell; Tar most impressed Farrell as "re-affirmation of self." At a meeting in New York in 1937, Anderson spoke of fancy in fiction and demonstrated integrity. Their second and last meeting, in 1940, was brief. Reprinted: 1954.B9.

9 _____. "A Note on Sherwood Anderson." Reflections at Fifty and Other Essays. New York: Vanguard Press, pp. 164-68.

Reprint of 1954.B8.

10 FENTON, CHARLES A. The Apprenticeship of Ernest Hemingway: The Early Years. New York: Farrar, Straus & Young, pp. 100, 103-105, 107, 116-20, 122, 126, 145-50, 156, 203, 225, 226, 236, 248.

Anderson encouraged Hemingway to return to Europe, from where Anderson had recently come. Hemingway went to Paris with letters of introduction from Anderson to Stein and other writers; from them he learned the work of writing, whereas Anderson had claimed to write spontaneously. Hemingway told Fitzgerald that Winesburg, Ohio was his first literary model.

11 GELFANT, BLANCHE H. "Sherwood Anderson, Edith Wharton, and Thomas Wolfe." The American City Novel. Norman: University of Oklahoma Press, pp. 95-132.

Anderson's novels, treating "personal dissociation and the failure of love" and set in small towns or in cities, belong to the study of city fiction. Anderson dramatized anomie and analyzed it from economic and social causes; he examines the social individual in both past and present, especially in Poor White. Reprinted: 1974.A3.

12 GRILLO, GIUSEPPE. "Ingenuità e Vigio in Sherwood Anderson." Idea: Settimanale di Cultura, 6 (18 April), 3-4.

American naturalism is native and can lead to a false picture of life. In Anderson's works naturalism verges on evasion and is best in the short story form; his characters are figures buried in the limbo of provincial life. Anderson's art consists of imperfection and simplicity.

*13 GUIDO, AUGUSTO. "Sherwood Anderson." Mondo Occidentale, No. 5 (November).

Cited: 1955.B32.

1954

14 HART, ROBERT CHARLES. "Writers on Writing: The Opinions of Six Modern American Novelists on the Craft of Fiction." Dissertation, Northwestern University, 489 pp.

Anderson had an unformulated but workable theory of the role of the writer--fiction presents what could well happen, fiction is not photographic but romantic, fiction is imagination fed by reality, fiction is therapeutic for writer and readers, and the writer senses humanity above self. The writer acts as a "priest" to promote understanding and reconciliation.

15 HECHT, BEN. A Child of the Century. New York: Simon and Schuster, pp. 225-32, 234, 247, 329, 331, 339, 341, 344.

Hecht believed few of the personal tales Anderson told. The two writers in Chicago tried to collaborate on a play about Cellini, but Anderson seemed not to worry about difficulty in being published. Anderson's mistress tried to kill herself when he ignored her; Anderson had merely "experimented" in the affair. Later Anderson suggested that he and Hecht play enemies instead of friends, and their last meeting was just before Anderson's death.

16 HOFFMAN, FREDERICK J. "Sherwood Anderson: A 'Groping, Artistic, Sincere Personality.'" Western Review, 18 (Winter), 159-62.

Of two new biographies of Anderson, Howe's Sherwood Anderson is better criticism; Schevill's Sherwood Anderson: His Life and Work is more factual. What emerges from Anderson's successes is his power to present truth instinctively, to choose to write well; Anderson fails when he speculates upon his observations, creating a line of grossly failing novels.

17 LEARY, LEWIS, ed. Articles on American Literature, 1900-1950. Durham: Duke University Press, pp. 11-13.

[Fifty-nine articles on Anderson; nine articles by Anderson]

18 O'CONNOR, WILLIAM VAN. The Tangled Fire of William Faulkner. Minneapolis: University of Minnesota Press, pp. 20-25, 31-32, 164.

When Faulkner modeled Dawson Fairchild of Mosquitoes on Anderson, he did not do so admiringly. At a New York party, Faulkner proved more popular than Anderson, who once commented on Faulkner's height and another time warned Faulkner not to let talent overwhelm development.

19 OHASHI, KICHINOSUKE. "On Sherwood Anderson." American Literary Review (February), pp. 4-10.

Writers of nineteenth-century America tried to describe only the surface of lives in traditional ways, but Anderson tried to see beneath the surface of lives, and he drew in his plain and naive way men's secrets. In this respect Anderson is revolutionary; but, instead of pursuing secrets more deeply, he suddenly escaped into fancy. Anderson's infantilism led to his mysticism. [Takashi Kodaira]

20 SHERBO, ARTHUR. "Sherwood Anderson's I Want to Know Why and Messrs. Brooks and Warren." College English, 15 (March), 350-51.

In Understanding Fiction Brooks and Warren imply wrongly that Anderson is discussing humans' knowledge of right and wrong in "I Want to Know Why." Actually, Anderson is discussing a human's knowledge of and appreciation of animal beauty.

21 STEEN, JOS VAN DER. Amerikaanse Romanciers van Heden. Louvain: Davidsfonds, pp. 30, 31, 132.

Wolfe lacked the objectivity and careful word choice (much less economy) of Anderson.

22 TAKAMURA, KATSUJI. "Sherwood Anderson." An Introduction to the Modern American Novel. Tokyo: Kenkyusha, pp. 51-60.

Anderson is a writer who belonged to the Chicago group and who revolted against village life; he cursed the industrialization and standardization of the world. [Takashi Kodaira]

23 TANIGUCHI, RIKUO. "A Writer and His Wives: On Sherwood Anderson, I." Kanazawa English Studies [Society of English Literature], 1 (June), 59-65.

Lonely and sensitive, Anderson seeks women to avoid loneliness. When he becomes uncomfortable under a wife's influence, he seeks help from another woman. Thus, Anderson's four wives were different. More cultivated than Anderson, they were teachers rather than wives; but he never blamed them after the divorces. Relationships with the four wives influenced Anderson's works in realism of psychology, style, Freudianism, and so forth. [Takashi Kodaira] Reprinted revised: 1965.B30.

1955

1955 A BOOKS

1 ESCHELMÜLLER, VALERIE. "Sherwood Anderson: Versuch einer Kritischen Betrachtung Seines Prosawerkes." Dissertation, University of Vienna, 150 pp.

With Anderson the critic cannot separate biography and esthetics, for the writer was a very personal artist, using personal knowledge and feelings to create prose pictures of small lives in simple, eloquent style. When Anderson wrote *Winesburg, Ohio*, *Poor White*, and *The Triumph of the Egg*, he fused mankind, machine, and small town into spontaneous, genuine critique and fiction. Never a formal fictionist, Anderson came from the tradition of oral narrative; his best work is timeless and relevant and completely part of the eternal present.

1955 B SHORTER WRITINGS

*1 ANON. "Il Meglio." *Il Mondo* [Rome] (1 February), p. 8.
Cited: 1969.B3.

2 ARGUS. Review of *Winesburg, Ohio*. *Liitto* (1 November).
[Tauno Mustanoja]

3 BRUNO, FRANCESCO. "Il Mondo di Anderson." *La Fiera Letteraria* (20 February), p. 5.

Translation of *The Sherwood Anderson Reader* provides much of Anderson to Italian readers for the first time. The collection gives Anderson's world view, for in their buried lives the writer explored his characters through prose of heightened realism.

*4 _____. "Rasconti di Sherwood Anderson." *Roma d'Oggi* (3 June), p. 5.
Cited: 1969.B3.

5 -E. Review of *Winesburg, Ohio*. *Turun Päivälehti* (11 December).
[Tauno Mustanoja]

6 FELDMAN, EUGENE S. "Sherwood Anderson's Search." *Psychoanalysis*, 3 (1955), 44-51.

Anderson's heroes--like the author himself--searched for more satisfactory worlds after escaping from frustrations. The basis of Anderson's search for "belonging" is in his nomadic childhood and undependable parents.

7 FLANAGAN, JOHN T. "Hemingway's Debt to Sherwood Anderson." Journal of English and Germanic Philology, 54 (October), 507-20.
Hemingway broke with Anderson and wrote The Torrents of Spring because he wanted to write "hard," realistic fiction; and he deplored Anderson's sentimentality and lack of humor. Yet Hemingway resembled Anderson in treatment of sex, anti-genteelism, simple characters, and distrust of plot stories. Reprinted: 1955.B8; 1966.A3.

8 _____. "Hemingway's Debt to Sherwood Anderson." Studies by Members of the English Department, University of Illinois, in Memory of John Jay Parry. Urbana: University of Illinois Press, pp. 47-60.
Reprint of 1955.B7.

9 HANNULA, RISTO. Review of Winesburg, Ohio. Satakunnan Kansa (28 October).
[Tauno Mustanoja]

10 I., K. J. Review of Winesburg, Ohio. Uusi Suomi (16 October).
[Tauno Mustanoja]

11 K., P. Review of Winesburg, Ohio. Kansan Työ (16 November).
[Tauno Mustanoja]

12 KAJIWARA, HIDEO. "Sherwood Anderson: Winesburg, Ohio." Studies in the Humanities and Social Sciences [North and South Colleges, Osaka University], 3 (March), 1-15.
Analysis of the world of Anderson's grotesques shows that the author did not rebel against the village as such but against its industrialization. Anderson tried to empathize with his grotesques, groping toward something with intuitive mysticism. Difficulty arises from Anderson's poetic and symbolic method. [Takashi Kodaira]

13 KAZIN, ALFRED. "The Letters of Sherwood Anderson." The Inmost Leaf: A Selection of Essays. New York: Harcourt, Brace and Co., pp. 223-29.
Reprint of 1953.B21.

14 KILPI, RAILI. Review of Winesburg, Ohio. Savon Sanomat (26 October).
[Tauno Mustanoja]

15 KUNITZ, STANLEY J. and VINETA COLBY, eds. "Anderson, Sherwood." Twentieth Century Authors, First Supplement: A Biographical Dictionary of Modern Literature. New York: H. W. Wilson Co., p. 20.

1955

(KUNITZ, STANLEY J. and VINETA COLBY)
[List of one primary and thirteen secondary sources]

16 L., V. Review of Winesburg, Ohio. Uusi Aura (23 October).
[Tauno Mustanoja]

17 L-O, K. Review of Winesburg, Ohio. Savo-Karjala (10 November).
[Tauno Mustanoja]

18 LENNARTZ, FRANZ. "Anderson, Sherwood." Ausländische Dichter und Schriftsteller Unserer Zeit: Einzeldarstellungen zur Schönen Literatur in Fremden Sprachen. Stuttgart: Alfred Kröner Verlag, pp. 10-12.
A literary rebel and questioner, Anderson spoke for the new realism and developed the new short story based on inner life rather than surface detail. Advocate of sexual freedom and fulfilment, Anderson opposed industrialism and followed psychoanalysis.

19 LESSER, SIMON O. "The Image of the Father: A Reading of 'My Kinsman, Major Molineux' and 'I Want to Know Why.'" Partisan Review, 22 (Summer), 372-90.
As Hawthorne's "My Kinsman, Major Molineux" depends on understanding by the unconscious mind, Anderson's "I Want to Know Why" requires reading below the surface to discover that Anderson's boy-hero is denied a non-sexual father-surrogate at the story's climax. Reprinted: 1957.B17.

20 LEWIS, R. W. B. The American Adam: Innocence, Tragedy and Tradition in the Nineteenth Century. Chicago: University of Chicago Press, pp. 84, 115.
The basis for Anderson's "grotesque" characters appears in American literature as early as W. E. Channing--"a tension . . . between the eccentric, on the one hand, and the undifferentiated lump of solid citizenry, on the other." Even Anderson's lesson of escape from society as a ritual may be traced to Hawthorne.

21 M., K. Review of Winesburg, Ohio. Kirjastolehti, No. 10.
[Tauno Mustanoja]

22 MÄKI, EINO. Review of Winesburg, Ohio. Parnasso, pp. 332-33.
No such place as described in Winesburg, Ohio could exist. [Tauno Mustanoja]

23 MANNINEN, KERTTU. Review of Winesburg, Ohio. Aamulehti (8 November).
Understated and flawless, Winesburg, Ohio is artistically and technically harmonious. [Tauno Mustanoja]

24 MIYAMOTO, YOKICHI. "On Sherwood Anderson, I." Bulletin of the Faculty of Liberal Arts (Humanities), Ibaraki University, 5 (March), 1-9.
Faulkner was right that Anderson should have quit writing with Dark Laughter. Anderson's creative power declined rapidly because he was buried alive as a writer of the past by the new Lost Generation such as Hemingway and Faulkner. Yet Anderson handed down a literary fortune in plain style and original storytelling. His style influenced by Stein, Anderson's technique is the opposite of the American traditional story, being also realistic and at the same symbolic. [Takashi Kodaira]

25 N., E. Review of Winesburg, Ohio. Tapuli, No. 24.
[Tauno Mustanoja]

26 P., O. Review of Winesburg, Ohio. Turun Sanomat (3 November).
The most remarkable aspect of Winesburg, Ohio is Anderson's ability to reveal the guarded, hidden thoughts of his characters. [Tauno Mustanoja]

27 P., S. Review of Winesburg, Ohio. Ylä-Vuoksi (12 December).
[Tauno Mustanoja]

28 P-N. Review of Winesburg, Ohio. Uutisaitta, No. 12.
[Tauno Mustanoja]

29 PENNANEN, LAURI. Review of Winesburg, Ohio. Ylioppilaslehti (16 December).
[Tauno Mustanoja]

30 PHILLIPS, WILLIAM L. "Sherwood Anderson's Two Prize Pupils." University of Chicago Magazine, 47 (January), 9-12.
While Anderson's reputation declines, the reputations of Hemingway and Faulkner--Anderson's most famous followers--have risen. Needing to change publishers and repudiate Anderson, Hemingway parodied the older writer in The Torrents of Spring. From Anderson Faulker learned to create fiction and "province." Reprinted: 1966.A7.

31 RICHARDS, ROBERT FULTON, ed. "Anderson, Sherwood." Concise Dictionary of American Literature. New York: Greenwood Press, pp. 7-8.

1955

(RICHARDS, ROBERT FULTON)
Anderson rejected his Ohio business life "deliberately, abruptly, and permanently." Winesburg, Ohio "changed not only the personal history of the author but the course of American fiction," for Anderson influenced Faulkner, Wolfe, McCullers, and Hemingway.

32 ROSSI, SERGIO. "Sherwood Anderson." Aevum, 29 (September-December), 559-74.
After Winesburg, Ohio Anderson tired artistically and became repetitious. His style of heightened common language, his carefully crafted stories of provincial life were part of the anti-Puritan, plebeian stream of American literature.

33 S. Review of Winesburg, Ohio. Kaleva (9 November).
[Tauno Mustanoja]

34 S., K. Review of Winesburg, Ohio. Sosialistinen Aikakauslehti, No. 11-12.
[Tauno Mustanoja]

35 SAVOLAINEN, ERKKI. Review of Winesburg, Ohio. Savo (19 October).
[Tauno Mustanoja]

36 SKORPIONI. Review of Winesburg, Ohio. Haminan Lehti (16 November).
[Tauno Mustanoja]

37 SMITH, THELMA M. and WARD L. MINER. Transatlantic Migration: The Contemporary American Novel in France. Durham: Duke University Press, pp. 15-18.
Translations of Anderson's works in the 1920's gave French readers a view of modern America far different than the legends they had believed.

38 SPILLER, ROBERT E. The Cycle of American Literature: An Essay in Historical Criticism. New York: Macmillan Co., pp. 156, 167, 192, 214, 218.
Robinson's poems about Tilbury Town anticipated Winesburg, Ohio; Anderson's rejection of business became the legendary renunciation of corrupted American life. Later naturalists imitated Anderson, not Dreiser; Anderson taught Faulkner, especially in the art of indirect narration.

39 STARRETT, VINCENT. "Winesburg, Ohio by Sherwood Anderson." Best Loved Books of the Twentieth Century. New York: Bantam Books, pp. 92-94.

Only eight of the Winesburg, Ohio stories do not deal with sex--Anderson's answer to life's problems. Without humor, Anderson creates overdramatized stories of grotesques that are truly dull and morbid and humorless.

40 SUZUKI, SACHIO. "Sherwood Anderson." Bungakusha, 59 (June), 97-100.
Anderson is significant in the history of American literature for his stories, his novels, his legend, his connections with modern painting and literary predecessors. [Takashi Kodaira]

41 T., A. Review of Winesburg, Ohio. Työkansan Sanomat (2 November).
[Tauno Mustanoja]

42 T., T. W. Review of Winesburg, Ohio. Karjala (4 November).
[Tauno Mustanoja]

43 TAKEMURA, HISAO. "The Breakdown of Imagination: Sherwood Anderson and Winesburg, Ohio." Shuryu [Doshisha Eibungakukai] (February), 35-46.
All great literary works rebel against something; in Anderson's instance, it is resistance to industrialism. Anderson's grotesques are defeated people whose imaginations have broken down because of the monster of industrialism. In describing such a breakdown of imagination beautifully and concisely, Anderson gains honor in American literature. [Takashi Kodaira]

*44 UNSELD, SIEGFRIED. "An diesem Dienstag: Unvorgreifliche Gedanken über die Kurzgeschichte." Akzente, 2 (1955), 139-44.
Cited: Kvam, W. C. Hemingway in Germany. Athens: Ohio University Press, 1973, p. 82.

45 UNTERMEYER, LOUIS. Makers of the Modern World: The Lives of Ninety-Two Writers, Artists, Scientists, Statesmen, Inventors, Philosophers, Composers, and Other Creators Who Formed the Pattern of Our Century. New York: Simon and Schuster, pp. 461, 703, 717-18, 719, 722.
Anderson learned simplicity from Stein; he taught style to Faulkner and Hemingway.

46 V. E-L. Review of Winesburg, Ohio. Kaltio, No. 6.
[Tauno Mustanoja]

1955

47 WHICHER, GEORGE FRISBIE. Poetry and Civilization, Essays. Edited by Harriet Fox Whicher. Ithaca: Cornell University Press, pp. 134, 135, 136.

Anderson is one of the American writers who broods over doomed characters, creating in fiction "a kind of moral equivalent for psychotherapy." He has helped provide American writers with a "usable present."

48 WISH, HARVEY. Contemporary America: The National Scene Since 1900. New York: Harper & Brothers, p. 329.

Anderson became an outstanding short story writer in the 1920's, for Winesburg, Ohio "departed from the sex conventions of the American short story." Anderson "dismayed academic critics" with these psychoanalytic stories of "warped personalities in all their naked abnormalities."

1956 A BOOKS - NONE

1956 B SHORTER WRITINGS

1 ANON. "Karl Anderson, Painter, Is Dead." New York Times (19 May), p. 19.

Last of the Anderson family, Karl Anderson, "portrait and landscape painter who was dean of the Westport art colony," died May 18. Preceeding him in death were Sherwood Anderson, the author; "Earl, a poet; Ray, an editor, and Irwin, a business man. Their sisters were Stella, who wrote on art, and Fern."

2 BROOKS, VAN WYCK and OTTO L. BETTMAN. Our Literary Heritage: A Pictorial History of the Writer in America. New York: E. P. Dutton and Co., pp. 131, 146, 197, 206, 221.

Anderson's imaginative world was based on Adventures of Huckleberry Finn; his characters were lost examples of post-pioneer America.

*3 CADORESI, DOMENICO. "Anderson, Traven, Baudelaire." Nostro Tempo [Naples], No. 8-9 (August-September), pp. 36-37.

Cited: 1969.B3.

*4 CAMILUCCI, MARCELLO. "Novelle di Anderson e di Lardner." Il Popolo [Rome] (21 April), p. 3.

Cited: 1969.B3.

5 CANTWELL, ROBERT. Famous American Men of Letters. New York: Dodd, Mead and Co., pp. 184-85.

The dominant post-war tone of American fiction was realistic; but Anderson's Winesburg, Ohio stories "cast a curious, vague half-light over familiar American scenes that left them like a haunting and shadowy reflection of reality."

6 DeDOMINICIS, ANNA MARIA. "Lettere di Sherwood Anderson." Letterature Moderne, 6 (November-December), 711-20.
Anderson's early works treat grotesque characters, souls troubled by modern life; later the writer developed a social conscience. Art to Anderson was immediate and intuitive and meant to liberate the individual. The Letters are valuable for reasons social, esthetic, autobiographical, and journalistic.

7 ELDER, DONALD. Ring Lardner: A Biography. Garden City: Doubleday & Co., pp. 119, 130, 140, 231-34, 363.
Lardner admired Anderson but did not approve of sexual expression in books. On February 23, 1926, Lardner wrote to Fitzgerald that Anderson had entertained him in New Orleans; "On Meeting Ring Lardner" grew from this meeting. Anderson visited Lardner as he was ill before dying in 1933.

8 FAULKNER, WILLIAM. "The Art of Fiction XII." Paris Review, No. 12, pp. 44-45, 46.
When Jean Stein interviewed Faulkner, he spoke of Anderson's helping to publish Soldiers' Pay when the writers were together in New Orleans; to Faulkner, Dreiser followed Twain and led to Anderson, "the father of my generation of American writers and the tradition of American writing which our successors will carry on."

*9 FRANCIOSA, MASSINO. "Notarella su Sherwood Anderson." Il Punto nelle Lettere e nelle Arti, No. 2 (October-November), pp. 3-5.
Cited: 1969.B3.

10 GRANA, GIANNI. "Anderson e Dreiser." La Fiera Letteraria (15 January), p. 4.
Naturalism passé in Europe, America is having a reawakened interest in such authors as Anderson. Publication in Italian of The Sherwood Anderson Reader shows this writer as unconventional, anti-social and anti-industry, nostalgic for a fabled past, and proponent of the imaginative, psychological approach to fiction.

11 MAHONEY, JOHN J. "An Analysis of Winesburg, Ohio." Journal of Aesthetics and Art Criticism, 15 (December), 245-52.

1956

(MAHONEY, JOHN J.)
The author's voice predominates in Winesburg, Ohio; the few character speeches are essentially soliloquies for self-revelation, not response.

12 RAYMUND, BERNARD. "The Grammar of Not-Reason in Sherwood Anderson." Arizona Quarterly, 12 (Spring), 48-60; 12 (Summer), 136-48.
Always bewildered by his own complexity, Anderson was always clear about his craft. Yet of the seven novels, only Many Marriages deserves reprinting. In the stories--where craft glows brightly--Anderson deals with "not-reason," symbolic representation of inexplicable action.

13 ROSATI, SALVATORE. Storia della Letteratura Americana. Turin: Edizioni Radio Italiana, pp. 200, 233-35, 247, 248, 270.
Anderson is typical of the American literary revolt against society, using often in fiction his own escape from business. Critically successful but never rich, Anderson wrote best of quiet, repressed lives, giving himself an unquestioned central place among writers between the World Wars.

14 SINERVO, AIRA. Review of Winesburg, Ohio. Työläisopiskelija, No. 2.
[Tauno Mustanoja]

15 THURSTON, JARVIS. "Anderson and 'Winesburg': Mysticism and Craft." Accent, 16 (Spring), 107-28.
Not himself intellectual, Anderson trusted intuition as his way toward truth; and in Winesburg, Ohio he unified his stories by the mystic's attitude, at once "oracular" and "sympathetic." Reprinted in part: 1966.A3.

16 WALCUTT, CHARLES CHILD. American Literary Naturalism, A Divided Stream. Minneapolis: University of Minnesota Press, pp. 191, 222-39, 258, 279.
Reprint of 1952.B21.

17 ZARDOYA, CONCHA. Historia de la Literatura Norteamericana. Barcelona: Editorial Labor, pp. 237-41.
Anderson's stories are far better than his novels; best are the Winesburg, Ohio stories of psychological realism. Flawed with a bewildered style, Anderson's one theme is individual frustration.

1957 A BOOKS - NONE

1957 B SHORTER WRITINGS

1 ANDERSON, CARL L. The Swedish Acceptance of American Literature. Philadelphia: University of Pennsylvania Press, pp. 66, 67, 70, 71-73, 81, 87-88, 92, 96, 97, 98, 111, 149, 193.
When Dark Laughter and Tar were printed in Swedish in 1928, critics liked Anderson's social criticism and compared him to Hamsun.

2 ANDERSON, KARL JAMES. "My Brother, Sherwood Anderson." The Saturday Review Treasury. New York: Simon and Schuster, pp. 325-32.
Reprint of 1948.B2.

3 ANON. "Sherwood Anderson." American Writing Today. Edited by Allan Angoff. New York: New York University Press, pp. 351-53.
Reprint of 1922.B14.

4 ANON. "Camden's Noted Author." Dayton Daily News (15 December), p. 17.
Stephen Coombs of Camden, Ohio, has studied Anderson's life, found his birthplace, and worked to honor Anderson in Camden.

5 ANZILOTTI, ROLANDO. Storia della Letteratura Americana. Milan: Casa Editrice Dr. Francesco Vallardi, pp. 63-65, 73, 82.
Using impressionism and introspection, Anderson overcame the naturalistic formula present in his stories and thus rendered reality lyrically. He pioneered in psychological fiction and opened to new use America's provincial literature.

6 ASSELINEAU, ROGER. "Réalism, Rêve et Espressionism dans 'Winesburg, Ohio.'" Archives des Lettres Modernes, No. 2 (April), pp. 1-32.
Anderson's setting in Winesburg, Ohio is realistically delineated; but his characters' lives are described from within, so that reality is only Anderson's springboard to truth. These stories are Anderson's meditations, rendered expressionistically.

7 BROOKS, VAN WYCK. Days of the Phoenix: The Nineteen-Twenties I Remember. New York: E. P. Dutton and Co., pp. 7, 11-14, 17, 106, 124, 171.

1957

(BROOKS, VAN WYCK)

Anderson occasionally visited Brooks after they met in 1917, but Brooks was aware of Anderson's desire to wander over America, for he loved all humanity and wrote of the obscure and lovable grotesques. Anderson liked the Midwest and carried essential loneliness with him. Anderson's brother Ray hated Sherwood's fiction; but Karl Anderson, the painter, was imitative of Sherwood when he tried to write a novel.

8 CESTRE, CHARLES. "Sherwood Anderson." _La Littérature Américain_. Paris: Librairie Armand Colin, pp. 166-68.

Anderson uses naturalism heightened by symbolism to tell stories of interior lives; his characters are naturalistically trapped but seek escape to love and to craft. It is unfortunate that sex dominates Anderson's works.

9 FAULKNER, WILLIAM. _New Orleans Sketches_. Introduction by Carvel Collins. New Brunswick: Rutgers University Press, pp. 12-13, 15, 17-20, 21-22, 25, 30.

Anderson visited New Orleans briefly in 1922 and at length in 1924. Soon Anderson wrote of Faulkner in "A Meeting South," and the men became creative-writing friends in 1925. Probably _Sherwood Anderson & Other Famous Creoles_ damaged the friendship.

10 _____. "Sherwood Anderson." _Princeton University Library Chronicle_, 18 (Spring), 89-94.

Reprint of 1925.B33.

11 FUKUDA, MITSUHARU. "An Essay on _Winesburg, Ohio_." _St. Paul's Review Arts and Sciences_, 3 (1957), 30-54.

Adolescence is one of the subjects in _Winesburg, Ohio_, for Anderson tries to grasp "something like a dawn" in youth. A spirit of adolescence can aid in countering industrialism. When Anderson wrote _Winesburg, Ohio_, he used symbolism to transcend the limit of realism. [Takashi Kodaira]

12 GAUSS, CHRISTIAN. _The Papers of Christian Gauss_. Edited by Katherine Gauss Jackson and Hiram Hayden. New York: Random House, pp. 236-37.

In 1923 Gauss wrote Edmund Wilson that he disliked Anderson's work for being too sexual and dreamy, without humor or intellect.

13 HILTON, EARL. "Sherwood Anderson and 'Heroic Vitalism.'" _Northwest Ohio Quarterly_, 29 (Spring), 97-107.

Anderson's earliest fiction, influenced by Carlyle and Nietzsche, is of hatred; with Winesburg, Ohio he turned toward love of his characters.

14 HOFFMAN, FREDERICK J. Freudianism and the Literary Mind. Revised edition. Baton Rouge: Louisiana State University Press, pp. 90, 229-50, 257, 260.

Anderson preferred to live in his imagination rather than in the factual world. When Anderson met intellectuals in Chicago, he absorbed their talk of Freud but rejected "mechanization" of behavior. His fiction deals with repression, frustration, and anti-social acts; but Freudian interpretations of his own work must start with Anderson's own ideas instead of Freud's. Reprinted: 1966.A3; 1966.A7.

15 IZZO, CARLO. "Sherwood Anderson." Storia della Letteratura Nord-Americana. Milan: Nuova Accademia Editrice, pp. 622-24.

Unable to handle the "rules" of life, Anderson had a dreamy sense of the real and a sympathy for the weak and oppressed. He writes of fatally useless gestures of rebellion in works vague, primitive, imprecise, and informal. Influenced uselessly by Freud, Anderson made stories of the smallest germs of life, told poetically and with love.

16 KANEKO, HISAKAZU. "A Note on S. Anderson's Winesburg, Ohio." Rikkyo Review, Arts and Letters, 18 (March), 17-43.

The world of reality is inseparably bound up with the world of imagination in Winesburg, Ohio, art being art and not life. [Takashi Kodaira]

17 LESSER, SIMON O. "Conscious and Unconscious Perception." Fiction and the Unconscious. Boston: Beacon Press. pp. 224-34.

Reprint of 1955.B19.

18 LEVIN, HARRY. Contexts of Criticism. Cambridge: Harvard University Press, pp. 149-50, 154, 237.

The Torrents of Spring parodies Anderson and also shows Hemingway's knowledge of other literatures. Anderson and Hemingway improved the colloquial in fiction by identifying with their characters.

19 McCORMICK, JOHN. Catastrophe and Imagination: An Interpretation of the Recent English and American Novel. London: Longmans, Green, pp. 125-26, 180, 197, 211, 248-50, 264.

Anderson's view of isolation is sociological, and with Wolfe he "formed an American composite of D. H. Lawrence";

(McCORMICK, JOHN)
yet imitation of Lawrence's themes and style was ruinous to Anderson.

20 MINCHERO VILASARÓ, ANGEL. "Anderson, Sherwood." Diccionario Universal de Escritores: I. Estados Unidos. San Sebastian: Edidhe, pp. 30-31.

In clear, rhythmic, poetic style Anderson wrote of the forlorn characters of small towns. He studied repressed instincts and can be called the D. H. Lawrence of America.

21 MIYAMOTO, YOKICHI. "On Sherwood Anderson, II." Bulletin of the Faculty of Liberal Arts (Humanities), Ibaraki University, 7 (March), 39-53.

Discussion of Anderson's works after Dark Laughter may be useless. Yet, study of the later novels and the Memoirs is essential to understand Anderson's essence and to know the limitations of his attempts in literature. In fact, tracing patterns of Anderson's work after Dark Laughter is more valuable than studying works published before that novel. [Takashi Kodaira]

*22 NAPOLITANO, GIAN GASPARE. "Come Morì Anderson." Il Giorno [Milan] (18 July), p. 4.

Cited: 1969.B3.

23 R.[ICE], J.[OHN] A.[NDREWS]. "Winesburg, Ohio by Sherwood Anderson." American Panorama: Essays by Fifteen American Critics on 350 Books Past and Present which Portray the U. S. A. in Its Many Aspects. Edited by Eric Larrabee. New York: New York University Press, p. 17.

Winesburg, Ohio, dealing with post-pioneer America, "is a history of discontents," for the people are incomplete and lost.

24 SPRIGGE, ELIZABETH. Gertrude Stein: Her Life and Work. New York: Harper & Brothers, pp. 56, 123, 133, 137, 157, 194, 196, 201, 203, 223.

Anderson met Stein in Paris in 1921; and Stein invited Anderson to introduce Geography and Plays, for Anderson was the only one of the early post-war writers to feel her influence and become and remain her friend.

25 VITTORINI, ELIO. Diaro in Publico. Milan: Bompiani, pp. 136, 138-39, 145, 322.

Anderson's stories held the metaphysical ardor of obscure interior acts reproduced in plastic or musical images which surround the characters like the fragments of broken elements.

26 WAGNER, GEOFFREY. Wyndham Lewis: A Portrait of the Artist as the Enemy. New Haven: Yale University Press, pp. 46-47.
Lewis disagreed with Anderson about Negroes, believing that Negroes had no essential culture and could lower the civilization of the West.

1958 A BOOKS - NONE

1958 B SHORTER WRITINGS

1 AIKEN, CONRAD. "Anderson, Sherwood." A Reviewer's ABC: Collected Criticism of Conrad Aiken from 1916 to the Present. New York: Meridian Books, pp. 130-32.
Reprint of 1927.B1.

2 ANON. "Terrible Town." Time, 72 (21 July), 67.
Donald Saddler's dance-drama of Winesburg, Ohio focuses on four grotesque characters and is an "economical evocation of Anderson's mordant visions."

3 ARNOLD, ARMIN. D. H. Lawrence in America. New York: Philosophical Library, pp. 35, 111-12, 168, 172-73, 182, 194, 201.
Lawrence--so admired and imitated by Anderson--scarcely mentioned Anderson's name or read anything by him. The writers are linked in American criticism by Anderson's work, not the reverse. Anderson's review of Assorted Articles is "the highest compliment ever paid to Lawrence."

4 ATKINSON, BROOKS. "Theatre: Diffuse Drama." New York Times (6 February), p. 22.
Anderson's form in Winesburg, Ohio is difficult to dramatize, and the current production is disappointing.

5 BROOKS, VAN WYCK. From a Writer's Notebook. New York: E. P. Dutton and Co., pp. 80-81.
Perhaps Anderson's love of words--and of Stein's experiments--came from unfortunate years in journalism.

6 BURROW, TRIGANT. A Search for Man's Sanity: The Selected Letters of Trigant Burrow, With Biographical Notes. Edited by The Lifwyn Foundation. Foreword by Sir Herbert Read. New York: Oxford University Press, pp. x, 39, 53-63, 86-87, 269-70, 274, 442-43, 513, 523, 558-62, 564-65.
Anderson met Burrow in the New York mountains in 1916, and the men began corresponding in 1921, when the former apologized for being artistically too stern. Anderson tried to help Burrow publish work on psychoanalysis; and,

(BURROW, TRIGANT)
after Anderson's death, Burrow wrote scholars that Anderson had not read Freud and used psychology by intuition.

7 DYBOSKI, ROMAN. Wielcy Pisarze Amerikyanscy. Warsaw: Institut Wydawniczy Pax, 1958, pp. 444-53, 466, 469, 481, 486, 493, 502, 536, 605, 630, 631, 643-44.
While critics assess Anderson's literary contributions variously, all must concur that his originality and subtlety as well as his psychological insight place him far above his naturalistic predecessors. [James F. Cradler]

8 EISHISKINA, N. M. Amerikanskaia Novella XX Veka. Moscow, pp. 235-55, 526-27.
[Seen but not translated]

*9 FABIANI, ENZO. "Tutti Sognano per le Vie dell'Ohio." Gente [Milan] (7 May), p. 54.
Cited: 1969.B3.

10 FLANAGAN, JOHN T. "A Soil for the Seeds of Literature." The Heritage of the Middle West. Edited by John J. Murray. Norman: University of Oklahoma Press, pp. 218, 219, 221.
Midwestern writers such as Anderson succeeded in autobiography as well as in fiction. Although Anderson's poetry is unimpressive, in short stories he proved that intuition and tone outweigh plot.

11 GLASGOW, ELLEN. Letters of Ellen Glasgow. Edited by Blair Rouse. New York: Harcourt, Brace and Co., p. 69.
On August 23, 1923, Glasgow wrote to Hugh Walpole that "Nothing I think can be quite so bad, so pompous, so utterly devoid of a sense of the ridiculous as Mr. Sherwood Anderson."

12 GOLD, HERBERT. "The Purity and Cunning of Sherwood Anderson." Hudson Review, 10 (Winter 1957-58), 548-57.
Anderson loved to cultivate his fancy, for his stories are esthetically if not literally autobiographical, giving Americans a new image of themselves, flawed but romantically idealistic. Reprinted: 1962.B12; 1966.A3.

13 GUIDO, AUGUSTO. "Lyrismo di Sherwood Anderson." Occasioni Americane: Saggi di Letteratura Americana. Rome: Edizioni Moderne, pp. 122-27.
Anderson's best characteristic is lyricism; his topics were shocking and influenced by Lawrence. Anderson

violated tabu and called for individual freedom to live and create.

14 HASHIMOTO, FUKUO. "A Memorandum on Sherwood Anderson." Senshu University Bulletin, 16 (January), 47-54.

The grotesques in Winesburg, Ohio are ordinary people made grotesque by the author, who chose lonely people as subjects and wrote of their defeats through his imagination. In harmony with his characters, Anderson made Winesburg, Ohio successful. Yet Anderson could not find such harmony with industrial workers or moderns. A writer who could not write without being in phase with his object, Anderson failed in Dark Laughter and Beyond Desire. [Takashi Kodaira]

15 HEINEY, DONALD. "Sherwood Anderson." Recent American Literature. Great Neck, NY: Barron's Educational Series, pp. 296-301.

Anderson is suspicious of conventional values and hypocrisies; he is mystical instead of religious; he tries to write the colloquial style; he writes stories better than novels.

16 HERBST, JOSEPHINE. "Ubiquitous Critics and the Author." Newberry Library Bulletin, 5 (December), 1-13.

Probably because Anderson distrusted intellectuals, he learned nothing from his critics, for he had to change subject and style as he felt essential--not to fit either popular or critical taste.

17 HEWES, HENRY. "Do Books Make the Best Theatre?" Saturday Review, 41 (8 February), 26-27.

Sergel has tried to follow Anderson's own ideas in dramatizing Winesburg, Ohio--without great success.

18 ITAZU, YUKISATO. "On Sherwood Anderson's Style." English Grammar (November), pp. 18-23.

Passages in "Hands," "Adventure," "Terror," "Death in the Woods," and Dark Laughter show that Anderson's place in the history of literature is due to his style that was copied by Hemingway and to his psychological method that was copied by Faulkner. [Takashi Kodaira]

19 MILLER, HENRY. The Red Notebook. Highlands, NC: J. Williams, n. p.

While traveling to gather material for The Air-Conditioned Nightmare, Miller planned in "Places to Visit" to see "Sherwood Anderson / Troutdale / Marion, Va." He also

1958

(MILLER, HENRY)
noted near Mobile, Alabama "(and little town of Sherwood Anderson's)."

20 NORMAN, CHARLES. The Magic-Maker: E. E. Cummings. New York: Macmillan Co., pp. 119, 164, 198, 340.
Perhaps service in World War I accounted for the differences between Anderson and younger writers who had served, but Cummings admired Anderson's emotional response to life.

21 ROSATI, SALVATORE. L'Ombra dei Padri: Studi Letteratura Americana. Rome: Edizioni di Storia e Letteratura, pp. 88, 91, 100, 101-102, 104, 105, 112, 119, 120, 145, 200.
Until Anderson began using psychoanalytic theory in his work, the approach had belonged to only specialists. Faulkner's escape ideas closely resemble Anderson's; Anderson specifically influenced Steinbeck, Hemingway, and Jeffers.

22 SERGEL, CHRISTOPHER. "Haunting Voices." New York Times (2 February), 2, p. 3.
Anderson first visited Roger Sergel in 1923 and read a play by young Christopher Sergel. When Sergel later adapted Winesburg, Ohio into drama, he frequently recalled Anderson's talks at his father's home.

23 SUZUKI, KINTARO. "Sherwood Anderson, I." Waseda Commercial Review, 133 (March), 59-76.
Interest in Winesburg, Ohio creates interest in learning of the author's chronology, family, and boyhood. [Takashi Kodaira]

24 WILSON, EDMUND. American Earthquake. Garden City: Doubleday and Co., pp. 125-28.
Anderson's style probably came from his advertising work and from the New York authors of the early 1920's, but he never managed to write as well as he talked.

1959 A BOOKS

1 FERRES, JOHN H. "The Right Place and the Right People: Sherwood Anderson's Search for Salvation." Dissertation, Louisiana State University, 221 pp.
Anderson was concerned with more than finding achievement and joy in his own life; he sought spiritual salvation both of his own soul and the American soul. Anderson's

first books deal with "child-rearing and brotherhood"; then he investigates possible return to "an elemental, agrarian kind of existence"; his third quest is through sex--"universal communion and self-realization"; the final phase involves country journalism and labor causes. Anderson's search failed because of his determinism and inability to accept stasis.

1959 B SHORTER WRITINGS

1 ALLEN, LEE. "Sherwood Anderson's Hometown." Cincinnati Enquirer (25 January), H., p. 1.
Bert Ramsey, a retired farmer who lives in Anderson's place of birth, wonders who Anderson was. Almost no one in Camden, Ohio, knows of Anderson or his books.

2 ANKIST, A. A. Ocherki Novoi i Noveishei Istorii SShA. Moscow, pp. 217, 488, 494, 496-98, 504, 510, 511.
[Seen but not translated]

3 ANON. "Anderson, Sherwood." Literatur Handboken: Tredje Utökade och Omarbetade Upplagan. Stockholm: Bokförlaget Forum, p. 212.
While writing advertising copy in Chicago, Anderson began writing psychological studies in condensed fictional form.

*4 ANON. "Ritratto di Kit Brandon." Il Corriere d'Informazione (18-19 July), p. 5.
Cited: 1969.B3.

*5 ANON. "Una Donna Inquieta." Vita [Rome], 1 (30 July), 57.
Cited: 1969.B3.

*6 ANON. "Ritratto di Kit Brandon." La Lucerna [Rome], No. 9-10 (September-October), p. 24.
Cited: 1969.B3.

7 BEACH, SYLVIA. Shakespeare and Company. New York: Harcourt, Brace and Co., pp. 30-32, 42, 77, 111.
Beach entertained Anderson when he came to Paris in 1921 and introduced him to Stein. Anderson later wrote to introduce Hemingway to Beach.

*8 BERNOBINI, PAOLO. "Un Povero Bianco." Il Giorno [Milan] (5 May), p. 6.
Cited: 1969.B3.

1959

9 CENTRE CULTUREL AMÉRICAIN. Les Années Vingt: Les Écrivains Américains à Paris et Leurs Amis, 1920-1930. Paris: Centre Culturel Américain, pp. 46-48.
[Exhibit of thirteen of Anderson's books]

10 CHURCHILL, ALLEN. The Improper Bohemians: A Re-Creation of Greenwich Village in Its Heyday. New York: E. P. Dutton & Co., pp. 68, 227, 244-45.
Dell brought the manuscript of Windy McPherson's Son to New York in 1913. John Reed and Anderson talked of poets' roles when they met; usually Anderson acted as bohemian as he dressed.

*11 CIMATTI, PIETRO. "L'Ultimo Anderson." La Fiera Letteraria (2 August), p. 4.
Cited: 1969.B3.

12 CLARK, EDWARD. "Winesburg, Ohio: An Interpretation." Die Neueren Sprachen, New Series 8 (December), 547-52.
Winesburg, Ohio is an affirmative work because of "the people's relationship to the setting, the striving that is common to each person, and the special artistic function of one of them"--the young hero.

13 DERLETH, AUGUST. "Three Literary Men: A Memoir of Sinclair Lewis, Sherwood Anderson and Edgar Lee Masters." Arts and Society (Winter), pp. 11-46.
At lunch with Derleth in New York, Anderson spoke of Masters, of sex in his work, of criticism, of Dreiser, local-color, and the planned trip to South America. Reprinted: 1963.B10.

14 DICKIE, FRANCIS. "From Forest Fire to France." American Book Collector, 10 (September), 23-24.
Having met Anderson at a Paris bar, Dickie invited him and his wife to visit. Anderson was in Paris to gather information for a book and advised writing slowly and not selling out to commercial success.

15 DREISER, THEODORE. Letters of Theodore Dreiser: A Selection, 3 volumes. Edited by Robert H. Elias. Philadelphia: University of Pennsylvania Press, pp. 9, 279, 307, 310-11, 314, 347, 416-17, 422, 427, 586, 642, 645, 647, 653-56, 666-67, 753-55, 760-63, 768-69.
Dreiser helped Anderson to publish his first two books, did not like Poor White, and liked Anderson's preface to Free and Other Stories. He liked Anderson's stories and Many Marriages, worked with Anderson on The American

Spectator, and disagreed with Anderson's anti-industry sentiments.

16 EASTMAN, MAX. Great Companions: Critical Memoirs of Some Famous Friends. New York: Farrar, Straus and Cudahy, pp. 49-50, 72.
Lincoln Steffens defended Anderson against Hemingway to Eastman, who thought The Torrents of Spring very poor.

17 ELLMAN, RICHARD. James Joyce. New York: Oxford University Press, pp. 529, 543, 593.
Anderson, who had met Joyce "once or twice" in 1920, sent Hemingway to meet Joyce in 1921 with a letter of introduction. On March 9, 1922, Hemingway wrote to Anderson to praise Ulysses ; in Paris in 1927 Joyce fed oysters to Anderson, who hated that dish.

*18 FORLIVESI, PIERO. "L'Ultimo Anderson." Il Popolo [Rome] (22 July), p. 5.
Cited: 1969.B3.

19 HARKNESS, DAVID JAMES. The Great Lakes States and Alaska and Hawaii in Literature: A Manual for Schools and Clubs. Knoxville: University of Tennessee, pp. 6, 38, 44.
Anderson's experiences in Chicago are related in Marching Men, Mid-American Chants, and A Story Teller's Story; in five other books Anderson has written about "the seamy side of Ohio life among the poorly placed."

20 HEPBURN, JAMES G. "Disarming and Uncanny Visions: Freud's 'The Uncanny' with Regard to Form and Content in Stories by Sherwood Anderson and D. H. Lawrence." Literature and Psychology, 9 (Winter), 9-12.
The imagery of Anderson's "Death in the Woods" leads to viewing the old woman as a breast symbol repressed by the adult narrator.

21 LAWRY, JON S. "'Death in the Woods' and the Artist's Self in Sherwood Anderson." Publications of the Modern Language Association, 74 (June), 306-11.
"Death in the Woods" succeeds because Anderson uses his imagination to fuse boy-narrator and woman-girl-dogs into conscious awareness of reality. Reprinted: 1974.A3.

22 LOEB, HAROLD. The Way It Was. New York: Criterion Books, pp. 9, 59, 63, 80-81, 235, 246.
Loeb and Kreymborg liked Anderson and hoped to publish some of his work, and they reached Paris in 1921 just after

1959

(LOEB, HAROLD)
Anderson had gone to England. Later Hemingway may have resented Anderson's publication help.

23 MATTHEWS, JACK. "Winesburg Today." Columbus Dispatch Magazine [OH] (29 November), pp. 40-43.
Although Winesburg, Ohio is modeled on Clyde, Ohio, the characters are invented by Anderson. The landscape of the town is copied by Anderson and has changed little, while Anderson's book has become universal.

24 MAY, HENRY F. The End of American Innocence: A Study of the First Years of Our Own Time, 1912-1917. Chicago: Quadrangle Books, pp. 95, 247, 250, 257, 258, 259-62, 287, 289, 291, 316, 328, 380.
Anderson in 1917 called for a literature of "crudity," of rebellion, of simple form. He possibly got his mysticism from boyhood notice of evangelical religion; he even presents a new "religion" of his own--sex. The style of Winesburg, Ohio "was the beginning of contemporary American prose, deceptively simple, laconic, sharp, [and] brand-new."

25 MIYAMOTO, YOKICHI. "Winesburg, Ohio and Its Background." Journal of the Faculty of Literature, Chuo University, 6 (February), 27-46.
How could Anderson master the craft of fiction in Winesburg, Ohio after so amateurish efforts as Windy McPherson's Son and Marching Men? Winesburg, Ohio may have been written with the background of works by Norris and Dreiser and Masters--as well as Freudianism. Yet the influence of Stein was more important, for her conception is pictorial, especially cubistic. [Takashi Kodaira]

26 MOTODA, SHUICHI. "'Hands.'" The Analysis and Technique of the Short Story. Tokyo: Kaibunsha, pp. 211-41.
"Hands" is a story of neurotic angst and perversion, from the Freudian point of view. The hero is drawn as the image of the ego in the dilemma between id and super-ego. Perhaps all the other Winesburg, Ohio stories are about the conflict among these elements, but only the theme of this story can be interpreted by Freudian method, as theme must not be confused with motive, which is the human isolation in modern civilization. [Takashi Kodaira]

27 NASU, YORIMASA. "'Death in the Woods': The Background and Meaning." Review [Nagasaki Junior College of Foreign Language], 4 (1959), 41-63.
In "Death in the Woods" Anderson draws upon Darwinian theory and the world of beauty, the former representing

the world of industrialism; the latter, Anderson's "transcendental" world of imagination. These two worlds are organically united in this story; as the heroine moves from ugliness to beauty, so Anderson moved from business to writing. The theme being the power to live through loneliness with patience, the story has optimism and romanticism behind this idea of power. [Takashi Kodaira]

28 O'CONNOR, WILLIAM VAN. "The Grotesque in Modern American Fiction." College English, 20 (April), 343, 344.
Grotesque characters such as Anderson's in Ohio are not to be explained in socio-political terms, for Anderson had a diminished sense of American innocence and presents his grotesques as isolates.

29 RIDEOUT, WALTER B. "Why Sherwood Anderson Employed Buck Fever." Georgia Review, 13 (Spring), 76-85.
Anderson invented the reporter Buck Fever so that he could entertain readers of his Virginia newspapers on both the repertorial and imaginative levels. Reprinted: 1966.A7.

30 RINGE, DONALD A. "Point of View and Theme in 'I Want to Know Why.'" Critique, 3 (Spring-Fall), 24-29.
The narrator of "I Want to Know Why" unconsciously reveals himself as selfishly "sensuous" and self-centered; he then feels love and disillusion.

31 ROSATI, SALVATORE. Narratori Americani Contemporanei. Turin: Edizioni RAI Radiotelevisione Italiana, pp. 5-6, 98, 130, 143, 166, 167, 172, 133-41.
Anderson was among the first American writers to be influenced by Freud, and through Anderson's influence Freud reached many others. Many people liked Anderson because his unusual characters were different from those of genteel-tradition authors. Anderson influenced literature through style, theme, and setting.

32 RUGGLES, ELEANOR. The West-Going Heart: A Life of Vachel Lindsay. New York: W. W. Norton Co., pp. 208, 237-38.
Although Lindsay preceded Anderson in the Chicago Renaissance, Anderson later saw Lindsay walking in New York and determined that the pedestrian had to be Vachel Lindsay.

33 SUZUKI, KINTARO. "Sherwood Anderson, II." Waseda Commercial Review, 138 (January), 87-108.
The biographies of Anderson by Howe and Schevill make it possible to study the writer's manhood between the Spanish-American War and the nervous breakdown in 1912. [Takashi Kodaira]

1959

34 TAYLOR, DWIGHT. Joy Ride. New York: G. P. Putnam's Sons, pp. 221-33.

Taylor reprints Rascoe's account of Fitzgerald's first bringing whiskey to Dreiser to show that Anderson probably did not attend this party.

35 THURBER, JAMES. The Years with Ross. Boston: Little, Brown and Co., p. 78.

Ross bluntly told Anderson that no one since O'Henry had written a good story; Ross later bought five pieces from Anderson.

*36 VECCHI, MASSIMO. "Stupore di Anderson." Il Popolo [Rome] (9 June), p. 5.

Cited: 1969.B3.

37 WASSERSTROM, WILLIAM. Heiress of All the Ages: Sex and Sentiment in the Genteel Tradition. Minneapolis: University of Minnesota Press, pp. 100, 101, 102, 129.

By 1925 gentility was of no use to Anderson, who led younger "lost generation" writers; Anderson's trouble was in rejecting a past that he did not understand. Ironically, Anderson later evoked instead of denied the ideal of women.

38 WINTHER, S. K. "The Aura of Loneliness in Sherwood Anderson." Modern Fiction Studies, 5 (Summer), 145-52.

Loneliness is central to Anderson's characters and plots, originating in the author's own childhood. His typical symbol is the wall.

1960 A BOOKS

1 ANDERSON, DAVID D. "Sherwood Anderson and the Meaning of The American Experience." Dissertation, Michigan State University, 440 pp.

Study of the body of Anderson's works determines the author in his milieu and his understanding of that milieu. Anderson's works developed and grew as his career continued, he interpreted the American experience, and he reacted to that experience. From 1912 to 1919 he began his collection of observations, from 1919 to 1929 his powers of observation and analysis peaked, and from 1929 until his death in 1941 he formulated the results.

2 SHEEHY, EUGENE P. and KENNETH A. LOHF. Sherwood Anderson: A Bibliography. Los Gatos, CA: Talisman Press, 125 pp.

[Bibliographical description of Anderson's books and pamphlets, lists of translations and reprintings of these (over 68 items); contributions to periodicals, books, and newspapers (almost 400 items); secondary criticism from books, theses, dissertations, articles, and reviews (about 740)] Reprinted: 1968.A3.

3 SULLIVAN, JOHN H. "Sherwood Anderson's Idea of the Country Weekly Newspaper." Master's thesis, Marquette University, 154 pp.

After enjoying his country newspapers in Virginia, Anderson yearned to travel, to escape from his third unhappy marriage, and to lecture to young people about careers in small-town journalism.

1960 B SHORTER WRITINGS

1 ANON. "Anderson." Handbuch der Weltliteratur: Von den Anfangen bis zur Gegenwart. Third edition revised. Frankfurt am/M: Vittorio Klostermann, p. 668.

[Biography and list of translations]

2 ANON. "Anderson, Sherwood." Grand Larousse Encyclopédique, 1. Paris: Librairie Larousse, 387.

At forty, Anderson became a writer of literature and journalism; he helped free the modern American short story from the "well-made plot."

3 BENÉT, STEPHEN VINCENT. Selected Letters of Stephen Vincent Benét. Edited by Charles A. Fenton. New Haven: Yale University Press, pp. 336, 337, 344.

Benét defends his anthologies and the Institute of Arts and Letters by citing Anderson's place in them; and he acknowledges Anderson's writing about his own father.

4 BERNSTEIN, IRVING. The Lean Years: A History of the American Worker, 1920-1933. Boston: Houghton Mifflin Co., pp. 15, 341, 380, 435-36.

Anderson attended a union meeting to see induction of new members and praised brotherhood; later he felt guilty as the Depression hurt his unionization activities. Anderson contributed to defenses of Kentucky miners and was always amazed at the lack of bitterness among the unemployed.

5 BUDD, LOUIS J. "The Grotesques of Anderson and Wolfe." Modern Fiction Studies, 5 (Winter 1959-60), 304-10.

Wolfe claimed great admiration for Winesburg, Ohio, for he shared Anderson's view of life as essential loneliness.

1960

(BUDD, LOUIS J.)
When Wolfe wrote of his own town, he wrote of tragic grotesques instead of satiric figures.

6 COWLEY, MALCOLM. "Anderson's Lost Days of Innocence." New Republic, 142 (15 February), 16-18.
Anderson's influence on younger writers was to react emotionally to new areas of national and personal life. Winesburg, Ohio--Anderson's stories of moments in lives--is an affirmative work toward community. Reprinted: 1960.B7; 1966.A3; 1966.A7; 1974.A3.

7 _____. "The Living Dead--IX: Sherwood Anderson's Epiphanies." London Magazine, 7 (July), 61-66.
Reprint of 1960.B6.

8 DINAMOV, S. Zarubezhnaia Literatura. Moscow, pp. 367-95, 451-53.
[Seen but not translated]

9 DURHAM, PHILIP and TAUNO F. MUSTANOJA. American Fiction in Finland. Helsinki: Société Néophilologique, pp. 17, 24, 47-48, 53, 67, 106, 113-14, 116, 127, 179, 181.
Finns think that Anderson is a humanitarian, that he values all experience, and that he is benevolent. Winesburg, Ohio and Dark Laughter create enthusiasm among Finnish readers.

10 FUSSELL, EDWIN. "'Winesburg, Ohio': Art and Isolation." Modern Fiction Studies, 6 (Summer), 106-14.
The merits of Winesburg, Ohio lie beyond the work as Bildungsroman; the hero must accept isolation, while the grotesques cannot. The individual personality has to remain private. Reprinted: 1966.A3; 1966.A7; 1974.A3.

11 GOCHBERG, DONALD. "Stagnation and Growth: The Emergence of George Willard." Expression, 4 (Winter), 29-35.
Anderson makes the hero of Winesburg, Ohio average in order to point up the grotesques; the boy matures into awareness of life as "growth and decay." Reprinted: 1971.A2.

12 GROSS, SEYMOUR L. "Sherwood Anderson's Debt to Huckleberry Finn." Mark Twain Journal, 11 (Summer), 3-5, 24.
Anderson shared Twain's pessimism about humanity but portrayed characters as victims better than Twain. "I Want to Know Why" is indebted to Adventures of Huckleberry Finn for ironic point of view, "symbolic dichotomy" (race track

versus town), Negroes as moral centers, outside world as rotten, cruelties suffered, and final withdrawal from society.

13 H.[AGEN], BR.[IGITTE]. "Anderson, Sherwood." Der Romanführer, 11. Stuttgart: Anton Hiersemann, pp. 5-8.

Winesburg, Ohio, Anderson's impressions of small-town life, stands for all American towns; Poor White is a social novel; The Triumph of the Egg deals with individuals who are inarticulate characters.

14 HAMADA, SEIJIRO. "What Does Dark Laughter Mean?" Rising Generation (December), pp. 22-23.

Dark Laughter is characterized by a contrast between white love and black love. As subconscious flows beneath conscious, so does the black world flow beneath the plot. The black world is home for whites in the machine age; the river represents mother-love and also cuts beneath the plot symbolically. [Takashi Kodaira]

15 HOWARD, LEON. Literature and the American Tradition. Garden City: Doubleday and Co., pp. 266-67, 280.

Anderson rebelled against social and literary conventions, especially against "the well-knit formalism of Poe, Bierce, and O'Henry"; he made short fiction "the perceptive record of a significant moment of experience."

16 KOSHIKAWA, SEIZO. "An Observation of Horses and Men." Journal of the Society of English and American Literature, Kwansei Gakuin University, 9 (October), 92-105.

Horses and Men can demonstrate Anderson's outlook as person and author. In the industrial age, men sometimes forget their need to love and understand each other--Anderson's state of "impotence." Others take to loneliness in the industrial age--Anderson's grotesques. [Takashi Kodaira]

17 MODERN LANGUAGE ASSOCIATION OF AMERICA. American Literary Manuscripts: A Checklist of Holdings in Academic, Historical, and Public Libraries in the United States. Austin: University of Texas Press, pp. 19-20.

[Anderson manuscripts held by 33 libraries]

18 NASU, YORIMASA. "The Character of Winesburg, Ohio." Review [Nagasaki Junior College of Foreign Language], 5 (1960), 1-28.

The grotesques of Winesburg, Ohio are in conflict between the real world and the imaginative world. The central

1960

(NASU, YORIMASA)
character is Anderson's portrait of his spiritual self, the real world being Chicago and the imaginative world a small Ohio town. The book thus is a picture scroll of Anderson's groping, awakening, and escape, with Chicago and a small Ohio town as background. [Takashi Kodaira]

19 NOWELL, ELIZABETH. Thomas Wolfe: A Biography. New York: Doubleday and Co., pp. 28, 282, 391, 395, 408-409, 411-12.
Wolfe spent two days visiting Anderson in the fall of 1937, when he became ecstatic over the beautiful countryside of Southwest Virginia. Later the authors quarreled over Eleanor Anderson's innocent question about Wolfe's being Jewish.

20 PARRY, ALBERT. Garrets and Pretenders: A History of Bohemianism in America. Revised edition. New York: Dover Publications, pp. 188, 191, 193-94, 195, 198, 278, 303.
Anderson was from 1913 on part of Chicago's "Bohemia," reading his manuscripts and living colorfully. Anderson frequented Schlogl's, and Margaret Anderson published his "dark forebodings and blind gropings." In New York, Anderson merely passed through "Bohemia."

21 PRIESTLY, J. B. Literature and Western Man. New York: Harper & Brothers, pp. 431, 432-33.
Anderson escaped Ohio for Chicago and even Paris, but he ended as a newspaperman in America. Nearly always bewildered and dreamy, Anderson longed for a lost idyllic America and seems to be "a kind of folk-poet who has tried a lot of jobs, and has looked at Freud."

22 ROTHWEILER, ROBERT LIEDEL. "Ideology and Four Radical Novelists: The Response to Communism of Dreiser, Anderson, Dos Passos, and Farrell." Dissertation, Washington University, 289 pp.
Anderson's liberal political cast is indistinct. In his early works he is concerned with the laborer, but he did not become politically active until the early 1930's. Then he became a recorder of changes in American society, especially changes in small towns. As the New Deal reforms worked, Anderson became more and more disenchanted with Communism as an answer to workers' problems; thus Anderson never developed a set view of politics, politicians, or the place of authors in politics.

23 SINCLAIR, UPTON. My Lifetime in Letters. Columbia: University of Missouri Press, pp. 152-56, 341-42.

On December 12, 1916, Anderson wrote Sinclair against making literature and politics equal; in 1917 Anderson repeated his belief and expected to find no answers to life's confusions.

24 SPRINGER, ANNE M. The American Novel in Germany: A Study of the Critical Reception of Eight American Novelists Between the Two World Wars. Hamburg: Cram de Gruyter, pp. 6-8, 60, 61, 67, 72, 85.
Anderson was popular in Germany from the early 1920's as exponent of the new literature of America, especially Freudian literature.

25 SULLIVAN, JOHN A. "Winesburg Revisited." Antioch Review, 20 (Summer), 213-21.
Many present citizens of Clyde, Ohio, deny that their town is the setting for Winesburg, Ohio; but Anderson always remembered Clyde pleasantly.

26 THORP, WILLARD. American Writing in the Twentieth Century. Cambridge: Harvard University Press, pp. 26, 49, 168-70.
Publication of Winesburg, Ohio in 1919 was Anderson's debut as a major writer. Never objective, Anderson's novels handle industrialism emotionally. As a naturalist, Anderson differs in giving every character "at least a momentary flash of self-illumination, a glimpse of the wonder of life."

27 THURSTON, JARVIS, O. B. EMERSON, CARL HARTMAN, and ELIZABETH V. WRIGHT. Short Fiction Criticism: A Checklist of Interpretations Since 1925 of Stories and Novelettes. . . . Denver: Alan Swallow, pp. 7-11.
[List of criticism of 22 stories by Anderson]

28 TSUBOI, KIYOHIKO. "A Story Teller's Last Story: A Study on 'Death in the Woods.'" Transactions of Okayama University Junior College of Law and Economics, Literary Review, 2 (March), 1-15.
Only an oral storyteller could have created "Death in the Woods," Anderson's great work in 5,000 words and 355 sentences. About five out of six words are monosyllabic; such modifiers as epithets, similes, and metaphors are used to some extent. Anderson develops rhythm by using repeated words and accent of sentences. [Takashi Kodaira]

*29 V. H., J. Review of An American Tragedy drama. Münchner Neueste Nachrichten (7 December).
Cited: 1960.B24.

1960

30 WENTZ, JOHN C. "Anderson's Winesburg and the Hedgerow Theatre." Modern Drama, 3 (May), 42-51.

Anderson began dramatizing Winesburg, Ohio late in 1932 with Arthur Barton; but Anderson disliked the result by 1933. By August 10, 1933, Anderson had written his own play, produced forty-one times at the Hedgerow Theatre from 1934 through 1936.

1961 A BOOKS

1 LENOX, WINFIELD SCOTT. "The Significance of Sherwood Anderson's Poetry." Master's thesis, Loyola University, 94 pp.

Anderson's favorite theme--loss of love in industrialized society--dominates in his poetry. Central to understanding Anderson's poetic prose is knowledge of his two poetry volumes--Mid-American Chants and A New Testament. As Anderson experimented in poetry, his prose style became increasingly lyrical.

1961 B SHORTER WRITINGS

1 AARON, DANIEL. Writers on the Left: Episodes in American Literary Communism. New York: Harcourt, Brace and Co., pp. 29, 76, 98, 99-100, 102, 178, 179, 181, 187, 190, 192, 194, 206-207, 210, 237, 378.

Radicals wondered about Anderson's politics as he withdrew from life; they thought him "the pet of the Chicago literati, mystagogue of Middlewesternismus, the admirer of Gertrude Stein. . . ." In the 1930's, Anderson mirrored middle-class failures instead of presenting answers.

2 ANDERSON, DAVID D. "Emerging Awareness in Sherwood Anderson's Tar." Ohioana, 4 (Summer), 40-42, 51.

In Tar Anderson presents his hero as becoming aware of social matters and mystical matters, so that the story retells his view of the growth of America.

3 BOWDEN, EDWIN T. The Dungeon of the Heart: Human Isolation and the American Novel. New York: Macmillan Co., pp. 114-24.

Obsessed with the inner life of his characters, Anderson in Winesburg, Ohio creates only that; each story develops upon loneliness, usually psychologically induced. The only answer is escape.

4 BROOKS, VAN WYCK. From the Shadow of the Mountain: My Post-Meridian Years. New York: E. P. Dutton and Co., pp. 4, 8-9, 11, 38, 121-22, 139.

Brooks helped Karl Anderson try to write a novel; Anderson brought Anita Loos to visit Brooks. Anderson's stories came from life and suggestions in Borrow; Brooks tried to have Max Perkins become Anderson's editor.

5 BURTIS, MARY ELIZABETH and PAUL SPENCER WOOD. "Sherwood Anderson." Recent American Literature. Patterson, NJ: Littlefield, Adams, pp. 13-17.

With Winesburg, Ohio Anderson told of the loveless and the lonely; his later works deal with humans threatened by the machine age. When he succeeded, Anderson did so by instinct instead of discipline.

6 CUNLIFFE, MARCUS. The Literature of the United States. Revised edition. Baltimore: Penguin Books, pp. 236, 261, 266-69, 270, 271, 276, 280, 281, 291, 302, 362.

Anderson's favorite theme--based on his own life--was escape from repressive situations. His work combines Stein and Sandburg, giving craft and subject to his nearly incoherent intentions.

7 DELL, FLOYD. "On Being Sherwood Anderson's Literary Father." Newberry Library Bulletin, 5 (December), 315-21.

In Chicago Anderson was super-sensitive to criticism of his work. Dell helped get Windy McPherson's Son published and some Winesburg stories were published through his good offices, but Anderson's friendship left as Anderson became more famous.

8 HASSAN, IHAB. Radical Innocence: Studies in the Contemporary American Novel. New York: Harper & Row, pp. 49-51, 78, 170, 233.

Knowing instinctively what Freud formally systematized, Anderson created in Winesburg, Ohio stories of characters caught between Puritanism and the success ethic. Innocence is past; inarticulateness and frustration are the present. The grotesque is incomplete, in stasis, is uncreated--"innocence deformed and preying upon itself."

9 KUEHL, JOHN. "Scott Fitzgerald's Critical Opinions." Modern Fiction Studies, 7 (Spring), 5, 13.

Fitzgerald blamed Mencken and Anderson with encouraging a sickness in American fiction--that of caring more for subject than craft; Anderson was worth attention for style, not ideas. Many Marriages had good subject matter--"the

1961

(KUEHL, JOHN)
reaction of a sensitive, highly civilized man to the phenomenon of lust."

10 McALEER, JOHN J. "Christ Symbolism in Winesburg, Ohio." Discourse, 4 (Summer), 168-81.
In Winesburg, Ohio Anderson has each character suffer to teach the hero to choose wisely as he matures. The use of figures who speak of Christ or imitate him drives the boy toward spiritual values. Reprinted: 1971.A2.

11 MARCUS, MORDECAI. "What Is an Initiation Story?" Journal of Aesthetics and Art Criticism, 14 (1960-61), 221, 224, 227.
"I Want to Know Why" is a story of incomplete initiation, for the initiate must presumably solve his puzzlement after his shocking experience.

12 MEEHAN, JAMES. "Ohio's Literary Giant: Sherwood Anderson." Ohio Review, 1 (June), 6-7, 25-26.
Had Anderson died twenty years earlier, no one could have doubted that a poor boy from a small town in Ohio had become a great writer; but his later books, in which he tried to use modern, "adult" themes, are failures. Anderson's achievement is his method--"a lyrical naturalism which concentrated not on events but on the development of consciousness in seemingly ordinary or pathetic characters."

13 MENCKEN, H. L. Letters of H. L. Mencken. Edited by Guy J. Forgue. New York: Alfred A. Knopf, pp. 150, 207, 231, 245, 266, 285, 287, 385, 386, 391, 437, 464.
Mencken liked Winesburg, Ohio and Anderson's other stories but not his novels; he solicited contributions from Anderson for his magazines. Mencken distrusted Anderson's evaluation of other authors or Anderson himself.

14 MIYAKE, TSUNEO. "A Study of Sherwood Anderson, I: On Winesburg, Ohio." Fukuoka University Review of Literature and Science, 16 (October), 1-6.
The composition of Winesburg, Ohio, its reception, its structure and method, and its style. [Takashi Kodaira]

15 MIYAMOTO, YOKICHI. "Sherwood Anderson." Eibei Bungakushi Koza XI. Tokyo: Kenkyusha, pp. 186-96.
["A Tall Tale and Truth," "Father's Heritage," "The Collapse of a Small Town," "A Story Teller and Modern Novels," "Anderson's Position in the History of American Literature"] [Takashi Kodaira]

16 MUMMENDEY, RICHARD. Die Schöne Literatur der Vereinigten Staaten von Amerika in Deutschen Übersetzungen: Eine Bibliographie. Bonn: H. Bouvier, pp. 5-6.
[List of Anderson's books translated into German]

17 NYREN, DOROTHY, ed. A Library of Literary Criticism. Second edition. New York: Frederick Ungar, pp. 18-22.
[Brief extracts from several critical works on Anderson]

18 PIVANO, FERNANDA. La Balena Bianci e Altri Miti. Verona: Arnoldo Mondadori Editore, pp. 81, 107, 113-23, 152, 153, 157, 179, 192, 200, 201, 206, 229, 234-35, 238, 263, 275-76, 277, 283, 293-94, 298, 345, 391-92, 403, 419, 452-53, 484.
In A Story Teller's Story, fantasy is the basis for all truth. Anderson relates to Lardner, Masters, Stein, Lewis, Dreiser, Cabell, Faulkner, and Fitzgerald.

19 ROSS, DANFORTH. The American Short Story. Minneapolis: University of Minnesota Press, pp. 29-31.
Influenced by naturalism, Anderson wrote intuitively, using the colloquial style and psychological insights. His heroes want the experience denied by social conformity.

20 SALINGER, J. D. Raise High the Roof Beam, Carpenters and Seymour--An Introduction. Boston: Little, Brown and Co., p. 161.
The character Buddy Glass praises Anderson's "gentle and effective style," supposedly noticeable in one of Glass' early works.

21 SAROYAN, WILLIAM. Here Comes, There Goes, You Know Who. New York: Simon and Schuster, pp. 16, 126.
Saroyan resented Anderson, whom he saw lecturing to a club of women; yet he liked Anderson's story of eating cabbage soup as a child.

22 SCHORER, MARK. Sinclair Lewis: An American Life. New York: McGraw-Hill, pp. 3-4, 177, 274, 276-82, 288, 294, 303, 305, 319, 332, 335, 374, 380, 406, 433, 434, 464, 546, 553, 768.
In 1920 Anderson wrote Lewis over the pleasure Main Street had given him; Lewis responded kindly about Winesburg, Ohio. Perhaps Anderson became jealous of Lewis' financial success, for he began speaking ill of Lewis' attitude and talent; and the two writers never again sympathized with each other.

23 STERN, EDITH M. "Papa Flops." Esquire, 55 (February), 66.
Anderson violently objected when Liveright was willing to publish Hemingway's The Torrents of Spring.

1961

24 SUZUKI, KINTARO. "Sherwood Anderson's Breakdown." Eibungaku [Waseda Daigaku Eibungakukai], 19 (January), 298-312.
Anderson's nervous breakdown became part of the writer's legend. [Takashi Kodaira]

25 TANSELLE, G. THOMAS. "Fitzgerald Letters at Newberry." Fitzgerald Newsletter, No. 15 (Fall), p. 6.
The Newberry Library holds two Fitzgerald letters to Anderson and one to Malcolm Cowley.

26 WHITE, WILLIAM. "The Private Correspondence of Sherwood Anderson." Daily Collegian [Detroit] (10 October), p. 4.
The Detroit Feinberg Collection owns eight letters by Anderson--six to Noah Steinberg, one to J. G. Leippert, and one to Harvey Taylor.

27 WRIGHT, AUSTIN McGIFFERT. The American Short Story in the Twenties. Chicago: University of Chicago Press, pp. 2-3, 11, 14-16, 18, 21, 26, 28, 30, 39, 52, 63, 88, 134, 140, 142, 150, 151-52, 155, 157, 170, 218, 224-25, 239, 263, 267, 269-70, 297, 304, 306-308, 320, 324, 345, 369, 374, 380, 383, 385.
Anderson's stories do not seem dated now in comparison with those of traditional writers, for Anderson was experimenting without narrative tradition in telling subjective truth about imaginative reality.

1962 A BOOKS - NONE

1962 B SHORTER WRITINGS

1 ADAMS, RICHARD P. "The Apprenticeship of William Faulkner." Tulane Studies in English, 12 (1963), 123-29.
Anderson encouraged Faulkner to read recent literature instead of Renaissance and nineteenth-century work, to write fiction instead of poetry, and to submit Soldiers' Pay to Anderson's publisher.

2 ANDERSON, DAVID D. "Sherwood Anderson After 20 Years." Midwest Quarterly, 3 (January), 119-32.
Anderson's early work remains important because content and form were new and personal; when his later work became derivative in style, Anderson courted obscurity.
Reprinted: 1966.A6.

3 _____. "Sherwood Anderson's Use of the Lincoln Theme." Lincoln Herald, 64 (Spring), 28-32.

Always interested in Lincoln, Anderson used some Lincolnesque qualities in the hero of Poor White--the Midwestern mystic who questions current values.

4 ANON. "Library Notes." Newberry Library Bulletin, 6 (November), 31-32.
Mrs. E. Vernon Hahn has given The Newberry Library the typescript of Marching Men and almost three hundred letters written by Anderson from 1917 into the 1930's.

5 BLÖCKER, GUNTER. "Sherwood Anderson: Winesburg, Ohio." Kritisches Lesebuch: Literatur Unserer Zeit in Probe und Bericht. Hamburg: Leibniz-Verlag, pp. 67-70.
Written in a kaleidoscopic style, Winesburg, Ohio is unified by the newspaper reporter--the "opener of souls."

6 BROWN, DEMING. Soviet Attitudes toward American Writing. Princeton: Princeton University Press, pp. viii, 23, 29, 32, 48, 54, 66, 109-16, 120, 130, 131, 132, 177, 242, 250, 319.
Anderson's work began to appear in Russian in 1924, was popular into the 1930's, and now is read academically. In the 1930's, Anderson was accused of not being enough concerned with political causes of suffering.

7 CABELL, JAMES BRANCH et al. Between Friends: Letters of James Branch Cabell and Others. Edited by Padriac Colum and Margaret Freeman Cabell. New York: Harcourt, Brace & World, pp. 45, 136-37, 283.
Rascoe writes Cabell in 1918 about fighting over literature with Hecht in front of Anderson, who tries to do for America what great European authors attempt. Later Anderson and Cabell helped edit The American Spectator.

8 DETLEFSEN, HAROLD. "Herman Hurd of Clyde: Sherwood Anderson's Boyhood Chum." RFD News, 5 (8 October), 1, 2, 9.
Only Herman Hurd, now eighty-five, knew Anderson in boyhood. Clyde, Ohio--the basis of Winesburg, Ohio--hated Anderson and this book.

9 FEIBLEMAN, JAMES K. "Memories of Sherwood Anderson." Shenandoah, 13 (Spring), 32-45.
Anderson met Feibleman in New Orleans and talked of his home in Virginia, his third trip to Europe, and Lawrence. Anderson's poor luck was to have written only one great book; his power was to see cosmic importance in everything.

1962

10 FITZGIBBONS, CONSTANCE. "Roadside Markers Keep Memories Green; Ohio Great Remembered." Dayton Daily News (19 March).
A sign in Camden, Ohio, now shows the pride of Anderson's birthplace. A searcher for answers, Anderson found none but created "darkly disturbing but compassionate keyhole glimpses of small town Ohio personalities."

11 GELB, ARTHUR and BARBARA GELB. O'Neill. New York: Harper & Brothers, pp. 283, 328, 597-98, 766, 786, 794-95, 797, 810.
Anderson attended with O'Neill a New York party given by Donald Friede; Dreiser was uncomfortable but liked a ghost story that Anderson told. O'Neill and Anderson became friends and later worked together editing The American Spectator. In April, 1935, Anderson visited O'Neill in the South and later called him "a sick man," one who needed encouragement. Anderson was among the first to recognize O'Neill for winning the Nobel Prize.

12 GOLD, HERBERT. "The Fair Apple of Progress." The Age of Happy Problems. New York: Dial Press, pp. 56-67.
Reprint of 1958.B12.

13 HAAS, ROBERT BARTLETT. "Gertrude Stein Talking--A Transatlantic Interview." UCLAN Review, 8 (Summer), 7, 8.
Anderson was to have written an essay on Stein's style, but Haas and Stein dropped the project. In response to a question in 1946 about Anderson's essay of 1922, Stein gave an entire history of her development. Reprint: 1971.B20.

14 H.[AGOPIAN], J.[OHN] V. "Sherwood Anderson." Insight I. Edited by John V. Hagopian and Martin Dolch. Frankfurt am/M: Hirschgraben-Verlag, pp. 11-14.
"The Egg" is a parable in which Anderson tells the reader too much information and concludes morally.

15 HARDWICK, ELIZABETH. A View of My Own: Essays in Literature and Society. New York: Farrar, Straus and Cudahy, pp. 1-13.
Reprint of 1953.B17.

16 HOFFMAN, FREDERICK J. The Twenties: American Writing in the Postwar Decade. Revised edition. New York: Free Press, pp. 108, 150, 161, 217-18, 222, 224, 227, 238, 239, 298, 302-306, 358-59, 369, 376, 426, 451.
The use of colloquial idiom in American fiction can be traced from Twain to Stein to Anderson to Hemingway. Anderson explored technology's effect upon humans in Poor White (fictionally) and Perhaps Women (sociologically).

17 _____. "The Voices of Sherwood Anderson." Shenandoah, 13 (Spring), 5-19.
Anderson is important because he influenced other writers, theorized about art, wrote of loneliness and society, and "documented" America from 1870 to 1915. Reprinted: 1966.A7.

18 JOSEPHSON, MATTHEW. Life Among the Surrealists: A Memoir. New York: Holt, Rinehart and Winston, pp. 38, 63, 64, 89, 156, 257, 259, 312.
Anderson's need for comradeship comforted Hart Crane, still in Akron; later, Crane was hurt that Anderson could not understand his poetry. Anderson's letters of introduction for Hemingway approved the younger man's sobriety; Anderson's anti-industrialism helped form the liberalism of the 1920's.

19 KNOLL, ROBERT E. McAlmon and the Lost Generation: A Self-Portrait. Lincoln: University of Nebraska Press, pp. 6, 227, 228, 233, 367, 373.
McAlmon believed that Hemingway's "My Old Man" imitated Anderson's "I'm a Fool." Anderson in the 1920's wrote childlishly and may have cultivated that habit; sometimes Anderson give childish characters too much sophistication of sensibility.

20 KODAIRA, TAKASHI. "On the Escape of George Willard." Pursuit, 1 (December), 41-48.
To the grotesque characters of Winesburg, Ohio comes no release until death. Some have left elsewhere to come to Winesburg, but even they isolate themselves from the commonplace, once there. Anderson's hero and all the thousands of young men whom he represents leave the village for the city. Their futures are doubtful, for they are like the grotesques who stay in Winesburg after the reporter leaves. [Takashi Kodaira]

21 LAND, MYRICK. The Fine Art of Literary Mayhem: A Lively Account of Famous Writers and Their Feuds. New York: Holt, Rinehart and Winston, pp. 180-204.
After enjoying Anderson's friendship in Chicago and Stein's in Paris, Hemingway became jealous of Anderson's great reputation (based, he felt, on little talent) and parodied the older writer in The Torrents of Spring.

22 LAWRY, JON S. "Love and Betrayal in Sherwood Anderson's 'I Want to Know Why.'" Shenandoah, 13 (Spring), 46-54.
When the boy in "I Want to Know Why" can no longer love purely and simply, he must learn to live poised between primitive irresponsibility and convention.

1962

23 LEISY, ERNEST E. and JOHN T. FLANAGAN. A History of American Literature. Osaka: Kyoiku Kosho, pp. 82-83.
Anderson's novels are structurally flawed, yet his stories are memorable. In Poor White he contrasts artisan and industry; in Winesburg, Ohio he writes from the unconsciousness of characters to avoid mere plot.

24 McALEER, JOHN J. "Christ Symbolism in Anna Christie." Modern Drama, 4 (February), 389-96.
In Winesburg, Ohio Anderson makes the first twentieth-century use of fictional Christ symbolism, linking the characters to Christ's suffering to show the purposelessness of suffering. O'Neill's Anna Christie may be adapting Anderson's idea to drama.

25 MALIN, IRVING. New American Gothic. Preface by Harry T. Moore. Carbondale: Southern Illinois University Press, p. 6.
"The Book of the Grotesque" describes almost Gothic characters "who love themselves so much that they cannot enter the social world except to dominate their neighbors."

26 MILLER, HENRY. "Anderson the Storyteller." Stand Still the Hummingbird. Norfolk, CT: New Directions, pp. 174-80.
Reprint of 1941.B78.

27 MINAMIDA, SEIJI. "An Essay on Winesburg, Ohio: On Its Infantilism." Pursuit, 1 (December), 49-56.
There are two major themes in Winesburg, Ohio--the psychology of the grotesques and the hero's awakening to manhood. [Takashi Kodaira]

28 MITO, OSAMU. "'Crowded Solitude' in America: Sherwood Anderson's Case." English Literature Review [English Literary Society, Kyoto Women's University], 6 (March), 22-75.
Winesburg, Ohio is symbolic of a crowded American square, Anderson's miserable experience of departure and return showing his lack of success in overcoming the conventions and mechanization of civilization. But Anderson watched, loved, and wrote of the procession of the grotesques on the square. Impressionistic to express romanticism about nature and brotherhood, Anderson is aloof from most literary movements. [Takashi Kodaira]

29 NEWMAN, M. W. "Unwrap Sherwood Anderson's Love Letters." Chicago Daily News (31 March), p. 5.
A second volume of Anderson letters from The Newberry Library collection is to be published.

30 O'CONNOR, WILLIAM VAN. The Grotesque: An American Genre and Other Essays. Carbondale: Southern Illinois University Press, pp. 6-8, 21, 25, 36, 47-48, 115, 116-17.

Anderson never developed his theory of the grotesque characters about whom he wrote; yet in his stories there is lack of communication and love and fulfilment. Some of Anderson's grotesques would be so anywhere, not just in a village.

31 OHARA, HIROTADA. "Winesburg, Ohio and Main Street: Significant Contrasts in Expression between Them." Pursuit, 1 (December), 57-66.

Anderson and Lewis differ aurally and orally due to their approach to reality. Anderson uses psychological realism, and Lewis uses photographic realism. While Anderson is deductive, Lewis is inductive. Anderson was influenced by modern painting--especially cubism and expressionism. [Takashi Kodaira]

32 POGGI, VALENTINA. "Il Linguaggio Narrativo di Sherwood Anderson." Studi Americana, 8 (1962), pp. 93-109.

Not all of Anderson's work is of good stylistic quality. He carefully hunts the clearest expression of emotion for thought that values life. His prose is more impressionistic than descriptive.

33 RAVITZ, ABE C. Clarence Darrow and the American Literary Tradition. Cleveland: Press of Case Western Reserve University, pp. 100, 104.

Darrow's novel Farmington is a forerunner of Winesburg, Ohio in "artful analysis of the Buckeye personality in terms social and psychological," for in Farmington characters become warped by embracing truths.

34 RICHARDSON, H. EDWARD. "Faulkner, Anderson, and Their Tall Tale." American Literature, 34 (May), 287-91.

In later tributes to Anderson, Faulkner may have forgotten having included a tall tale in Mosquitoes that he and Anderson invented in New Orleans.

35 RIDEOUT, WALTER B. "Sherwood Anderson's 'Mid-American Chants.'" Aspects of American Poetry: Essays Presented to Howard Mumford Jones. Edited by Richard M. Ludwig. Columbus: Ohio State University Press, pp. 149-70.

Anderson wrote most of Mid-American Chants from February into April of 1917, perhaps inspired by recently having met literati in New York and having returned to Chicago determined to use the Midwest in poetry.

1962

36 RIDEOUT, WALTER B. "The Simplicity of Winesburg, Ohio." Shenandoah, 13 (Spring), 20-31.

Resembling in setting Clyde, Ohio, Winesburg, Ohio is imaginatively detailed, told in tones of "elegiac quietness," generally set at evening, full of repeated words and patterns, and based on the initiation of the hero into acceptance of all people. Reprinted: 1966.A3.

37 ROHRBERGER, MARY. "The Man, the Boy, and the Myth: Sherwood Anderson's 'Death in the Woods.'" Midcontinent American Studies Journal, 3 (Fall), 48-54.

The old woman in "Death in the Woods" is Demeter and Proserpine and Hecate--all used to effect initiation in the boy and remembrance-understanding in the narrator. Reprinted: 1966.B33.

38 ROSELIEP, RAYMOND. "Epitaph for Winesburg." Shenandoah, 13 (Spring), 31.

"Distilled significance defines / a lyric as well as a life."

39 SAITO, TADATOSHI. "In Search of 'Fellowship': A Note on Winesburg, Ohio." Hitotsubashi Review (August), pp. 100-103.

Winesburg, Ohio can be divided into two groups of stories--first, those in which the reporter does not appear; and second, those in which he does play some role. When he appears, the stories deal with the characters' searching for fellowship through him. When he does not appear, the stories deal with characters as victims of isolation. [Takashi Kodaira]

40 SINCLAIR, UPTON. The Autobiography of Upton Sinclair. New York: Harcourt, Brace & World, p. 252.

Anderson is among writers known by Sinclair who drank whiskey and suffered dire consequences.

41 SINGLETON, M. K. H. L. Mencken and The American Mercury Adventure. Durham: Duke University Press, pp. 4, 19, 73, 74, 76, 77, 144, 205, 210, 211.

Mencken, liking realism, published several Anderson stories in The American Mercury; but Mencken published even his favorite authors sparingly. Leftist critics later blamed Anderson for associating with the conservative Mercury people.

42 SUTCLIFFE, DENHAM. "Anderson, Sherwood." Ohio Books and Their Authors: Biographical Data and Selective Bibliographies for Ohio Authors, Native and Resident, 1796-1950.

Edited by William Coyle. Cleveland: World Publishing Co., pp. 12-14.

By the late 1920's, critics were unhappy with Anderson's writings, which they charged with becoming adolescent, sentimental, formless, and unintellectual. In the tradition of Whitman, Anderson is defended as mystical, primitive, innovative, and intuitive.

43 TAKIGAWA, MOTOO. "From Anderson to Hemingway and Faulkner." Journal of the Society of English and American Literature, Kwansei Gakuin University, 13 (October), 68-75.

Anderson pursued study of reality less deeply than Hemingway and Faulkner; thus, the two younger writers had to outgrow Anderson's influence, but their characteristics are the same--pictorial instead of explanative. [Takashi Kodaira]

44 TANSELLE, G. THOMAS. "Additional Review of Sherwood Anderson's Work." Publications of the Bibliographical Society of America, 56 (Third quarter), 358-65.

[Unannotated reviews (322) of Anderson's work not in 1960.A2]

45 _____. "The First Notice of Sherwood Anderson." Notes & Queries, 9 (August), 307-309.

Dell's first notice about Anderson--omitting his name--probably was "New Novels: A First Glimpse," Chicago Evening Post (5 September), 1913, p. 9.

46 _____. Review of Sherwood Anderson: A Bibliography. Wisconsin Studies in Language and Literature, 3 (Fall), 106-12.

Sheehy and Lohf in their bibliography provide incomplete information, they are inconsistent in form, and they are inadequate in coverage.

47 UMEGAKI, KIYOSHI. "Winesburg, Ohio." Osaka Literary Review, 1 (April), 70-82.

As a spirit of youth saved the old man in "The Book of the Grotesque," so the grotesques in Winesburg, Ohio can recover momentarily a spirit of youth. The theme of the book is loneliness for egotistical persons. [Takashi Kodaira]

48 WILLIAMS, CRATIS D. "Kit Brandon, A Reappraisal." Shenandoah, 13 (Spring), 55-61.

In Kit Brandon Anderson returns to the structure of his first three novels but implements the style with primitivistic or experimental techniques from his mid-1920's novels.

1963

1963 A BOOKS

1 ANON. Winesburg, Ohio: A Critical Commentary. New York: American R. D. M. Corporation, 50 pp.
[Students' guide, plot summaries]

2 LEWIS, JANE KAREN. "Sherwood Anderson's Concept of Art and the Artist: Its Influence on the Style and Form of His Novels." Master's thesis, University of Texas, 108 pp.
The only structure that Anderson understood was the loose, organic form of the short story as he wrote it. Novels were beyond his ability to structure well or to overcome fascination with words as words.

3 STEELE, BETTY JEAN. "The Industrial World of Sherwood Anderson." Master's thesis, Duke University, 95 pp.
Study of five classes--"the inventor, the entrepreneurs, the professional men, the craftsmen, and the workers"--reveals that in his works Anderson sees degradation and discouragement as the price of industrialism. Only through craftsmanship and the erotic can humans be free.

1963 B SHORTER WRITINGS

1 ANDERSON, DAVID D. "Sherwood Anderson's Idea of the Grotesque." Ohioana, 6 (Spring), 12-13.
Anderson may have adopted the term "grotesque" from the 1915 play Grotesque by Cloyd Head and Maurice Brown.

2 ANON. "Bronze Plaque Now Marks Local House Where Sherwood Anderson, Famous Author, Was Born 87 Years Ago." Preble County News [OH] (12 September), p. 1.
The Camden Progressive Club has bought Anderson's birthplace and set up a marker. The remodeled and repainted house was once visited by Anderson, in 1934.

3 ASSELINEAU, ROGER. "Introduction." Revue des Lettres Modernes, No. 78-80 (1963), pp. 7-9.
Although Anderson is much forgotten, he was a pioneer in helping later writers, among them Faulkner, Hemingway, Wolfe, Saroyan, Miller, Steinbeck, and Caldwell. Often gauche, slow, and prolix, Anderson above all was passionately sincere and dedicated to creativity, exploring the interior infinite.

4 _____. "Langue et Style de Sherwood Anderson dans Winesburg, Ohio." Revue des Lettres Modernes, No. 78-80 (1963), pp. 121-35.

Much as Anderson loved words, he resisted their power to avoid matter. Thus, much of his imagery and style in Winesburg, Ohio is deliberately dull. Anderson occasionally used technical words; often he sounds biblical; overall, his style is artificially crafted to evoke emotions. Reprinted in translation: 1966.A3.

5 _____. "Sélection Bibliographique des Études Consacrées à Sherwood Anderson." Revue des Lettres Modernes, No. 78-80 (1963), pp. 137-57.
[Extensive list of secondary works]

6 BAKER, CARLOS. Hemingway: The Writer as Artist. Third edition. Princeton: Princeton University Press, pp. 4, 5-6, 7, 12, 25-26, 31-34, 36-37, 39, 40, 42-43, 44, 45-46, 78, 175.
Hemingway claimed Winesburg, Ohio as his first pattern, but by 1923 he had broken beyond Anderson and by 1926 he was ready to protect literature and negotiate a better contract by publishing The Torrents of Spring.

7 BOGOSLOVSKII, V. N. Istoriia Zarubezhnoi Literatury XX Veka. Moscow, pp. 602-603, 850-54.
Anderson's lonely, restless heroes search for love but can not find it in the gray existence of the American provinces. [James F. Cradler]

8 CALLAGHAN, MORLEY. That Summer in Paris: Memoirs of Tangled Friendships with Hemingway, Fitzgerald, and Some Others. New York: Coward-McCann, pp. 31, 37, 48-49, 56, 113, 123-24.
Callaghan had admired Anderson and regretted Hemingway's parody in The Torrents of Spring. At a New York party Callaghan called Anderson his "father" and gratified the older writer. After a later dinner, Anderson imagined Callaghan defending Hemingway's Catholicism.

9 DAVIDSON, DONALD. "Sherwood Anderson's A Story Teller's Story." The Spyglass: Views and Reviews. Edited by John Tyree Fain. Nashville: Vanderbilt University Press, pp. 61-63.
In A Story Teller's Story Anderson reveals himself as wistful and idealistic about creativity.

10 DERLETH, AUGUST. Three Literary Men: A Memoir of Sinclair Lewis, Sherwood Anderson, Edgar Lee Masters. New York: Candlelight Press, 56 pp.
Reprint of 1959.B13.

11 DURHAM, JOHN. "Did the 'Lionel Trilling Syndicate' Murder Sherwood Anderson?" Forum, 4 (Winter), 12-14.

Cowley may have misjudged Anderson's critical death at the pens of Trilling, Kazin, Klein, and Howe, for less "rationalist" critics still value Anderson highly.

12 FITZGERALD, F. SCOTT. The Letters of F. Scott Fitzgerald. Edited by Andrew Turnbull. New York: Charles Scribner's Sons, pp. 174, 179, 186-87, 191, 194-95, 197, 199, 475-76.

In spite of Anderson, the short story in the mid-1920's is "at its lowest ebb as an art form." In 1917 Anderson discovered the American present in Ohio. Critics are wrong to say that Anderson is profound; with no ideas, "he is one of the very best and finest writers in the English language today." Fitzgerald disliked A Story Teller's Story and encouraged Scribner's to publish Hemingway.

13 GOLDHURST, WILLIAM. F. Scott Fitzgerald and His Contemporaries. Cleveland: World Publishing Co., pp. 23-24, 29, 32, 157, 160, 204.

Anderson's "great and redeeming virtue" was his vanity; yet he was helpful to young Hemingway and Faulkner. Anderson scarcely exaggerated the tragedy of writers in America.

14 HECHT, BEN. Gaily, Gaily. Garden City: Doubleday, pp. 163, 166-67, 169-70, 172-73.

Hecht was with Dreiser and Anderson at a party in Chicago before Anderson had published. Anderson looked like a barber but was "a moony sort of Socrates" with immense superiority. Many women loved his ego; one claimed that Anderson read Winesburg, Ohio stories to her when intimate. Reprint of 1963.B15.

15 _____. "Letitia." Playboy, 10 (July), 88, 124.

Reprinted: 1963.B14.

16 IMADA, JUNZO. "Psychoanalysis of 'Loneliness' by Sherwood Anderson." Faculty of Foreign Languages Kita-Kyushu University Bulletin, 7 (March), 1-9.

"Loneliness" may be interpreted through use of psychological terms such as "Oedipus complex," "womb-fantasy," and "ambivalence." The central character of this story could not mature beyond the Oedipal stage. [Takashi Kodaira]

17 KITAGAKI, MUNEHARU. "Truth into Falsehood: An Essay on Winesburg, Ohio." Essays Presented to Naozo Ueno in Honor

of His Sixtieth Birthday. Edited by Jiro Takimoto. Tokyo: Nanundo, pp. 447-67.
The grotesques of Winesburg, Ohio can be understood through Anderson's use of the words "truth" and "adventure." [Takashi Kodaira]

18 LÜDEKE, HENRY. Geschichte der Amerikanischen Literatur. Second edition. Bern: Franke Verlag, pp. 407, 411, 420.
Anderson longed for an agrarian America, a lost utopia with personal freedom. The "hobo" of American literature, Anderson writes of himself in each work, seeking liberation in the erotic, in the artistic, and in psychology.

19 MIYAMOTO, YOKICHI. "Shiro Ozaki and Sherwood Anderson." Gakuto [Maruzen] (December), pp. 50-53.
There is a parallel to be drawn between Winesburg, Ohio and Ozaki's Life's a Stage and A Fancy Village. As did Hemingway and Faulkner, Ozaki used Anderson to seek his own theme and stimulate his own imagination.

20 MORGAN, H. WAYNE. "Sherwood Anderson: The Search for Unity." Writers in Transition: Seven Americans. New York: Hill and Wang, pp. 82-104.
Anderson's divided loyalty was to business and art. He saw good in business if it did not hurt creativity. Best at stories, Anderson cared more for character than form. He liked misfits and had a fatalistic philosophy tempered by humanism.

21 MORRIS, WRIGHT. The Territory Ahead. New York: Atheneum, pp. 24, 237-39, 240-41.
Winesburg, Ohio may keep its appeal from the artist-material tension. Hemingway's The Torrents of Spring is "a sustained, carefully planned, and extremely clever effort of annihilation," written by a scared man.

22 O'CONNOR, FRANK. The Lonely Voice: A Study of the Short Story. Cleveland: World Publishing Co., pp. 16, 18, 39-41, 113.
Anderson is the only story teller who may not be a great writer, for he had craft in dealing with his "submerged population--the lonely dreamers of the Middle West"--and in having communication become problem and danger; from Winesburg, Ohio "the modern American short story develops."

23 RICE, ELMER. Minority Report: An Autobiography. New York: Simon and Schuster, pp. 226, 327.

(RICE, ELMER)
Rice met Anderson frequently and liked his sensitivity; later, Anderson supported Foster and Ford, while Rice did not openly do so.

24 RIDEOUT, WALTER B. and JAMES B. MERIWETHER. "On the Collaboration of Faulkner and Anderson." American Literature, 35 (March), 85-87.
Faulkner used his own part of the Anderson-Faulkner oral tall tale when he wrote Mosquitoes.

25 ROBERTSON, NAN. "Books Selected for White House." New York Times (16 August), pp. 3-5, 22.
The collection of American books for the White House library includes Winesburg, Ohio, Dark Laughter, and Letters of Sherwood Anderson.

26 SAN JUAN, EPIFANIO, JR. "Vision and Reality: A Reconsideration of Sherwood Anderson's Winesburg, Ohio." American Literature, 35 (May), 137-55.
Winesburg, Ohio is valuable intrinsically because Anderson's grotesques demonstrated the imagination he so admired; all aspects of the book are devoted to the emotional quality of the characters. Reprinted: 1966.A3.

27 SPILLER, ROBERT E., WILLARD THORP, THOMAS H. JOHNSON, HENRY SEIDEL CANBY, and RICHARD M. LUDWIG, eds. Literary History of the United States. Third revised edition. New York: Macmillan Co., pp. 1229-33, 1234, 1236, 1296, 1359, 1385, 1424, 1442, 1476.
H. S. Canby says that Anderson's best biography is the self-study A Story Teller's Story. Using one technique for narrative--"loose, sprawling, and repetitive"--Anderson sometimes created great art in short stories. His characters are ordinary people bearing secret psychological wounds. His answer was acceptance and love that could overcome standardization, repression, and convention. In life's failures are the best studies of character.

28 TADA, TOSHIO. "Sherwood Anderson: A Grotesque Buried in History?" Studies in English Language and Literature [Kansai University], 7-8 (April), 89-116.
Anderson's best works are set in late-nineteenth-century America, when industrialism was changing the Midwest. The period about which he wrote is as adolescent as is Anderson's writing, and Anderson is buried in the grotesque history of America. [Takashi Kodaira]

29 TANSELLE, G. THOMAS. "Realist or Dreamer: Letters of Sherwood Anderson and Floyd Dell." Modern Language Review, 58 (October), 532-37.

Four hitherto unpublished letters exchanged in 1920-21 by Anderson and Dell further show Dell's disappointment at Anderson's poetic prose.

30 TOKLAS, ALICE B. What Is Remembered. New York: Holt, Rinehart and Winston, pp. 109-10, 128, 138, 151.

Anderson brought his second and third wives and two of his children to meet Stein, as well as introducing Ralph Church and Hemingway to her. Anderson compared Stein's short hair to a monk's; in America he escorted the two women around New Orleans.

31 TSUJIMOTO, ICHIRO. "Sherwood Anderson: His Position in the History of the American Short Story." Memoirs of the Faculty of Liberal Artsand Education, Shiga University, 13 (December), 125-31.

Using Rahv's paleface-redskin dichotomy, the idea may be advanced that the paleface developed the form of the American short story; then the redskin enriched its contents. Anderson is a redskin but differs from other redskins by doing away with the traditional form of the American short story. [Takashi Kodaira]

32 TURNER, SUSAN J. A History of the Freeman: Literary Landmark of the Early Twenties. New York: Columbia University Press, pp. 24, 60, 90-91, 135, 139-41.

Having aided the Chicago Renaissance, Anderson moved to New York and won the Dial award. The Dial reviewers--Brooks and Mary Colum--appreciated Anderson's fiction.

33 WASSERSTROM, WILLIAM. The Time of The Dial. Syracuse: Syracuse University Press, pp. 37, 81, 82, 95, 97, 137.

As Anderson had contributed an essay on Stieglitz, "I'm a Fool," and "The Triumph of the Egg" to The Dial, Schofield Thayer solidly supported Anderson's Dial prize as indicative of future support for the arts in America.

34 WEST, PAUL. The Modern Novel. Two volumes. London: Hutchinson University Library, pp. 29, 192, 222, 238, 239-40, 243, 296, 365, 409.

Stein helped Anderson by "demonstrating where the impossible began." Hemingway's The Torrents of Spring is "gibing literary prattle." Anderson's novels are "those of an expatriot who stayed home" and fail through lack of "heroic pretensions"; yet Anderson's work is a relief to "the American cult of violence."

1963

35 WINTER, ELLA. And Not to Yield: An Autobiography. New York: Harcourt, Brace & World, p. 176.

At a dinner at Anderson's, Winter heard Wolfe and Max Eastman arguing over anti-Semitism; and Wolfe asked Winter to introduce him to "some Jews."

1964 A BOOKS

1 BURBANK, REX. Sherwood Anderson. New York: Twayne Publishers, 159 pp.

Product of the culturally deprived, rootless Midwest, Anderson moved from prairie Midland boyhood to Chicago excitement to New York City sophistication. Bored by small towns, upset by industry, and self-conscious with intellectuals and other artists, Anderson went discontentedly across the face of America. Windy McPherson's Son and Marching Men show naturalistic heroes rising to conscience; Winesburg, Ohio combines grotesque characters and psychic consciousness; Poor White, Horses and Men, and The Triumph of the Egg illustrate use of narrative perspective; Many Marriages, Dark Laughter, Beyond Desire, and Kit Brandon concern need for "psychological and moral solutions to the problems of modern industrial society. . ."; and A Story Teller's Story and Sherwood Anderson's Memoirs are "confessions" about the author's place in American society. Reprinted in part: 1966.A7; 1974.A3.

2 LOVE, GLEN ALLEN. "Sherwood Anderson's American Pastoral." Dissertation, University of Washington, 204 pp.

Anderson fits into the pastoral mode--the urbanite viewing the rustic--because of his idealism, his primitivism, and his dislike for the standardized and mechanical. Beginning with works on the corruption of the pastoral dream by greed and industry, Anderson moves backward into honest nostalgia for the pastoral village, and then forward into urban, industrialized complexities, ending his career with a clear-eyed vision in Home Town.

3 RESER, JAMES A. "Sherwood Anderson: Country Newspaper Editor-Owner-Publisher." Master's thesis, East Tennessee State University, 76 pp.

Being unable to write "to order," Anderson gave up his book contracts and ran two country-town newspapers in Marion, Virginia, from 1927 through 1929. The experience--while he enjoyed it--allowed him to renew his feeling for small-town people and lives.

4 WEBER, BROM. Sherwood Anderson. Minneapolis: University of Minnesota Press, 48 pp.

Anderson's great theme is "death in life"--humanity without community or love or imagination; as Anderson felt reborn after his breakdown in 1912, so his fictional heroes re-enact the same reawakening. His work is uneven, his tone is emotional, his style is lyrical--and many consider him a failure after the early 1920's.

1964 B SHORTER WRITINGS

1 AIYAMA, YOSHIFUMI. "Notes on Winesburg, Ohio, I." Sapporo Tanki Daigaku Ronsyu, 11 (March), 163-78.

Anderson could not find in Winesburg, Ohio solution to the problem of isolation; he wrote Dark Laughter and Poor White to find the solution. [Takashi Kodaira]

2 ALLEN, WALTER. The Modern Novel in Britain and the United States. New York: E. P. Dutton & Co., pp. 66, 69, 77-81, 82, 86.

Anderson's reputation must now stand on Winesburg, Ohio, influenced by Masters, Turgenev, Twain, Stein, and the Bible and written in "a prose freer, more idiomatic, more lyrical, less 'literary', than anyone had written since Mark Twain." The archetypal story is "'Queer.'"

3 ANDERSON, DAVID D. Critical Studies in American Literature: A Collection of Critical Essays. Karachi: University of Karachi, pp. 99-141.

From 1912 to 1927, Anderson covered three themes: individual rebellion against materialism, individual isolation, and possible spirituality beneath naturalism. Happy during these years, Anderson was not politically active. The Depression brought him into politics as he saw the failure of the so-called "American dream." Winesburg, Ohio deals with loneliness in terms of very human characters; Poor White deals with the effects of industrialism on a Midwestern town. Reprinted in part: 1966.A3.

4 ARMOUR, RICHARD. American Lit Relit. New York: McGraw Hill, pp. 110, 135, 153-54.

Squalor in American literature is depicted "at great length" and in Winesburg, Ohio; perhaps Stein's portrait inspired Anderson, as Cézanne inspired Stein; the Stein-Anderson-Hemingway influence will end God knows where.

1964

5 ASSELINEAU, ROGER. "Sherwood Anderson: Grandeur et Misère d'un Romancier." Information et Documents, No. 195 (1 March), pp. 23-27.

In Winesburg, Ohio Anderson wrote well, for he released the dreamer in himself, exploring inner reality without losing surface actuality. Only Anderson's stories are well handled, his characters being unfulfilled dreamers. Because Anderson dealt in "moments," he could not do well in novels. Knowing life to be absurd, Anderson expressed love and acceptance.

6 BRASHERS, HOWARD C. An Introduction to American Literature for European Students. Stockholm: Svenska Bokförlaget, pp. 128-29, 135, 172.

The grotesques of Winesburg, Ohio are repressed by society, but "they themselves make up that iron vice." All of Anderson's novels are weak or sentimental; the best, Dark Laughter, "is finally unsatisfying because it moves by clairvoyance and wish-fulfillment."

7 CECCHI, EMILIO. Scrittori Inglesi e Americani: Saggi, Note e Versioni. Fourth edition. Milan: Alberto Mondadori Editore, pp. 190-91, 197, 199-200, 206-207, 217, 224, 234, 246, 370.

When Anderson saw Chartres, he realized the modern loss of a spiritual past. American criticism was reborn because of such literature as Anderson's works. Knowing few rules of writing, Anderson innovated in style and showed the poison of provincial Puritanism. Whereas Lewis helped to overcome the Puritans' influences intellectually, Anderson did so emotionally.

8 CIANCIO, RALPH A. "The Grotesque in Modern American Fiction: An Existential Theory." Dissertation, University of Pittsburgh, 203 pp.

Winesburg, Ohio is the clearest literary example of the grotesque in American fiction. In original style Anderson uses the commonest distorting factor--fanaticism--as the origin of grotesquerie; he creates grotesque characters in non-grotesque art; and he views loss of communication as resulting from psychological forces rather than cosmic ill.

9 DAHLBERG, EDWARD. Alms for Oblivion. Minneapolis: University of Minnesota Press, pp. 3-19.

An "Ohio populist and sex rebel," Anderson spiritually descended from Whitman and feared what money could do to his creativity and freedom. Thoroughly Midwestern, Anderson had "manual intelligence" but not "speculative intellect." Reprint of 1951.B17.

10 EASTMAN, MAX. Love and Revolution: My Journey Through an Epoch. New York: Random House, pp. 17, 139, 140-41.

Eastman scarcely knew Anderson while working with The Liberator; Anderson's stories arrived through Dell. Friends later, Eastman recalls Anderson as a genial questioner of life. At a 1930's dinner, Anderson and Wolfe disagreed over being at ease--Wolfe with men; Anderson, with women.

11 FIEDLER, LESLIE A. Waiting for the End. New York: Stein and Day, pp. 10, 13, 34, 78, 84, 129.

The Torrents of Spring is one of Hemingway's "central achievements," not just a parody of Anderson; Anderson had influenced the Hemingway style through his "passionate provincial stutter." Even To Have and Have Not may parody Beyond Desire.

12 GULLASON, THOMAS H. "The Short Story: An Underrated Art." Studies in Short Fiction, 2 (Fall), 17, 22.

Studies of short stories lately have concentrated on cycles such as Winesburg, Ohio. Anderson's stories were written for escape; his attempted novels deserved such scorn as Hemingway's The Torrents of Spring provided.

13 HECHT, BEN. "About Sherwood Anderson." Letters from Bohemia. Garden City: Doubleday, pp. 87-103.

Anderson told Hecht that he abandoned business in Ohio when his factory burned down, that he grew up in the Ozarks, and that an ex-mistress killed herself. No writer had (and usually deserved) more self-confidence about his talent in writing or in sex.

14 HEMINGWAY, ERNEST. "Une Generation Perdue." A Moveable Feast. New York: Charles Scribner's Sons, pp. 25-31.

Stein first liked Anderson as a person; Hemingway liked him as the author of fine short stories about characters whom Anderson loved. Anderson's novels were very bad, and Hemingway parodied Dark Laughter in The Torrents of Spring. Basically, Anderson and Stein lacked creative discipline.

15 HIGGS, ROBERT JACKSON. "Sports and the Athlete in the Work of Sherwood Anderson, Ring Lardner, and F. Scott Fitzgerald." Master's thesis, University of Tennessee, 80 pp.

The athlete became an American hero due in part to the World War. Anderson gives to athletes "the gallant and noble qualities of Spenser's knights." In baseball Anderson found comraderie, and in horseracing drivers he found mystical understanding of beauty and craft.

1964

16 HUEBSCH, B. W. "From a Publisher's Commonplace Book." American Scholar, 33 (Winter 1963-64), 122, 124, 126.

Even scholars now study Anderson, as do those fascinated by the man's personality. Anderson's letters often show misunderstanding of publishing or apparent awareness of audience. Lawrence responded negatively to Winesburg, Ohio, sent at Anderson's insistence. Not Huebsch but Hart Crane met Anderson in New Orleans.

17 JOOST, NICHOLAS. Schofield Thayer and The Dial: An Illustrated History. Carbondale: Southern Illinois University Press, pp. 36, 38, 47-48, 52, 64, 65-72, 84, 105-106, 110, 111, 112, 115, 116, 140, 145, 169, 196, 262.

Before receiving the Dial award, Anderson had condescended to the journal and to Schofield Thayer's wealth. Soon thereafter Many Marriages appeared serially. This and other Anderson items caused much editorial debate.

18 LIBMAN, V. A. "Anderson, Sherwood." Problemy Istorii Literatura SShA. Moscow: Izdatel'stvo "Nauka," pp. 390-91.

[Bibliography of translations of Anderson's works into Russian and of studies on him in Russian] Reprinted in translation: 1969.B29.

19 MENDELSON, M. Sovremenny Amerikanskii Roman. Moscow, pp. 6, 28, 30, 65, 79, 108, 147, 152, 220, 272, 351, 353, 432, 438, 504.

Anderson shares many ideas with his contemporaries. His antipathy for machines as instruments of spiritual and physical enslavement, for example, strikes a sympathetic response from John Steinbeck. [James F. Cradler]

20 MILLGATE, MICHAEL. American Social Fiction: James to Cozzens. London: Oliver & Boyd, pp. 84-85, 87-93, 101, 106, 112, 134, 136-37, 197, 210.

Anderson "often seems attractive without being admirable," for he presented vague ideas about society more often than correct pictures. In Winesburg, Ohio are Anderson's best images of social commentary, the writer assuming innocent, intuitive understanding of human nature.

21 MOORE, GEOFFREY. American Literature and the American Imagination. Hull: University of Hull Publications, pp. 13, 20.

A "redskin" rebel in literature, Anderson was "particularly interested in the poignance of the transition from innocence to experience, and communicates the idealism and despair of adolescence without whimsy."

22 NASU, YORIMASA. "Sherwood Anderson and J. D. Salinger." Studies in Humanities [Doshisha University], 71 (March), 21-34.

The central characters of Winesburg, Ohio and The Catcher in the Rye are aloof from the world and act as camera eyes to photograph the world. Severed from families, teachers, and lovers, they differ from each other in courses of escape, the Anderson character leaving a town for a city and the Salinger character trying to become a savior of children. [Takashi Kodaira]

23 POTTER, HUGH McCLELLAN. "The 'Romantic Nationalists' of the 1920's." Dissertation, University of Minnesota, 294 pp.

Anderson saw his role as writer as leading first himself and then others to full flowering of all potentials to become more natural, more liberated from conventions and strictures. Especially in his autobiographies Anderson reveals his concept of "bardic" leader toward individual and social fulfillment of the American dream. Anderson as a romantic nationalist in the 1920's rebelled against "pragmatism, industrialism, and Victorian moral precepts."

24 PEDEN, WILLIAM. The American Short Story: First Line in the National Defense of Literature. Boston: Houghton Mifflin Co., pp. 9, 11, 21, 25, 35-36, 39, 90, 112, 165.

The short story descends from Hawthorne and Poe to Bierce and Anderson; Dubliners and Winesburg, Ohio are important forces in development.

25 PIVANO, FERNANDA. America Rossa e Nera. Florence: Vollecchi Editore, pp. 61, 78, 81, 165-66, 220, 233, 237, 238.

Father of modern American literature, Anderson presented blacks and whites and in his autobiography writes of the origin of Dark Laughter.

26 RICHARDSON, H. EDWARD. "Anderson and Faulkner." American Literature, 36 (November), 298-314.

Anderson influenced Faulkner to write fiction about the South and to write lyrically and psychologically--in other words, he exercised general instead of specific influence on the younger writer.

27 TUCK, DOROTHY. Crowell's Handbook to Faulkner. New York: Thomas Y. Crowell Co., pp. 127, 130, 197, 235, 237-38.

Perhaps Faulkner went to New Orleans in 1925 in order to meet Anderson, who agreed to help Faulkner publish Soldiers' Pay and became Dawson Fairchild in Mosquitoes.

1964

28 VOLPE, EDMUND L. A Reader's Guide to William Faulkner. New York: Farrar, Straus and Giroux, pp. 10-11, 58-59, 141.

Admiring Anderson's casual life in New Orleans and willing to have Anderson help publish Soldiers' Pay, Faulkner used New Orleans scenes and possibly Anderson himself in Mosquitoes--as a figure who magnifies trivialities in his native state into imposing fiction.

29 WALKER, WILLIAM E. and ROBERT L. WELKER, eds. Reality and Myth: Essays in American Literature in Memory of Richard Croom Beatty. Nashville: Vanderbilt University Press, pp. 181, 214, 221-22, 223, 224, 230, 233, 234, 242, 246, 249.

Faulkner and Anderson became friends in New Orleans, and Anderson contributed dull "testaments" to The Double Dealer; yet Anderson spotted and encouraged Faulkner's talent.

1965 A BOOKS

1 COLE, JANICE ELLEN. "Many Marriages: Sherwood Anderson's Controversial Novel." Dissertation, University of Michigan, 229 pp.

Many Marriages is not just a poor novel about sex. Instead, the hero of the novel awakens to life, sex, and the need to be free of conventions that have become stultifying. The novel must not be read realistically but symbolically, as Anderson's experiment in imaginative development of the quest for liberation.

1965 B SHORTER WRITINGS

1 ADAMS, J. DONALD. Speaking of Books and Life. New York: Holt, Rinehart and Winston, pp. 8, 11, 17, 21, 269.

Good as Anderson was in fiction, he "could think no more clearly than Dreiser." The generation of "exile" had read and responded to Anderson's works; to Anderson's male characters women are "confused symbols in the minds of baffled and thwarted men"; as with most American writers, Anderson lacked a sense of humor.

2 AIYAMA, YOSHIFUMI. "Notes on Winesburg, Ohio, 2." Sapporo Tanki Daigaku Ronsyu, 12 (March), 130-40.

Aid in understanding Winesburg, Ohio comes from the subjects of "the young thing," sex, night, the wall, the dream, and the form.

1965

*3 ANON. "Tak Prikhodit Vaska Minuta." Voprosy Literatury, No. 2 (1965), pp. 171-78.
Cited: 1969.B29.

4 BABB, HOWARD S. "A Reading of Sherwood Anderson's 'The Man Who Became a Woman.'" Publications of the Modern Language Association of America, 80 (September), 432-35.
The youth in "The Man Who Became a Woman" must undergo experiences that develop beyond adolescent homosexuality into adult "integrity."

5 BERTHOFF, WARNER. The Ferment of Realism: American Literature, 1884-1919. New York: Free Press, pp. 29, 83, 91, 221, 262, 281-82, 283, 290-93.
In the local color of Winesburg, Ohio Anderson balances harsh criticism with nostalgia. Anderson later chronicles the effects of change from agrarian to industrial towns, giving his work the confessional and documentary tone. Anderson presents the essentially moral call for psychological purification to exorcise materialism, greed, and convention. Anderson's metier of writing short stories reinforces his roots in regional vernacular.

6 BROOKS, VAN WYCK. An Autobiography. Introduction by Malcolm Cowley. Foreword by John Hall Wheelock. New York: E. P. Dutton & Co., pp. 259, 263-66, 267, 269, 272, 363, 458.

7 CONNOLLY, CYRIL. The Modern Movement: One Hundred Key Books From England, France and America 1880-1950. London: Andre Deutsch / Hamish Hamilton, pp. 45-46, 53, 123, 124.
Even Anderson showed up in exciting Paris in the 1920's--at Sylvia Beach's bookstore. Anderson influenced Hemingway to write In Our Time and thus "gave the Modern Movement one of its few men of action."

8 FAULKNER, WILLIAM. Essays, Speeches & Public Letters. Edited by James B. Meriwether. New York: Random House, pp. 3-10, 173-75.
Reprint of 1953.B12.

9 _____. Faulkner in the University: Class Conferences at the University of Virginia, 1957-1958. Edited by Frederick L. Gwynn and Joseph L. Blotner. New York: Vintage Books, pp. 11, 21-22, 23, 57, 70, 150, 229-34, 259-60, 281.
Faulkner recalls meeting and learning from Anderson in New Orleans in 1924; the act of writing was so intense that Anderson got little pleasure; Anderson perhaps admired

1965

(FAULKNER, WILLIAM)
Stein's literary knowledge, being, he felt, uneducated; Anderson became unhappy trying to move beyond yet equal Winesburg, Ohio.

10 FEIBLEMAN, JAMES K. "Literary New Orleans Between World Wars." Southern Review, New Series 1 (Summer), 704, 709, 710-12, 714.
When Feibleman met Anderson in New Orleans, Anderson mainly liked to talk each evening with people who appreciated his stories. Anderson did not talk of Faulkner to these New Orleans friends, but he bragged of Stein's influence.

11 FORD, FORD MADOX. Letters of Ford Madox Ford. Edited by Richard M. Ludwig. Princeton: Princeton University Press, p. 319.
Ford and Anderson attended together a 1939 dinner to honor E. E. Cummings.

12 HICKS, GRANVILLE. Part of the Truth. New York: Harcourt, Brace & World, pp. 34, 101.
Winesburg, Ohio was one of Hicks' independent literary discoveries; he and Anderson later signed a statement backing Foster and Ford.

13 HIGASHIDA, CHIAKI. "Dark Laughter's Style." Joshidai Bungaku, Gaikoku Bungaku Hen [Osaka Joshidaigaku Eibungakuka] 17 (March), 1-16.
With Anderson the novel depends first on causes which hinder characters from living fully and then with the way to remove these causes; the former is fact, and the latter is fancy. Anderson gives more emphasis to ideal than real in his fiction. Dark Laughter is not impressive because it is artistically flawed, lacking in beauty and fragrance as literary art. [Takashi Kodaira]

14 HOWE, IRVING. "Sherwood Anderson: Winesburg, Ohio." The American Novel from James Fenimore Cooper to William Faulkner. Edited by Wallace Stegner. New York: Basic Books, pp. 154-65.
In Winesburg, Ohio Anderson's fragile stories "capture something that is universal, a note of nostalgia and loss, a quality of rare tenderness."

15 JOSEPH, GERHARD. "The American Triumph of the Egg: Anderson's 'The Egg' and Fitzgerald's 'The Great Gatsby.'" Criticism, 7 (Spring), 131-40.

Independently Anderson and Fitzgerald use the egg as symbol--Anderson, of frustration and failure of a grotesque father who resents Christopher Columbus; Fitzgerald, of an American dreamer who triumphs and loses and dies.

16 KAZIN, ALFRED. Starting Out in the Thirties. Boston: Little, Brown and Co., p. 136.

"Like so many writers who came of age in the Thirties, I took for granted the continuing spirit of the Twenties that I knew from Winesburg, Ohio. . . ."

17 KODAIRA, TAKASHI. "The Grotesque in Society, I: On Winesburg, Ohio." Studies and Essays by the Faculty of Law and Literature, Literature, Kanazawa University, 12 (March), 55-67.

The grotesques of Winesburg, Ohio are so individual that they can snatch up one of the truths and live their lives by it. Alone in society or mistaken by others in searching for understanding, they have no release until death. Others leave for the city; some come to Winesburg from elsewhere to live in isolation as before. [Takashi Kodaira]

18 LOWRY, MALCOLM. Selected Letters of Malcolm Lowry. Edited by Harvey Breit and Margerie Bonner Lowry. Philadelphia: J. B. Lippincott, pp. 85-86.

Anderson once said that a writer could become exotic and say just anything, art or not.

19 LUCOW, BEN. "Mature Identity in Sherwood Anderson's 'The Sad Horn-Blowers.'" Studies in Short Fiction, 2 (Spring), 291-93.

In "The Sad Horn-Blowers" Anderson uses cornet playing as the hero's search for identity as an individual in "a world in which mature identity paradoxically means absorption into a homogeneous mass."

20 McALEER, JOHN J. "Biblical Symbolism in American Literature: A Utilitarian Design." English Studies, 46 (August), 316-20.

With symbolic use of Christ images in Winesburg, Ohio, Anderson created twentieth-century Christ references in literature, influencing O'Neill, Hemingway, and Faulkner.

21 MacSHANE, FRANK. The Life and Work of Ford Madox Ford. New York: Horizon, pp. 215, 253, 265-67, 269.

Ford solicited essays by Anderson and also taught at Olivet College, but Anderson never referred to Ford's

1965

(MacSHANE, FRANK)
books, only to his "tendency to invite people to be guests of his at a great southern manor which did not exist."

22 MILLER, HENRY. Letters to Anias Nin. Edited by Gunther Stuhlmann. New York: G. P. Putman's Sons, pp. 49, 213, 259.
Miller encourages Nin in 1932 to find out the psychological meaning of Many Marriages. On November 19, 1940, Miller visited Anderson's country home in Virginia.

23 MORRIS, WRIGHT. "The Lunatic, the Lover, and the Poet." Kenyon Review, 27 (Autumn), 727-28, 733, 735-36.
By writing Winesburg, Ohio about grotesques, Anderson liberated the type from humorous use and made grotesques into people.

24 PARISH, JOHN E. "The Silent Father in Anderson's 'I Want to Know Why.'" Rice University Studies, 51 (Winter), 49-57.
Contrary to most opinion, Anderson in "I Want to Know Why" admires and approves the quiet father's distant yet loving treatment of the son.

25 ROGERS, W. G. Wise Men Fish Here: The Story of Frances Steloff and the Gotham Book Mart. New York: Harcourt, Brace & World, pp. 114, 116-17, 209.
Anderson had complained about selling his best Winesburg, Ohio stories cheaply to The Seven Arts. When he died, Anderson was planning to write a work about Faulkner.

26 SCHLUETER, PAUL. "Between Book Ends: Sherwood Anderson's First Novel." St. Louis Post-Dispatch (21 December).
Republication of Windy McPherson's Son shows the 1916 work as apprenticeship for Anderson; yet the hero is "not quite like anyone else in American fiction."

27 STARRETT, VINCENT. Born in a Bookshop: Chapters from the Chicago Renaissance. Norman: University of Oklahoma Press, pp. 175, 176-78, 183, 186, 200, 202, 223, 226.
Starrett regrets knowing Anderson only slightly. Anderson lacked humor and took his work with high seriousness. Winesburg, Ohio elicited Starrett's "purient enthusiasm," and Anderson "mistook an obsession with sex for a philosophy of life."

28 SWANBERG, W. A. Dreiser. New York: Charles Scribner's Sons, pp. 146-47, 165, 177, 187, 188, 202, 210-11, 239, 249, 251, 262, 263, 269, 272, 280, 286, 292, 310, 313-14, 345, 347,

367, 403, 405, 406, 409, 410, 413, 419, 424, 429, 435, 436, 438, 440, 456, 465-66, 475-76, 500.

Dreiser met Anderson at a Chicago party early in 1913 and later tried to find him a publisher for Windy McPherson's Son: he did not care for Poor White, served only beer at the famous party, imitated "Tandy," disliked Anderson's dirty stories, advised him on film rights, disliked Winesburg, Ohio as drama, exposed himself in Pennsylvania, and praised science.

29 TAKANO, KAZUNORI. "An Analysis of the Characters in Winesburg, Ohio." Research Reports of Sasebo Technical College, 2 (December), 53-66.

The characters of Winesburg, Ohio may be analyzed according to isolation, daydreaming, repression, negativism, regression, identification, substitution, attention-getting, and rationalization. They differ from average people in appearance; yet they have average psychological mechanisms. To ease tension and keep self-respect, they try to fulfill their needs indirectly. [Takashi Kodaira]

30 TANIGUCHI, RIKUO. "A Writer and His Four Wives: An Essay on Sherwood Anderson." Kikan Eibungaku, 3 (Autumn), 13-26.

Reprint of 1954.B23. [Takashi Kodaira]

31 TANNER, TONY. "Sherwood Anderson's Little Things." The Reign of Wonder: Naïvety and Reality in American Literature. Cambridge: Cambridge University Press, pp. 205-227.

The "little things" of which the hero of Winesburg, Ohio thinks are representative of the simple style of Anderson's language, the simple truths revealed in his stories, the simple way to present localized characters with universal significance. Writing of "little things"--moments of wonder and thus life--the writer might leave incomplete a broader view.

32 TANSELLE, G. THOMAS. "The Letters of Sherwood Anderson and August Derleth." Notes & Queries, 12 (July), 266-73.

In 1939 and 1940 Anderson and Derleth exchanged several letters (hitherto unpublished) that "form a discussion of honesty and freedom in literature that is eloquent in its own right."

33 ULANOV, BARRY. The Two Worlds of American Art: The Private and the Popular. New York: Macmillan Co., pp. 190, 193-94, 202, 258-61, 263-65.

Anderson's procedures in Winesburg, Ohio are themselves grotesque, for he too obviously guides the reader's

1965

(ULANOV, BARRY)
response; but in some of the other, non-Winesburg, Ohio stories, Anderson pares his prose to lean essentials. These stories Hemingway knew and learned from; and Carson McCullers, worsening even Anderson's grotesques, created nightmare.

34 UNTERMEYER, JEAN STARR. Private Collection. New York: Alfred A. Knopf, pp. 90-91, 194, 230, 292.
Soon before his death, Anderson told Untermeyer of a Chicago walk with Sandburg; Alys Bentley, the dance teacher, appealed to Anderson the artist. When Anderson died, the Olivet College writer's chair went to Untermeyer, whose nicest compliment from her son resembled one in Anderson's story "Death."

35 UNTERMEYER, LOUIS. Bygones: The Recollections of Louis Untermeyer. New York: Harcourt, Brace & World, pp. 37-40.
Frank encouraged Anderson to publish Winesburg, Ohio stories in The Seven Arts; "'Queer'" graced an early issue.

36 WHITE, RAY LEWIS. "The Original for Sherwood Anderson's Kit Brandon." Newberry Library Bulletin, 6 (December), 196-99.
The heroine of Kit Brandon is based on a bootleg queen whose last days Anderson reported in his Virginia newspapers and in Hello Towns!

37 ZUTHER, H. W. Eine Bibliographie der Aufnahme Amerikanischer Literatur in Deutschen Zeitschriften 1945-1960. Munich: Dissertationsdruck Franz Frank, pp. 10, 19.
[Brief list of Anderson studies in German.]

1966 A BOOKS

1 CARLSON, G. BERT, JR. "Sherwood Anderson's Political Mind: The Activist Years." Dissertation, University of Maryland, 288 pp.
In 1930--after declaring himself apolitical in the 1920's--Anderson became concerned with southern textile and coal strikes; he was "a political commentator without credentials." With concern as motivation Anderson produced social commentary instead of either propaganda or good fiction; his topics were "machine-induced standardization, striking workers, Communist uprisings, bootlegging, and the ever-present New Deal."

2 CRIST, ROBERT LENHART. "Sherwood Anderson's Dark Laughter: Sources, Composition, and Reputation." Dissertation, University of Chicago, 207 pp.

Dark Laughter is influenced by Anderson's boyhood in Ohio, his war experience, his Chicago jobs, his marriage and family, his trips to Europe and New Orleans; among literary influences are Twain, Joyce, Lawrence, Stein, Maugham, Toomer, Gauguin, Borrow, and Brooks. The novel was a best-seller because of publicity and "scandal," and it became Anderson's most profitable book.

3 FERRES, JOHN H., ed. Sherwood Anderson: Winesburg, Ohio: Text and Criticism. New York: Viking Press, 511 pp. [criticism, pp. 253-511]

Reprint of 1919.B1, B6, B9, B16-17; 1922.B46; 1941.B54; 1942.B77; 1950.B16; 1951.A1, B30; 1953.B12; 1955.B7; 1956.B15; 1957.B14; 1958.B12; 1960.B10; 1962.B36; 1963.B4, B26; 1964.B3; 1966.B20.

4 HOWE, IRVING. Sherwood Anderson. Stanford: Stanford University Press, 271 pp.

Reprint of 1951.A1.

5 LINDROTH, JAMES R. and COLETTE LINDROTH. Anderson's Winesburg, Ohio and Other Works (A Critical Commentary). New York: Monarch Press, 70 pp.

[Brief biography, reading list, study questions; detailed plot summary of Winesburg, Ohio; short summaries of Poor White, Tar, A Story Teller's Story, Dark Laughter, and The Triumph of the Egg; brief summaries of five critics' comments]

6 TRAYNHAM, LINDA CAROL. "'The Chosen of His Race': The Horse as Symbol in Sherwood Anderson's Fiction." Master's thesis, University of South Carolina.

Anderson uses the horse as subject and symbol. As he left race-tracks to find meaning, Anderson later abandoned the industrial world, finding truth in horse versus machine--that is, horses are primitive, natural, and good; machines are modern, artificial, and inhuman.

7 WHITE, RAY LEWIS, ed. The Achievement of Sherwood Anderson: Essays in Criticism. Chapel Hill: University of North Carolina Press, 270 pp.

Reprint of 1916.B9; 1917.B12; 1919.B1; 1925.B43; 1941.B54; 1950.B16; 1951.A1, A2, B30; 1953.B12; 1954.B6; 1955.B30; 1957.B14; 1959.B29; 1960.B6, B10; 1962.B2, B17; 1964.A1.

1966

1966 B SHORTER WRITINGS

1 ANGOFF, CHARLES. The Tone of the Twenties and Other Essays. Foreword by Thomas Yoseloff. New York: A. S. Barnes, pp. 11, 18-19, 21, 29, 37-38, 52, 199.
A vital part of the 1920's, Anderson was "one of the supreme literary artists of the English language in the past one hundred years" and equal to Hardy, Chekhov, and de Maupassant. No critic has yet understood Anderson as well as Mencken did.

2 ANON. "Anderson, Sherwood." Brockhaus Enzyklopädie, 1. Wiesbaden: F. A. Brockhaus, 501.
Winesburg, Ohio influenced modern short story techniques; in all of his work Anderson exposed the materialism and sterility of modern life.

3 ANON. "In Brief." New York Times Book Review (25 December), p. 20.
Publication of recent evaluations in The Achievement of Sherwood Anderson will show earlier, totally negative criticism as irrelevant.

4 BRIDGMAN, RICHARD. The Colloquial Style in America. New York: Oxford University Press, pp. 10, 146, 151, 152-64, 195, 196, 197, 198, 199, 201, 202, 212, 218, 222, 239, 240.
Anderson used vernacular style through self-justification of "environment, language, and self" and became "the first writer since Mark Twain to take the vernacular as a serious way of presenting reality." As Anderson experimented with becoming omniscient instead of "limited" narrator, his style became confused and worthless.

5 BROWN, JOHN et al. Hemingway. Paris: Librairie Hachette, pp. 17, 18, 22, 83-84, 87, 88, 91-92, 156-57, 226-27.
Although Hemingway loved Anderson and Winesburg, Ohio, he published The Torrents of Spring after discussing Dark Laughter with Dos Passos.

6 BRYER, JACKSON R. "F. Scott Fitzgerald as Book Reviewer." Papers of the Bibliographical Society of America, 60 (Third quarter), 369-70.
Fitzgerald's review of Many Marriages shows the young author's concern with the craft and theory of literature.

7 BUCCO, MARTIN. "A Reading of Sherwood Anderson's 'Hands.'" Colorado State Review, 1 (Spring), 5-8.
In Anderson's poetic story "Hands," he uses a circular structure to emphasize the boy's bewilderment, curiosity, and respect.

8 BUDDINGH, C. "Anderson, Sherwood." Grote Winkler Prins, 2. Amsterdam: Elsevier, 74.

His reputation begun with Winesburg, Ohio--a success he never managed to repeat--Anderson influenced Hemingway, Wolfe, Fitzgerald, and Steinbeck. Although he later became interested in industrialism, Anderson wrote best of common people in simple, naturalistic style.

9 CABAU, JAQUES. La Prairie Perdue: Histoire du Roman Américain. Paris: Éditions du Seuil, pp. 33, 142, 223, 264.

In Anderson, God and Nature are more important to the Midwest than Washington, D. C.; Harvard intellectuals; or the Broadway theater. To Twain Anderson owes the impulse to create native literature.

10 CHAPMAN, ARNOLD. The Spanish American Reception of United States Fiction, 1920-1940. Berkeley: University of California Press, pp. 5, 6, 74-97, 175-80, 188-90, 209-11.

Anderson was known in Spanish America through French translations in the 1920's. In 1928 his first translated work appeared in Spanish; in 1929 all of Poor White appeared. After 1942 his voice in South America became diffused.

11 COWLEY, MALCOLM. The Faulkner-Cowley File: Letters and Memories, 1944-1962. New York: Viking Press, pp. 3, 109, 153.

Anderson had discovered Faulkner's talent long before Cowley did, drank with and taught Faulkner, helped publish his first novel; Phil Stone very early in young Faulkner's life gave him Anderson books to read.

12 CRANE, HART. The Complete Poems and Selected Letters and Prose of Hart Crane. Edited by Brom Weber. New York: Liveright Publishing Corporation, pp. 205-206, 208-13.

Reprint: 1919.B11; 1921.B20.

13 DOS PASSOS, JOHN. The Best Times: An Informal Memoir. New York: New American Library, pp. 128-29, 157-58.

Dos Passos met Anderson at Fitzgerald's apartment and complimented Anderson's writing. Later Fitzgerald talked to Dos Passos of Anderson's work, "admiringly but critically." Dos Passos did not like Hemingway's printing the amusing parody The Torrents of Spring; Hemingway said he did not want to hurt Anderson.

1966

14 GOR.[LIER], C.[LAUDIO]. "Anderson, Sherwood." Grande Dizionario Enciclopedico Utet, 1. Turin: Union Tipografico-Editrice Torinese, 683-84.

Many of Anderson's works are not first-rate, and his best writing concerns dull small-town life. Influenced by Freud and Jung, Anderson created characters at once realistic and archetypal. Influenced stylistically by Stein, Anderson in turn taught use of the colloquial style to Hemingway.

15 GRIFFITH, MALCOLM ANSTETT. "The Grotesque in American Fiction." Dissertation, Ohio State University, 222 pp.

The only common trait of the characters in Winesburg, Ohio is "psychological quirks," but Anderson is sure that their condition is not normal.

16 HAGA, KAORU. "'Contrast' and 'Unity' in Sherwood Anderson's Winesburg, Ohio." Bulletin of Aomori Junior College, 4 (June), 29-38.

Anderson is emotional and not fitted for the novel form, as he is also intentionally against the traditional novel structure. Anderson first writes fragmentary sketches and then tries to unify them--hence, his struggle with traditional narrative method. Winesburg, Ohio is the intellectually unified accumulation of the literary craft. [Takashi Kodaira]

17 HICKS, GRANVILLE. "A New Look at Three Lives." Saturday Review, 49 (15 October), 27-28.

The denial of significance to Sherwood Anderson in American literature will become less tenable with publication of The Achievement of Sherwood Anderson.

18 HIPKISS, ROBERT ARTHUR. "The Values of Expatriation for the Major American Novelists, 1914-1941." Dissertation, University of California, Los Angeles, 218 pp.

Visiting Europe had little effect on Anderson's technique, for he was already an established author. He appreciated Europe for art, for freedom, and for tradition; but he was in Europe for only a few months in the 1920's. Only in new friendships such as with Stein did Anderson change his career after visiting Europe.

19 JACKSON, PAUL R. Review of The Achievement of Sherwood Anderson. Chicago Tribune Books Today (2 October), p. 8.

The Achievement of Sherwood Anderson "supports the judgment that Anderson's canon consists of a collection of admirable short stories and a cluster of inferior writing."

20 JOSELYN, SISTER M. "Sherwood Anderson and the Lyric Story." The Twenties: Prose and Poetry. Edited by Richard E. Langford and William E. Taylor. DeLand, Fl.: Edward Everett Press, pp. 70-73.

Winesburg, Ohio is "an uneven collection," "a special kind of amalgam of naturalism and lyricism," for Anderson's best stories involve epiphany, ritual-dialogue, symbols, and suggestiveness. Reprinted: 1966.A3.

21 KODAIRA, TAKASHI. "The Grotesque in Society, II: On Poor White." Studies and Essays by the Faculty of Law and Literature, Literature, Kanazawa University, 13 (January), 46-62.

Poor White is a kind of sequel to Winesburg, Ohio, for Anderson writes of the qualities of the city in the industrialization of a town. The hero of Poor White is a grotesque obsessed with poor-white consciousness, on the road to the kind of impotence Anderson would use in Perhaps Women. The husband-wife relationship in Poor White becomes one of child-mother. [Takashi Kodaira]

22 KRAMER, DALE. Chicago Renaissance: The Literary Life in the Midwest, 1900-1930. New York: Appleton-Century, pp. 37-51, 167-73, 232-43, 249, 259, 288-308, 313, 323-29, 333-42, 346, 349-50, 354.

Anderson built his legends on invented parents (flamboyant yet pathetic father, martyr mother) and fictionalized escape from business. As part of Chicago's literati after 1913, Anderson quickly learned to dramatize and promote himself. As Chicago faded from Renaissance days, Anderson moved to New York and New Orleans.

23 LASS, ABRAHAM H. "Winesburg, Ohio." A Student's Guide to 50 American Novels. New York: Washington Square Press, pp. 115-22.

Only the main character in Winesburg, Ohio may achieve maturity and communication. [Plot summary, character descriptions, brief biography]

24 LAWRY, JON S. "The Artist in America: The Case of Sherwood Anderson." Ball State University Forum, 7 (Spring), 15-26.

Instead of denigrating America in Winesburg, Ohio, Anderson shows the individual seeking fulfillment--a "democratic aesthetic" that would bind into brotherhood book, reader, and author.

25 LOOS, ANITA. A Girl Like I. New York: Viking Press, pp. 219-20, 228, 256.

(LOOS, ANITA)

John Emerson recounted Anderson's desertion of his washing-machine factory and his early reading of Dostoevski. While an itinerant laborer, Anderson wrote Winesburg, Ohio; reviews of this book put Anderson back in touch with his abandoned family. Invited to write publicity for the Emersons, Anderson's publicity may not have been written. Unfortunately, Anderson preferred psychotic to normal characters.

26 MARESCA, CAROL J. "Gestures as Meaning in Sherwood Anderson's Winesburg, Ohio." College Language Association Journal, 9 (March), 279-83.

Because there is little dialogue in Winesburg, Ohio, gestures become especially important as characters attempt to end their emotional isolation.

27 MAYFIELD, SARA. "Another F.[itzgerald] Myth Exploded by Mencken." Fitzgerald Newsletter, No. 32 (Winter), p. 1.

Mencken has annotated his copy of Sherwood Anderson's Memoirs to disagree with Anderson's story of the mistreatment of Fitzgerald at Dreiser's party.

28 MILLGATE, MICHAEL. The Achievement of William Faulkner. New York: Random House, pp. 9, 13-20, 30, 68, 72-73, 75, 87-88, 122, 290, 291, 299, 305, 313, 330.

Perhaps Anderson and Faulkner met in New Orleans before 1924, but they probably met there early in November, 1924; and they exchanged tall-tale letters that were used in Mosquitoes. The writers had disagreed over some matter before Faulkner parodied Anderson.

29 MIYAKE, TSUNEO. "Sherwood Anderson: Dark Laughter." Kyushu American Literature, 9 (July), 34-41.

Dark Laughter contains Anderson's idyllic and superficial view of the Negroes' life and lacks architectonic quality. [Takashi Kodaira]

30 NOLTE, WILLIAM. H. L. Mencken: Literary Critic. Middletown, CT: Wesleyan University Press, pp. 28, 58, 115, 130, 154, 157, 168, 169, 171-72, 192, 231, 232, 240, 245.

A defender of Anderson for realism if not style, Mencken defended him against charges of immorality by S. P. Sherman--to the point of snubbing Sherman at a New York party for Anderson. Mencken approved of Anderson the storyteller but not of Anderson the social reformer.

31 OKUMURA, HIROSHI. "Three Patterns in Sherwood Anderson's Works and Winesburg, Ohio." Annual Reports of Takamatsu Technical College, 1 (March), 73-79.

Anderson's works may be divided into three patterns: that of pilgrimage, that of adolescence, and that of the grotesque. In Winesburg, Ohio Anderson could get rid of mystical evils and make impressionistic technique compatible with novel structure. [Takashi Kodaira]

32 RAGAN, SAM. "Anderson's Place in Our Literature." Raleigh News and Observer (9 October).

A fascinating book about "one of the most fascinating characters in American literature." The Achievement of Sherwood Anderson "needed to be published."

33 ROHRBERGER, MARY. Hawthorne and the Modern Short Story: A Study in Genre. The Hague: Mouton, pp. 9, 14, 56-57, 58, 91-98.

Reprint of 1962.B37.

34 SCHLAUCH, MARGARET. "Sherwood Anderson and a Case of 'Icelandic Realism.'" Germanica Wratislaviensia, 10 (1966), 207-20.

In A Story Teller's Story Anderson discusses a translation of the Old Icelandic Flateyjarbók.

35 SELIGMANN, HERBERT J. Alfred Stieglitz Talking: Notes on Some of His Conversations, 1925-1931. New Haven: Yale University Press, pp. v, 24, 143-44.

On January 26, 1926, Stieglitz had a Dove painting, "Penetration," finished by the artist at Anderson's request after Anderson had seen an earlier work by Dove. On May 26, 1931, Stieglitz told Anderson of his awe of Frieda Lawrence.

36 SPRATLING, WILLIAM. "Chronicle of a Friendship: William Faulkner in New Orleans." Texas Quarterly, 9 (Spring), 35, 36, 38, 40.

When Anderson tired of living with Faulkner, he encouraged Faulkner to live with Spratling. Anderson and Faulkner together planned a nonsense novel. Anderson did not enjoy Sherwood Anderson & Other Famous Creoles; Anderson's one-day yachting party inspired Mosquitoes.

37 STONE, EDWARD. Voices of Despair: Four Motifs in American Literature. Athens: Ohio University Press, pp. 68, 201, 210, 231.

Anderson had lived through industrialization and found standardization repellent. "Out of Nowhere into Nothing" illustrates Freud's vogue.

1966

38 SUTTON, WILLIAM A. "Sherwood Anderson's Second Wife." Ball State University Forum, 7 (Spring), 39-46.

Tennessee Mitchell Anderson wrote an autobiographical fragment (unpublished) about her youth in Michigan, becoming a piano tuner in Chicago, and men; the marriage to Anderson, from 1916 into 1924, failed because of Anderson's egotism.

39 TAYLOR, W. D. "Outstanding Critique of Sherwood Anderson." Richmond Times-Dispatch (20 November).

The Achievement of Sherwood Anderson contains essays that measure the author's achievement and essays that are historical or analytical.

40 THOMSON, VIRGIL. Virgil Thomson. New York: Alfred A. Knopf, pp. 89, 175, 417.

Thomson was thirty when he met Anderson in Paris and attended a Christmas tea with Anderson and Faÿ. Stein and Anderson remained friends "always, though I do not think she ever took him seriously as a writer."

41 TSUJIMOTO, ICHIRO. "The Revolt from Formalism and Anderson." The American Short Story. Tokyo: Azuma Shuppansha, pp. 106-121.

Reprint with revision of 1963.B31.

42 YARBROUGH, TOM. "Reading & Writing." St. Louis Post-Dispatch (2 October).

The Achievement of Sherwood Anderson is "a fine addition to literary criticism, a good starting point for any reader who might want to make his first evaluation of Sherwood Anderson or to revise an earlier judgment."

43 YOUNG, PHILIP. Ernest Hemingway: A Reconsideration. University Park: Pennsylvania State University Press, pp. 80-82, 138, 141, 174, 177, 178, 179, 186, 215.

The Torrents of Spring is funny only after one reads Dark Laughter. Anderson had taught Hemingway to write from pity; he had to learn to write with discipline.

1967 A BOOKS

1 ANDERSON, DAVID D. Barron's Simplified Approach to Winesburg, Ohio. Woodbury, NY: Barron's Educational Series, 57 pp.

[Chronology; brief biography; selected themes; summary and interpretation of each story; study questions; brief bibliography]

2 _____. Sherwood Anderson: An Introduction and Interpretation. New York: Holt, Rinehart and Winston, 182 pp.

Anderson's whole attempt in writing was to expose the undercurrent of reality beneath life's surface. In his earliest books he compares the American dream to American reality; in Winesburg, Ohio he more closely examines individual lives hurt by American myths and finds his own place forever in small-town America instead of in industrial cities. Anderson's philosophy became understanding that walls of isolation must be destroyed to allow communication and empathy. Not perfection but acceptance of life "was the only meaning man could know, but it was far from a petty or ignoble meaning."

3 SUTTON, WILLIAM A. Exit to Elsinore. Muncie: Ball State University, 45 pp.

After Anderson left his office in November, 1912, to wander around the countryside of Ohio suffering amnesia, he kept a diary of thoughts that might elucidate his state of mind while lost. Reprinted: 1972.A2.

1967 B SHORTER WRITINGS

1 ANON. "Hemingway's Papa." Edinburgh Scotsman (10 June).

The Achievement of Sherwood Anderson renews interest in Anderson--so often a failure but valuable for "meticulous tenderness" and ability to see life freshly and with wonder.

2 ANON. "In Brief." New York Times Book Review (22 October), p. 44.

The pieces of country journalism in Return to Winesburg are simple but habit-forming.

3 BIRCHFIELD, JAMES. "Weekly Editors Should Read New Anderson Book." Publishers' Auxiliary (21 October), p. 4.

Sherwood Anderson's son Robert Lane Anderson had his own personality and literary style, contrary to editorial statements in Return to Winesburg.

4 BORGES, JORGE LUIS. Introducción a la Literatura Norteamericana. Buenos Aires: Editorial Columba, pp. 34-35.

Anderson wrote Windy McPherson's Son under Sandburg's influence. The related stories in Winesburg, Ohio are Anderson's chief work. Later in life Anderson edited newspapers in Marion, Virginia.

1967

5 BROOKS, GLADYS. If Strangers Meet: A Memory. New York: Harcourt, Brace and World, p. 38.
After Van Wyck Brooks edited a manuscript novel by Karl Anderson, he found that the prose resembled Sherwood Anderson's.

6 CARNEVALI, EMANUEL. The Autobiography of Emanuel Carnevali. Edited by Kay Boyle. New York: Horizon Press, pp. 14, 168-70, 177, 183, 185, 251.
Perhaps Carnevali liked Anderson so much because the younger writer was foreign. When ill in Chicago, Carnevali received grapefruit and sympathy from Anderson, who later denied shelter but gave an overcoat to the "insane" poet.

7 CHRISTIAN, HENRY A. "Ten Letters to Louis Adamic." Princeton University Library Chronicle, 28 (Winter), 90-91.
On November 9, 1939, Anderson wrote Adamic his appreciation for the latter's My America.

8 COAN, OTIS W. and RICHARD G. LILLARD. American Fiction: An Annotated List of Novels That Interpret Aspects of Life in the United States, Canada, and Mexico. Fifth edition. Palo Alto: Pacific Books, pp. 37, 80, 89, 162.
Winesburg, Ohio--"Sentimental and bitter"--fights "the hypocrisies and the pharisaic code of villagers." The stories in The Triumph of the Egg imitate the form of Spoon River Anthology; Poor White and Windy McPherson's Son deal with the effects of industrialization.

9 COWLEY, MALCOLM. Think Back on Us . . . A Contemporary Chronicle of the 1930's. Edited by Henry Dan Piper. Carbondale: Southern Illinois University Press, pp. 88, 248, 272.
Anderson left the revolutionary political movement as suddenly as he had joined it. He had contributed to the legendary journal The Smart Set; never honored by a Pulitzer Prize, Anderson--along with Dreiser, Dos Passos, Lewis, and Hemingway--"contributed most to the development of American fiction."

10 CROMIE, ROBERT. "Cromie Looks at Authors and Books." Chicago Tribune (9 October).
Return to Winesburg is valuable for preserving "literary ephemera."

11 DAHLBERG, EDWARD. Epitaphs of Our Times: The Letters of Edward Dahlberg. New York: George Braziller, pp. 27, 103, 124-25, 155, 196, 222, 235, 265, 267, 268-69, 270.

Dahlberg owes political awareness to having read Sherwood Anderson's Notebook; he agreed with Anderson's distrust of industry and his theory of American loneliness. At one time Dahlberg alone defended Anderson's books; in 1939 Anderson often felt obscure as a literary name.

12 DANIELSEN, ERIC. "Sherwood Anderson." Fremmede Digtere i det 20. Arhundrede. Edited by Sven M. Kristensen. Copenhagen: G. E. C. Gad, pp. 451-62

Anderson kept alive and returned fictionally to his escape from business. This myth demonstrates Anderson's preference for fancy over fact. Influences on Winesburg, Ohio were Turgenev, Twain, and Stein, as well as Masters; and the book became the universal symbol of an imaginary town. Anderson remains the acclaimed literary artist of psychoanalysis.

13 DERLETH, AUGUST. "Books of the Times." Madison Capital Times (28 September).

Return to Winesburg reflects Anderson's country journalism and his views on small-town life.

14 FORGUE, GUY JEAN. H. L. Mencken: L'Homme, l'Oeuvre, l'Influence. Paris: Mirard Lettres Modernes, pp. 14, 228, 253, 280, 286, 289, 311, 316, 318, 328, 335-38, 341, 350, 351, 352, 402.

In 1922 Mencken praised Anderson as a leading American novelist whose style was surpassed by Cather and whose work became flawed with sex and confusion. Anderson disagreed with Mencken's bitterness to provincials; but Anderson was a dreamer, and Mencken was a satirist.

15 GÁLLEGO, CÁNDIDO PEREZ. "Los Alrededores de Winesburg, Ohio." El Heroe Solitario en la Novela Norteamericana. Madrid: Editorial Prensa Española, pp. 107-121.

The small-town sketches of Winesburg, Ohio present dark aspects of life, dramatic images of reality. The young hero forms community among grotesques, and Anderson captures moments of rebellion against conventions and situations. With "Sophistication" the key story in the work, Winesburg, Ohio presents a society of anomie, the town becoming as it was, once the hero departs.

16 HAHN, EMILY. Romantic Rebels: An Informal History of Bohemianism in America. Boston: Houghton Mifflin Co., pp. 165, 180-81, 225, 228-29, 280.

Anderson disliked Dell's imitation of his attire after the latter moved to New York. Friend of Stein and the

(HAHN, EMILY)
Double Dealer group, Anderson had driven Carnevali from his house to save Anderson's own sanity.

17 HICKS, GRANVILLE. "Small Towns as Points of Departure." Saturday Review, 50 (9 December), 23.
Return to Winesburg provides a selection of Anderson's country journalism--an adventure that "did not revive his literary powers, as Kit Brandon (1936) proves, but it gave him some solid satisfactions."

18 HURD, THADDEUS B. "Sherwood Anderson, American Author." Sandusky County Historical Society History Leaflet No. 3 (April).
Anderson used Clyde, Ohio, as the setting for Winesburg, Ohio; and "in these sensitive sketches of the lives of small town people, against a background which is unmistakably Clyde, he paints a deep and moving picture of the Ohio small town in the closing years of the nineteenth century." Because he feared ridicule, Anderson seldom came to Clyde after 1919.

19 JOSELYN, SISTER MARY. "Some Artistic Dimensions of Sherwood Anderson's 'Death in the Woods.'" Studies in Short Fiction, 4 (Spring), 252-59.
The narrator of "Death in the Woods" evolves from Ohio child to youth in Illinois to older artist. The woman becomes girl and then statue; the dogs almost become wolves; and all this transformation becomes fiction.

20 JOSEPHSON, MATTHEW. Infidel in the Temple: A Memoir of the Nineteen-Thirties. New York: Alfred A. Knopf, pp. 112, 139-40, 151, 281.
Anderson objected publicly to charges of criminal syndicalism against writers who aided striking miners in Harlem, Kentucky. Anderson offered Hamilton Basso the chance to become a country journalist.

21 KATO, AKIHIKO. "A Study of Sherwood Anderson." Studies [Anjo Gakuen], 1 (March), 61-72.
Understanding of Anderson's environment and biography is essential to understanding of the personal statements in Winesburg, Ohio. [Takashi Kodaira]

22 KITAYAMA, AKIMASA. "Sherwood Anderson." Study of English (June), pp. 13-14.
Anderson's biography and milieu contribute to understanding his short fiction. [Takashi Kodaira]

23 KOSHIKAWA, SEIZO. "On the Part of 'Godliness' in Winesburg, Ohio." Journal of the Society of English and American Literature, Kwansei Gakuin University (December), pp. 14-24.
A microcosm of Winesburg, Ohio, "Godliness" differs from the other stories by being written from historical rather than geographical perspective. Grotesqueness belongs to time; "Godliness" becomes indispensable to the work, giving it completion in time and space. [Takashi Kodaira]

24 LAUGHLIN, ROSEMARY M. "Godliness and the American Dream in Winesburg, Ohio." Twentieth Century Literature, 13 (July), 97-103.
"Godliness" fits into Winesburg, Ohio through symbolism, theme, setting, and history; the story is almost an allegory of Protestant American pioneers or settlers. Reprinted: 1971.A2.

25 MARUSSIG, ANTÔNIO. "Winesburg, Ohio, A New Way of Writing Short Stories." ITA Humanidades, 3 (1967), 83-85.
In writing Winesburg, Ohio, Anderson "broke the pattern of writing folk tales, that is to say, those stories in which events are more important than emotions."

26 MURAMATSU, NOBUO. "On Winesburg, Ohio by Sherwood Anderson." Bulletin of the Faculty of Humanities [Wako University], 2 (March), 163-72.
As America became industrialized after the Civil War, terms changed from space to time in social orientation; the grotesques in Winesburg, Ohio in relating to the young hero demonstrate national anguish and loneliness. Unable to serve as a priest of life, as does Huckleberry Finn, this Anderson hero is victim of his nation's transition period. [Takashi Kodaira]

27 MURPHY, GEORGE D. "The Theme of Sublimation in Anderson's Winesburg, Ohio." Modern Fiction Studies, 13 (Summer), 237-46.
Instead of being sexually explicit or advanced, Winesburg, Ohio is instead full of "an extremely hesitant, almost puritanical attitude toward physical sexuality," the characters responding to sex with repulsion, complacency, blocked idealism, and quasi-Platonic transcendance.

28 NABUCO, CAROLINA. Retrato dos Estados Unidos a Luz da Sua Literatura. Rio de Janeiro: Livraria José Olympio Editora, pp. 78, 105-109, 113, 114, 115, 166.
Anderson presented melancholy characters, filled with introspection and frustrations. He concentrated on Midwestern scenes, describing post-pioneer industrialization

1967

(NABUCO, CAROLINA)
and urbanization; a small town is actually the cast of characters in Winesburg, Ohio.

29 OHARA, HIROTADA. "Remaining Vestiges of an Eggshell: Sherwood Anderson and the Problem of Adolescence." Amerika Bungaku [Amerika Bungakukai], 1 (January), 87-103.
Anderson's characters are extremely sensitive and naive, like chickens with fragments of eggshell on their backs. They plunge from the world of fact into the world of fancy, the author's ideal world being the world of the egocentric child, covered with a beautiful shell. [Takashi Kodaira]

30 ORSZAGH, LASZLO. Az Amerikai Irodalom Törtenete. Budapest: Gondolat Kiadó, pp. 281-82, 296, 297, 302-305, 306, 334, 344, 398, 411, 412, 414.
Reared in a small town, Anderson became a writer in the tradition of revolt against the village. His novels deal with social conventions that oppress common people. His heroes are lonely, grotesque failures, warped by traumas and behavioral expectations. Greed and mechanization prevent community. Apostle of primitivism, Anderson questioned capitalism; but pessimism prevented his advocacy of revolution.

31 PANDEYA, S. M. "Hemingway's The Torrents of Spring: Significance of a Parody." Indian Responses to American Literature. Edited by C. D. Narasimhaiah. New Delhi: United States Educational Foundation in India, pp. 149-69.
Hemingway wrote The Torrents of Spring to hold up literary standards, and this act proves the author's devotion to craft. In parodying Anderson, Hemingway attacks primitivism, free association, internal monologues, stream-of-consciousness, echolalia, and "poster art."

32 PICHT, DOUGLAS R. "Anderson's Use of Tactile Imagery in Winesburg, Ohio." Research Studies, 35 (June), 176-78.
In Winesburg, Ohio touch becomes a way for isolated individuals to establish momentary community. Reprinted: 1971.A2.

33 POLI, BERNARD J. Ford Madox Ford and the Transatlantic Review. Syracuse: Syracuse University Press, pp. 90, 91, 160, 168.
In using the story-cycle form in Winesburg, Ohio, Anderson was trying to present an entire milieu and way of life.

34 REID, RANDALL. The Fiction of Nathanael West: No Redeemer, No Promised Land. Chicago: University of Chicago Press, pp. 139-49, 161.
West's use of Anderson in structure, theme, and even grotesque characters is so obvious and frequent that he may intend variation upon or sequel to Winesburg, Ohio.

35 SCHÖNE, ANNEMARIE. Abriss der Amerikanischen Literaturgeschichte in Tabellen. Franfurt am/M: Athenäum Verlag, pp. 104, 151-52, 172, 175, 176, 214.
Part of the rebellious group of writers who opposed Puritanism, Anderson learned his impressionistic technique from Stein and preached his theme of liberation from conventions as well as from industrialism; but Anderson was essentially pessimistic.

36 SPRATLING, WILLIAM. File on Spratling: An Autobiography. Introduction by Budd Schulberg. Boston: Little, Brown and Co., pp. 17-18, 21-30, 120-23.
Of the New Orleans writers of the early 1920's, Anderson "was our star performer, a sort of magnet who attracted luminaries from afar. He was the story-teller oracle and his wonderful wife Elizabeth was the priestess of the temple." Anderson and Faulkner told tall tales at parties, but Anderson did not like Faulkner's parody. Later, in Mexico, Anderson did not want to see his ex-wife Elizabeth.

37 STEM, THAD. "Pieces From Papers in Virginia Town." Raleigh News and Observer (24 September).
Return to Winesburg proves that even as country journalist Anderson "is much too valuable to be lost in the modern, frenetic literary shuffle."

38 TAKIGAWA, MOTOO. "Sherwood Anderson." American Literature and Sex. Tokyo: Azuma Shuppansha, pp. 41-57.
Anderson's writing is based on his keen sensuousness rather than on his intellect. Because he realizes that nature does not exist in a machine civilization, he advocates sexual liberation and natural living. Because Anderson is sentimentally lyrical, his work is not so rich in intellect as is Lawrence's. [Takashi Kodaira]

39 TAYLOR, WELFORD D. "Anderson Collection Fails in Its Purpose." Richmond Times-Dispatch (1 October).
Return to Winesburg provides a less fair picture of Anderson's small-town newspapers than does Hello Towns!

1967

40 TURNBULL, ANDREW. Thomas Wolfe. New York: Charles Scribner's Sons, pp. 126, 173, 208, 223, 273-74, 282-83, 312.
After reading Of Time and the River, Anderson wrote Wolfe that he "knew why he could never write a novel" himself. Wolfe disagreed when Anderson confessed to feeling not himself with women. When Wolfe visited Anderson in Virginia he still admired Anderson's early stories; later in New York Wolfe broke with Anderson over a Semitism quarrel.

41 WALKER, WARREN S., ed. "Sherwood Anderson." Twentieth-Century Short Story Explication: Interpretations of Short Fiction Since 1800, 1900-1966. Hamden, CT: Shoestring Press, pp. 5-14.
[Criticism of 31 stories by Anderson]

42 WELLS, ROBERT W. "Sherwood Anderson, the Publisher, Also Followed a Different Drummer." National Observer (16 October).
Return to Winesburg contains journalism by Sherwood Anderson--"this reluctant refugee from Winesburg, speaking across the years."

43 WEST, THOMAS REED. Flesh of Steel: Literature and the Machine in American Culture. Nashville: Vanderbilt University Press, pp. xi, 3-4, 12, 15, 21-34, 35, 51-52, 71, 75, 91, 108, 111, 122-23, 131, 135.
With his interest in the poetic qualities in technology, Anderson could fear the standardization of machinery and admire the "delicacy and ordered grace," eventually observing land-and-machine as harmony.

44 WHITE, RAY LEWIS. "Hemingway's Private Explanation of The Torrents of Spring." Modern Fiction Studies, 13 (Summer), 261-63.
Five unpublishable letters from Hemingway to Anderson (or about Anderson) contain Hemingway's advance apology and simultaneous defense of The Torrents of Spring.

1968 A BOOKS

1 MENKIN, GABRIEL A. "Structure in Sherwood Anderson's Fiction." Dissertation, University of Pittsburgh, 267 pp.
The structure of Anderson's best published stories centers on the device of developing "episodes which are expressed with dramatic and visual power." Often details

in succession build to crucial scenes; and often life-summaries fuse with final situations. Some structures come from first-person point of view, although Anderson could well use the ominiscient-narrator voice. Anderson's novels suffer from attempting epic sweep and summary narration.

2 OHASHI, KICHINOSUKE, ed. Sherwood Anderson. Tokyo: Kenkyusha, 244 pp.

[The first Japanese book completely about Sherwood Anderson is divided into three sections: "A Critical Biography," "Works," and "Appraisal." Each work is compactly summarized and then commented on by an expert on Anderson.]

OHASHI, KICHINOSUKE. "A Critical Biography," pp. 1-27. [Six parts of the critical biography are entitled "Foreword," "The Early Years," "The Success Dream, An Escape," "The Birth of a Story Teller," "A Success as a Story Teller," and "The Later Years." Reprinted in part in revised form of 1968.B29.

HASHIGUCHI, YASUO. "Windy McPherson's Son," pp. 30-37. The hero of Anderson's first novel seeks something outside himself for happiness; then he learns that happiness must come from within himself. Perhaps this change reflects Anderson's growth from objective realism toward Winesburg, Ohio.

_____. "Marching Men," pp. 37-46. People who have experienced the shock of recognition are united, no longer individuals. The heroine is typical of women in all of Anderson's works.

MIYAMOTO, YOKICHI. "Winesburg, Ohio," pp. 47-65. A Bildungsroman, Winesburg, Ohio is first the story of a small town and then the revelation by pieces of real life. Anderson uses the cycle form to have the best features of stories and novels.

SUYAMA, SHIZUO. "Poor White," pp. 66-83. Anderson's own violent transition period affects this novel, giving the ending much confusion. Whereas Anderson lived through his 1912 crisis, he could not take his characters beyond similar crises.

KATO, HIROKAZU. "Many Marriages," pp. 83-94. This novel fails because the public has never liked it even though Anderson liked it; perhaps the heated atmosphere of the work should be appraised.

TOKUNAGE, SHOZO. "Dark Laughter," pp. 94-107. Influenced by Stein, Joyce, and Lawrence, this novel is a primitive, instinctive, and healthy "dark laugh" at the sophisticated "white smile" of moderns.

(OHASHI, KICHINOSUKE)

SUYAMA, SHIZUO. "Beyond Desire," pp. 107-18. Of unbalanced framework and repetitive style, the novel becomes indefinite--apparently for both characters and author.

YAMAMOTO, AKIRA. "The Triumph of the Egg," pp. 119-132. [Various approaches from American critics are given for "I Want to Know Why," "The Egg," "Unlighted Lamps," "Out of Nowhere into Nothing," and "The New Englander."]

MIZUGUCHI, SHIGEO. "Horses and Men," pp. 132-41. [Approaches by American critics to "I'm a Fool," "The Man Who Became a Woman," "An Ohio Pagan."]

_____. "Death in the Woods and Other Stories," pp. 142-46. [Commentary by American critics and Anderson himself on "Death in the Woods" and "A Meeting South."]

HARAKAWA, KYOICHI. "Three Autobiographical Volumes," pp. 146-51. Anderson's three autobiographies are his best biography; they relate to the autobiographies of Henry Adams and J. S. Mill, and they are filled with poetry and truth.

OYAMADA, YOSHIFUMI. "A Story Teller's Story," pp. 151-64. This autobiography is full of psychological realism, revealing Anderson in the process of creation and with his peculiar vision.

HARAKAWA, KYOICHI. "Tar: A Midwest Childhood," pp. 164-74. Basically autobiographical, Tar yet distorts facts artistically. Unlike A Story Teller's Story, there is in Tar no organic mixture of vision and actuality and hence no literary reality.

_____. "Sherwood Anderson's Memoirs," pp. 175-83. Neither fiction nor autobiography, Anderson's Memoirs is not complete and satisfying, for the imagination is not successful.

MIYAMOTO, YOKICHI. "Appraisal," pp. 185-201. The critical reaction against Anderson in the late 1920's now seems unexpected. It occurred because Anderson had carelessly adopted methods of modernism at a time when social realism was becoming dominant. With the 1940's came criticism of the author's fiction as immature. Making his papers available in 1947 started proper study of Anderson. In the 1950's scholars studied him, and other writers expressed admiration. With his value for all humanity, Anderson now obviously is appealing.

OHASHI, KICHINOSUKE and AKIRA YAMAMOTO. "Chronology and Bibliography," pp. 215-44. [The first comprehensive Japanese bibliography on Anderson, listing 9 books and 93 sections of books, 3 special issues, 68 articles--all in English; and listing 10 sections of Japanese books and 25 Japanese articles]

MIURA, SHUMON. "Anderson and Nobuo Kojima," Supplement, pp. 1-4. Anderson's "The Egg" influenced Shotaro Yasuoka's "Toy Rabbits." As one trait of Japanese writing is the irrational and as the Japanese do not like plot-stories, their tradition in fiction is closer to Anderson than Poe.
IIJIMA, YOSHIHIDE. "Notes on Anderson," Supplement, pp. 4-7. Use of the Mississippi River as symbol and as reality in Dark Laughter differs from Faulkner's use of the River. [Takashi Kodaira]

3 SHEEHY, EUGENE P. and KENNETH A. LOHF. Sherwood Anderson: A Bibliography. New York: Kraus Reprint Corporation, 125 pp. Reprint of 1960.A2.

1968 B SHORTER WRITINGS

1 ABCARIAN, RICHARD. "Innocence and Experience in Winesburg, Ohio." University Review Kansas City, 35 (December), 95-105.

Although the hero is important in Winesburg, Ohio, Anderson's picture of "blighted hope, of frustrated and wasted human worth and, most profound and universal, of lost innocence" unifies the book.

2 ANON. "Back to Ol' Virginny." Journalist (April).

Return to Winesburg contains journalism "of a dated and escapist flavor. But Anderson could put some things splendidly."

3 BEACHCROFT, T. O. The Modest Art: A Survey of the Short Story in English. London: Oxford University Press, pp. 104, 234, 235, 240-41, 246, 252, 260.

Although Maugham disliked Anderson's stories, many people credit Anderson with renovating and being most influential on the American short story. With simple outlook, Anderson "is reminiscent of a primitive painter or a colonial period craftsman."

4 BINNI, FRANCESCO. "Il 'Personaggio' di Sherwood Anderson." Studi Americani, 14 (1968), 265-87.

Anderson's naturalistic art did not fall to pieces in his later years, for he deserves a high position as poetic, subjective naturalist. He becomes involved with his narrators, desiring to render emotional experiences.

5 BOUSQUET, ELIZABETH. "The Twain Tradition: Sherwood Anderson, Ernest Hemingway, Stephen Crane." Master's thesis, University of Montreal, 141 pp.

1968

(BOUSQUET, ELIZABETH)
"Whenever we find in writers such as Stephen Crane, Anderson, and Hemingway himself, a style that flows with the easy grace of colloquial speech and gets its directness and simplicity by leaving out subordinate words and clauses, we will be right in thinking that this is the language of Mark Twain." In line with Twain, Anderson painted decadent characters from the agrarian age; and many of his heroes are in Twain's Adamic tradition.

6 BROWNING, CHRIS. "Kate Swift: Sherwood Anderson's Creative Eros." _Tennessee Studies in Literature_, 13 (1968), 141-48.
The heroine of "The Strength of God" and "The Teacher" is Anderson's ideal woman in terms both human and creative-spiritual. Reprinted: 1971.A2.

7 BUCHLOH, PAUL G. "Sherwood Anderson." _Amerikanische Erzählungen von Hawthorne bis Salinger: Interpretationen_. Edited by Paul G. Buchloh. Neumünster: Karl Wachholz Verlag, pp. 48-51.
Anderson is a transition figure between the generation of American realists including Twain and Howells and that generation including Hemingway and Faulkner. Most known for short stories, Anderson based _Winesburg, Ohio_ on his boyhood life.

8 BURHANS, CLINTON S., JR. "The Complex Unity of _In Our Time_." _Modern Fiction Studies_, 14 (August), 326, 328.
Hemingway's "My Old Man" imitates Anderson's stories of adolescence; all of _In Our Time_, modeled on _Winesburg, Ohio_, uses irony and "contradictory actuality" to reflect of the whole world what Anderson's book had shown of the Midwest.

9 FAULKNER, WILLIAM. _Lion in the Garden: Interviews with William Faulkner, 1926-1962_. Edited by James B. Meriwether and Michael Millgate. New York: Random House, pp. 12, 62, 66, 95, 101, 117-19, 120, 168, 186, 198, 218, 233, 249-50.
In 1931 Faulkner admitted that Anderson did not read _Soldiers' Pay_ before helping to have it published. Anderson's real help was in having proved the validity and viability of non-Seaboard American literature, even though he created one good book, _Winesburg, Ohio_; but Anderson had great dedication to writing.

10 FIEDLER, LESLIE A. _The Return of the Vanishing American_. New York: Stein and Day, pp. 145-46.
Instead of ridiculing only Anderson in _The Torrents of Spring_, Hemingway is parodying also "his own dearest and most absurd affectations," especially when a naked Indian woman cures the hero of European impotence.

11 GILBERT, JAMES BURKHART. Writers and Partisans: A History of Literary Radicalism in America. New York: John Wiley and Sons, pp. 28, 53, 75, 82.

Among the literary radicals publishing in The Masses was Anderson, who later followed the trend to live in Greenwich Village.

12 GILDZEN, ALEX. "Sherwood Anderson, Elyria, and the Escape Hunch." Serif, 5 (March), 3-10.

Anderson became obsessed with "the escape hunch" while learning to write fiction as a businessman in Elyria, Ohio; in his published fiction, escape into creativity becomes the way to overcome living death.

13 GREGORY, HORACE. "On Sherwood Anderson." Talks with Authors. Edited by Charles F. Madden. Carbondale: Southern Illinois University Press, pp. 12-22.

Gregory met Anderson when young in Milwaukee; he repaid Anderson's kindness by editing The Portable Sherwood Anderson in 1947. Of the Chicago Renaissance school, Anderson was the storyteller, for "he had a particular kind of story to tell, poetic in its symbolic reference." Anderson's controlling theme is the emergence and effects of industrialism. Influential upon younger writers, Anderson presented the American adolescent better than anyone before him.

14 GUERIN, WILFRED L. "'Death in the Woods': Sherwood Anderson's 'Cold Pastoral.'" College English Association Critic, 30 (May), 4-5.

"Death in the Woods" is about the creative ability that shapes remembered incident into understood meaning.

15 GURKO, LEO. Ernest Hemingway and the Pursuit of Heroism. New York: Thomas Y. Crowell and Co., pp. 16-18, 21, 26, 29, 30, 137-38, 141, 142, 175.

In Chicago personally and by literary example Anderson taught Hemingway "the direct statement of immediate emotion in sentences that were brief, stripped, and economical"; without knowledge of Dark Laughter or Stein's middle-period prose, the reader would make little sense of The Torrents of Spring.

16 HAYASHI, SHIGEO. "Winesburg, Ohio as the Work Based on the Dreams of the Author." Studies in Foreign Literatures [Research Institute of the Cultural Sciences, Ritsumeikan University], 16 (April), 11-30.

With dream characteristics, Winesburg, Ohio deals with two types of dreams: the young hero is an example of

1968

(HAYASHI, SHIGEO)
autobiographical dream; the grotesques exemplify reverse-wishful dreams. Anderson formed the Winesburg stories of fellow-lodgers in a Chicago rooming house and a dream-self back in Anderson's boyhood town.

17 L., H. J. "Winesburg, Ohio." Lexikon der Weltliteratur, 2. Edited by Gero von Wilpert. Stuttgart: Alfred Kröner Verlag, 1165.
Winesburg, Ohio is unified by the recurring young male character, the idea of the grotesque, and the setting. Not a realistic picture of the American small town, these stories deal with anomie and being unloved.

18 JANSSENS, G. A. M. The American Literary Review: A Critical History. The Hague: Mouton, pp. 34-35, 37, 43, 45-47, 49, 50, 197.
When the editor of The Dial promised Anderson to pay all contributors equally, Pound objected that Anderson and George Moore were less meritorious than himself. Anderson's Dial award received excellent publicity, but critics for that magazine reflected the immediate denigration of Anderson's work.

19 JOOST, NICHOLAS. Ernest Hemingway and the Little Magazines: The Paris Years. Barre, MA: Barre Publishers, pp. 3-5, 6, 15, 18, 21-31, 39, 40, 42-43, 49, 62, 63, 66, 94, 129, 144, 151-54, 160, 166.
Anderson used his own friendship with editors of such magazines as The Dial and The Double Dealer to encourage Hemingway's work, as he shared introductions to his new European friends with the younger man.

20 KATO, AKIHIKO. "A Study of Sherwood Anderson, 2." Studies [Anjo Gakuen College], 2 (March), 41-56.
Among Anderson's literary affiliations were the Chicago Renaissance group of writers, Gertrude Stein, post-impressionist painters, the Bible, and Trigant Burrow; of the Chicago writers, only Anderson remained true to the dream of total liberation. [Takashi Kodaira]

21 LORCH, THOMAS M. "The Choreographic Structure of Winesburg, Ohio." College Language Association Journal, 12 (September), 56-65.
Winesburg, Ohio is unified by "common patterns of characters and action," for in using symbolic technique Anderson depends on "small, relatively static units such as tableaux and descriptive portraits, symbolic gestures, physical settings, and natural backgrounds."

22 LOVE, GLEN A. "Winesburg, Ohio and the Rhetoric of Silence." American Literature, 40 (March), 38-57.
In Winesburg, Ohio Anderson turns from the "shrillness and disorder of industrialism" to the pastoral village of his youth; paradoxically, the artist is forced to use words instead of expressive silence for healing communication.

23 MAYFIELD, SARA. The Constant Circle: H. L. Mencken and His Friends. New York: Delacourt Press, pp. 17, 30, 42-43, 68-69, 84, 185, 286.
In 1918 Mayfield found Sara Haardt enthusiastic over Anderson's Winesburg, Ohio stories in periodical form. Mencken disagreed with Anderson's account of the drunk Fitzgerald at Dreiser's party. Anderson told Mencken and Mayfield of his rejection of business, of his early fiction, and of having met Faulkner.

24 MELLARD, JAMES M. "Narrative Forms in Winesburg, Ohio." Publications of the Modern Language Association of America, 83 (October), 1304-12.
In Winesburg, Ohio Anderson uses four narrative forms--"a form (1) that focuses on a central symbol, (2) that portrays a character type, (3) that delineates a quality, state, or 'truth,' and (4) that depicts a simple plot development."

25 MENCKEN, H. L. H. L. Mencken's Smart Set Criticism. Edited by William Nolte. Ithaca: Cornell University Press, pp. 11, 175, 272-78.
Reprint of 1919.B17; 1920.B13; 1923.B47.

26 MIYAMOTO, YOKICHI. "The Background of Winesburg, Ohio." Journal of the Faculty of Literature [Chuo University], 23 (January), 1-22.
Among influences on Sherwood Anderson were Clyde and Elyria, Ohio; the Chicago Renaissance authors; Freud, Stein, Twain, the Bible; and other reading, all coming together in Winesburg, Ohio.

27 NACHIGAMI, TASUKU. "Sympathy and Antipathy in Winesburg, Ohio: Grotesque and Paradox of Grotesque." Bulletin of the Faculty of Education, Fukyshima University, Liberal Arts, 20 (November), 86-95.
Of three hypotheses on the goal of Winesburg, Ohio, the first is appeal for sympathy and understanding of the grotesques, the second is the necessity for understanding the grotesques, and the third is that those unable to understand the grotesques are themselves grotesque. [Takashi Kodaira]

1968

28 OHARA, HIROTADA. "A Sense Which Repels 'Maturity': A Study of Anderson's Midwestern Trait." American Literature [Tokyo Chapter of the American Literature Society of Japan], 17 (Spring), 15-22.

The point of view in Anderson being the typically Midwestern egocentric, Anderson thus declined after Winesburg, Ohio; he repels maturity and fell behind as the "eternal child." [Takashi Kodaira]

29 OHASHI, KICHINOSUKE. "A Note on Sherwood Anderson." Geibun-Kenkyu, 25 (March), 78-92.

Man of fancy rather than of imagination, Anderson can draw impressive fictional pictures; but he will not be able to connect these pictures into a unified whole without imagination. The value of Winesburg, Ohio lies in the fact that these stories are beautiful pictures framed by the setting. Worth little as a novelist, Anderson has importance as a writer of short stories. [Takashi Kodaira]

30 PRICE, ROBERT. Review of Return to Winesburg. Indiana Magazine of History, 64 (March), 83-84.

In best and worst style, never matching Winesburg, Ohio, Return to Winesburg contains moments of humane reporting.

31 ROBINSON, ELEANOR M. "A Study of 'Death in the Woods.'" College English Association Critic, 30 (January), 6.

"Death in the Woods" reveals Anderson's idea of creation: an event is observed, the mind cannot resolve its meaning, experience is gained, the meaning emerges.

32 SANDBURG, CARL. The Letters of Carl Sandburg. Edited by Herbert Mitgang. New York: Harcourt, Brace and World, pp. 232, 260-62, 331.

Sandburg asked Anderson's advice in 1925 about including some "dirty stuff" in the former's work. In 1928 Sandburg promised to visit Anderson in Virginia and praised Anderson's three story collections and A Story Teller's Story. Shortly, Sandburg subscribed to Anderson's country newspaper and promised to consult Anderson on Virginia matters in Lincoln's day. When Sandburg did visit Anderson in 1934-35, Anderson was cynical about Hecht and Willian Allen White.

33 SAROYAN, WILLIAM. I Used to Believe I Had Forever Now I'm Not So Sure. [n.p.]: Cowles Publishing Corporation, pp. 30-31, 90, 135-36.

Saroyan told his brother Henry that he courted a woman while pretending to be Anderson, whom Saroyan once saw lecturing but never met. Anderson--like all great writers--was a "loner."

34 SCHORER, MARK. The World We Imagine: Selected Essays. New York: Farrar, Straus and Giroux, pp. 299-382.

Stein abandoned medicine for art and writing; after giving up commerce for writing, Anderson learned technique from Stein. Both taught Hemingway, who admired Stein and Anderson but parodied them. Fitzgerald would sell out for society and money, unlike the other three writers.

35 SCHULZE, MARTIN. Wege der Amerikanischen Literatur: Eine Geschichtliche Darstellung. Frankfurt am/M: Verlag Ullstein, pp. 343, 344-46, 353, 354, 360, 375, 377, 386, 393.

Following Anderson's interest in primitivism, Steinbeck imitated Anderson's story-cycle form in Tortilla Flat. Welty uses the same Anderson form in The Golden Apples.

36 STEPHENS, ROBERT O. Hemingway's Nonfiction: The Public Voice. Chapel Hill: University of North Carolina Press, pp. 6, 16-17, 120, 125, 222, 232, 239.

In 1922 Hemingway complained to Anderson that journalism was tiresome; Anderson parodied, Hemingway turned his parodic talent on Bromfield. He thought that Anderson and Fitzgerald had suffered from believing what their critics wrote.

37 STEWART, RANDALL. Regionalism and Beyond: Essays of Randall Stewart. Edited by George Core. Nashville: Vanderbilt University Press, pp. 191, 257-58.

Anderson gave the first acceptability of unfinished endings to American literature. When Anderson revered New York literati above Midwestern writers, the "spectacle of the Middle Western genius bowing down before the demi-gods of New York" is pathetic.

38 SULLIVAN, BARBARA W. "A Gallery of Grotesques: The Alienation Theme in the Works of Hawthorne, Twain, Anderson, Faulkner, and Wolfe." Dissertation, University of Georgia, 218 pp.

"Hawthorne presented the Romantic alien; Mark Twain portrayed the Realistic alien," and "It remained for Sherwood Anderson to merge the two traditions." Anderson's grotesques are often psychologically "bizarre and eccentric," but they are presented realistically. His grotesques are non-heroic sufferers from community pressures.

39 TANSELLE, G. THOMAS. "Anderson Annotated by Brooks." Notes & Queries, 15 (February), 60-61.

(TANSELLE, G. THOMAS)
In Van Wyck Brooks' copies of Perhaps Women and A Story Teller's Story are brief responses--here described bibliographically--from Brooks' readings of the books.

40 TAYLOR, WELFORD DUNAWAY. Review of Return to Winesburg. American Literature, 40 (March), 99-100.
Return to Winesburg is less impressive than Hello Towns!, being inadequately documented and organized chronologically instead of artistically.

41 WAGER, WILLIS. American Literature: A World View. New York: New York University Press, pp. 198, 228-29, 238.
Influenced in Winesburg, Ohio by Stein's Three Lives and in Poor White by Twain's Adventures of Huckleberry Finn, Anderson gives sharp delineation to the transition of America from agrarian to urban society.

42 WEST, MICHAEL D. "Sherwood Anderson's Triumph: 'The Egg.'" American Quarterly, 20 (Winter), 675-93.
Perhaps "The Egg" is influenced by Dubliners; and this story, composed in 1918 and influenced in style by Anderson's advertising writing, the Bible, Freud, and autobiography, through the narrator reflects on the father's failed masculinity and his own childish wish to substitute with the mother.

43 WYLDER, DELBERT E. "The Torrents of Spring." South Dakota Review, 5 (Winter 1967-68), 23-35.
The Torrents of Spring parodies Dark Laughter and Many Marriages, especially Anderson's narrative perspective and primitivism.

44 YASUKOCHI, HIDEMITSU. "Sherwood Anderson's 'Death in the Woods': On the Solidarity of Life." Cairn, 11 (June), 53-72.
In "Death in the Woods" Anderson creates a world of the old dead woman and the narrator. Emphasis on death gives only the theme of the story; stress on the narrator as a boy would ignore the theme. Combining both emphases organically gives better understanding of Anderson's real meaning--rediscovery of the natural and of the past. [Takashi Kodaira]

45 YOUNG, PHILIP. "Scott Fitzgerald on His Thirtieth Birthday Sends a Small Gift to Ernest Hemingway." Modern Fiction Studies, 14 (Summer), 229-30.
In a letter to Hemingway, Fitzgerald may parody the interchapters of In Our Time as Hemingway had parodied Anderson in The Torrents of Spring.

1969 A BOOKS

1 HUMPHRIES, DAVID MARSHALL. "Winesburg, Ohio: The Struggle for Dignity." Master's thesis, Bucknell University, 80 pp.

A sense of dignity had been established on "realistic" criteria of "wealth, position, and education"; in Winesburg, Ohio Anderson wrote from respect for buried, psychological, integrated dignity--needed by his characters.

2 KRAFT, ROBERT GEORGE. "Sherwood Anderson, Bisexual Bard: Some Chapters in a Literary Biography." Dissertation, University of Washington, 200 pp.

Anderson's idea of the creative artist as "bard"--singer of primitive, transcendent elements of people's common life--shaped his work into the 1920's. Diffuse sexuality allowed Anderson to share ideally all life and "sing" that life poetically. Other writers and Anderson's second wife contributed to the growing conception of bard; when Anderson abandoned the bardic role and Tennessee Mitchell, his work declined.

3 MILLER, WILLIAM VAUGHN. "The Technique of Sherwood Anderson's Short Stories." Dissertation, University of Illinois, 277 pp.

Using ninety-six published stories, with minor attention to Winesburg, Ohio, it is possible to study each story in regard to Anderson's theory of art as crafted writing and expression of imaginative truth; scene as "time, objective location, and psychological 'place'"; character as predominant concern of fiction; theme as barriers to communication and community; style as lyricism; and oral narration and the colloquial style as organic form.

4 WHITE, RAY LEWIS, comp. The Merrill Checklist of Sherwood Anderson. Columbus: Charles E. Merrill Co., 36 pp.

[Unannotated, selected checklist of 172 primary and 409 secondary books, chapters, articles, and reviews]

1969 B SHORTER WRITINGS

1 ALLEN, WALTER. The Urgent West: The American Dream and Modern Man. New York: E. P. Dutton and Co., pp. 195-97, 200.

Anderson is "the founding father of the modern short story in America." In Winesburg, Ohio the characters suffer loneliness, defeat, distortion, and self-consciousness.

1969

2 ANDERSON, ELIZABETH and GERALD R. KELLY. Miss Elizabeth: A Memoir. Boston: Little, Brown and Co., pp. 34-35, 41, 47-195, 205, 206, 245, 290, 304, 314-15.

Elizabeth Prall was the third Mrs. Sherwood Anderson--from 1924 to 1933. Together the Andersons lived in New Orleans and Virginia, knowing Stein, Hemingway, Faulkner, and other famous authors, until in 1929 Sherwood advised Elizabeth never to return to him. The divorce became final in 1933, and Elizabeth eventually settled near William Spratling in Mexico.

3 ANON. "Anderson, Sherwood." Repertorio Bibliografico della Letteratura Americana in Italia. Rome: Edizioni di Storia e Letteratura, volumes 1-2 [1966], 39-40; volume 3 (1969), 68-69.

[Checklist of 7 articles, 20 reviews, and 7 translations; additional references to Anderson discussed with other subjects]

4 ANON. "Anderson's 'Tar.'" Madison Capital Times (5 June).

Tar: A Midwest Childhood, A Critical Text makes the work available for the first time in forty years and provides scholarly apparatus to make the work comprehensive.

5 ANON. "1969: Twelve Books of Uncommon Excellence." New York Times Book Review (7 December), p. 1.

Sherwood Anderson's Memoirs: A Critical Edition is one of a dozen books published in 1969 and previously reviewed in The New York Times Book Review that is now judged "especially outstanding."

6 BAKER, CARLOS. Ernest Hemingway: A Life Story. New York: Charles Scribner's Sons, pp. 78, 82-84, 86-87, 100, 118-19, 134, 147, 158-60, 163, 165, 170-71, 181, 239, 364, 585, 588.

After returning from Paris, Anderson encouraged Hemingway to return there and meet Anderson's new literary friends; later Hemingway weaned himself by publishing The Torrents of Spring and still pretended to be Anderson's friend, even to regretting Anderson's death in 1941.

7 BALDESHWILER, EILEEN. "The Lyric Short Story: The Sketch of a History." Studies in Short Fiction, 6 (Summer), 451, 453.

At his best in certain Winesburg, Ohio tales, Anderson freed the short story in America from "the tale, the moral fable, the romantic reverie, the journalistic jeu" and fused naturalism with lyricism.

8 BENSON, JACKSON S. Hemingway: The Writer's Art of Self-Defense. Minneapolis: University of Minnesota Press, pp. 32-33, 62.

As almost all of Hemingway's prose up to The Sun Also Rises is satire, The Torrents of Spring reflects Hemingway's unfortunate "moral energy" and sense of duty in satirizing Anderson's sentimentality. Even Hemingway was not a totally dispassionate writer.

9 BRADLEY, VAN ALLEN. "Gold in Your Attic." Nashville Banner (29 August).

Tar: A Midwest Childhood, A Critical Text will become not only a resource for scholars but a collector's item.

10 _____. "A Modern Classic." Chicago Daily News (30 August).

Publication of Sherwood Anderson's Memoirs: A Critical Edition provides, "finally, the towering, magnificently orchestrated autobiography that Sherwood Anderson must have envisioned."

11 _____. "The Year's twelve best books." Chicago Daily News (6-7 December), Panorama, p. 6.

Sherwood Anderson's Memoirs: A Critical Edition joins 1969's list of twelve-best for the book is a "re-edited version of a classic work, in which the vintage Anderson emerges. A mellow and rewarding book of memories by a great writer of fiction."

12 BRADY, JOHN. "Sherwood Anderson's Memoirs Revisited." American Book Collector, 20 (November-December).

Sherwood Anderson's Memoirs: A Critical Edition is valuable to literary historians and invaluable to Anderson enthusiasts.

13 _____. "When Sherwood Anderson's Mudguards Were Dented." American Book Collector, 19 (Summer), 20-22.

As Anderson's books from Winesburg, Ohio on were not welcome in the public library of Clyde, Ohio, Anderson explained the financial failure of his publisher (Horace Liveright, in 1933) as his "dented mudguards"--his inability to donate a set of his books. Soon after Anderson's death, the library began shelving his books.

14 CHIDA, AKIO. "Notes on Sherwood Anderson's 'The Egg.'" Toho Gakuen Faculty Bulletin, 11 (July), 12-21.

"The Egg" and Anderson's other works have four characteristics: "the rail road," "a success dream," "the grotesque," and the "hope of women." Anderson is ambivalent

1969

(CHIDA, AKIO)
toward the railroad. The success dream is shattered in the machine age. The grotesques expect salvation from women in crises. Yet Anderson's conscience is incomplete; he may have been satisfied with "seeing beneath the surface of lives" as a storyteller. [Takashi Kodaira]

15 COUSIN, JOHN W. and D. C. BROWNING. "Anderson, Sherwood." Everyman's Dictionary of Literary Biography: English & American. London: J. M. Dent & Sons, p. 14.
[Brief biographical sketch]

16 CONNELL, EVAN S., JR. "Sherwood Anderson's Memoirs." New York Times Book Review (10 August), pp. 1, 24.
White's edition of Sherwood Anderson's Memoirs is thorough in presenting properly a great deal of material written by Sherwood Anderson, but not every word written by Sherwood Anderson deserves to be printed.

17 CURLEY, DOROTHY NYREN, MAURICE KRAMER, and ELAINE FIALKA KRAMER, eds. "Anderson, Sherwood." A Library of Literary Criticism: Modern American Literature, 1. Fourth edition revised. New York: Frederick Ungar, 37-43.
[Reprints of 20 brief passages from critics of Anderson]

18 FEIBLEMAN, JAMES K. The Way of a Man: An Autobiography. New York: Horizon Press, pp. 83, 119-20, 159-67, 179, 263, 270, 272, 273, 274-76, 291.
Anderson dressed flamboyantly in New Orleans in 1924, became Feibleman's friend, and lived up to his protested integrity as an artist. Yet "intellectual" friends and critics ruined Anderson after their early praise.

19 FERRES, JOHN H. "Winesburg, Ohio at Fifty." Hofstra Review, 4 (Autumn), 5-10.
Published fifty years ago, Winesburg, Ohio still has appeal because of its anti-Puritanism, new story form, and true nostalgia. Reprinted: 1971.B13.

20 FROHOCK, W. F. "Sherwood Anderson e l'elegia americana." Translated by Mario Maffi. Strumenti Critici, 3 (1969), 286-99.
Anderson's basic tone in Winesburg, Ohio, Poor White, and A Story Teller's Story is idyllic elegy; his symbolist style evokes simplicity of response for rural ambience.

21 GOTO, SHOJI. "Imagination and Style: Sherwood Anderson's Case." American Literature [Tokyo Chapter of the American Literature Society of Japan], 22 (Winter), 8-14.

Anderson's imagination is as simple, plain, and fundamental as his style. He thinks the industrialization of America will produce "impotence"--a keen insight into modern life. [Takashi Kodaira]

22 HASHIGUCHI, YASUO. "Anderson and Ohio." Study of English (August), pp. 34-35.

Because of his character and nationality, Anderson's relationship to his region is in flux, yet he cherishes the memory of Ohio. [Takashi Kodaira]

23 HERRON, IMA HONAKER. The Small Town in American Drama. Dallas: Southern Methodist University Press, pp. xvii, 193, 195, 213, 238, 239, 256-62.

Anderson's work examines the effects of prosperity on village characters; when he dramatized Winesburg, Ohio he maintained the tone but abandoned the pattern of the stories. The stories were better.

24 HILFER, ANTHONY CHANNELL. The Revolt from the Village, 1915-1930. Chapel Hill: University of North Carolina Press, pp. 3, 27, 28, 29, 32, 33, 135, 147-57, 204, 212, 213, 218, 235-43, 247, 248, 249, 252, 253.

Anderson's stories of village life are "low mimetic tragedy, the modern naturalistic tragedy of ordinary people, a form characterized by the prevalence of pathos and irony." In Winesburg, Ohio Anderson reveals the buried life with sympathy but without sentimentality or bitterness.

25 HORTON, ALAN. "Ohio's Literary Man: Anderson." Cleveland Press (29 August).

Sherwood Anderson's Memoirs: A Critical Edition shows that with Anderson, "Ohio has made a big contribution to 20th Century literature."

26 JUNKER, HOWARD. "Growing Up in Winesburg." Newsweek, 74 (25 August), 82, 82D.

Publication of Sherwood Anderson's Memoirs: A Critical Edition again proves that Anderson was no great autobiographer; he must stand--and shall stand--high for Winesburg, Ohio.

27 LANDOR, M. "Škola Šervuda Andersona." Voprosy Literatury, 13 (1969), 141-72.

Anderson's letters reflect his entire artistic life. To trace his influence on contemporaries and those following him is in large measure to illuminate American literary dynamics of our age. [James F. Cradler] Translated: 1970.B18.

1969

28 LEARY, LEWIS. "Sherwood Anderson: The Man Who Became a Boy Again." Literatur und Sprache der Vereinigten Staaten: Aufsätze zur Ehren von Hans Galinsky. Edited by Hans Helmcke, Klaus Lubbers, Renate Schmidt-von Bardeleben. Heidelberg: C. Winter, pp. 135-43.
Reversing the American myth of rags-to-riches, Anderson abandoned his business and sought the simple truths of adolescence--love, community, pity at injustice, and some irresponsibility. His artistic hope became to listen to people and record their secret moments of unexpressed aspiration. Anderson's weakness was in recognizing but never plumbing life's mystery.

29 LIBMAN, VALENTINA A. Russian Studies of American Literature: A Bibliography. Translated by Robert V. Allen. Edited by Clarence Gohdes. Chapel Hill: University of North Carolina Press, pp. 4, 40-42, 65, 68.
Translation of 1964.B18.

30 ____. Sovremennoe Literaturovedenie SŠA. Moscow: Nauka, pp. 183, 185, 189, 201, 205.
V. W. Brooks remained true not only to the esthetic principles but the philosophical and ethical canons of the great critical realists of the 1920's--Lewis, Dreiser, Anderson, and Hemingway. [James F. Cradler]

31 McDonald, Walter R. Review of Sherwood Anderson's Memoirs: A Critical Edition. North American Review, 254 (Winter), 70-71.
Reading this new edition of Anderson's Memoirs is a literary "voyage of discovery" about "this life relived once more with feeling . . . an exciting adventure."

32 ____. "Winesburg, Ohio: Tales of Isolation." University Review Kansas City, 35 (March), 237-40.
The typical character in Winesburg, Ohio is yearning for community, attempted communication, and moments of illumination.

33 MILLER, HENRY. The Books in My Life. New York: New Directions, pp. 41, 217-19.
When Miller re-read The Triumph of the Egg, the book "came near to being a rotten egg." Yet he still admires Winesburg, Ohio and Many Marriages and sympathizes with Anderson's loneliness. When Miller met Anderson, he liked his ease and honest Americanism.

34 MIYAMOTO, YOKICHI. "Sherwood Anderson's Appraisal." American Literature [Tokyo Chapter of the American Literature Society of Japan], 22 (Winter), 14-19.

Although Anderson is incompetent, he does form a link between Stein and the writers of the Lost Generation. He is useful, and he fathered a new generation of American writers. Anderson was courageous enough to adopt the new craft of fiction. [Takashi Kodaira]

35 NAKAMURA, KAZUO. "A Study of Winesburg, Ohio." Amerika Bungaku [American Literature Society of Tokyo University of Education], 9 (Winter), 31-38.

Important points in Winesburg, Ohio are grotesque, comic aspects, primitivism, the hero's role, the plotless story, comparison with Twain and Hemingway, monologues, and so forth. [Takashi Kodaira]

36 OHARA, HIROTADA. "The Awakening of Anderson in the Chicago Renaissance." American Literature [Tokyo Chapter of the American Literature Society of Japan], 22 (Winter), 1-8.

Awakening to literature in the Chicago Renaissance, Anderson wrote Winesburg, Ohio. An experimentalist, he was too proud to settle down in the fictional town and went on the road again for self-discovery. Had he not left the home nest too quickly, he could have continued to fly against the storm of the red thirties. [Takashi Kodaira]

37 POPESCU, PETRU. "Sherwood Anderson: Winesburg in Ohio." România Literară (16 October), p. 23.

Anderson was the typical, autobiographical writer of the period 1900-1930, when literary naturalism was in vogue. Not widely read today but remembered for Winesburg, Ohio, he was too closely bound with the delusions of American society; yet in one book he blames industry / capitalism for human suffering. The characters have unreasoning minds; they are uprooted and somnolent and confused--typical products of America.

38 RAHV, PHILIP. Literature and the Sixth Sense. Boston: Houghton Mifflin Co., pp. 3-4, 5, 23, 30-31, 62-63, 96, 268-69.

Anderson suffers from his ability to write from experience only. He writes only of shut-in people from such observation, and his women are simply escape dreams; his theme is the American dream versus American reality.

39 RAVITZ, ABE C. "With Sherwood Anderson." Cleveland Plain Dealer (24 August).

1969

(RAVITZ, ABE C.)
Now Sherwood Anderson's Memoirs: A Critical Edition will "stand as a testimonial to the value of Sherwood Anderson, Clyde's significant legacy to American literature."

40 REED, KENNETH T. Review of Sherwood Anderson's Memoirs: A Critical Edition. American Notes & Queries, 8 (October), 30-31.
Perhaps over-edited, Sherwood Anderson's Memoirs: A Critical Edition is yet magnificently presented and enriches all of American literary studies.

41 RICHARDSON, H. EDWARD. William Faulkner: The Journey to Self-Discovery. Columbia: University of Missouri Press, pp. 28, 91, 116-38, 166, 171, 178, 189, 190, 209, 216, 218-21, 227.
Anderson was the "major literary influence on William Faulkner's early fiction," the younger writer gaining literary introductions, publication, and sense of prose-writing from the older. Above all, Faulkner must credit Anderson for "steering his early work in the direction of regionalistic impressionism and away from the futility of his post-war disillusionment."

42 RIDEOUT, WALTER B. "The Sherwood Anderson Story." Virginia Quarterly Review, 45 (Summer), 537-40.
Discovery of the real text of Sherwood Anderson's Memoirs and presentation of that text in a new critical edition again reminds that here "we touch not only a gifted writer but a gifted man."

43 SPENCER, BENJAMIN T. "Sherwood Anderson: American Mythopoeist." American Literature, 41 (March), 1-18.
Anderson's idea of America was a mixture of devotion and despair that the Jeffersonian dream had become vulgarity, materialism, and loss of community. To demonstrate the possible "repository of archetypal emotions and situations," Anderson used as setting the small Midwestern town and as mythic symbol the cornfields. Reprinted: 1974.A3.

44 STONE, EDWARD. A Certain Morbidness: A View of American Literature. Preface by Harry T. Moore. Carbondale: Southern Illinois University Press, pp. xii, 116, 153-55, 176.
In "The Strength of God" Anderson casts religious symbolism over the story of a peeping preacher; in Dark Laughter he uses Freudian thought-association in a sophisticated manner.

45 STOUCK, DAVID. "Winesburg, Ohio and the Failure of Art." Twentieth Century Literature, 15 (October), 145-51.

In each Winesburg, Ohio story, both public and private "modes of perception" work, ultimately to mutual disadvantage. Anderson does not present art--writing--as able to solve loneliness and despair. Reprinted: 1971.A2.

46 SULLIVAN, JOHN H. "Sherwood Anderson: Man for This Season." Washington Post (9 August), D, p. 4.

A new edition of Anderson's Memoirs now must rank the work among his very best writing.

47 UNTERECKER, JOHN. Voyager: A Life of Hart Crane. New York: Farrar, Straus and Giroux, pp. 88, 144, 152-55, 157-59, 162-64, 167-68, 170, 174, 190, 192-94, 210-12, 217-18, 222-23, 225-26, 230, 237, 245-46, 249-52, 255, 390, 622, 644.

After praising Winesburg, Ohio, Crane needed Anderson's literary associations and encouragement, although Anderson probably failed to understand Crane's difficult, abstract poetry.

48 WEBER, BROM. "Personal History." Saturday Review, 52 (23 August), 38-39.

Sherwood Anderson's Memoirs: A Critical Edition captures the "poignant lyricism" of Winesburg, Ohio and provides "a version of the Memoirs that probably comes as close to its author's conception of the work as an editor can hope to do."

49 WYLDER, DELBERT E. Hemingway's Heroes. Albuquerque: University of New Mexico Press, pp. 11-30, 37, 51-52, 178, 223-25, 228-29.

The Torrents of Spring, written after The Sun Also Rises, parodies Many Marriages and Dark Laughter; though sometimes psychologically grotesque, Hemingway's characters differ from Anderson's in lack of self-absorption.

1970 A BOOKS

1 APPELL, PAUL P., ed. Homage to Sherwood Anderson, 1876-1941. Mamaroneck [NY]: Paul P. Appel, Publisher, 212 pp.

Reprint of Story, 19 (September-October), 1941, with the addition of The Modern Writer and a selection of letters from Anderson written from 1931 through 1936.

2 SOMERS, PAUL PRESTON, JR. "Sherwood Anderson and Ernest Hemingway: Influences and Parallels." Dissertation, Pennsylvania State University, 194 pp.

Hemingway was aiming toward the "Hemingway" style before Anderson influenced him; both writers shared concern for the individual, simple (or primitive) characters, and nature. Both dealt with adolescents, Blacks, and initiation. Both emphasized the present and impressionism.

1970 B SHORTER WRITINGS

1 ANON. Review of *Tar: A Midwest Childhood, A Critical Text*. *Choice*, 7 (March), 70.

Tar "may well be as representative a literary autobiography of the first half of the 20th century as any."

2 ARLEN, MICHAEL J. *Exiles*. New York: Farrar, Straus & Giroux, pp. 117-18.

One summer Arlen courted a woman named Amy whose sophisticated mother "had known Sherwood Anderson 'personally.'"

3 BENNETT, JOSIAH Q. "Winesburg Revisited." *Serif*, 3 (September), 80-82.

Investigation of multiple copies of the early printings of *Winesburg, Ohio* confirms conclusions reported earlier by William L. Phillips.

4 BERRY, THOMAS ELLIOTT. *The Newspaper in the American Novel, 1900-1969*. Metuchen, NJ: Scarecrow Press, pp. 61, 62, 77.

In *Dark Laughter* Anderson's hero is a newspaper reporter who seeks a new name, life, and job; Anderson "is another author who makes no examination of the institution but does use a character from the newspaper world occasionally."

5 BORT, BARRY D. "*Winesburg, Ohio*: The Escape from Isolation." *Midwest Quarterly*, 11 (Summer), 443-56.

Not interested in hunting truth or experience nor impelled by self-discovery, *Winesburg, Ohio* characters deal with possibilities of community and communication.

6 COWLEY, MALCOLM. *A Many-Windowed House: Collected Essays on American Writers and American Writing*. Edited by Henry Dan Piper. Carbondale: Southern Illinois University Press, pp. xiv, 145, 166-77, 214, 240.

In the late 1920's Cowley feared that "irrationalism" such as Anderson's would damage literature. Traditional naturalism failed to explore inner worlds as Anderson did. Brooks described Anderson "heroically"; the anti-village movement followed naturally upon the "muckraking" movement.

7 DUFFEY, BERNARD I. Review of Sherwood Anderson's Memoirs: A Critical Edition. American Literature, 42 (March), 113-16.
Sherwood Anderson's Memoirs: A Critical Edition provides a good text but--most important of all--"accomplishes in fact what we are often told textual editing should accomplish, a recovery of authorial sense in the work."

8 DURANT, WILL and ARIEL DURANT. Interpretations of Life: A Survey of Contemporary Literature. New York: Simon and Schuster, pp. 29, 54.
Anderson introduced Hemingway by letter to Stein, Dos Passos, and Joyce; in 1925 Anderson, O'Neill, Eastman, Brooks, and Sandburg started The New Masses.

9 EARNEST, ERNEST. The Single Vision: The Alienation of American Intellectuals. New York: New York University Press, pp. x, 25, 37, 43, 52-53, 63, 139-40, 154-56, 187, 200, 203, 205, 218.
In Winesburg, Ohio Anderson links current tragedies to industrial evils, but essentially the book proves the evils of poor transportation. In Poor White Anderson tries to present humanism amid industry through anti-intellectualism. Both Winesburg, Ohio and Many Marriages attack Victorian conventions.

10 GILMER, WALKER. Horace Liveright: Publisher of the Twenties. New York: David Lewis, pp. vii, 9, 27, 31, 43, 88, 101, 106-19, 121, 122, 123, 124, 125, 126, 129, 168, 188, 234, 235, 237.
Anderson began his association with Liveright when the publisher included Winesburg, Ohio in the Modern Library; Huebsch had not made enough money for Anderson, and Liveright promised and delivered publicity, advances, and royalties until he lost control of his company in 1933.

11 GRIBANOV, B. Xeminguej. Moscow: Molodaja gvardija, pp. 78-83, 94-98.
Hemingway respected and admired Anderson, but he disagreed with Anderson on many aspects of writing and resented being cast in the role of Anderson's follower. [James F. Cradler]

1970

12 HOWE, IRVING. The Decline of the New. New York: Harcourt, Brace and Co., pp. 153-54.

Although Anderson belonged to the pre-World War generation, his stories of loneliness prepared the milieu for the 1920's writers. Winesburg, Ohio is not about a crisis of morals or values, but instead it presents the damaged result of that crisis.

13 INGRAM, FORREST L. "The Dynamics of Short Story Cycles." New Orleans Review, 2 (Spring), 7-12.

In study of short-story cycles, "Anderson's Winesburg best represents the center of the short-story cycle spectrum. For one discovers in his handling of setting, action, theme, time, character, and symbol the typical pattern of story cycles--the pattern of recurrence and development as a single integrated movement."

14 JOOST, NICHOLAS and ALVIN SULLIVAN. D. H. Lawrence and The Dial. Carbondale: Southern Illinois University Press, pp. 121, 131, 197.

The Dial liked to publish Anderson's work because the editor shared Anderson's interest in psychological fiction; hence, Many Marriages appeared serially.

15 KRONENBERGER, LOUIS. No Whippings, No Gold Watches: The Saga of a Writer and His Jobs. Boston: Little, Brown and Co., pp. 4-5, 6, 12, 16, 17-18, 25, 29, 189, 261.

As part of the post-War literary scene, Anderson had wisely joined forces with Boni & Liveright as well as introduced Faulkner's work to that firm, at whose headquarters Kronenberger first saw Anderson.

16 KUMAGAI, KEIKO. "On Some Literary Techniques of Sherwood Anderson." Jissen Bungaku, 40 (June), 60-73.

Analysis of conjunction and, repetition of words, phrases, clauses, and sounds shows that Anderson formed his original style in close connection with stream-of-consciousness technique. [Takashi Kodaira]

17 LACEY, JAMES F. Review of The Achievement of Sherwood Anderson. Zeitschrift für Anglistik und Amerikanistik, 18 (1970), 436-37.

The Achievement of Sherwood Anderson is a balanced anthology of the best criticism of Anderson and "says everything that anyone but a specialist would care to know about Anderson."

18 LANDOR, M. "Die Schule Sherwood Andersons." Translated by Wilfried Braumann. Kunst and Literatur, 18 (1970), 841-55; 961-75.

Translation of 1969.B27.

19 LEARY, LEWIS, CAROLYN BARTHOLET, and CATHARINE ROTH. Articles on American Literature 1950-1967. Durham: Duke University Press, pp. 15-18.

[List of 100 articles about Anderson]

20 LEMMON, DALLAS M., JR. "The Rovelle, or the Novel of Interrelated Stories: M. Lermontov, G. Keller, S. Anderson." Dissertation, Indiana University, 226 pp.

Besides devices like setting, central character, minor characters, unifying idea, and initial-terminal balance, Winesburg, Ohio gains further cyclic unity through "extensive and subtle patterns of interrelationships" of "repetitions and variations," these patterns being both large and small, static and dynamic, scattered and clustered.

21 LIBMAN, V. Problemy Literatura SShA XX Veka. Moscow, pp. 217, 221, 230, 258, 266, 302, 313, 315, 317, 319, 321, 322, 325, 350, 372, 376, 382, 391-403, 405-406.

[Translations of Anderson works into Russian]

22 MADDEN, DAVID, ed. American Dreams, American Nightmares. Carbondale: Southern Illinois University Press, pp. xxx, 24, 26, 45, 49-50, 52, 76, 101.

"The Egg" is in short-story form classic expression of common people's dreams of success. Faulkner and Hemingway had to rebel against Anderson as senior writer. Later disenchanted by failure of the American Dream, Anderson retreated to small-town Virginia; yet in Puzzled America and his Memoirs he gave "perhaps the best documentary account of the depression years."

23 MASSA, ANN. Vachel Lindsay: Fieldworker for the American Dream. Bloomington: Indiana University Press, pp. 35, 191-92.

Tar perhaps condemns "human weakness" instead of the Midwest; although Lindsay probably read Anderson's works, the poet did not agree with the anti-village bias.

24 MONIGLE, MARTHA. "Sherwood Anderson in Boulder." Michigan Quarterly Review, 9 (Winter), 55-56.

In the summer of 1937, Monigle heard Anderson lecture on the short story at the writers' conference at the University of Colorado. Shy and modest, Anderson said, "The

1970

(MONIGLE, MARTHA)
theme in all my stories . . . is how a man tries to recapture his lost innocence."

25 NAKAMURA, KAZUO. "Two Towns: Poor White and Main Street." Amerika Bungaku [American Literature Society of Tokyo University of Education], 10 (April), 46-53.
Poor White is lively, even now, compared to Main Street. Lewis' craft was realism, while Anderson's was to mix realism with symbolism. Anderson uses such symbols as cars and bright stones. Both authors are against standardization. [Takashi Kodaira]

26 OHASHI, KICHINOSUKE. "A Note on Anderson." Eigo Bungaku Sekai (March), 18-21.
Reprint with revision of 1968.B29.

27 PARKER, DOROTHY. Constant Reader. New York: Viking Press, pp. 16-17, 36-37, 56, 114-15.
"I'm a Fool" is "one of the four great American short stories"; except for Anderson, Lardner, and Hemingway's work, all stories are alike.

28 PAVESE, CESARE. American Literature: Essays and Opinions. Translated by Edwin Fussell. Berkeley: University of California Press, pp. vi, viii, xi, xiv, xviii, xix, xx, xxi, 4, 13, 30-41, 43, 56, 75-78, 90, 107-108, 124, 142, 144-45, 147, 148, 170, 177, 184, 189-91, 199.
Translation of 1951.B29.

29 REA, PAUL WESLEY. "A Teacher's Guide to the Modern American Short Story." Dissertation, Ohio State University, 213 pp.
Using "Hands," "I Want to Know Why," "The Egg," and "I'm a Fool," the teacher can analyze the technical aspects of Anderson's craft and then place Anderson as an author more interested in society than art.

30 ROSS, ISHBEL. The Expatriots. New York: Thomas Y. Crowell Co., pp. 223-24.
When Stein discussed writers with Hemingway, she praised few who had not praised her; she liked Anderson's personality better than his prose.

31 SILVERMAN, RAYMOND JOEL. "The Short Story Composite: Forms, Functions, and Applications." Dissertation, University of Michigan, 347 pp.
Winesburg, Ohio is unified into a short story composite by the maturing of the central character from ignorance to

sophistication. Other characters occur once and then remain isolated by self. Each story terminates firmly, reflecting the "walls between the Winesburg people."

32 SIMONSON, HAROLD P. The Closed Frontier: Studies in American Literary Tragedy. New York: Holt, Rinehart and Winston, pp. 105-106.
The work of West resembles that of Anderson, The Day of the Locust sharing with Winesburg, Ohio longing for an edenic past and the conclusion that grotesquerie is normal.

33 TAKEDA, SHOICHI. "A Study on Sherwood Anderson's Short Story: On 'I Want to Know Why.'" Eibungaku Ronko [Rissho Daigaku Eibungakukai], 6 (November), 56-71.
"I Want to Know Why" can be analyzed from psychological realism. The relation between mankind and nature in Anderson is too romantic, but Anderson was not the least important figure in the transition from naturalistic realism to psychological realism. [Takashi Kodaira]

34 TAYLOR, WELFORD DUNAWAY. "Sherwood Anderson." Virginia Cavalcade, 19 (Spring), 42-47.
With the profits of Dark Laughter, Anderson built his country home (designed by Spratling) in rural Virginia. Writing for his country newspapers allowed Anderson to create humor, benefit the town, earn an interesting living, and meet his future wife, Eleanor Copenhaver, who encouraged Anderson's social concern.

35 TURNER, SUSAN J. "The Anderson Papers." American Scholar (Winter 1969-70), 152-53, 156, 158, 160.
Although the editorial apparatus in Sherwood Anderson's Memoirs: A Critical Edition is often too obvious, restoration of Anderson's text makes the work "strong and free and good." Tar: A Midwest Childhood, A Critical Text makes the work available again but in a less usable scholarly edition.

36 VALVERDE, JOSÉ MARÍA. Historia de la Literatura Universal, III. Del Romanticismo a Nuestros Dias. Second edition. Barcelona: Editorial Planeta, pp. 434-435.
Presenting small-town characters without authorial judgment and in simple style in Winesburg, Ohio accounts for this classic book's appeal.

37 WALKER, WARREN S., ed. Twentieth-Century Short Story Explication: Supplement I to Second Edition, 1967-1969. Hamden [CT]: Shoe String Press, pp. 9-17.
Criticism of 22 stories by Anderson]

1970

38 WOLFE, DON M. The Image of Man in America. New York: Thomas Y. Crowell Co., pp. 9, 223, 235-36, 345, 359, 391.
Anderson wrote of sexuality as essentially noble; he praised Dreiser for objective (but compassionate) description; Faulkner lacked Anderson's possibility of inherited gentleness; even Anderson in superb treatment of sex fails to surpass Faulkner's obsession with aberration.

39 WOLFE, THOMAS. The Notebooks of Thomas Wolfe. Edited by Richard S. Kennedy and Paschal Reeves. Chapel Hill: University of North Carolina Press, pp. 113, 172, 243, 288, 337, 877, 882, 886, 887, 888-89, 920.
In 1927 Wolfe listed Anderson and A. E. Coppard as "The Best Shortstory Writers"; in 1928 he thought that Anderson had been able to suggest best the "strangeness and variety of this life" but that he had become "too fancy since Winesburg, Ohio." Wolfe visited Anderson in Virginia in September, 1937; the writers disagreed in New York in December, 1937.

1971 A BOOKS

1 FANNING, MICHAEL. "France and Sherwood Anderson." Dissertation, University of Arkansas, 405 pp.
The first translations of Anderson's works were into French, and Anderson was considered by the French to be a major author until 1928. French commentary on Anderson is often factually wrong and personally biased but "emotionally accurate."

2 WHITE, RAY LEWIS, comp. The Merrill Studies in Winesburg, Ohio. Columbus: Charles E. Merrill Publishing Co., 113 pp.
Reprint of 1919.B1-2, B7, B16-17, B19-20; 1941.B54; 1943.B4; 1951.A1, B30; 1960.B11; 1961.B10; 1967.B24, B27, B32; 1968.B6; 1969.B45.

3 YANCEY, ANITA VIRGINIA RISH. "Winesburg, Ohio and The Pastures of Heaven: A Comparative Analysis of Two Studies on Isolation." Dissertation, University of Southern Mississippi, 229 pp.
Both Winesburg, Ohio and The Pastures of Heaven deal with isolation; but, whereas Winesburg, Ohio is intricately constructed, The Pastures of Heaven is simply constructed and not very subtle. Neither Anderson nor Steinbeck gives environmental dominance, but both authors allow human potential to be wasted in pastoral settings. Anderson's characters are more complex; both writers use central

characters for unity. Winesburg, Ohio uses nine motifs; The Pastures of Heaven uses only two. The works are alike in using narrators and framework.

1971 B SHORTER WRITINGS

1 ANDERSON, DAVID D. "Sherwood Anderson: Virginia Journalist." Newberry Library Bulletin, 6 (July), 251-62.

Hello Towns! is important to show Anderson's recognition that factual matters (ordinary journalism) are only part of life; Anderson's imaginative journalism made his country newspapers part of literature.

2 BEJA, MORRIS. Epiphany in the Modern Novel. Seattle: University of Washington Press, pp. 20, 48-49.

Anderson, Mansfield, and Woolf are masters of the "epiphany" form--stories with little plot or length and with abrupt endings.

3 BERTHOFF, WARNER. Fictions and Events: Essays in Criticism and Literary History. New York: E. P. Dutton & Co., pp. 173, 174, 179, 260-61, 313, 326.

Anderson's Winesburg, Ohio characters are in line with isolates in Hawthorne and Melville; yet not these characters but their social milieu (not setting) makes the work magic.

4 BRYAN, JAMES. "Sherwood Anderson and The Catcher in the Rye: A Possible Influence." Notes on Contemporary Literature, 1 (November), 2-6.

Salinger's story "I'm Crazy" from 1945 echoes "I'm a Fool" in style and character and may lead into The Catcher in the Rye.

5 C., D. "Anderson, Sherwood." The Penguin Companion to American Literature. Edited by Malcolm Bradbury, Eric Mottram, and Jean Franco. New York: McGraw-Hill, p. 19.

Heroes in Anderson's novels parallel the writer's life, moving to city, success, disillusionment, rejection, and exploration. The result is often community, mysticism, and personal freedom. Anderson's artistic problem was finding the best narrator's role in his fiction.

6 CHANNICK, HERBERT. "The Great Adventure: Sherwood Anderson and Harness Racing." Hoof Beats (December), pp. 31-33, 66, 67.

A fan of harness racing from boyhood on, Anderson often wrote of racing, for he equated craft and racing.

1971

7 CHURCHILL, ALLEN. The Literary Decade. Englewood Cliffs: Prentice-Hall, pp. 3, 13-14, 17, 21, 29, 57, 80, 86, 90, 98, 122, 170, 172, 179, 184, 192-93, 203, 210-12, 237-38, 293-94, 320-21.

Anderson published from 1916 on and "did much to bring naturalism, colloquialism, and the sex urge" to American books; he never forgave Lewis for imitating an oral tale by Anderson. Among Chicago writers helped by Anderson were Hecht and young Hemingway. Lewis praised Anderson in his lectures. Influential by personal example as well as stories, Anderson profited greatly from Dark Laughter but terminated Liveright's generous advances. Hemingway broke with Anderson and Stein, who thought him homosexual; even Faulkner turned on Anderson.

8 DAHLBERG, EDWARD. The Confessions of Edward Dahlberg. New York: George Braziller, pp. 40, 201, 202, 204, 213, 245, 264.

Anderson had "adjustive" brown eyes; Cummings disliked Anderson's neglected face; Anderson considered Ford M. Ford "a gargantuan liar"; Dahlberg could imitate Anderson's speech; Anderson was one of the few literate authors in the 1930's.

9 ______. "Dahlberg on Dreiser, Anderson and Dahlberg." New York Times Book Review (31 January), pp. 2, 30.

Anderson imitated Dreiser's mannerisms for the amusement of Dahlberg, but Anderson always suffered charges of being a confused thinker.

10 DAY, MARTIN S. History of American Literature From 1910 to the Present. Garden City: Doubleday & Co., pp. 4-8, 244, 369.

Anderson's one controlling theme was how to have unity that would restore brotherhood in the midst of mechanization and materialism. In short stories few writers equal Anderson's ability to present inarticulate natures suffering in small towns.

11 DeJOVINE, F. ANTHONY. The Young Hero in American Fiction: A Motif for Teaching Literature. New York: Appleton-Century Crofts, pp. 26-27, 42-44, 60-61, 65-66, 86, 149.

The hero of "Hands" is not necessarily homosexual; the hero of Winesburg, Ohio is Anderson's alter ego and at the end of the work is mature and escapes grotesquerie by "managing" experience.

12 DENISOVA, T. N. Na Puti k Čeloveku. Kiev: Naukova dumka, pp. 109-11.
Anderson influenced Hemingway thematically and in fostering his interest in the democratic hero. Hemingway parodied Anderson's Dark Laughter. [James F. Cradler]

13 FERRES, JOHN H. "The Nostalgia of Winesburg, Ohio." Newberry Library Bulletin, 6 (July), 235-42.
Reprint of 1969.B19.

14 FITZGERALD, F. SCOTT. "Sherwood Anderson on the Marriage Question." F. Scott Fitzgerald in His Own Time: A Miscellany. Edited by Matthew J. Bruccoli and Jackson R. Bryer. Kent: Kent State University Press, pp. 138-40.
Reprint of 1923.B26.

15 FITZGERALD, F. SCOTT and MAXWELL PERKINS. Dear Scott / Dear Max: The Fitzgerald-Perkins Correspondence. Edited by John Kuehl and Jackson Bryer. New York: Charles Scribner's Sons, pp. 12-13, 90, 95, 97, 106, 110, 111, 126, 127, 130, 134, 135, 142.
Despite Anderson's efforts, the short story genre is ebbing; Mencken did not speak to Sherman at Huebsch's party for Anderson; Anderson's life was "a mess"; Anderson had style but few ideas; Perkins should purchase Hemingway; Hemingway forwarded through Fitzgerald a letter about The Torrents of Spring.

16 FRIDDELL, GUY. "Sherwood Anderson and His Smyth County Sidekick: Buck Fever." Commonwealth, 38 (November), 32-36.
The Buck Fever Papers, collected by W. D. Taylor, will prevent Anderson's fictional country journalist from being forgotten.

17 GERVASI, FRANK. "The Liberation of Gertrude Stein." Saturday Review, 54 (21 August), 13-14.
Gervasi knew Stein's influence on Anderson and little else about her in 1944 France. He found her healthy and aware of Anderson's death--and Toklas' food delicious.

18 GLICKSBERG, CHARLES I. The Sexual Revolution in Modern American Literature. The Hague: Martinus Nijhoff, pp. 4, 8, 15, 20, 21, 31, 34, 46, 47-57, 58, 69, 74, 113, 137, 142, 145, 154, 227, 236, 244, 246.
Anderson became the "anointed prophet" of sex-as-salvation, picturing the whole individual fictionally. The characters of Winesburg, Ohio are intended as ordinary villagers, not special cases, suffering from loneliness and

1971

(GLICKSBERG, CHARLES I.)
frustrations. In Many Marriages Anderson declares the subconscious and necessary liberation of it.

19 GROSS, THEODORE L. The Heroic Ideal in American Literature. New York: Free Press, pp. 143, 146-47.
Winesburg, Ohio influenced the theme of the disillusionment in Toomer's Cane as well as the work's form and tone; Cane is the only "Negro Awakening" book of significance.

20 HAAS, ROBERT BARTLETT, ed. A Primer for the Gradual Understanding of Gertrude Stein. Los Angeles: Black Sparrow Press, pp. 20, 21, 31, 33.
Reprint of 1962.B13.

21 HOWARD, MICHAEL S. Jonathan Cape, Publisher: Herbert Jonathan Cape / G. Wren Howard. London: Jonathan Cape, pp. 40, 45, 46, 79, 102, 110.
Cape declined to publish Many Marriages, but he did publish Windy McPherson's Son, Poor White, and Winesburg, Ohio. Anderson contributed evidence to defend publication of Radclyffe Hall's The Well of Loneliness.

22 INGRAM, FORREST L. Representative Short Story Cycles of the Twentieth Century: Studies in a Literary Genre. The Hague: Mouton, pp. 14, 17, 18, 19, 20-23, 25, 32, 33, 34, 35, 40, 41, 105, 116, 128, 139, 143-99, 200-203.
Winesburg, Ohio is neither novel nor disparate stories; the work is a cycle, united by recurring theme--"the gradual emergence . . . of a fictive community in the distortive memory of the book's single narrator"; narrative voice, stylistic repetition, setting, mythic departure of central character.

23 JOHNSON, RICHARD COLLES. "The Achievement of Sherwood Anderson: An Anniversary Exhibition." Newberry Library Bulletin, 6 (July), 268-87.
[Catalog of 134 Anderson items exhibited at The Newberry Library in 1969]

24 KINGSBURY, STEWART A. "A Structural Semantic Analysis of the 'Punch Line' of Sherwood Anderson's Short Story, The Egg." Papers from the Michigan Linguistics Society Meeting October 3, 1970. Edited by David Lawton. Mt. Pleasant: Central Michigan University, pp. 52-61.
The semantic analysis of one line of "The Egg" is "based upon the Firthian concepts of collocation and context and incorporates aspects of structural semantics. . . ."

25 KRONENBERGER, LOUIS and EMILY BECK MORISON. "Anderson, Sherwood." Atlantic Brief Lives: A Biographical Companion to the Arts. Boston: Little, Brown and Co., p. 13.
Anderson's dominant theme is "conflict between instinctive forces in human nature and inhibiting effects of organized industrial society."

26 LIGHT, JAMES F. Nathanael West: An Interpretative Study. Second edition. Evanston: Northwestern University Press, p. 68.
In 1927 West told John Sanford that he had become acquainted with Anderson's writing.

27 McCORMICK, JOHN. The Middle Distance: A Comparative History of American Literature, 1919-1932. New York: Free Press, pp. 1, 5, 16-28, 32, 36, 40, 45, 47-48, 60, 75, 98, 168, 170, 174-75, 215.
Author of one good book and a few other good stories, Anderson created good feeling for himself as a legendary ex-businessman artist. His essence, however, was to be devious and posing for attention. The Anderson style is not descended from Twain and is not poetic, and only parts of Winesburg, Ohio are well written.

28 MARRINER, GERALD L. "Sherwood Anderson: The Myth of the Artist." Texas Quarterly, 14 (Spring), 105-16.
Child of ordinary parents, product of conventional background, Anderson created the myth of sensitive child and frustrated businessman who later escaped dramatically into writing and bohemian life.

29 MAYFIELD, SARA. Exiles from Paradise: Zelda and Scott Fitzgerald. New York: Delacourt Press, pp. 59, 82, 93, 140-41.
Dreiser's party with Anderson present was dull until Fitzgerald arrived; Dos Passos met Anderson at Fitzgerald's New York apartment; Hemingway repaid Anderson's help with The Torrents of Spring; Zelda hated Hemingway and his parody of Anderson.

30 MERIWETHER, JAMES B. The Literary Career of William Faulkner: A Bibliographical Study. Columbia: University of South Carolina Press, pp. 5, 11, 12, 14; figures 27-29.
[An undated letter from Anderson, and several other items owned by Faulkner or about Anderson and Faulkner]

31 NAKAMURA, KAZUO. "The Groping People in an Age of Confusion: An Essay on Sherwood Anderson's Novels." Studies in

1971

(NAKAMURA, KAZUO)
American Literature [American Literature Society of Japan], 7 (March), 56-74.
A theme of Winesburg, Ohio is the central character's growth to maturity. Anderson's novels may be considered as the extension of this theme. In spite of their defects, one can trace in them people groping for true values amid confusion. [Takashi Kodaira]

32 _____. "Longing for a Primitive World: On Dark Laughter." Amerika Bungaku [American Literature Society of Tokyo University of Education], 11 (August), 20-28.
The style of Dark Laughter is experimental, Anderson trying to express the rhythm of the river and the Blacks. The temptation to interpret the behavior of hero and heroine is dangerous. The theme of the work is at best longing for a primitive world, and the novel is more a prose poem than a novel. [Takashi Kodaira]

33 NEUWEILER, SIEGFRIED. "Sherwood Anderson's 'I Want to Know Why': Die Strukturelle Eigenart einer 'Story of Initiation.'" Studien und Materialen zur Short Story. Edited by Paul Goetsch. Frankfurt am/M: Verlag Moritz Diesterweg, pp. 76-84.
Using psychological realism in "I Want to Know Why," Anderson relates content and form to combine structure and meaning. The fateful final scene seems to bring to the hero a moment of recognition, causing his reassimilation into society after a period of alienation.

34 PAWLOWSKI, ROBERT S. "The Process of Observation: Winesburg, Ohio and The Golden Apples." University Review Kansas City, 37 (June), 292-98.
Winesburg, Ohio and Welty's The Golden Apples are alike in small-town setting, central character, visiting strangers, and motifs of life-death and desire-yearning; in technique both authors resemble cubistic painters.

35 RIDEOUT, WALTER B. "'The Tale of Perfect Balance': Sherwood Anderson's 'The Untold Lie.'" Newberry Library Bulletin, 6 (July), 243-50.
The narrator of "The Untold Lie" is an unnamed citizen of Anderson's imaginary town of Winesburg, one who can be both objective and subjective storyteller, telling of revolt against convention in past history and present action.

36 SAKUMA, YOSHIKAZU. "On Winesburg, Ohio." Teoria [Hosei Daigaku Daigakuin Eiyukai], 3 (September), 55-66.

Anderson's setting in Winesburg, Ohio becomes cold and gray, for his ideal society consists of both freedom in the city and solidarity in the town. Two characters escape from his imaginary town, one thinking and speaking freely; the other, to observe life innocently. [Takashi Kodaira]

37 SAMOKHVADOVA, N. I. Istoria Amerikaniskia Literatura, 2. Moscow, 106-12.

[Seen but not translated]

38 SATYANARAYANA, M. R. "From Winesburg to Salinas Valley in Search of Love." Osmania Journal of English Studies, 8 (1971), 19-28.

Steinbeck's The Long Valley lacks the central character present in Winesburg, Ohio; but the books are similar in "the theme of loneliness, an atmosphere of melancholy, and a complete absence of humour."

39 STENERSON, DOUGLAS C. H. L. Mencken: Iconoclast from Baltimore. Chicago: University of Chicago Press, pp. 5, 15, 198-99, 206, 214, 218, 220.

Mencken attracted Anderson's work to his magazines, for he admired use of colloquial style, the "gusto" of Windy McPherson's Son, Winesburg, Ohio, and "I Want to Know Why."

40 TAYLOR, WELFORD D. "Kit Brandon: A Reidentification." Newberry Library Bulletin, 6 (July), 263-67.

Not an episode in Marion, Virginia, in the late 1920's, but instead Treasury Department trials in 1935 provided Anderson the original character of Kit Brandon.

41 TOMKINS, CALVIN. Living Well Is the Best Revenge. New York: Viking Press, p. 27.

In Paris Hemingway read The Torrents of Spring manuscript to Gerald and Sara Murphy. Gerald felt that the parody of Anderson was not in good taste, and Sara slept through Hemingway's reading.

42 TOWNER, LAWRENCE W. "Preface." Newberry Library Bulletin, 6 (July), 233.

The Newberry Library in 1969 celebrated acquisition of the Winesburg, Ohio manuscript and the fiftieth anniversary of publication of the book.

43 WAY, BRIAN. "Sherwood Anderson." The American Novel and the Nineteen Twenties. Edited by Malcolm Bradbury and David Palmer. London: Edward Arnold, pp. 107-26.

1971

(WAY, BRIAN)
One of "the great masters of the American short story," Anderson deserves study as more than an influence. Especially good at writing of loneliness, and eloquent about himself as an observer of America's changing scene, Anderson cannot structure long fiction or create good dialogue.

44 WEBER, ALFRED. "Sherwood Andersons Reflexionen über die Dichtung." Amerikanische Literatur im 20. Jahrhundert. Edited by Alfred Weber and Dietmar Haack. Göttingen: Vanderhoeck & Ruprecht, pp. 29-55.
Combining Anderson's statements on literature presents a "theory"--that fiction and fact need proper form, that truth is properly a creative expression, that reflection is the bridge from outward observation to inward truth.

45 WHITE, RAY LEWIS. "A Checklist of Sherwood Anderson Studies, 1959-1969." Newberry Library Bulletin, 6 (July), 288-302.
[293 items--editions, translations, essays, studies, index]

46 _____. "Sherwood Anderson." The Politics of Twentieth-Century Novelists. Edited by George A. Panichas. Foreword by John W. Aldridge. New York: Hawthorne Books, pp. 251-62.
Anderson claimed that he proposed Socialism as an Ohio businessman, he wrote apprentice novels about political "order" while personally unhappy in Ohio, he ignored politics from 1918 until the Depression, and he resisted Communism while championing labor in the 1930's.

47 YAMAMOTO, AKIRO. Review of Sherwood Anderson's Memoirs: A Critical Edition. Studies in English Literature [English Literary Society of Japan] (March), 293-300.
White's new edition of the Anderson Memoirs has just appeared, and the old one has just passed away. [Takashi Kodaira]

1972 A BOOKS

1 SEBASTIAN, DILLARD FLOYD, JR. "Sherwood Anderson's Theory of Art." Dissertation, Louisiana State University, 185 pp.
To Anderson art is to restore "instinct and emotion in a civilization which subordinates human vitality to impersonal structures of materialism." Anderson equated art with "life, love, and beauty," beauty being humanistic instead of esthetic. The artist ultimately hopes to revitalize and better order American life.

2 SUTTON, WILLIAM A. The Road to Winesburg: A Mosaic of the Imaginative Life of Sherwood Anderson. Metuchen, NJ: Scarecrow Press, 645 pp.

[Extension to 1919 of Sutton's 1943 dissertation, documenting Anderson's relationships with members of the Chicago Renaissance group and publishing histories of his first four books] Reprint with revision of 1943.A1. Reprint of 1919.B16, B20-22; 1967.A3

1972 B SHORTER WRITINGS

1 ANDERSON, DAVID D. "Sherwood Anderson and the Coming of the New Deal." Criticism and Culture: Papers of the Midwest Modern Language Association. Edited by Sherman Paul. Iowa City: Midwest Modern Language Association, pp. 88-96.

After the Depression began, Anderson never became a revolutionary but continued his "search for illumination and insight that he had begun when he started to write," so that dehumanization and isolation as factors could be named and obliterated.

2 ANON. "Literary Landmarks." New York Times (16 April), X, p. 34.

Anderson's home in Virginia has become a National Historic Landmark.

3 ANON. "Anderson Found His Dream." Smyth County News (25 July), Supplement, p. [3].

Not able to be a "country squire," Anderson bought his two newspapers in Virginia. Later--wherever he traveled--"Always he came home."

4 ANON. "Local Recognition Given to Sherwood Anderson." Clyde Enterprise [OH] (20 September), pp. 1, 12.

Thaddeus B. Hurd chaired events for Sherwood Anderson Day, which Anderson's children and last wife attended. Clyde had not previously honored the author. The speaker was William Sutton, who described Anderson's writing as done for emotional self-therapy.

5 ANON. Review of The Buck Fever Papers. Virginia Quarterly Review, 48 (Winter), xxxvi.

The Buck Fever Papers contain Anderson's wit and "personal" journalism.

6 BACH, BERT C. Review of The Road to Winesburg. Library Journal, 97 (1 September), 2735.

1972

(BACH, BERT C.)
Although turgid, mannered, poorly structured, and unintegrated, Sutton's The Road to Winesburg contains "virtually every known detail about Anderson" and is "For specialists in the field."

7 BAKER, CARLOS. "Sherwood Anderson's Winesburg: A Reprise." Virginia Quarterly Review, 48 (Autumn), 568-79.
To create Winesburg, Ohio, Anderson had to "brood like a great mother bird over a Mid-American town until it hatched into palpable existence," inspired by Romain Rolland's call for bravery in American writing. Anderson's bravery showed in his sexual subjects in conventional language. Other subjects in Winesburg, Ohio are escape, discovery, varieties of love, rejection, and loyalty--all under the "key terms" of deprivation, search, release, and repression.

8 BLAKE, FAY M. The Strike in the American Novel. Metuchen, NJ: Scarecrow Press, pp. 72, 90, 109-11, 118, 122, 143, 160, 163, 165, 166-67, 172, 174, 237, 238, 240, 248-49, 257.
Anderson's early novels reflect his concern for labor problems, along with his "politically uncommitted" stance; the industrial strike is for Anderson but a literary device. In Beyond Desire Anderson shows actual concern for labor.

9 BLUEFARB, SAM. "George Willard: Death and Revolution." The Escape Motif in the American Novel: Mark Twain to Richard Wright. Columbus: Ohio State University Press, pp. 42-58.
In Winesburg, Ohio the escape from town of the central character symbolizes the young man's death (loss of boyhood) and rebirth (into maturity).

10 BUTCHER, FANNY. Many Lives--One Love. New York: Harper & Rowe, pp. 76, 101, 102, 411, 427.
In March, 1914, Anderson attended Margery Currey's inaugural party for The Little Review. Anderson left his family to marry Tennessee Mitchell, who had a sense of humor in contrast to Masters' bitterness and Anderson's "blackly dour" personality.

11 CALHOUN, MEG. "Authentic American Voice." Smyth County News (25 July), Supplement, p. [16].
Anderson met Eleanor Copenhaver in Marion in 1929, spent mornings writing at his country house, and is buried in Marion because he liked the view.

12 CIANCIO, RALPH. "'The Sweetness of the Twisted Apples': Unity of Vision in Winesburg, Ohio." Publications of the Modern Language Association of America, 87 (October), 994-1006.

The characters' fanaticism in Winesburg, Ohio has Anderson's sympathy for spiritual fulfillment. The central character comes to share the vision of the prologue and to transcend it to become--"symbolically at least"--the old writer.

13 DUFFY, MARTHA. "Then and Now." Time, 100 (18 September), 99-100.

Republication of Hemingway's The Torrents of Spring shows the author's ingratitude to Anderson, as well as deserved parody of Anderson's "lapidary dialogue, his reverence for the little town . . . even his anxious asides to the reader."

14 FITZGERALD, F. SCOTT and HAROLD OBER. As Ever, Scott Fitz--Letters Between F. Scott Fitzgerald and His Literary Agent Harold Ober 1919-1940. Edited by Matthew J. Bruccoli et al. Philadelphia: J. B. Lippincott Co., p. 125.

On February 9, 1929, Ober suggested that Bennett Cerf wanted a Fitzgerald story to go with stories by Anderson and others in Great Modern Short Stories, edited by Grant Overton.

15 FORD, HUGH, ed. The Left Bank Revisited: Selections from the Paris Tribune, 1917-1934. University Park: Pennsylvania State University Press, pp. xx, 45, 81-83, 98, 99, 158-59, 168, 257, 265, 267, 279.

Interviewed by William Shirer in Paris in 1926, Anderson assumed that the United States was in no danger of becoming cultured. Anderson actually created the chance for exploration of Stein's charm.

16 HUBBELL, JAY B. Who Are the Major American Writers? A Study of the Changing Literary Canon. Durham: Duke University Press, pp. 175, 208, 209, 213, 217, 219, 221, 249, 280, 304.

P. E. More hated Anderson's lack of formal education; but Anderson rated high in various 1920's polls and lower in 1930's polls.

17 INGRAM, FORREST L. "American Short Story Cycles: Foreign Influences and Parallels." Proceedings of the Comparative Literature Symposium, V: Modern American Fiction. Insights and Foreign Lights. Edited Wolodymyn T. Zyla and Wendell M. Aycock. Lubbock: Texas Tech University, pp. 19-37.

Winesburg, Ohio is a story cycle unified by "character, theme, setting, and symbolism," resembling internally Turgenev's Hunting Sketches.

1972

18 JOHNSON, RICHARD COLLES. "Addenda to Sheehy and Lohf's Bibliography of Sherwood Anderson." Papers of the Bibliographical Society of America, 66 (First quarter), 61.
The July, 1971, issue of The Newberry Library Bulletin and Sutton's 1941 dissertation provide additional information about Anderson items.

19 LONGSTREET, STEPHEN. We All Went to Paris: Americans in the City of Light, 1776-1971. New York: Macmillan Co., pp. 17, 267, 307, 308, 310, 335.
Besides sending Hemingway to Paris with introductions to Stein and Joyce, Anderson himself visited the French salons of Stein and Natalie Barney.

20 McHANEY, THOMAS L. "Anderson, Hemingway, and Faulkner's The Wild Palms." Publications of the Modern Language Association of America, 87 (May), 465-74.
In The Wild Palms Faulkner alludes to Anderson's Dark Laughter and presents "a full portrait of Anderson's second wife, Tennessee Mitchell, who seems to be the model for Faulkner's heroine, Charlotte Rittenmeyer."

21 MOORE, HARRY T. "Gertrude to Sherwood." St. Louis Globe-Democrat Books (18-19 November), A, p. 10.
Sherwood Anderson / Gertrude Stein is interesting in itself and as "A valuable footnote to the literary history of the 1920's."

22 NAKAGAWA, HOJO. "The Ordeal of Sherwood Anderson: His Frustration in Humanization." Journal of Ryukoku University, 398 (February), 69-90.
Focusing on Beyond Desire shows that the dream of humanization is shattered in the spiritual crises of the modern age. Both Anderson and his hero have an ambiguous attitude toward the labor strike; it is very difficult to liberate poor whites from social bondage. After the hero's death, a death ceremony instead of a departure ceremony casts shadows on the dream of humanization. Yet Anderson sees integrity and freedom in death ceremonies; his belief in humanity is so strong that he can maintain his dream. [Takashi Kodaira]

23 NAKIJIMA, SHIGEO. "Sherwood Anderson and Communism." Kyoyoronso [Keiogijuku Daigaku Hogaku Kenkyukai] 34 (March), 48-62.
Before 1930 Anderson's conscience was literary instead of social; due to the influence of Eleanor Copenhaver he then developed a social concern. He came to approve of the

New Deal. American nationalism is probably stronger than American socialism or communism. [Takashi Kodaira]

24 PAPINCHAK, ROBERT ALLEN. "Beginnings, Middles, and Ends: A Study of the American Short Story." Dissertation, University of Wisconsin, 366 pp.
Neither realist nor naturalist, Anderson created grotesque characters formed by fanatical true-belief and industrialism-standardization. In _Winesburg, Ohio_ Anderson used a new form of story cycle, a new style of colloquial serious simplicity, the concept of grotesque character, and the imagery of fertility.

25 ROGERS, DOUGLAS R. "Development of the Artist in _Winesburg, Ohio_." _Studies in the Twentieth Century_, No. 10 (Fall), 91-99.
The central character of _Winesburg, Ohio_ does more than unify Anderson's stories; he gives promise of maturing into a creative artist, one who can combine fact and imagination.

26 SAKUMA, YOSHIKAZU. "S. Anderson and J. D. Salinger: From Innocence as a Means to Innocence Itself." _Studies in English Literature_ [English Literary Society of Hosei University], 14 (February), 121-33.
Considering _Winesburg, Ohio_, _The Catcher in the Rye_, and _Nine Stories_, Anderson and Salinger differ in attitude toward the salvation of moderns. Anderson seeks to fulfill self-realization through innocence as a means, while Salinger seeks to recover innocence above the means and the end. [Takashi Kodaira]

27 SANDOS, MITCHELL. "A Loner, But He Loved People." _Smyth County News_ (25 July), Supplement, p. [3].
Anderson was "a loner with few friends, yet a man who loved people; his closest Virginia friends were Bob Williams and Andy Funk.

28 _____. "Today Anderson Would See New Faces, Change." _Smyth County News_ (25 July), p. 7.
Most of Anderson's friends in Marion, Virginia, are dead; the changed town would now be "disturbingly strange" to the writer.

29 SCHULBERG, BUDD. _The Four Seasons of Success_. Garden City: Doubleday, pp. 3, 12, 13, 21, 50-51, 77.
Hemingway treated badly anyone who had helped him to success; _The Torrents of Spring_ is "a snotty little novel." Anderson needs to be understood, not rated.

1972

30 [SNELLING, PAULA]. "Sherwood Anderson . . . A Composite Picture." From the Mountain. Edited by Helen White and Redding S. Suggs. Memphis: Memphis State University Press, pp. 159-62.
Reprint of 1937.B45.

31 SPILLER, ROBERT E., WILLARD THORP, THOMAS H. JOHNSON, HENRY SEIDEL CANBY, and RICHARD M. LUDWIG. Literary History of the United States, Bibliography Supplement II. New York: Macmillan Co., pp. 106-107.
[32 items dealing with Anderson--letters, editions, biographies, bibliographies, criticism]

32 STERN, JEROME H. "Letters Between Friends." Tallahassee Democrat (10 December), E, p. 16.
Sherwood Anderson / Gertrude Stein "neither reveals any secrets nor changes our estimation of its subjects. But it is a graceful, useful, and above all charmingly readable volume, and we never can have too many of those."

33 STEWART, MAAJA. "Scepticism and Belief in Chekhov and Anderson." Studies in Short Fiction, 9 (Winter), 29-40.
Anderson and Chekhov share the common themes of "isolation, inarticulateness, and ineffectiveness of action" of the individual unhelped by society; beliefs of individuals contradict "social codifications and assertions of value."

34 TSUTSUMI, KOJI. "The Conflict between Man and Machine in Perhaps Women, I." Heron, 6 (March), 49-64.
[Abridged Japanese paraphrasings of parts of Perhaps Women] [Takashi Kodaira]

35 WALDHORN, ARTHUR. A Reader's Guide to Ernest Hemingway. New York: Farrar, Straus and Giroux, pp. 9-10, 12, 31, 43-44, 85-88, 153-54, 214, 232.
Hemingway owes Anderson introductions to Chicago writers, Stein, and Anderson's publisher, as well as the stylistic debt of simple diction and colloquial speech. The Torrents of Spring parodies Anderson's primitivism, "stiff-backed intellectuals," and ritualized sex.

36 WESCOTT, GLENWAY. "Memories and Opinions." Prose, No. 5 (1972), pp. 197-98.
When Stein and Anderson discussed Hemingway as cowardly, Hemingway avenged himself on Stein in Green Hills of Africa and For Whom the Bell Tolls.

1973 A BOOKS

1 KLEIN, MARIE ANNETTE. "The Stalled Traveller: A New Approach to the Full-Length Works of Sherwood Anderson." Dissertation, University of Illinois, 195 pp.

Anderson's fiction reveals that he had a child's sensibilities and a child's psychological needs. For example, Anderson had to fight always to overcome unacceptable mother and father memories or images. He never resolved conflict with the "insanity" of American culture and attempted psychic rebirth as primitive artist. He romantically worshipped youth, but his obsessions ultimately destroyed man and work.

2 SMITH, PHILIP ALAN. "Dark Laughter: A Prose Poem." Master's thesis, Adelphi University, 30 pp.

Because _Dark Laughter_ thematically and stylistically resembles Anderson's published poetry, it is possible to rewrite as poetry the lyrical passages upon which Anderson lavished most attention.

1973 B SHORTER WRITINGS

1 ANDERSON, DAVID D. "The Real World of Sherwood Anderson." _Ohioana_, 16 (Autumn), 120-22.

Republication of Anderson's non-fiction from the 1930's proves the error of critics who assumed that Anderson turned to non-fiction because his fiction failed.

2 ANON. "Anderson, Sherwood." _New Standard Encyclopedia_, 1. Chicago: Standard Educational Corporation, 408-409.

In _Winesburg, Ohio_ Anderson describes frustrations of townspeople "in simple, forthright language with a touch of lyricism." Anderson proposed primitivism against industrialism.

3 ANON. Review of _The Road to Winesburg_. _Choice_, 9 (January), 1450.

The Road to Winesburg is "far from the definitive biography of Anderson we have long awaited, but it should at least supply an abundance of raw material for that book when it is eventually written."

4 ANON. "Sherwood Anderson / Gertrude Stein." _New York Times Book Review_ (8 April), p. 30.

"The value of this small sheaf of letters and essays" published in _Sherwood Anderson / Gertrude Stein_ "lies in

1973

(ANON)
the revelation of how mutual confidence helped to link the Revolution of the Word with a vision of the Great American novel."

5 CASH, EARL A. Review of _Sherwood Anderson / Gertrude Stein_. _Best Sellers_, 32 (15 March), 564-65.
The result of _Sherwood Anderson / Gertrude Stein_ is "a perspective on the two literary figures which, because of its honesty, intimacy, humor, and sometimes passion, no secondary criticism could hope to give."

6 COWLEY, MALCOLM. _A Second Flowering: Works and Days of the Lost Generation_. New York: Viking Press, pp. 49, 50, 67, 114, 132, 254.
Whereas the Anderson character wants to know _why_, the Hemingway character wants to know _how_.

7 DAVIDSON, MARSHALL B. et al. _The American Heritage History of the Writer's America_. New York: American Heritage Publishing Co., pp. 276, 283, 298, 323-24, 325, 329, 332, 333, 334, 336.
By the time of the World War, Anderson was writing of the spread of corruption from cities into villages. First novelist to treat the subconscious (especially sex) well, Anderson contributed psychology to American fiction.

8 DENISOVA, T. N. _Pro Romantickize U Realizni_. Kiev, pp. 3-4.
[Seen but not translated]

9 DICKERSON, MARY JANE. "Sherwood Anderson and Jean Toomer: A Literary Relationship." _Studies in American Fiction_, 1 (Autumn), 163-65.
Winesburg, Ohio and _Cane_ are similar in structure, theme, narrator-observer, exphasis on inner life, and rural setting. Perhaps _Cane_ influenced Anderson's theme in _Dark Laughter_.

10 DINGMAN, LARRY. _Bibliography of Limited and Signed Editions in Literature, Twentieth Century American Authors_. Stillwater, MN: James Cummings, pp. 7-8.
[Descriptions of 9 items by Anderson]

11 DOS PASSOS, JOHN. _The Fourteenth Chronicle: Letters and Diaries of John Dos Passos_. Boston: Gambit, pp. 339, 345, 382, 391-92, 515-16, 521, 636.
Dos Passos tried to keep Hemingway from publishing _The Torrents of Spring_. In 1922 Dos Passos wrote Anderson to

recall their 1921 meeting in Paris; he wrote Wilson in 1929, however, that Anderson had "softening of the brain"; in 1965 he recalled that Anderson might have introduced him to Faulkner in 1924.

12 DuBOIS, W. E. B. The Correspondence of W. E. B. DuBois, Volume I: Selections, 1877-1934. Edited by Herbert Aptheker. Amherst: University of Massachusetts Press, 342.

In 1926 Anderson stated that Negroes should create art without thinking of being Negro and that artists of both races are probably equally badly treated.

13 FINKEL, JAN M. "Techniques of Portraying the Grotesque Character in Selected Writings of Nathaniel Hawthorne, Sherwood Anderson, and Joseph Heller." Dissertation, Indiana University, 185 pp.

Anderson's grotesque characters do not cope with life or probe life's meanings. Instead they suffer anomie at society's bid, although they remain more sweet than horrible. Industrialism and the business world cause Anderson's grotesques to occur.

14 FRANK, WALDO. Memoirs of Waldo Frank. Edited by Alan Tractenberg. Introduction by Lewis Mumford. Amherst: University of Massachusetts Press, pp. viii, xvi, xix, 62, 86-87, 91, 99-100, 108, 146, 193, 239, 250.

Frank always felt sorry that Anderson so much admired New York intellectuals, for the Midwestern writer early had a narrative gift later spoiled by sentimental self-indulgence.

15 GADO, FRANK, ed. First Person: Conversations on Writers & Writing. Schenectady: Union College Press, pp. ix, xiv, 3-4, 11, 48.

Glenway Wescott knew and admired Anderson but could not equal Anderson in writing the vernacular.

16 GOLD, ROBERT S. "S. Anderson." McGraw-Hill Encyclopedia of World Biography, 1. New York: McGraw-Hill, 177-78.

Anderson's work is "graced by a psychological complexity absent from earlier American fiction. His stories stress character and mood, and his style is laconic and colloquial."

17 HAYASHI, SHIGEO. "On the Themes of Poor White." Studies in Foreign Literatures [Research Institute of the Cultural Sciences, Ritsumeikan University], 26 (March), 45-62.

1973

(HAYASHI, SHIGEO)
The theme of Poor White is the industrial history of a town, as well as the self-realization of the hero and the relationship of hero and heroine. To Anderson the secondary themes may have seemed unresolved at the end of his novel; yet the symbols of brightly colored stones would seem to make the novel complete. [Takashi Kodaira]

18 INOUE, HIROTSUGU. "Sherwood Anderson's Style." Shigaku Kenshu, 60 (September), 48-61.
Analysis of Anderson's style according to functional grammar shows that the style is emotional and subjective, compared with that of Hemingway. Winesburg, Ohio is the world of artistic truth conjured by the author's active fancy.

19 JOHNSON, CHRISTIANE. "Langage et Point de Vue dans la Nouvelle de Sherwood Anderson: 'The Strength of God.'" Études Anglaises, 26 (April-June), 187-94.
In "The Strength of God" Anderson uses each word deliberately to indicate states of mind of the central character, for this story could not be told in first-person style.

20 KNOEPFLE, JOHN. "Crossing the Midwest." Regional Perspectives: An Examination of America's Literary History. Edited by John Gordon Burke. Chicago: American Library Association, pp. 113-14, 121.
The setting based on Anderson's boyhood town of Clyde, Ohio, Winesburg, Ohio broke from traditional romantic plots; motivated toward "beauty, truth, and goodness," Anderson's characters live in "a turmoil of erotic energy and rural loneliness."

21 L., M. "Anderson, Sherwood." Webster's New World Companion to English and American Literature. New York: World Publishing Co., pp. 12-13.
Winesburg, Ohio presents eccentric characters obsessed by a "truth"; Poor White deals with social fragmentation after industrialization.

22 LANDOR, M. "M. Gor'kij o Šervude Andersone." Voprosy literatury, 17 (1973), 176-88.
Gorky's interest in Anderson was unfailing and multi-faceted. [James F. Cradler]

23 LEIGHTON, BETTY. "A Sincere, Superficial Friendship." Winston-Salem Journal and Sentinel (25 February), D., p. 4.

Sherwood Anderson / Gertrude Stein reveals much of Anderson but little of Stein. In fact, the fabled relationship is now shown to be a mutual-admiration society.

24 MANN, ELIZABETH L. "Very Different People, But Good Friends." Greensboro Daily News (4 February).
Sherwood Anderson / Gertrude Stein is entertaining and informative, as the reader can trace the development of the two writers' friendship.

25 PEARSALL, ROBERT BRAINERD. The Life and Writings of Ernest Hemingway. Amsterdam: Rodopi NV, pp. 9, 34, 46, 47, 51, 60, 70, 72, 83, 85-86.
By publishing The Torrents of Spring and The Sun Also Rises, Hemingway broke off friendship with Anderson and Stein, as well as with his new, younger crowd of Parisian admirers and friends.

26 P.[HELP]S, W.[ILLIAM] L. "Anderson, Sherwood." Encyclopaedia Britannica, 1. Chicago: Encyclopaedia Britannica, 894.
His best work the stories in Winesburg, Ohio, The Triumph of the Egg, and Death in the Woods, Anderson wrote of Midwestern townspeople "warped into inarticulate grotesques by isolation and frustration of love and creativity."

27 POWNALL, DAVID E. "Anderson, Sherwood." Articles on Twentieth Century Literature: An Annotated Bibliography, 1954 to 1970, 1. New York: Kraus-Thompson Organization, 55-67.
[58 Annotated entries]

28 SAKUMA, YOSHIKAZU. "S. Anderson and J. D. Salinger, II: On Initiation and Innocence." Teoria [Hosei Daigaku Daigakuin Eiyukai], 5 (November), 1-12.
The initiation of Anderson's hero in Winesburg, Ohio is from what Hassan would call "the Utopian motive"; that of Salinger's hero in The Catcher in the Rye is from "the Edenic motive." Anderson seems Western; Salinger, Eastern. [Takashi Kodaira]

29 SAMSELL, R. L. "Paris Days with Ralph Church." Fitzgerald / Hemingway Annual 1972. Edited by Matthew J. Bruccoli and C. E. Frazer Clark, Jr. Washington, DC: Microcard Editions, pp. 145-46.
Rediscovery and publication of Church's manuscript memoir of Anderson's 1926 visit to Paris reconstructs Anderson's conversation soon after the appearance of The Torrents of Spring.

1973

30 SMITH, ANNELIESE H. "Part of the Problem: Student Responses to Sherwood Anderson's 'I Want to Know Why?'" Negro American Literature Forum, 7 (Spring), 28-31.
Smith's students failed to recognize Anderson's feminization (and, hence, denigration) of Negroes in "I Want to Know Why."

31 SOKOLOFF, ALICE HUNT. Hadley: The First Mrs. Hemingway. New York: Dodd, Mead and Co., pp. 40-41, 42, 44, 49, 83.
Hadley Hemingway disagreed with Anderson's comparison of Ernest's work to Kipling's; Anderson advised the couple to move to Paris in 1921 and wrote introductory letters to Pound, Beach, Stein, and Galantière. In Paris they stayed at the hotel Anderson had recommended and finally used his introductions. Pauline Pfeiffer encouraged Ernest to publish The Torrents of Spring against Hadley's advice.

32 TANSELLE, G. THOMAS. Review of The Road to Winesburg. American Literature, 45 (March), 126-28.
In The Road to Winesburg William A. Sutton has made available the materials for Anderson's biography through 1919; but he has not composed a straightforward biography of the assembled (and valuable) materials.

33 TOKLAS, ALICE B. Staying on Alone: Letters of Alice B. Toklas. Edited by Edward Burns. Introduction by Gilbert A. Harrison. New York: Liveright Publishing Corporation, pp. 15, 62, 95, 96, 364, 382.
Anderson's letters to Stein were "very sweet not long and not literary." Anderson introduced Ralph Church to Stein, and Lloyd Lewis asked for Anderson's letters for The Newberry Library. Stein told Hemingway that he should support his early writing by "running a laundry."

34 TSUTSUMI, KOJI. "The Conflict Between Man and Machine in Perhaps Women, II." Heron, 7 (February), 57-64.
[Further abridged paraphrases of Perhaps Women]

35 VOSS, ARTHUR. The American Short Story: A Critical Survey. Norman: University of Oklahoma Press, pp. 23, 86, 183-98, 209, 220, 221, 243, 267, 275, 279, 284, 288, 316.
In Winesburg, Ohio Anderson attempted to let subject and tone impose form; in form, lyricism, innovation, and "personality," Anderson helped lead American fiction away from the "plot" story.

36 WALKER, WARREN S., ed. Twentieth-Century Short Story Explication: Supplement II to Second Edition, 1970-1972. Hamden [CT]: Shoe String Press, pp. 3-4.

[Criticism of 14 Anderson stories]

1974 A BOOKS

1 McNEELY, DARRELL W. "Jean Toomer's Cane and Sherwood Anderson's Winesburg, Ohio: A Black Reaction to the Literary Conventions of the Twenties." Dissertation, University of Nebraska, 148 pp.

As Winesburg, Ohio provided a new style and form for "mainstream" writers of the 1920's, so Cane served for Black writers of the Harlem Renaissance. Considering Winesburg, Ohio as touchstone, the creation, composition, and reception of Cane is demonstrated through innovation, experimentation, and rebellion against tradition.

2 MORRIS, ANN R. Winesburg, Ohio: Notes. Lincoln, NB: Cliffs Notes, 61 pp.

[Biography, character descriptions, commentaries, setting, ideas of initiation, style, study questions, bibliography--students' guide]

3 RIDEOUT, WALTER B., ed. Sherwood Anderson: A Collection of Critical Essays. Englewood Cliffs, NJ: Prentice-Hall, 177 pp.

Reprint of 1916.B9; 1922.B35; 1925.B40, B59; 1928.B54; 1950.B16; 1951.A1, B30; 1953.B12; 1954.B11; 1959.B21; 1960.B6, B10; 1964.A1; 1969.B43.

4 SCHORR, MARK. "Sherwood Anderson's Imagination: History and Fiction." Dissertation, Harvard University, 241 pp.

"Anderson's fiction is history in the sense that it continually portrays the settings, feelings, and forms of behavior that are characteristic of a particular form of historical reality, and represents them in an idiom that is faithful to their natures." In using fiction as history Anderson influenced such authors as Wright Morris, Philip Roth, Walker Percy, and Evan Connell.

5 THISSEN, JOHN HUGHES. "Sherwood Anderson and Painting." Dissertation, Northwestern University, 189 pp.

Anderson responded to painting esthetically and let it influence his work. Appreciation of painting gave Anderson artistic friends. romantic escape, $700--all biographical;

(THISSEN, JOHN HUGHES)
understanding of artistic minds, moments, colors, self-understanding, pleasure--all psychological; self-reliance, subject-matter, and critical analogy--literary.

1974 B SHORTER WRITINGS

1 ANON. "Anderson, Sherwood." Encyclopedia Americana: International Edition, 1. New York: Americana Corporation, 809-10.
With Winesburg, Ohio Anderson gave his dominant idea--"the conflict between the instinctive forces of human nature and the inhibiting effects of a narrowly conventional industrial society."

2 ANON. "Anderson, Sherwood." Encyclopaedia Britannica, Micropaedia, 2. Chicago: Encyclopaedia Britannica, 355.
Anderson developed his prose style from ordinary speech and from the example of Stein. Going beyond the genteel tradition in American writing, Anderson pushed naturalism into psychological techniques in stories of common people.

3 ANON. "Anderson, Sherwood." Webster's American Biographies. Springfield, MA: G. & C. Merriam, p. 29.
Winesburg, Ohio, Poor White, and The Triumph of the Egg constitute Anderson's best work; his theme is constraining life in small towns.

4 BALDANZA, FRANK. "Northern Gothic." Southern Review, 10 (July), 566-82.
James Purdy and Anderson are both Ohio writers but with differences. Purdy is a confident writer; Anderson is confused. Purdy writes allegories; Anderson writes plotless sketches. Purdy heightens language; Anderson transcribes it. Purdy uses broad settings; Anderson uses places. Purdy gives detail; Anderson gives social history.

5 BLAIR, WALTER, THEODORE HORNBERGER, JAMES E. MILLER, JR., and RANDALL STEWART. American Literature: A Brief History. Glenview, IL: Scott, Foresman and Co., pp. 203, 234, 261, 284, 292, 301, 310.
Anderson's contributions to literature are in his unconventional, intense stories; Winesburg, Ohio may be the first Freudian literature in America, for all of the characters suffer from sexual repression.

6 BLOTNER, JOSEPH. Faulkner: A Biography. New York: Random House, pp. 164, 319, 349, 366-71, 374, 388-89, 391-94, 396, 400-406, 408-18, 420-21, 423, 425, 430-31, 450, 478, 488, 496-502, 505, 507, 516-17, 521, 522, 524, 527, 534-36, 600, 666, 688, 694, 706, 707, 709-11, 713, 714, 938, 974-75, 980, 1016, 1056, 1230-31, 1257, 1268, 1313, 1342, 1351, 1357, 1414, 1420, 1451, 1594; "Notes," pp. 58-59, 62, 63, 68, 71, 76, 95, 155, 175, 183.

Anderson gave generous sympathy, time, and advice to Faulkner in New Orleans in 1924; "A Meeting South" developed from one of their adventures. In 1925 Faulkner and Anderson discussed writing and made up plots together for fun. By background, temperament, friends, and age, Anderson and Faulkner differed enough not to feel close from 1926 on.

7 BLUE, ADRIANNE. "Critical Tools: Adrianne Blue on Sherwood Anderson / Gertrude Stein. Fiction International, 2 (March), 155-56.

Sherwood Anderson / Gertrude Stein shows Anderson as the greater egoist of the two writers. Stein is the intelligent and accepting writer, and she shows "a more steadfast regard for Anderson."

8 DONAGHEV, MEG. "Taxco: The Silver City." Mexico City News Vistas (8 December), pp. 3-4.

Elizabeth Prall liked "penniless Sherwood Anderson," and their divorce resulted from his not being able to meet her standards.

9 GUNN, DREWEY WAYNE. American and British Writers in Mexico, 1556-1973. Austin: University of Texas Press, pp. 123, 181-82.

Anderson was familiar with Lawrence's works about Mexico; and Anderson visited Acapulco in February and March, 1938.

10 HAAS, RUDOLF. Amerikanische Literaturgeschichte, 2. Heidelberg: Quelle & Meyer, 209, 221, 298, 305.

Anderson uses the initiation theme and the idea of anomie in his fiction. His characters are picaresque and must find assimilation. In Winesburg, Ohio all of the urban neuroses are located in a small town.

11 HICKS, GRANVILLE. Granville Hicks in The New Masses. Edited by Jack Alan Robbins. Port Washington, NY: Kennikat Press, pp. xi, 44.

Although Anderson had "flashes of insight," his Many Marriages takes "the confused psycho-analytical approach."

1974

12 KANAZAWA, YUTAKA. "On Dark Laughter." English Literature [Waseda University English Literary Society], 40 (March), 96-105.

Anderson's method in Winesburg, Ohio is transitional, for he cannot write Dark Laughter in the short-story form. With new method, Dark Laughter fails because Anderson cannot use Stein and Joyce; his method continues to seek he knew not what. [Takashi Kodaira]

13 KONOMURA, KIYOAKI. "Sex in Sherwood Anderson's Beyond Desire." General Education Review, College of Agriculture and Veterinary Medicine, Nihon University, 9 (March), 69-76.

Considering Beyond Desire from the standpoint of the handling of sex, Anderson presents the hero as unwilling to feel equal to the heroine. Sex in this novel is passive, violent, homosexual, and frustrated--and important to understanding Anderson's works. [Takashi Kodaira]

14 MELLOW, JAMES R. Charmed Circle: Gertrude Stein & Company. New York: Praeger, pp. 249, 257-58, 259-61, 262, 264, 270, 271-73, 277-78, 301, 316, 336, 349, 352, 355, 362, 400, 401, 403, 405.

Stein had great joy at Anderson's praise and understanding when they met in 1921; she soon invited him to introduce Geography and Plays. Stein sided with Anderson when Hemingway turned against them ungratefully in 1926. Anderson's second visit in 1926 gave them both joy.

15 MILLER, WILLIAM V. "Earth Mothers, Succubi, and Other Ectoplasmic Spirits: The Women in Sherwood Anderson's Short Stories." Midamerica I. Edited by David D. Anderson. East Lansing: Midwestern Press, pp. 64-81.

Most influenced by five women--his mother and four wives--Anderson portrayed mother-figures as strong, suffering martyrs and his wife-figures as mother-wives. Women became fictional managers, home-defenders, supporters of males, and aspiring thinkers.

16 _____. "In Defense of Mountaineers: Sherwood Anderson's Hill Stories." Ball State University Forum, 15 (Spring), 51-58.

Thirteen Anderson stories written after 1926 and set in the Eastern mountains show the author's continued ability to write well. In these stories Anderson wanted to write realistically about hill people and to show how industrialism affected their lives.

17 OHARA, HIROTADA. "Anderson and 'Understanding': A Comparative Study of His Three Stories about a Farm Woman's Death in the Woods." Journal of Human and Cultural Sciences [Society

for the Human and Cultural Sciences in Musashi University] (March), pp. 75-103.

Comparing the chapter in Tar with "Death in the Woods" shows that Anderson's progress can be traced from the admiration and longing for an urban success to the understanding and sympathy for moral failure through them. Against the Progressive movement after World War I, Anderson earnestly continued to seek truth and "understanding." [Takashi Kodaira]

18 ONO, MICHIO. "On Winesburg, Ohio: The Escape Motif." Bulletin of Aichi Shukutoku Junior College, 13 (March), 1-16.

Escape-oriented people, the grotesques in Winesburg, Ohio expect the young hero to escape for them. [Tokashi Kodaira]

19 PETERSON, RICHARD. "The Pastures of Heaven." A Study Guide to Steinbeck: A Handbook to His Major Works. Metuchen, NJ: Scarecrow Press, pp. 88, 89, 90, 104.

Steinbeck's The Pastures of Heaven most closely resembles Winesburg, Ohio, characters being united by external contact with others. Anderson uses frustrated hopes to give action; Steinbeck uses present hopes.

20 REED, P. LARUS. "The Integrated Short-Story Collection: Studies of a Form of Nineteenth- and Twentieth-Century Fiction." Dissertation, Indiana University, 313 pp.

Winesburg, Ohio achieves unity through the maturing of the central character, who is either in or touched by the related stories. Horses and Men, The Triumph of the Egg, and Death in the Woods approach unity through the artist-teller's intimate involvement and through the ordering of stories.

21 RIDEOUT, WALTER B. "Sherwood Anderson." Sixteen Modern American Authors: A Survey of Research and Criticism. Edited by Jackson R. Bryer. Durham: Duke University Press, pp. 3-28.

[Discursive bibliography of editions, manuscripts, letters, biographies, criticism, and bibliographies]

22 ROUGÉ, ROBERT. L'Inquiétude Religieuse dans le Roman Américain Moderne. Paris: Librairie C. Klincksieck, pp. 14, 58, 90, 199, 203, 212, 213, 217, 219, 247, 251-76, 302, 311, 329, 331, 421.

Anderson's work demonstrates the extension of Transcendentalism. He discovered the philosophy of power and the truth of the imagination. Yet he recognized the contradictions of the American dream of plenty and innocence,

1974

(ROUGE, ROBERT)
making ambiguity fundamental to his writings. Where love is both present and absent, Anderson has found inspiration for poetic, imaginative work. The artist's role is to give through pity, love, and imagination the feeling of communion and solitude and suffering.

23 SAKUMA, YOSHIKAZU. "On _The Triumph of the Egg_: Its World and Style." _Eibungakushi_ [Hosei Daigaku Eibungakukai], 16 (January), 57-72.
Stories in _The Triumph of the Egg_ concern fear or unease from loneliness under the pressure of convention or industry. Instinct will rule both grotesques aware of their condition and those aware of grotesquerie. [Takashi Kodaira]

24 SCHEICK, WILLIAM J. "Compulsion toward Repetition: Sherwood Anderson's 'Death in the Woods.'" _Studies in Short Fiction_, 11 (Spring), 141-46.
The narrator-boy of "Death in the Woods" psychologically dies and is reborn (matures), remaining inconclusive about the essential meaning of his experience; the boy fears becoming a "feeder," a user of women.

25 SCHEVILL, JAMES. "Anderson, Sherwood." _Collier's Encyclopedia_, 2. New York: Macmillan Educational Corporation, 184.
Winesburg, Ohio is unified by the author's perspective on the village and by the idea of grotesque characters, people "defeated by false dreams." In his stories Anderson demonstrated direct observation and use of mood and fragmented action.

26 SOMERS, PAUL P., JR. "Anderson's Twisted Apples and Hemingway's Crips." _Midamerica I_. Edited by David D. Anderson. East Lansing: Midwestern Press, pp. 82-97.
In several _Winesburg, Ohio_ stories and in such Hemingway stories as "Soldier's Home," initiation is painful; and the resulting characters are "grotesque" or "crips" (cripples).

27 _____. "The Mark of Sherwood Anderson on Hemingway: A Look at the Texts." _South Atlantic Quarterly_, 73 (Autumn), 487-503.
Using Anderson's example of colloquial understatement, Hemingway learned how to express emotion as simply as possible.

28 TURNER, DARWIN T. "An Intersection of Paths: Correspondence Between Jean Toomer and Sherwood Anderson." College Language Association Journal, 17 (June), 455-67.
When Anderson wrote complimenting Toomer in 1922, the latter responded with great praise for Winesburg, Ohio. Toomer advised Anderson that the white author had created unreal Negro characters, and he moved on to write of neurotic whites.

29 WOODRESS, JAMES. "Sherwood Anderson." American Fiction, 1900-1950: A Guide to Information Sources. Detroit: Gale Research Co., pp. 37-41.
[Bibliography of bibliographies, edition, reprints, biographies, and criticism]

1975 A BOOKS - NONE

1975 B SHORTER WRITINGS

1 ALSEN, EBERHARD. "The Futile Pursuit of Truth in Twain's 'What is Man?' and Anderson's 'The Book of the Grotesque,'" Mark Twain Journal, 17 (Winter 1974-75), 12-14.
The "old man" or "writer" represents Anderson in "The Book of the Grotesque" and Twain's "What is Man?" Anderson may have considered Twain "grotesque" for holding the "truth" of a mechanistic world-view.

2 ANDERSON, DAVID D. Review of The "Writer's Book." Winesburg Eagle, 1 (November), 3.
Martha Curry's edition of Anderson's manuscript "Writer's Book" makes available many of the author's late 1930's ideas on creativity.

3 _____. "The Uncritical Critics: American Realists and the Lincoln Myth." Midamerica II. Edited by David D. Anderson. East Lansing: Midwestern Press, pp. 17-23.
In Poor White Anderson used elements of Abraham Lincoln in the central character; both work toward human freedom, one from anti-slavery, the other from pro-industrialism. Anderson never completed his planned book on Lincoln.

4 DENT, GENE H. "Sherwood Anderson / A Story Teller's Town: The Filming of a Documentary." Midwestern Miscellany III. Edited by Paul J. Ferlazzo and Nancy H. Pogel. East Lansing: Midwestern Press, pp. 50-53.
Preparatory to filming Clyde, Ohio, for documentary purposes, Dent found that in Winesburg, Ohio Anderson had used the area's geography very closely.

1975

5 EDEN, WALTER ANTHONY. "A Critical Approach to Autobiography: Technique and Themes in Sherwood Anderson, Benedetto Croce, Jean-Paul Sartre, and Richard Wright." Dissertation, New York University, 231 pp.

In A Story Teller's Story Anderson tries to determine his identity as an American. He rebels against traditions of materialism, convention, and tradition; and he learns from a fictional judge and Stein love of people and language. He equates artistic integrity with moral character and defines himself as an artist in a difficult age; he "confesses" his inner, buried self.

6 FARRELL, JAMES T. "The 1920's in American Life and Literature." Fitzgerald / Hemingway Annual 1974. Edited by Matthew J. Bruccoli and C. E. Frazer Clark, Jr. Englewood, CO: Microcard Editions Books, pp. 120, 122, 124, 125, 126.

Winesburg, Ohio is probably based on Camden, Ohio, Anderson's birthplace, and is filled with grotesque characters who do not fit society and who have a creative feeling to express or repress. Anderson discusses the small town with "remembered humanity."

7 FORD, HUGH. Published in Paris: American and British Writers, Printers, and Publishers in Paris, 1920-1939. Foreword by Janet Flanner. New York: Macmillan Co., pp. 12-13, 55, 62-63, 75, 108, 221.

As Ulysses had not yet appeared, Beach was happy to introduce Anderson to Stein in 1921. McAlmon's Village was compared to Anderson's treatment of the Midwest. Anderson wrote the catalog copy for Hemingway's In Our Time.

8 FREEDMAN, RICHARD. The Novel. New York: Newsweek Books, pp. 106-107.

Winesburg, Ohio is a story collection and a "coherent novel" written in prose as "limpid and colloquial as Willa Cather's"; his later works are sentimental failures.

9 HAMAMOTO, TAKEO. "Anderson's Understanding of Reality." American Literature [Tokyo Chapter of the American Literature Society of Japan], 30 (Spring), 1-6.

The business of the artist is to make things stay still, and through examining life when still Anderson created method for understanding reality. He is gifted with insight and tenderness enough to write of the discrepancy between humans and society, but he does not discuss what reality is; perhaps he cannot express it in words. [Takashi Kodaira]

10 HOBHOUSE, JANET. Everybody Who Was Anybody: A Biography of Gertrude Stein. New York: G. P. Putnam's Sons, pp. 114, 116, 121, 122, 128-30, 139-40, 157, 167, 187, 190, 217.

Anderson and Stein were friends after Sylvia Beach introduced them in Paris in 1921, and Anderson soon introduced Geography and Plays. Stein sided with Anderson in the Hemingway quarrel and entertained him again in 1927. They next met in Minnesota in 1934 and later that year in New Orleans.

11 KISNER, SISTER MADELEINE. "Color in the Worlds and Works of Poe, Hawthorne, Crane, Anderson, and Welty." Dissertation, University of Michigan, 183 pp.

Color appears in Winesburg, Ohio only in moments of intense feeling, the basic tone being drab: color equals emotion. Anderson tried to record color objectively and impressionistically.

12 LIGHT, MARTIN. The Quixotic Vision of Sinclair Lewis. West Lafayette: Purdue University Press, pp. 14, 24, 47.

Lewis may have read some of Anderson's work before writing Main Street; Anderson never understood Lewis' bitterness toward small towns. Perhaps the school teacher in Main Street is modeled on some of Anderson's characters.

13 LUEDTKE, LUTHER S. "Sherwood Anderson, Thomas Hardy, and 'Tandy.'" Modern Fiction Studies, 20 (Winter 1974-75), 531-40.

"Tandy" is the work by Anderson that most clearly reflects Hardy's influence, for the mysterious stranger speaks philosophy similar to that of the hero in Jude the Obscure.

14 MIYAMOTO, YOKICHI. "A New Craft of Fiction in 'Hands.'" American Literature and Language. Edited by the Society for Essays Presented to Professor Masaji Onoe in Honor of His Sixtieth Birthday. Tokyo: Nanundo, pp. 159-65.

Anderson rebelled against the plot story, which in his day was optimistic and moralistic. Anderson's method of story construction is to join scenes together out of chronological order and to interchange the past and the present, using a narrator. [Takashi Kodaira]

15 NAKAMURA, KAZUO. "On Carson McCullers, I: The Heart Is a Lonely Hunter and Winesburg, Ohio." American Literature [Tokyo Chapter of the American Literature Society of Japan], 30 (Spring), 41-50.

The Heart Is a Lonely Hunter and Winesburg, Ohio are alike in treatment of loneliness, but McCullers tries to

1975

(NAKAMURA, KAZUO)
express her thought allegorically, while Anderson tries to express the lonely aspect of life through psychological realism. [Takashi Kodaira]

16 NAKANO, KEIJI. "Sherwood Anderson's Cult of Womanhood." Hiyoshi Kiyo [Keiogijuku Daigaku Kogakubu], 16 (March), 34-40.

Anderson's thought about men and women in Perhaps Women had already been expressed in Winesburg, Ohio; his view of womanhood is deeply connected with his view of Nature, as in "The Untold Lie." [Takashi Kodaira]

17 OHARA, HIROTADA. "The Effect of Modern Paintings on Sherwood Anderson's Novels." American Literature [Tokyo Chapter of the American Literature Society of Japan], 30 (Spring), 6-16.

Anderson experimented in words and forms, and modern paintings made him experiment on "new and strange combinations of words" before Stein influenced him. Anderson's form is impressionistic and deeply connected with modern paintings. [Takashi Kodaira]

18 OHASHI, KICHINOSUKE. "Sherwood Anderson and Three Japanese." Rising Generation (July), 12-13.

Nine letters written by three Japanese to Anderson and one letter from Anderson are in The Newberry Library. Correspondence with Shinkichi Takahashi concerned Takahashi's reactions to The Triumph of the Egg, which struck the reader so deeply with its touch of Chekhov that he wrote Anderson, who mailed back a "little book." [Takashi Kodaira]

19 _____. "Sherwood Anderson and Three Japanese, 2." Rising Generation (August), pp. 7-8.

Takahashi thanked Anderson for the gift book on October 4, 1925, and was eager to translate the work into Japanese. Kinetaro Yoshida first wrote to Anderson on June 20, 1924, to have permission to translate some stories from The Triumph of the Egg and Horses and Men. On September 11, 1924, he regrets that the Japanese publisher of The Triumph of the Egg could not pay royalties to Anderson. [Takashi Kodaira]

20 _____. "Sherwood Anderson and Three Japanese, 3." Rising Generation (September), 21-22.

Given permission to translate Anderson into Japanese without paying royalties, Yoshida sends Anderson two copies of The Triumph of the Egg. [Takashi Kodaira]

21 _____. "Sherwood Anderson and Three Japanese, 4." Rising Generation (October), pp. 12-14.
On October 5, 1927, Yoshida wrote Anderson that he and Takagaki are doing all possible to further Anderson's Japanese reputation. He asks Anderson for a contribution and receives "The Future of Japanese and American Writing"--about the curse of standardization that results from capitalism and the need to search for truth in life. [Takashi Kodaira]

22 _____. "Sherwood Anderson and Three Japanese, 5." Rising Generation (November), pp. 25-27.
[Summaries of Anderson's article in 1975.B21; and references to 1934.B28] [Takashi Kodaira]

23 _____. "Sherwood Anderson and Three Japanese, 6." Rising Generation (December), pp. 11-13.
Because Anderson was by the late 1920's considered socialistic, Winesburg, Ohio was translated into Japanese and critics debated whether he was or was not socialistic. [Takashi Kodaira]

24 OMOTO, MITATE. "On Perhaps Women: Anderson's Mechanical View." Kagawa Kyoiku Gakubu Kenkyu Hokoku, Ichibu, 38 (March), 21-31.
More than forty years have passed since Anderson published Perhaps Women, but his view of technology is as effective now as then. [Takashi Kodaira]

25 OTSU, EIICHIRO. "Grotesqueness in Winesburg, Ohio." American Literature and Language. Edited by The Society for Essays Presented to Professor Masaji Onoe in Honor of His Sixtieth Birthday. Tokyo: Nanundo, pp. 150-58.
People become grotesque when their "integrity" collapses; it is characteristic of the modern novel that novelists began to write of the grotesque, and Winesburg, Ohio marked this turning point in the history of the American novel. Anderson was aware that his own life had made him grotesque; expression might regain his "integrity." [Takashi Kodaira]

26 SHIMURA, MASAO. "Private Notes on Anderson." American Literature [Tokyo Chapter of the American Literature Society of Japan], 30 (Spring), 17-24.
While the influence of Joyce on Winesburg, Ohio is in the use of epiphanies, the influence of Emerson is present, also. These stories are of the best moments of life that reveal God. Further interest lies in the possible

1975

(SHIMURA, MASAO)
relationship between Rainer Maria Rilke and Anderson, Emerson being geographically between the two writers. [Takashi Kodaira]

27 SMOLLER, SANFORD R. _Adrift Among Geniuses: Robert McAlmon, Writer and Publisher of the Twenties_. University Park: Pennsylvania State University Press, pp. 25, 91, 102-103, 138, 142-43, 173, 243-44.
Anderson aided Carnevali after his breakdown in Chicago, but McAlmon probably did not meet Anderson there. McAlmon disliked Hemingway's stories derived from Anderson's example, and Stein never ranked McAlmon as high as she did Anderson. Michaud and Herron compared _Village_ to _Winesburg, Ohio_.

28 STRONKS, JAMES. Review of _Sherwood Anderson / Gertrude Stein_. _Journal of the Illinois State Historical Society_, 65 (June), 296-97.
Sherwood Anderson / Gertrude Stein shows the authors' friendship to have been sincere if not worthy of legend.

29 SUTTON, WILLIAM A. "New Directions for Anderson Scholarship." _Winesburg Eagle_, 1 (November), 4.
The Sherwood Anderson Society should coordinate research, for even the Anderson letters provide ever-expanding opportunities.

30 [TAYLOR, WELFORD D.] "Centennial Events." _Winesburg Eagle_, 1 (November), 1-2.
The Sherwood Anderson Centennial Year of 1976 will be celebrated through a conference, special issues of journals, and publication of a volume of original essays.

31 [_____.] "An Editorial Bow." _Winesburg Eagle_, 1 (November), 1.
Publication of _The Winesburg Eagle_ by The Sherwood Anderson Society is "to help further Anderson scholarship and to broaden interest in the man and his work" and "to evoke something of the spirit of the man."

32 [_____.] "From the Membership." _Winesburg Eagle_, 1 (November), 2-3.
Anderson's centennial year will see publication of a selected bibliography, a volume of Anderson correspondence, and a monograph on "Seeds."

1975

33 UMPHLETT, WILEY LEE. The Sporting Myth and the American Experience. Lewisburg, PA: Bucknell University Press, p. 94.

When Lardner writes of sports figures who seek success in "the game," his characters resemble Anderson's grotesques who fall for the American myth of success.

34 WHITE, RAY LEWIS. Review of Sherwood Anderson: A Collection of Critical Essays. Old Northwest, 1 (September), 327-30.

Walter B. Rideout's Collection of Critical Essays on Anderson is the fifth such anthology on the author; the introduction by Rideout and B. T. Spencer's article on Winesburg, Ohio are most valuable work included.

35 _____. "A Sherwood Anderson Checklist, 1970-71." Winesburg Eagle, 1 (November), 4-5.

[Checklist of 10 books and dissertations; 30 chapters and articles].

Index

INDEX

Index

Index

Index

Index

INDEX

Index

662975